WHO
PLAYED
WHO
ON THE
SCREEN

Roy Pickard

WHO PLAYED WHO ON THE SCREEN

Hippocrene Books, Inc.
New York

First published in the U.K. by B.T. Batsford 1988

Published in the U.S.A. by Hippocrene Books, Inc. 1989

ISBN 0-87052-789-4
Typeset by
Lasertext Ltd., Stretford, Manchester, England
and printed in Great Britain by
Anchor Brendon, Tiptree, Essex.

Hippocrene Books, Inc.
171 Madison Ave.
New York, N.Y. 10016

INTRODUCTION

When my earlier book, *Who Played Who In The Movies,* first appeared in print, I received more correspondence about its contents than I had for any previous book I had then written. Overall, you seemed to be pleased to have at your fingertips a book that provided you with information that you could not find elsewhere. All of which was highly gratifying for the research had been both exhaustive and exhausting. There was, however, just one small problem: accompanying all your good wishes and congratulations was a sting in the tail. And on every occasion that 'sting' began with the words 'Why didn't you include?' or, 'Surely, if you included him, why didn't you include her?'

Since receiving those letters and your frequent requests for an update I have wondered many times as to how I could best revise the book (taking into account all your suggestions) and come up with a volume that was comprehensive in scope, easy to use and very nearly a new book in its own right. The following pages are the end result of long deliberations and more labours – an A–Z guide of many hundreds of entries that answer such questions as 'How many times has Sherlock Holmes been played on screen? Or Dr Watson? Or Abraham Lincoln? Or Tarzan? Or Indiana Jones? Or James Bond? Or The Phantom Of The Opera?

The net has been cast as wide as possible, incorporating major characters of fiction and real life people who have had a film biography devoted to them. The concentration is on sound cinema (although as many silent portrayals as possible are also included) and is international in scope. Each entry is prefaced by an introductory paragraph about each character, followed by comprehensive listings, detailing the number of times the character has been played on film. These listings are broken down thus: name of actor, name of film (as it appeared in its country of origin), its director, country of origin and year of release. To the right of the character entry, I have also included a boxed letter F or R, indicating whether the character is real or fictitious.

As before, porn movies have been omitted as they bear little or no resemblance to serious screen interpretations. So too have ballet and opera films. Made-For-TV films, however, now occupy a much larger place in the book for, in recent years, the standard of many TV films (although in general still lamentably low) has risen and several, such as Schlesinger's *An Englishman Abroad,* are as good if not better than anything made for the big screen.

As to how many entries to include and how many to leave out? Well, personal choice must obviously play a large part in things, although I have tried to be as liberal as possible and cater for all tastes. I have also taken the opportunity to embellish, wherever possible, single entries of fiction e.g. the entry for Miss Havisham in Dickens' *Great Expectations* is followed by entries devoted to other characters (and their screen interpreters) who play an important part in the novel – Pip, Estella, Magwitch and Jaggers. Other new additions include characters that have become famous through the medium of film itself such as *The Magnificent Seven* and *Twelve Angry Men.*

I am indebted to people across the world who have taken the trouble to write to me with suggestions for new entries and pointing out performances that I have previously overlooked. All of these have duly been taken into account and, together with the revised and updated entries, plus the new additions which take the book right up to 1988, make *Who Played Who On Screen* virtually a new book. It has been a delight to work on because I have been operating in what is mostly unexplored territory and dealing with aspects of film reference that have not been touched upon previously. In an age when film books repeat again and again information that can be found elsewhere many times over, this work, I think, proves that there are still avenues of film research worth exploring. The book boasts 300 new illustrations and has given me so much pleasure to compile that I am loathe to hand it over to my publishers. But, if it is to be published at all, I must do so now and immediately start a file for the next version. In the meantime, I hope that you find the book both useful and entertaining and that you find what you want from its pages. Happy browsing.

Roy Pickard, 1988

Misty Rowe as Marilyn Monroe in the 1976 biography *Goodbye, Norma Jean*

ACKNOWLEDGEMENTS

The pictures in this book were originally issued to publicize or promote films or TV material made or distributed by the following companies, to whom I gratefully offer acknowledgement: Allied Artists, American-International, Anglo-Amalgamated, Artificial Eye, Associated British-Pathé, ATP, ATV, Avco-Embassy, BIP, Brent-Walker, British and Dominions, Butchers, Cannon-Classic, Cinerama, Columbia, Walt Disney/Buenea Vista, Eagle-Lion, Ealing Studios, EMI, Filmmakers Associates, First National, Gainsborough, Gala, Gaumont/Gaumont-British, Goldwyn, Granada TV, Grand National, Hammer, Hemdale, Lippert, London Films, London Weekend TV, Lorimar, Metro-Goldwyn-Mayer, Miracle, Monogram, New World, Orion, Palace Pictures, Paramount, PRC, The Rank Organization, Rediffusion, Republic, RKO/RKO Radio, Hal Roach, Selznick, 20th Century-Fox, UIP, United Artists, Universal/Universal-International, Virgin Films, Warner Brothers and Yorkshire TV.

Ben Kingsley in the title role of Richard Attenborough's 1982 biography *Gandhi*

Adams, Nick

[F]

The central character in Ernest Hemingway's 1924 collection of short stories, 'In Our Time', a young man, closely modelled on the author himself, who reaches an early maturity when he leaves home in Michigan to serve as an ambulance driver In Italy in World War 1. Martin Ritt's 145-minute film of his experiences combined several of the Nick Adams stories including 'The Battler' (played by Paul Newman), 'Big Two-Hearted River' and 'Indian Camp'.

Richard Beymer	*Hemingway's Adventures Of A Young Man*	(Ritt)	USA, 62

Virginia McKenna, plus lioness Elsa in *Born Free,* the first of the two films made about Joy Adamson and the rearing of lion cubs in Kenya

Susan Hampshire and Nigel Davenport as Joy Adamson and George Adamson in the 1972 sequel *Living Free*

Adamson, Joy

[R]

The wife of a senior game warden in Kenya who raised a wild lion cub (named Elsa) to maturity and then had the painful task of reconditioning it to life in the wild. Her rearing of the baby lioness was filmed in 1966 as *Born Free,* her subsequent caring for Elsa's own cubs related in the sequel *Living Free.*

Virginia McKenna	*Born Free*	(Hill)	GB, 66
Susan Hampshire	*Living Free*	(Couffer)	GB, 72

Note: Diana Muldaur appeared as Adamson in a 1974 TV series; Game warden George Adamson was played on screen by Bill Travers (66) and Nigel Davenport (72), and on TV by Gary Collins.

Adler, Polly

[R]

The most notorious (and successful) New York bordello madam of the 20s, known for her line-up of beautiful girls and renowned clientele which included the rich, the famous and the infamous, e.g. Mafia boss 'Lucky Luciano. Shelley Winters played her in the 1964 biography, *A House Is Not*

A Home, a film not helped by Miss Winters having to deliver such lines as 'I pin my diamonds on my loneliness and despair'. Still, as madams go, she remains one of the few to get her life story on the screen.

Shelley Winters — *A House Is Not A Home* (Rouse) USA, 64

Ahab, Captain F

The half-crazed, vengeful sea captain of Herman Melville's 'Moby Dick' (1851), a man obsessed with his search for the great white whale that has maimed him and who takes his schooner 'Pequod' on its last doomed voyage. With its dark, symbolic overtones, one of the most difficult roles to interpret satisfactorily on screen. John Barrymore made two attempts, one silent, one sound, Gregory Peck just one in John Huston's near perfect adaptation of 1956.

John Barrymore — *Moby Dick* (Bacon) USA, 30
Gregory Peck — *Moby Dick* (Huston) USA, 56

Note: John Barrymore first appeared as Ahab in 1926 in Millard Webb's *The Sea Beast;* Gregory Peck was the final choice of John Huston who had originally wanted to make the film with his father Walter Huston in the pivotal role.

Alexandra, Feodorovna 

(1872–1918) German-born wife of Tsar Nicholas II, much hated by the Russian people and who gained notoriety when she fell under the influence of the peasant monk Rasputin. Eventually imprisoned and shot with her family in July 1918, she was portrayed with distinction by Janet Suzman in *Nicholas And Alexandra* which encompassed the events that precipitated the collapse of the dynasty.

Hermine Sterler — *Rasputin* (Trotz) Ger, 32
Ethel Barrymore — *Rasputin And The Empress* (Boleslawsky) USA, 32
Lucie Hoeflich — 1914: *The Last Days Before The War* (Oswald) Ger, 32
Marcelle Chantal — *Rasputin* (L'Herbier) Fra, 39
Isa Miranda — *Rasputin* (Combret) Fra, 54
Gianna Maria Canale — *The Nights Of Rasputin* (Chenal) Fra/It, 60

Gregory Peck as the obsessed Captain Ahab battling with great white whale in John Huston's 1956 production *Moby Dick*

Renee Asherson — *Rasputin – The Mad Monk* (Sharp) GB, 66
Janet Suzman — *Nicholas And Alexandra* (Schaffner) USA, 71
Velta Linei — *Agony* (Klimov) USSR, 75

Note: Julia Dean in *Rasputin, The Black Monk* (USA, 17), Elinor Vanderveer in *Into Her Kingdom* (USA, 26) and Diana Karenne in *Rasputin And The Holy Devil* (Ger, 28) all appeared as Alexandra in silent productions.

Alexander The Great 

(356–23 BC) King Of Macedonia (educated by Aristotle) who extended the Greek civilization into the East and founded an empire that stretched through Syria and Egypt and into India. Robert Rossen's ambitious film of his conquests was not a success, but it did at least have the distinction of being the first intelligent epic at a time when the genre was dominated by slave girls, crashing temples and fatal haircuts!

Richard Burton — *Alexander The Great* (Rossen) USA, 56

Distraught at the news of Rasputin's murder, Alexandra (Janet Suzman) fears for the health of her young son Alexis (Roderic Noble) whose miraculous recoveries from haemophiliac attacks had been attributed to the healing powers of the notorious peasant monk. A scene from the Sam Spiegel epic *Nicholas and Alexandra*

A young Richard Burton and Danielle Darrieux in Robert Rossen's 1956 biographical epic of the Greek conqueror *Alexander The Great*

Alice In Wonderland F

One of literature's most enduring heroines, a little girl who experiences a remarkable series of adventures when she tumbles down a rabbit hole and discovers a world dominated by a fantastic illogicality. No film-maker has quite managed to come to terms with the fantasy elements of the tale, although Disney's animated version of 1951 continues to improve with age. Most films combine incidents from the two Lewis Carroll novels 'Alice's Adventures In Wonderland' (1865) and 'Through the Looking Glass' (1871).

Ruth Gilbert	*Alice In Wonderland*	(Pollard) USA, 31
Charlotte Henry	*Alice In Wonderland*	(McLeod) USA, 33
Carol Marsh	*Alice In Wonderland*	(Bower) Fra/GB, 50
Kathryn Beaumont (voice only)	*Alice In Wonderland*	(Disney) USA, 51
Anne-Marie Mallik	*Alice In Wonderland*	(Miller) GB/TV, 66
Fiona Fullerton	*Alice's Adventures in Wonderland*	(Sterling) GB, 72
Natalie Gregory	*Alice In Wonderland*	(Harris) USA/TV, 85

Note: The performance of Carol Marsh was in a part puppet, part live-action version of the story; in *Dreamchild* (GB, 85) Amelia Shankley played the child Alice in flashback sequences from the novel and Coral Browne the aged Alice Hargreaves on whom Lewis Carroll had based his girl character.

Both May Clark (GB, 03) and Mary Fuller (USA, 10) played Alice on the silent screen.

The bizarre characters and animals Alice encountered in her adventures down the rabbit hole included The White Rabbit, The Cheshire Cat, Mock Turtle and The Mad Hatter. These and other main characters in Carroll's novel have been played as follows:

The White Rabbit

Ralph Hertz — *Alice In Wonderland* (Pollard) USA, 31
Skeets Gallagher — *Alice In Wonderland* (McLeod) USA, 33
Ernest Milton (voice) — *Alice In Wonderland* (Bower) Fra/GB, 50
Bill Thompson (voice) — *Alice In Wonderland* (Disney) USA, 51
Wilfrid Brambell — *Alice In Wonderland* (Miller) TV/GB, 66
Michael Crawford — *Alice's Adventures in Wonderland* (Sterling) GB, 72
Red Buttons — *Alice In Wonderland* (Harris) USA/TV, 85

The Cheshire Cat

Tom Corliss — *Alice In Wonderland* (Pollard) USA, 31
Richard Arlen — *Alice In Wonderland* (McLeod) USA, 33
Felix Aylmer (voice) — *Alice In Wonderland* (Bower) Fra/GB, 50
Sterling Holloway (voice) — *Alice In Wonderland* (Disney) USA, 51
Primrose — *Alice In Wonderland* (Miller) TV/GB, 66
Roy Kinnear — *Alice's Adventures In Wonderland* (Sterling) GB, 72
Telly Savalas — *Alice In Wonderland* (Harris) TV/USA, 85

The Mock Turtle

Gus Alexander — *Alice In Wonderland* (Pollard) USA, 31
Cary Grant — *Alice In Wonderland* (McLeod) USA, 33
John Gielgud — *Alice In Wonderland* (Miller) TV/GB, 66
Michael Hordern — *Alice's Adventures In Wonderland* (Sterling) GB, 72
Alan Bennett (voice) — *Dreamchild* (Gavin Millar) GB, 85

No portrayals in the 1950 and 51 films, nor in the 1985 TV movie of Harry Harris.

The Mad Hatter

Leslie T. King — *Alice In Wonderland* (Pollard) USA, 31
Edward Everett Horton — *Alice In Wonderland* (McLeod) USA, 33
Raymond Bussieres (voice) — *Alice In Wonderland* (Bower) Fra/GB, 50
Ed Wynn (voice) — *Alice In Wonderland* (Disney) USA, 51
Peter Cook — *Alice In Wonderland* (Miller) TV/GB, 66
Robert Helpmann — *Alice's Adventures in Wonderland* (Sterling) GB, 72
Anthony Newley — *Alice In Wonderland* (Harris) TV/USA, 85
Tony Haygarth (voice) — *Dreamchild* (Gavin Millar) GB, 85

The Queen Of Hearts

Vie Quinn — *Alice In Wonderland* (Pollard) USA, 31
May Robson — *Alice In Wonderland* (McLeod) USA, 33
Pamela Brown (voice) — *Alice In Wonderland* (Bower) Fra/GB, 50
Verna Felton (voice) — *Alice In Wonderland* (Disney) USA, 51
Alison Leggatt — *Alice In Wonderland* (Miller) TV/GB, 66
Flora Robson — *Alice's Adventures In Wonderland* (Sterling) GB, 72
Jayne Meadows — *Alice In Wonderland* (Harris) TV/USA, 85

The March Hare

Meyer Beresen — *Alice In Wonderland* (Pollard) USA, 31
Charlie Ruggles — *Alice In Wonderland* (McLeod) USA, 33
Jerry Colonna (voice) — *Alice In Wonderland* (Disney) USA, 51
Michael Gough — *Alice In Wonderland* (Miller) TV/GB, 66
Peter Sellers — *Alice's Adventures In Wonderland* (Sterling) GB, 72
Roddy McDowall — *Alice In Wonderland* (Harris) TV/USA, 85
Ken Campbell (voice) — *Dreamchild* (Gavin Millar) GB, 85

No portrayal in the 1950 puppet version.

The Duchess

Mabel Wright — *Alice In Wonderland* (Pollard) USA, 31

Alison Skipworth	*Alice In Wonderland* (McLeod)	USA, 33
Joyce Grenfell (voice)	*Alice In Wonderland* (Bower)	Fra/GB, 50
Leo McKern	*Alice In Wonderland* (Miller)	TV/GB, 66
Peter Bull	*Alice's Adventures in Wonderland* (Sterling)	GB, 72
Martha Raye	*Alice In Wonderland* (Harris)	TV/USA, 85

No characterization in Disney's animated feature of 1951.

The Dormouse

Raymond Schultz	*Alice In Wonderland* (Pollard)	USA, 31
Jackie Searl	*Alice In Wonderland* (McLeod)	USA, 33
James MacDonald (voice)	*Alice In Wonderland* (Disney)	USA, 51
Wilfrid Lawson	*Alice In Wonderland* (Miller)	TV/GB, 66
Dudley Moore	*Alice's Adventures In Wonderland* (Sterling)	GB, 72
Arte Johnson	Alice In Wonderland (Harris)	TV/USA, 85
Julie Walters (voice)	*Dreamchild* (Gavin Millar)	GB, 85

Lewis Carroll (the pen name for the Rev. Charles Dodgson) has been played on screen by Stephen Murray in the live-action/puppet film of 1951, George Baker in Dennis Potter's TV play *Alice* (65) and Ian Holm in *Dreamchild* (85).

No characterization in Bower's 1951 puppet/live action adaption.

Ian Holm as the Reverend Charles Dodgson (Lewis Carroll) and Amelia Shankley as Alice Hargreaves in a scene from *Dreamchild,* Gavin Millar's sensitive account of the later years and childhood of the girl who inspired the heroine for Carroll's *Alice In Wonderland*

Anastasia

R

(1901–18) The youngest of the four daughters of Tsar Nicholas and Alexandra, supposedly murdered by the Bolsheviks in July, 1918, but later rumoured to have survived the massacre. Two films of 1956, one German, one American, investigated the possibility of Anastasia being alive. The latter starred Ingrid Bergman as an amnesiac refugee who is passed off by a group of con men as the last of the Romanovs. In more recent years Amy Irving has essayed the role in Marvin Chomsky's 1986 TV film *Anastasia – The Mystery of Anna.*

Dawn O'Day	*Rasputin And The Empress* (Bolelawsky)	USA, 32
Lilli Palmer	*Is Anna Anderson Anastasia?* (Harnack)	Ger, 56
Ingrid Bergman	*Anastasia* (Litvak)	USA, 56
Fiona Fullerton	*Nicholas And Alexandra* (Schaffner)	USA, 71
Amy Irving	*Anastasia – The Mystery of Anna* (Chomsky)	TVM/USA, 86

Note: Dawn O'Day later changed her name to Anne Shirley; on the silent screen Lee Parry played Anastasia in a 1928 German production.

Anastasia, Alberto

A Mafia boss, featured prominently in the recent spate of movies about organized crime in the United States. Known as the 'Lord High Executioner' for his ruthless methods of killing, he rose to power through his association with Mafia king, Lucky Luciano, and in the 50s challenged for the top spot in Murder Inc. Like most Mafia leaders he met his end in a grisly fashion – shot to death in a New York hotel barber shop in 1957. Richard Conte's performance in *My Brother Anastasia* is the most detailed screen portait to date.

Howard I. Smith	*Murder, Inc.* (Balaban/Rosenberg)	USA, 60
Fausto Tozzi	*The Valachi Papers* (Young)	Fra/It, 73
Richard Conte	*My Brother Anastasia* (Vanzina)	It, 73
Gianni Russo	*Lepke* (Golan)	USA, 75

Andersen, Hans Christian

R

(1805–75) Danish poet and teller of fairy tales; the subject of a large-scale Technicolor Goldwyn musical of the 50s and an animated feature of 1972. Goldwyn's film starred Danny Kaye as the story teller in love with a ballerina and adapted several of Andersen's stories into musical numbers e.g. 'The Ugly Duckling' and 'The King's New Clothes'.

Joachim Gottschalk	*Die Schwedische Nachtigall* (Brauer)	Ger, 40
Danny Kaye	*Hans Christian Andersen* (Charles Vidor)	USA, 52
Paul O'Keefe	*The Daydreamer* (Bass)	USA, 66
Richard Wordsworth	*Song Of Norway* (Stone)	USA, 70
Jesper Klein	*Hans Christian Andersen in Italy* (Cavaterra)	Den/It, 79

Note: Hetty Galen voiced the role in *The World of Hans Christian Andersen,* the '72 cartoon of Chuck McCann and Al Kilgore.

Annie

Depression America's most famous foundling; a cartoon character first introduced in the comic strip of Harold Gray and subsequently turned into the heroine of a Broadway musical. Mitzi Green and Ann Gillis appeared in two straight versions of the strip, Aileen Quinn in John Huston's 1982 version of the Charles Strouse/Martin Charnin musical.

Mitzi Green	*Little Orphan Annie* (Robertson)	USA, 32
Ann Gillis	*Little Orphan Annie* (Holmes)	USA, 38
Aileen Quinn	*Annie* (Huston)	USA, 82

Note: Daddy Warbucks, the billionaire tycoon who takes Annie under his wing after she has survived a kidnapping by two jailbirds, was played by Edgar Kennedy in 1932 and Albert Finney in the Huston film. The character did not appear in the 1938 production. Gray's comic strip was first published in 1924.

Antony, Mark

(*c.* 82–30 BC) Roman soldier and politician who avenged the murder of Caesar by destroying Cassius and Brutus at Philippi, then lost his influence in Rome when he became infatuated with Egyptian Queen, Cleopatra, and opted for a dissipated rather than a distinguished way of life. Marlon Brando

Bald-headed tycoon meets red-headed waif. Albert Finney as Daddy Warbucks and Aileen Quinn as the orphan *Annie* in John Huston's musical of 1982

delivered Shakespeare's 'Friends, Romans, Countrymen' speech in Mankiewicz's 1953 film; Richard Burton dallied with Elizabeth Taylor in the same director's *Cleopatra*, made a decade later. Charlton Heston has been drawn to the character on three occasions, twice in Shakespeare's *Julius Caesar* and once in *Antony And Cleopatra* which he also directed in 1972.

Henry Wilcoxon	*Cleopatra* (DeMille)	USA, 34
Charlton Heston	*Julius Caesar* (Bradley)	USA, 50
Marlon Brando	*Julius Caesar* (Mankiewicz)	USA, 53
Raymond Burr	*Serpent Of The Nile* (Castle)	USA, 53
Helmut Dantine	*The Story Of Mankind* (Allen)	USA, 57
Georges Marchal	*Legions Of The Nile* (Cottafavi)	It/Spa/Fra, 59
Bruno Tocci	*Caesar The Conqueror* (Anton)	It, 62
Richard Burton	*Cleopatra* (Mankiewicz)	USA, 63
Sidney James	*Carry on Cleo* (Thomas)	GB, 65
Charlton Heston	*Julius Caesar* (Burge)	GB, 70
Charlton Heston	*Antony And Cleopatra* (Heston)	Swi/Spa/GB, 72

Note: Philip Saville appeared as the Antony character in *An Honourable Murder* (GB, 60), a modernized version of *Julius Caesar*; Maurice Costello (USA, 08). Frank Benson (GB, 11) and Amleto Novelli (It, 13 & 16) all featured in the role on the silent screen.

Richard Johnson (72) and Colin Blakely (81) both portrayed Antony in TV adaptations of Shakespeare's play.

Aramis [F]

The most elegant of Alexandre Dumas' Three Musketeers, a poetry-writing womanizer who is forever vowing to renounce his adventurous ways for a more pious life in a monastery. In the movies he is simply a well-bred swashbuckler, more dandyish than most but still rallying to the call, 'All For One and One For All!' Richard Chamberlain has come the closest to capturing the true Aramis on screen.

Gino Corrado	*The Iron Mask* (Dwan)	USA, 29
Jean-Louis Allibert	*The Three Musketeers* (Diamant-Berger)	Fra, 32
Onslow Stevens	*The Three Musketeers* (Lee)	USA, 35
John King	*The Three Musketeers* (Dwan)	USA, 39
Miles Mander	*The Man In The Iron Mask* (Whale)	USA, 39
Robert Coote	*The Three Musketeers* (Sidney)	USA, 48
Carlo Ninchi	*The Gay Swordsman* (Freda)	It, 50
Keith Richards	*Sword of D'Artagnan* (Boetticher)	USA, 52
Judd Holdren	*Lady In The Iron Mask* (Murphy)	USA, 52
Jacques Francois	*The Three Musketeers* (Hunebelle)	Fra, 53
Paul Campbell	*The Knights Of The Queen* (Bolognini)	It, 54
Jacques Toja	*The Three Musketeers* (Borderie)	Fra, 61
Giacomo Rossi Stuart	*Zorro And The Three Musketeers* (Capuano)	It, 63
Roberto Risso	*Revenge Of The Musketeers* (Tulli)	It, 64
Richard Chamberlain	*The Three Musketeers* (Lester)	Panama/Spa, 74

Richard Chamberlain	*The Four Musketeers* (Lester) Panama/Spa, 75
Lloyd Bridges	*The Fifth Musketeer* (Annakin) Aus, 79

Note: Dan O'Herlihy starred as the son of Aramis in *At Sword's Point* (52); Harold Shaw (USA, 11), Eugene Pallette in *The Three Musketeers* (USA, 21) and Pierre de Guingand in the French serials, *The Three Musketeers* (22) and *Twenty Years After* (22), featured as Aramis on the silent screen.

Arrowsmith, Dr Martin

F

An idealistic young doctor who struggles against public apathy, corruption and the hypocrisies of his colleagues in his search for a cure for bubonic plague. One of Sinclair Lewis' most intricate characters created in 1925 and transferred to the screen just once—by John Ford in 1931.

Ronald Colman	*Arrowsmith* (Ford)	USA, 31

D'Artagnan

F

The prince of swashbucklers, brought to life in three novels by Alexandre Dumas—'The Three Musketeers' (1844), 'Twenty Years After' (1845) and 'The Viscount of Bragelonne' (1848–50)—and then again in the twentieth century when a host of actors (notably Douglas Fairbanks) recreated him for the screen. A quick tempered young Gascon who takes up service with the King's Musketeers, he was based on a real historical personage who lived in sixteenth century France. Dumas' novels follow D'Artagnan's exploits from his days as a young man to his death as Comte d'Artagnan, Master Of France. The films have generally concentrated on his earlier adventures.

Douglas Fairbanks	*The Iron Mask* (Dwan) USA, 29
Aime Simon-Girard	*The Three Musketeers* (Diamant-Berger) Fra, 32

(Left to right) Van Heflin as Athos, Gene Kelly as D'Artagnan, Gig Young as Porthos and Robert Coote as Aramis in George Sidney's 1948 production of *The Three Musketeers.*

Walter Abel	*The Three Musketeers* (Lee) USA, 35
Warren William	*The Man In The Iron Mask* (Whale) USA, 39
Don Ameche	*The Three Musketeers* (Dwan) USA, 39
Gene Kelly	*The Three Musketeers* (Sidney) USA, 48
Robert Clarke	*Sword Of D'Artagnan* (Boetticher) USA, 52
Louis Hayward	*Lady In The Iron Mask* (Murphy) USA, 52
Georges Marchal	*The Three Musketeers* (Hunebelle) USA, 53
Jeff Stone	*The Knights Of The Queen* (Bolognini) It, 54
Gerard Philipe	*Versailles* (Guitry) Fra, 54
Jacques Dumesnil	*Le Vicomte de Bragelonne* (Cerchio) Fra/It, 55
Gerard Barray	*The Three Musketeers* (Borderie) Fra, 61
Jean-Pierre Cassel	*Cyrano and D'Artagnan* (Gance) Fra, 62
Jean Marais	*The Iron Mask* (DeCoin) Fra, 62
George Nader	*The Secret Mark Of D'Artagnan* (Marcellini) It/Fra, 62
Franco Fantasia	*Zorro And The Three Musketeers* (Capuano) It, 63
Fernando Lamas	*Revenge Of The Musketeers* (Tulli) It, 64
Michael York	*The Three Musketeers* (Lester) Panama/Spa, 74
Michael York	*The Four Musketeers* (Lester) Panama/Spa, 75
Cornel Wilde	*The Fifth Musketeer* (Annakin) Aus, 79

Note: Louis Jourdan featured as D'Artagnan in the TV movie *The Man In The Iron Mask* (77); Cornel Wilde appeared as his son in *At Sword's Point* (52).

Douglas Fairbanks, in the 1921 version of *The Three Musketeers,* remains the most famous of the silent portrayals. Amleto Palermi (It, 09), Sydney Booth (USA, 11), M. Dehelly (Fra, 13), Max Linder (USA, 22), Aime Simon-Girard (Fra, 22) and Yonnel (Fra, 22) were others who featured in the role.

Arthur, King [F]

British king, possibly legendary, who was reputed to have defeated the invading Saxons in sixth century Britain. Much better known, however, as the mythical figure who extracted the sword 'Excalibur' from the rock and presided over the famous knights of the round table. The screen has presented him in various moods–heroic, cynical and through the song 'How To Handle A Woman' in *Camelot,* sadly embittered.

William Farnum	*A Connecticut Yankee* (Butler) USA, 31
Cedric Hardwicke	*A Connecticut Yankee In King Arthur's Court* (Garnett) USA, 49
Brian Aherne	*Prince Valiant* (Hathaway) USA, 54
Mel Ferrer	*Knights Of The Round Table* (Thorpe) GB, 54
Anthony Bushell	*The Black Knight* (Garnett) GB, 54
Brian Aherne	*Lancelot And Guinevere* (Wilde) GB, 63
Mark Dignam	*Siege Of The Saxons* (Juran) GB, 63
Richard Harris	*Camelot* (Logan) USA, 67
Anthony Sharp	*Gawain And The Green Knight* (Weeks) GB, 73

Nigel Terry as a young King Arthur, the once and future king, in John Boorman's realistic epic of the knights of the round table, *Excalibur*

Vladimir Antolek-Oresek	*Lancelot du lac* (Bresson) Fra/It, 74
Graham Chapman	*Monty Python And The Holy Grail* (Gilliam/Jones) GB, 75
Marc Eyraud	*Perceval Le Gallois* (Rohmer) Fra, 78
Kenneth More	*The Spaceman And King Arthur* (Mayberry) GB, 79
Nigel Terry	*Excalibur* (Boorman) USA, 81
Mr Kent	*Stuck On You!* (Herz/Weil) USA, 82
Trevor Howard	*Sword Of The Valiant: The Legend Of Gawain And The Green Knight* (Weeks) GB, 83

Note: Rickie Sorensen voiced the boy Arthur in Disney's *The Sword In The Stone* (63); Charles Clary featured as the king in the 1921 silent version of *A Connecticut Yankee At King Arthur's Court.* On TV Malcolm McDowell appeared in Clive Donner's television film *Arthur The King* (83).

Athos F

The most introspective of Dumas' three musketeers, moody, embittered and forever haunted by the memory of a romance with a woman who turned out to be an unscrupulous whore. When sober, possibly the best swordsman of the three; when drunk, an irresponsible saturnine woman hater. Van Heflin admirably caught the varied moods of the character in MGM's lavish colour spectacular of 1948.

Leon Barry	*The Iron Mask* (Dwan) USA, 29
Henri Rollan	*The Three Musketeers* (Diamant-Berger) Fra, 32
Paul Lukas	*The Three Musketeers* (Lee) USA, 35
Douglas Dumbrille	*The Three Musketeers* (Dwan) USA, 39
Bert Roach	*The Man In The Iron Mask* (Whale) USA, 39
Van Heflin	*The Three Musketeers* (Sidney) USA, 48
Rossano Brazzi	*Milady And The Musketeers* (Cottafavi) It, 51
John Hubbard	*Sword Of D'Artagnan* (Boetticher) USA, 52
Steve Brodie	*Lady In The Iron Mask* (Murphy) USA, 52
Jean Martinelli	*The Three Musketeers* (Hunebelle) Fra, 53
Domenico Modugno	*The Knights Of The Queen* (Bolognini) It, 54
Georges Descrieres	*The Three Musketeers* (Borderie) Fra, 61
Gianni Rizzo	*Zorro And The Three Musketeers* (Capuano) It, 63
Franco Fantasia	*Revenge Of The Musketeers* (Tulli) It, 64
Oliver Reed	*The Three Musketeers* (Lester) Panama/Spa, 74
Oliver Reed	*The Four Musketeers* (Lester) Panama/Spa, 75
Jose Ferrer	*The Fifth Musketeer* (Annakin) Aus, 79

Note: Maureen O'Hara featured as Claire, daughter of Athos in *At Sword's Point* (52); Leon Bary was also a silent Athos in *The Three Musketeers* (21) and Henri Rollan appeared in the role in Henri Berger's *The Three Musketeers* (22) and *Twenty Years After* (22).

Attila The Hun R

(*c.* 406–53) Fifth century Hunnish king, known affectionately as the 'Scourge Of God', who overran much of Europe with his Asian hordes, creating terror and devastation in his wake. Ideal for the movies one would have thought, but until Miklos Jancso's *Young Attila,* strictly a formularized villain whose intriguing paganism was lost among the usual cast of thousands!

Jack Palance	*The Sign Of The Pagan* (Sirk) USA, 54
Anthony Quinn	*Attila The Hun* (Fransisci) Fra/It, 55
Jozsef Madaras	*Young Attila* (Jancso) It, 71

Aylward, Gladys R

English servant girl who assisted at a remote mission station in China in the days prior to World War II and became world famous through her best-selling book 'The Small Woman'. A victim of the Hollywood soap opera treatment in *The Inn Of The Sixth Happiness* but not, luckily, the Japanese from whom she escaped with some orphaned children on a dangerous trek over the mountains. She died in 1970, aged 68.

Ingrid Bergman	*The Inn Of The Sixth Happiness* (Robson) GB, 58

Ingrid Bergman as Gladys Aylward in *The Inn of the 6th Happiness* (1958), the story of an English servant girl who became a missionary in China just prior to World War II

Bader, Douglas [R]

(1910–82) RAF fighter pilot who lost both legs in a flying accident in 1931 and bravely overcame his disability through the use of artificial limbs. The 1956 film with Kenneth More covered ten years in Bader's life, from the time of his accident to when he rejoined the airforce and became one of the heroic 'few'.

Kenneth More	*Reach For The Sky* (Gilbert) GB, 56

Barabbas 

The criminal condemned to death on the cross and released instead of Jesus by Pontius Pilate. A 'cameo' role in biblical epics, a major one in Richard Fleischer's 1962 film which traced Barabbas' life from the time of his release through his years as a slave and gladiator to his eventual ironic death by crucifixion.

Anthony Warde	*The Day Of Triumph* (Pichel/Coyle) USA, 54
Harry Guardino	*King Of Kings* (Ray) USA, 61
Livio Lorenzon	*Ponzio Pilato* (Callegari) It/Fra, 61
Anthony Quinn	*Barabbas* (Fleischer) It, 62
Richard Conte	*The Greatest Story Ever Told* (Stevens) USA, 65
Stacy Keach	*Jesus of Nazareth* (Zeffirelli) GB, 77

Note: George Seigmann played Barabbas in DeMille's 1927 silent film, *King Of Kings*.

Barker, Kate 'Ma' 

(1880–1935) Queen of the 'lady' gangsters of the 30s. Together with her four sons and Alvin Karpis, she executed several quarter-of-a-million bank jobs in Kansas, Missouri and Minnesota before coming to a bloody end in a shootout with the FBI at her Florida hideout. Shelley Winters' massive performance in Roger Corman's *Bloody Mama* is the definitive screen portrayal and likely to remain so for many years to come.

Jean Harvey	*Guns Don't Argue* (Karn/Kahn) USA, 55
Lurene Tuttle	*Ma Barker's Killer Brood* (Karn) USA, 60
Shelley Winters	*Bloody Mama* (Corman) USA, 70

Note: Blanche Yurka's Ma Webster was closely based on Barker in the 1940 production, *Queen Of The Mob;* the characters of Irene Dailey in *The Grissom Gang* (71) and Angie Dickinson in *Big Bad Mama* (74) were also loosely derived from that of the notorious woman outlaw. On TV Eileen Heckart appeared as Barker in Marvin Chomsky's TV film *The FBI Versus Alvin Karpis, Public Enemy Number One* (74).

Barnum, Phineas Taylor 

(1810–91) Brash American showman who helped put the word 'razzmatazz' into show business and joined with rival James Anthony Bailey in forming the famous Barnum and Bailey Circus. His efforts proved worthwhile: when he died he was worth five million dollars. Wallace Beery played him twice in the early 30s, first in *A Lady's Morals* in which he managed international singing star Jenny Lind, second in *The Mighty Barnum* in which he created his massive circus.

Wallace Beery	*A Lady's Morals* (Franklin) USA, 30
Wallace Beery	*The Mighty Barnum* (Walter Lang) USA, 34
Raymond Brown	*High, Wide And Handsome* (Mamoulian) USA, 37
Gus Partos	*Semmelweis* (De Toth) Hung, 39
Burl Ives	*Jules Verne's Rocket To The Moon* (Sharp) GB, 67

Note: Maclyn Arbuckle featured as Barnum in J. Searle Dawley's silent film *Broadway Broke* (23); Grace Moore (30) and Virginia Bruce (34) played Jenny Lind in the two Barnum films starring Wallace Beery.

On TV Burt Lancaster starred as *Barnum* in the 1986 TV film of Lee Philips; Hanna Schygulla appeared as Jenny Lind.

Barrymore, John 

(1882–1942) Another in the long line of great Hollywood actors who literally drank themselves into the grave. Before alcohol took control he was known as 'The Great Profile' and portrayed many famous literary characters on the screen i.e. Dr Jekyll And Mr Hyde, Captain Ahab, Raffles, Svengali, Arsene Lupin. In *Too Much, Too Soon,* the screen biography of Barrymore's daughter Diana, Errol Flynn stole the honours with his portrait of the once great actor in the final throes of disintegration.

Errol Flynn	*Too Much, Too Soon*	(Napoleon)	USA, 58
Jack Cassidy	*W. C. Fields And Me*	(Hiller)	USA, 76

Note: John Barrymore was the model for the character of Tony Cavendish, played by Fredric March in *The Royal Family Of Broadway,* directed by George Cukor and Cyril Gardner in 1930.

Bates, Norman F

Not the kind of guy you want to meet up with on a dark rainy night as Janet Leigh found to her cost in Alfred Hitchcock's *Psycho;* a young motel owner who resides with the corpse of his long dead mother in an old gothic house and periodically disposes of anyone unwise enough to stay the night. To-date, his gruesome activities have been essayed three times on screen by Anthony Perkins. Robert Bloch's macabre novel on which Hitchcock's original film was based was first publishd in 1959. It derived from a newspaper story about a man who kept his mother's body in a house somewhere near Wissconsin!

Still not quite right! Anthony Perkins imprisoned in the role of the crazed taxidermist Norman Bates in the second of the three Psycho films *Psycho II*

Anthony Perkins	*Psycho*	(Hitchcock)	USA, 60
Anthony Perkins	*Psycho II*	(Franklin)	USA, 83
Anthony Perkins	*Psycho III*	(Perkins)	USA, 86

Batman F

Masked crime fighter who, together with his young aide Robin, fought a never ending 'lone battle against the evil forces in society'. Hooded, caped and muscular, he was created by Bob Kane in a 1939 issue of Detective Comics and continued his crusades in screen serials of the 40s and a popular, long-running TV series of the 60s.

Lewis Wilson	*Batman*	(Hillyer)	USA, 43
Robert Lowrey	*Batman And Robin*	(Bennet)	USA, 49
Adam West	*Batman*	(Martinson)	USA, 66

Note: Robin was played by Douglas Croft (43) and John Duncan (49) in the 1940 serials; by Burt Ward in Martinson's 1966 feature film.

In the 1966 production the chief members of the 'opposition' were played by Burgess Meredith (The Penguin), Cesar Romero (The Joker), Frank Gorshin (The Riddler) and Lee Meriwether (Catwoman).

Bean, Judge Roy R

(1825–1903) 'Justice Of The Peace' in the town of Vinegaroon (later Langtry), Texas, during the 1880s and 90s but, in reality, a minor despot who referred to himself as the sole law 'West Of The Pecos'. Not without a sense of humour, he once acquitted a man for killing a Mexican because 'it served the deceased right for getting in front of the gun'. The fact that he lived until he was 78 proved that, for him at least, his system worked very well. Favourite hobbies: hanging horse thieves and worshipping actress Lily Langtry. Portrayed at length by Paul Newman in Huston's 1972 film *The Life And Times*

The hanging judge Paul Newman in John Huston's *The Life And Times Of Judge Roy Bean*

Of Judge Roy Bean. An Oscar to Walter Brennan in 1940 for his portrayal in *The Westerner.*

Walter Brennan	*The Westerner* (Wyler) USA, 40
Victor Jory	*A Time For Dying* (Boetticher) USA, 69
Paul Newman	*The Life And Times Of Judge Roy Bean* (Huston) USA, 72

Becket, Thomas R

(1118–70) Archbishop of Canterbury in twelfth century England, murdered by soldiers in his cathedral on the orders of his former friend King Henry II. The turbulent relationship between Becket and Henry, from the time they drank and whored together, to their clash of wills over matters of state, was examined in Peter Glenville's version of Anouilh's 1959 stage play. Richard Burton and Peter O'Toole (Henry) both received Oscar nominations for their portrayals.

Father John Groser	*Murder In The Cathedral* (Hoellering) GB, 52
Richard Burton	*Becket* (Glenville) GB, 64

Note: Sir Frank Benson starred in George Ridgwell's silent biography, *Becket* (GB, 23).

Beethoven, Ludwig van R

(1770–1827) German composer of outstanding genius, famous for his development of the symphony and his inspired work in many other musical forms, including chamber music, sonatas and concertos. Ewald Balser offered a sensitive portrayal of the composer in the 1949 Austrian film, *Eroica;* in 1970, the bicentennial of Beethoven's birth, Hans Conrad Fischer produced the documentary *Ludwig van Beethoven.* In 1960 Hollywood looked at episodes in the life of the young composer and referred to him as *The Magnificent Rebel.*

Harry Baur	*The Life And Loves Of Beethoven* (Gance) Fra, 36
Auguste Boverio	*Schubert's Serenade* (Boyer) Fra, 40
Albert Basserman	*New Wine* (Schunzel) USA, 41
Rene Deltgen	*Whom The Gods Love* (Hartl) Ger, 42
Memo Benassi	*Rossini* (Bonnard) It, 46
Ewald Balser	*Eroica* (Kolm-Veltee) Aus, 49
Erich von Stroheim	*Napoleon* (Guitry) Fra, 54
Ewald Balser	*Das Dreimaderlhaus* (Marischka) Aus, 58
Carl Boehm	*The Magnificent Rebel* (Tressler) USA, 60
Wolfgang Reichmann	*Beethoven's Nephew* (Morrissey) Fra/W. Ger, 85

Note: Fritz Kortner played Beethoven twice on the silent screen, first in an Austrian film of 1918 and then in the 1926 biography, *The Life Of Beethoven* (Austria, 26).

Beiderbecke, Bix 

(1903–31) One of the legendary jazz musicians of the 20s, a self-taught cornet player whose life was as tragic as it was brilliant and which was brought to an untimely end through chronic alcoholism when Beiderbecke was only 28. Only one feature film has been based on his life and then only loosely, the uneven *Young Man With A Horn,* adapted from the novel by Dorothy Baker. Kirk Douglas featured as the Beiderbecke character (renamed Rick Martin) and Harry James performed the trumpet solos. Hoagy Carmichael, a close friend and colleague of Beiderbecke in real life, also featured in the film as a veteran jazz musician and on-screen narrator.

Kirk Douglas — *Young Man With A Horn* (Curtiz) USA, 50

Note: A documentary study of Beiderbecke's life was filmed by Brigitte Berman in 1981. Entitled *Bix,* it combined old footage and old records with present day interviews with, among others, Carmichael, Artie Shaw, Spiegel Willcox, piano player Jess Stacy and Doc Cheatham.

Bel Ami F

Guy de Maupassant's unscrupulous young scoundrel who uses his power over women to reach the top in Parisian society during the 1880s. Real name: Georges Duroy. Four portrayals on film, the most accomplished being that of George Sanders in Albert Lewin's 1947 production, the most recent being a modern update which recast Duroy as an unsuccessful journalist/poet who works on a sex magazine named 'Playhouse'.

Willi Forst — *Bel Ami* (Forst) Ger, 39
George Sanders — *The Private Affairs Of Bel Ami* (Lewin) USA, 47
Jean Danet — *Bel Ami* (Daquin) Fra/Aus, 55
Harry Reems — *Bel Ami* (Torn) Swe, 75

Bell, Alexander Graham R

(1847–1922) Scottish-born American physicist whose invention of the telephone in 1876 brought him wealth, fame and a posthumous Hollywood biography starring Don Ameche!

Don Ameche — *The Story Of Alexander Graham Bell* (Cummings) USA, 39
Jim Ameche — *The Story Of Mankind* (Allen) USA, 57

Belle de Jour F

The central character of Joseph Kessel's 1928 novel; a frigid young wife (real name Severine Serizy) who is driven by her masochistic desires to become a part-time prostitute in a Paris brothel, earning the nickname Belle de Jour because she can only work in the afternoons from two to five! Portrayed by Catherine Deneuve in the 1967 film of Luis Bunuel who later commented that he was unimpressed with the original novel but that it allowed him to translate sexual fantasies into pictorial images and draw a serious portait of a female bourgeois masochist!

Catherine Deneuve, the beautiful but masochistic housewife who seeks afternoon relief in a brothel in Luis Bunuel's *Belle de Jour*

Catherine Deneuve — *Belle de Jour* (Brunel) Fra/It, 67

Belvedere, Lynn F

The most famous babysitter of them all, a self-confessed genius who answers an advertisement to look after the children of an all-American family and then proceeds to write an all-revealing bestseller about the gossipy neighbourhood in which he lives. Clifton Webb first played Belvedere in the 1948 comedy *Sitting Pretty.* He later repeated the role on two further occasions but found it impossible to top his supreme moment in *Sitting Pretty* i.e. tipping a bowl of porridge over the head of a baby that has been flicking the cereal at him throughout breakfast!

Clifton Webb — *Sitting Pretty* (Walter Lang) USA, 48

Clifton Webb — *Mr Belvedere Goes To College* (Nugent) USA, 49
Clifton Webb — *Mr Belvedere Rings The Bell* (Koster) USA, 51

Note: The Clifton Webb films derived from the novel 'Belvedere' by Gwen Davenport; in the recent TV series (1985–) Christopher Hewett has starred as the haughty childminder.

Ben-Hur, Judah [F]

Legendary hero of General Lew Wallace's 1880 novel; a man falsely convicted of trying to murder the Roman Governor of Palestine and who serves as a slave on the Roman galleys before eventually defeating his former friend Messala in an epic chariot race in Judaea. Ramon Novarro (silent) and Charlton Heston (sound) have played Ben-Hur in the two major versions of the story although a third, unknown actor also essayed the part in a 1907 production (directed by Sidney Olcott) and which recreated 16 scenes from the book.

Ramon Novarro — *Ben-Hur* (Niblo) USA, 25
Charlton Heston — *Ben-Hur* (Wyler) USA, 59

Note: Heston won an Oscar for his 1959 performance; Burt Lancaster, Rock Hudson and Cesare Danova were all considered prior to his casting. Francis X. Bushman played Messala on the silent screen, Stephen Boyd in William Wyler's film.

Bernadette of Lourdes 

(1844–79) Real name, Bernadette Soubirous. The humble French peasant girl who, in 1858, saw visions of the Virgin Mary and discovered a miraculous healing spring at Lourdes. Jennifer Jones won a best actress Academy Award for her visions of 1943; Daniele Ajoret featured in a little-known French/Italian film of 1960.

Jennifer Jones — *The Song Of Bernadette* (King) USA, 43
Daniele Ajoret — *Bernadette Of Lourdes* (Darene) Fra/It, 60

Bernhardt, Sarah 

(1844–1923) In the words of Oscar Wilde, 'The Divine Sarah', regarded by many who saw her as the greatest of all French actresses. Eccentric (she often slept in a rosewood coffin) and energetic (she

Jennifer Jones as the young French peasant girl Bernadette Soubirous who saw visions of the Virgin Mary and discovered a miraculous healing spring at Lourdes

reputedly enjoyed a thousand lovers), she just managed to be recorded on film for posterity in *Camille* (10), *Queen Elizabeth* (12), *Jeanne Dore* (15). In the 1976 biography by Richard Fleischer her lovers were reduced by 997 to three!

Colette Regis — *Trois Valses* (Berger) Fra, 38
Glenda Jackson — *The Incredible Sarah* (Fleischer) USA, 76

Bernstein, Carl and Woodward, Bob [R]

The young Washington Post reporters who stumbled onto the story of the Watergate burglary and then uncovered a terrifying trail of corruption that led to the Department of Justice, the FBI and finally the President of the United States. In Pakula's political thriller, *All The President's Men,* Dustin Hoffman is Carl Bernstein, Robert Redford Bob Woodward.

Dustin Hoffman and Robert Redford — *All The President's Men* (Pakula) USA, 76

Note: Jack Nicholson's Washington columnist Mark Forman in *Heartburn* (USA, 86) was based on the

Rescue at sea! Jack Hawkins' Roman commander and Charlton Heston's galley slave welcome the sight of a ship after almost perishing during a massive sea battle. A scene from MGM's epic *Ben Hur*, the story of a young jewish prince who seeks revenge on his former boyhood friend Messala and eventually achieves his ambition during the film's climactic chariot race

character of Bernstein and derived from Nora Ephron's novel about the infidelities of her husband; in *All The President's Men* Bob Woodward's secret political source, known as Deep Throat, was played by Hal Holbrook.

Biggles [F]

Daredevil British pilot adventurer, first created by Captain W. E. Johns in the 1930s and the central character of more than a hundred novels until Johns' death in 1968. He was neglected by film-makers until the 80s when he was brought to the screen as a 'time twin' involved in a time warp with a young New York businessman and became embroiled in modern day adventures, whilst his colleague returned the compliment by helping out on the Western Front during World War I. A pipe-smoking, gung-ho hero with plenty of imperialist attitudes, he was once mentioned as a possible subject for Dudley Moore! Full name: James Bigglesworth, DSO, DFC, MC.

Neil Dickson *Biggles* (Hough) GB, 86

Biko, Steve [R]

A young black South African and man of peace who, at university, became the leader of the Black Consciousness Movement and fought against the government policy of apartheid or 'separate development' instituted in 1948. Subsequently arrested and 'interrogated' by the South African security police, he died in September 1977 from horrific wounds sustained in police custody. The final two years of Biko's life were movingly portrayed in Richard Attenborough's scathing epic *Cry Freedom*; Denzel Washington, a young American actor best

Stephen Biko (Denzel Washington) in the clutches of the South African security police in Richard Attenborough's *Cry Freedom*

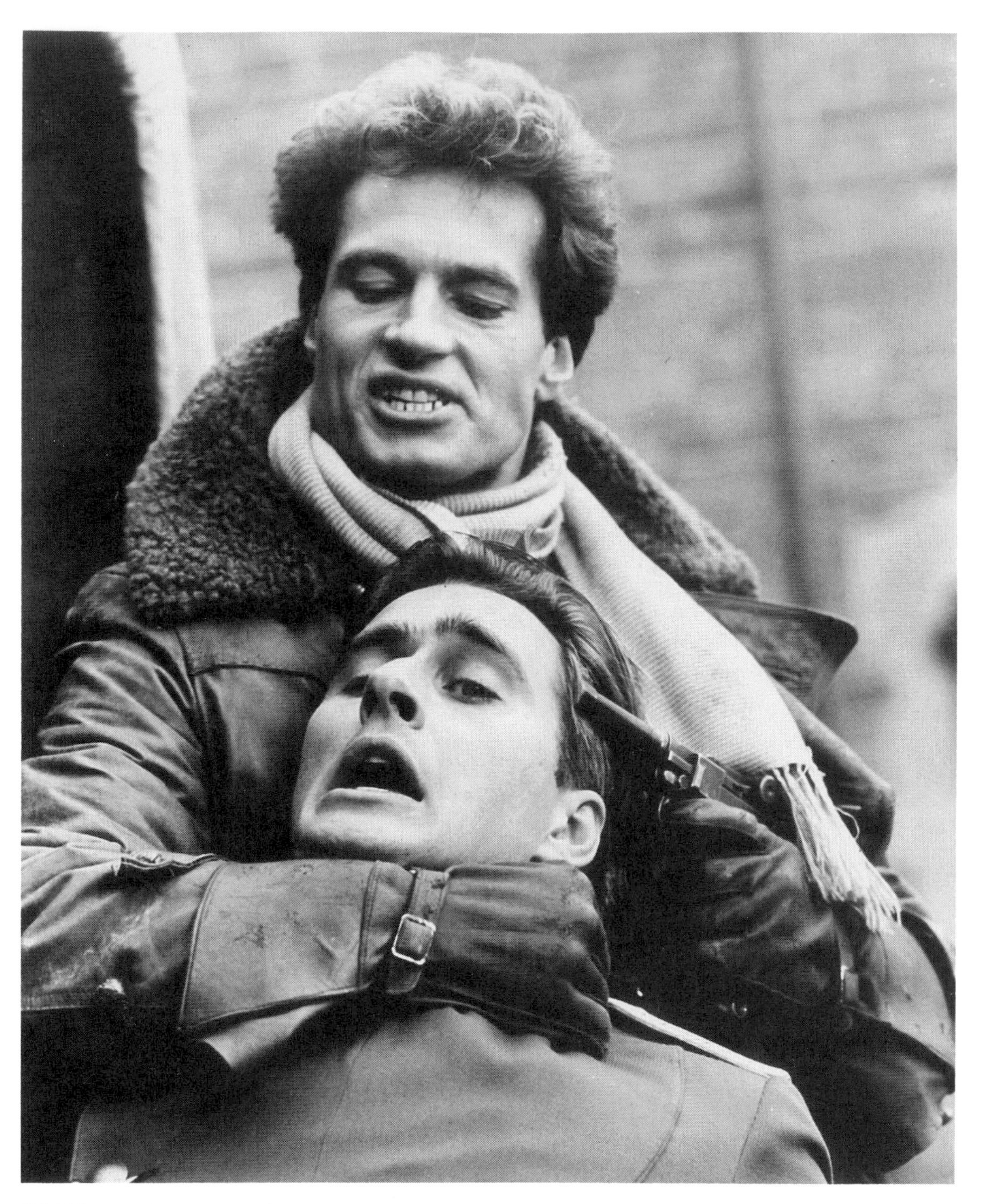

Neil Dickson as Captain W. E. John's archetypal British hero James Bigglesworth, first created by the author in the 1930s but not brought to the screen until 1986 in John Hough's fantasy adventure *Biggles*

known for his performances in the TV series *St Elsewhere,* played Biko.

Denzel Washington *Cry Freedom* (Attenborough) GB, 87

Note: Donald Woods, the liberal white newspaper editor who befriended Biko and was forced to flee the country in order to get his book on the black leader published, was played by Kevin Kline. His two books – his autobiography *Asking For Trouble* and *Biko* – formed the basis of John Briley's screenplay.

Billy The Kid

(1859–81) Outlaw of the American West who, if legend is to be believed, might have stayed on the right side of the law had his boss, rancher John Tunstall, not been killed in the Lincoln County War. Thereafter, it was a life of crime and a final boast that he had killed one man for every day of his young life. Screen portrayals have become less romantic and more realistic with the passing of time, i.e. Michael J. Pollard in *Dirty Little Billy* and Kris Kristofferson in Peckinpah's *Pat Garrett And Billy The Kid.* Real name: William Bonney.

Johnny Mack Brown *Billy The Kid* (King Vidor) USA, 30
Roy Rogers *Billy The Kid Returns* (Kane) USA, 38
Robert Taylor *Billy The Kid* (Miller) USA, 41
Jack Buetel *The Outlaw* (Hughes) USA, 43
Buster Crabbe *Raiders Of Red Rock* (Newfield) USA, 46
Dean White *Return Of The Badmen* (Enright) USA, 48
Don Barry *I Shot Billy The Kid* (Berke) USA, 50
Audie Murphy *Texas Kid Outlaw* (Neumann) USA, 50
Scott Brady *The Law vs Billy The Kid* (Castle) USA, 54
Tyler MacDuff *The Boy From Oklahoma* (Curtiz) USA, 54
Nick Adams *Strange Lady In Town* (LeRoy) USA, 55
Anthony Dexter *The Parson And The Outlaw* (Drake) USA, 57
Paul Newman *The Left-Handed Gun* (Penn) USA, 58
Jack Taylor *Billy The Kid* (Klimovsky) Spa, 62
Johnny Ginger *The Outlaws Is Coming* (Maurer) USA, 65
Chuck Courtenay *Billy The Kid vs Dracula* (Beaudine) USA, 66
Peter Lee Lawrence *The Man Who Killed Billy The Kid* (Buchs) Spa/It, 67
Geoffrey Deuel *Chisum* (McLaglen) USA, 70
Jean-Pierre Leaud *A Girl Is A Gun* (Moullet) Fra, 71
Michael J. Pollard *Dirty Little Billy* (Dragoti) USA, 72
Kris Kristofferson *Pat Garrett And Billy The Kid* (Peckinpah) USA, 73

Bismarck, Otto von

(1815–98) Prussian statesman and diplomat, a key figure in German nationalism and responsible for the unification of Germany in 1871. Not surprisingly, his achievements attracted Hitler's Third Reich and two major biographies, one featuring Paul Hartmann, the other Emil Jannings, appeared in the early 40s. In *Royal Flash,* Oliver Reed played Bismarck in his younger years, before his rise to power.

Lyn Harding *Spy Of Napoleon* (Elvey) GB, 36
Friedrich Otto Fischer *Robert Koch* (Steinhoff) Ger, 39
Paul Hartmann *Bismarck* (Liebeneiner) Ger, 40
Emil Jannings *The Dismissal* (Liebeneiner) Ger, 41
Friedrich Otto Fischer *Carl Peters* (Selphin) Ger, 41
Lyn Harding *The Prime Minister* (Dickinson) GB, 41
Kurt Katch *Salome, Where She Danced* (Lamont) USA, 45
Friedrich Domin *Ludwig II* (Käutner) W. Ger, 55
Oliver Reed *Royal Flash* (Lester) GB, 75

Note: On the silent screen Bismarck was played by Franz Ludwig in German productions of 1915 and 1926 and by Josef Schreiber in the 1922 Austrian film *Konig Ludwig II.*

Blackbeard

(*d.* 1718) Fierce, wild-looking English pirate (real name, Edward Teach) who operated with barbaric success in the Caribbean in the early years of the eighteenth century. Just one screen biography, by

Raoul Walsh in 1952, a film with one of the most gruesome last scenes in movie history – Blackbeard buried up to his neck in sand and unable to prevent his drowning by the incoming tide.

Louis Bacigalupi	*Double Crossbones* (Barton)	USA, 50
Thomas Gomez	*Anne Of The Indies* (Tourneur)	USA, 51
Robert Newton	*Blackbeard The Pirate* (Walsh)	USA, 52
Murvyn Vye	*The Boy And The Pirates* (Gordon)	USA, 60
Peter Ustinov	*Blackbeard's Ghost* (Stevenson)	USA, 67

Blaine, Rick

F

The archetypal embittered anti-hero, a disillusioned American who shuts himself off from the war and his lost love by running the Cafe Americain in Casablanca, playing host to Vichy France officials, Nazi officers, refugees and leaders of the French underground movement. Played to perfection by Humphrey Bogart in Michael Curtiz's 1943 film which derived from 'Everybody comes to Rick's', an unpublished play authored by Murray Burnett and Joan Alison.

Humphrey Bogart	*Casablanca* (Curtiz)	USA, 43

Note: In 1955 Charles McGraw played Rick Blaine in a short-lived (8 episode) TV series of *Casablanca;* David Soul starred as Blaine in an even less successful series (five episodes) in 1983.

Blaise, Modesty

F

Female counterpart to 007, Matt Helm, etc., a voluptuous super-agent/adventuress who runs a successful international crime network. The one film made about her exploits has her hired by the British Secret Service to protect a shipment of diamonds. Knifings, druggings, chases and general bed-hopping result. She first appeared in the 1963 Evening Standard comic strip of Peter O'Donnell and Jim Holdaway.

Monica Vitti	*Modesty Blaise* (Losey)	GB, 66

Blandish, Barbara

F

Heroine, if that is the correct word, of the James Hadley Chase novel 'No Orchids For Miss Blandish',

Here's looking at you kid! Bogart as Rick Blaine bids a final farewell to Ingrid Bergman in the last scene in *Casablanca*

A cartoon strip comes to life. Monica Vitti as the adventure-seeking Modesty Blaise, a heroine first created in the Evening Standard comicstrip of Peter O'Donnell and Jim Holdaway

a beautiful young heiress who falls in love with one of her captors when she is kidnapped by a brutal mob of gangsters. The 1948 version of the book, made in England, was filmed straight; Robert Aldrich's remake *The Grissom Gang,* was set in rural America during the early Depression years. Chase's thriller, published in 1939, remains one of the best-selling mysteries ever published.

Linden Travers	*No Orchids For Miss Blandish* (Clowes)	GB, 48
Kim Darby	*The Grissom Gang* (Aldrich)	USA, 71

Note: Claire, daughter of Barbara, carried on from where her mother left off in *The Flesh Of The Orchid,* made by Patrice Chereau in France in 1975. Charlotte Rampling featured as Claire.

Bligh, William [R]

(1754–1817) Sadistic captain of HMS Bounty, relieved of his command in 1789 and, along with eighteen men, set adrift in a small boat. A master seaman, he navigated nearly 3600 miles of open sea and succeeded in returning to England. Charles Laughton's famous leer and the accompanying 'Fifty lashes Mr Christian' earned him world fame and an Oscar nomination; Anthony Hopkins' more humane Bligh in the 1984 version of the story remains the most convincing interpretation.

Mayne Lynton	*In The Wake Of The Bounty* (Chauvel)	Australia, 33
Charles Laughton	*Mutiny On The Bounty* (Lloyd)	USA, 35
Trevor Howard	*Mutiny On The Bounty* (Milestone)	USA, 62
Anthony Hopkins	*The Bounty* (Donaldson)	GB, 84

Note: George Cross played Bligh in the 1916 Australian silent, *The Mutiny On The Bounty.*

Blixen, Karen [R]

(1883–1962) Celebrated Danish short story writer who for some 17 years (1914–31) ran, almost single handed, a coffee plantation in British East Africa (now Kenya). She later recalled her experiences in her 1937 memoir *Out Of Africa,* a book that defeated many film-makers until director Sydney Pollack and writer Kurt Luedtke brought it to the screen in an Oscar-winning style in 1985. Blixen, under the pen name of Isak Dinesen, published her first collection of stories, *Seven Gothic Tales,* in 1934 and followed it with *Winter's Tales* some eight years later. Meryl Streep featured as Blixen in Pollack's film; Robert Redford appeared as her British adventurer lover Denys Finch Hatton, a role originally offered to Jeremy Irons.

Meryl Streep	*Out Of Africa* (Pollack)	USA, 85

Blofeld, Ernst [F]

Supreme controller of SPECTRE, the international criminal organization bent on world domination in Ian Fleming's series of James Bond novels. A shadowy, background figure in movies (only his voice – belonging to Eric Pohlmann – was heard and his hands seen stroking his white cat) until Donald Pleasence arrived on the scene in *You Only Live Twice.*

Donald Pleasence	*You Only Live Twice* (Gilbert)	GB, 67
Telly Savalas	*On Her Majesty's Secret Service* (Hunt)	GB, 69
Charles Gray	*Diamonds Are Forever* (Hamilton)	GB, 71
Max Von Sydow	*Never Say Never Again* (Kershner)	GB, 83

Note: Apart from Blofeld, 007's chief adversaries have included the modern Midas Auric Goldfinger, the handless Chinese scientist Dr No and the high kicking Russian agent Rosa Klebb. The full list of Bond villains is as follows:

Dr No	Joseph Wiseman *(Dr No)*	GB, 62
Rosa Klebb	Lotte Lenya *(From Russia With Love)*	GB, 63
Red Grant	Robert Shaw *(From Russia With Love)*	GB, 63
Auric Goldfinger	Gert Frobe *(Goldfinger)*	GB, 64
Oddjob	Harold Sakata *(Goldfinger)*	GB, 64
Largo	Adolfo Celi *(Thunderball)*	GB, 65
	Klaus Maria Brandauer *(Never Say Never Again)*	GB, 83
Mr Kidd and Mr Wint	Putter Smith and Bruce Glover *(Diamonds Are Forever)*	GB, 71
Dr Kananga	Yaphet Kotto *(Live and Let Die)*	GB, 73
Scaramanga	Christopher Lee *(The Man With The Golden Gun)*	GB, 74

Meryl Streep as the Danish author Karen Blixen who for 17 years ran a coffee plantation in British East Africa. A scene from Sydney Pollack's award-winning *Out of Africa*

Stromberg	Curt Jurgens *(The Spy Who Loved Me)*	GB, 77
Jaws	Richard Kiel *(The Spy Who Loved Me)*	GB, 77
	(Moonraker)	GB, 79
Hugo Drax	Michael Lonsdale *(Moonraker)*	GB, 79
Kristatos	Julian Glover *(For Your Eyes Only)*	GB, 81
Kamal	Louis Jourdan *(Octopussy)*	GB, 83
Max Zorin	Christopher Walken *(A View To A Kill)*	GB, 85

Anne Boleyn R

(1507–36) The second wife of Henry VIII and the only one of the six to be afforded a full-scale film biography i.e. *Anne Of The Thousand Days.* A lady of honour to Henry's first queen, Catherine of Aragon, she bore the king a daughter (later Queen Elizabeth I) and a still-born son. Made to stand trial for adultery and witchcraft when Henry eventually tired of her, she was executed on the scaffold.

Merle Oberon	*The Private Life Of Henry VIII* (Korda)	GB, 33
Barbara Shaw	*The Pearls Of The Crown* (Guitry/Jaque)	Fra, 37
Elaine Stewart	*Young Bess* (Sydney)	USA, 53
Vanessa Redgrave	*A Man For All Seasons* (Zinnemann)	GB, 66
Genevieve Bujold	*Anne Of The Thousand Days* (Jarrott)	GB, 69
Charlotte Rampling	*Henry VIII And His Six Wives* (Hussein)	GB, 72

Geneviève Bujold as the ill-fated Anne Boleyn, the second wife of Henry VIII and who eventually stood trial for adultery and witchcraft and was executed on the scaffold. A scene from Charles Jarrott's 1969 production, *Anne of the Thousand Days*

Note: Anne was played on the silent screen by Laura Cowie in *Henry VIII* (GB, 11), Clara Kimball Young (USA, 12) and Henny Porten in Lubitsch's *Anna Boleyn* (Ger, 20).

The other wives have been played on screen as follows:

Catherine of Aragon (1483–1536)

Rosalie Crutchley	*The Sword And The Rose* (Annakin) GB, 53
Irene Papas	*Anne Of The Thousand Days* (Jarrott) GB, 69
Frances Cuka	*Henry VIII And His Six Wives* (Hussein) GB, 72

Jane Seymour (1509–1537)

Wendy Barrie	*The Private Life Of Henry VIII* (Korda) GB, 33
Helen Valkis	*The Prince And The Pauper* (Keighley) USA, 37
Lesley Paterson	*Anne Of The Thousand Days* (Jarrott) GB, 69
Jane Asher	*Henry VIII And His Six Wives* (Hussein) GB, 72

Anne Of Cleves (1515–1557)

Elsa Lanchester	*The Private Life Of Henry VIII* (Korda) GB, 33
Jenny Bos	*Henry VIII And His Six Wives* (Hussein) GB, 72

Catherine Howard (*c.* 1520–1542)

Binnie Barnes	*The Private Life Of Henry VIII* (Korda) GB, 33
Dawn Addams	*Young Bess* (Sidney) USA, 53
Monica Dietrich	*Carry On Henry* (Thomas) GB, 71
Lynne Frederick	*Henry VIII And His Six Wives* (Hussein) GB, 72

Catherine Parr (1512–1548)

Everley Gregg	*The Private Life Of Henry VIII* (Korda) GB, 33
Deborah Kerr	*Young Bess* (Sidney) USA, 53
Barbara Leigh-Hunt	*Henry VIII And His Six Wives* (Hussein) GB, 72

Napoleon Bonaparte [R]

(1769–1821) Emperor of France and possibly the only historical figure to have been viewed from every standpoint on screen. Boyer and Brando concentrated on his romantic excesses, Herbert Lom and Vladislav Strzhelchik on his retreat from Moscow, Rod Steiger his defeat at Waterloo and Kenneth Haig his imprisonment on St Helena. The recent *Adieu Bonaparte* centred on Napoleon's Egyptian campaign of 1798. Stanley Kubrick's long promised biography has yet to materialize.

The following is a list of the main actors to have played Napoleon on film. When two names appear against the pictures of Sacha Guitry, the first refers to the actor who played the young Bonaparte, the second to the performer who appeared as the older Napoleon.

Emile Drain	*L'Aiglon* (Tourjansky) Fra, 31
Paul Gunther	*Luise, Königin von Preussen* (Froelich) Ger, 31
Gianfranco Giachetti	*Cento Di Questi Giorni* (Camerini) It, 33
Paul Irving	*The Count Of Monte Cristo* (Lee) USA, 34
Esme Percy	*Invitation To The Waltz* (Merzbach) GB, 35
Rollo Lloyd	*Anthony Adverse* (LeRoy) USA, 36
Claude Rains	*Hearts Divided* (Borzage) USA, 36
Charles Boyer	*Maria Walewska* (Brown) USA, 37
Jean Louis Barrault Emile Drain	*The Pearls Of The Crown* (Guitry-Jaque) Fra, 37
Claude Martin Emile Drain	*Champs-Elysées* (Guitry) Fra, 38
Pierre Blanchar	*A Royal Divorce* (Raymond) GB, 38
Albert Dieudonne	*Madame Sans-Gêne* (Richebe) Fra, 41
Jean-Louis Barrault Sacha Guitry	*Le Destin Fabuleux de Désirée Clary* (Guitry) Fra, 42
Herbert Lom	*The Young Mr Pitt* (Reed) GB, 42
Sergei Mezhinsky	*Kutuzov*/1812 (Petrov) USSR, 44
Charles Sauten	*Kolberg* (Harlan) Ger, 45
Emile Drain	*La Diable Boiteux* (Guitry) Fra, 48
Arnold Moss	*The Reign Of Terror* (Anthony Mann) USA, 49
Paul Dahlke	*Begegnung Mit Werther* (Stroux) W. Ger, 49
Gerard Oury	*Sea Devils* (Walsh) GB, 53
Daniel Gelin Raymond Pellegrin	*Napoleon* (Guitry) Fra, 54
Marlon Brando	*Desiree* (Koster) USA, 54

(Above) Marlon Brando (centre) as a 'method' Napoleon in the 1954 CinemaScope production *Desiree* – co-starring Michael Rennie and Jean Simmons. (Right) Rod Steiger as a Napoleon defeated by the Duke of Wellington and the ravages of illness in Sergei Bondarchuk's 1971 epic *Waterloo*

Emile Drain	*Versailles* (Guitry) Fra, 54
Robert Cornthwaite	*The Purple Mask* (Humberstone) USA, 55
Herbert Lom	*War And Peace* (King Vidor) USA/It, 56
Dennis Hopper	*The Story Of Mankind* (Allen) USA, 57
Rene Deltgen	*Queen Luise* (Liebeneiner) W. Ger, 57
Pierre Mondy	*Austerlitz* (Gance) Fra/It,Yug, 60
Julien Bertheau	*Madame Sans-Gêne* (Christian-Jaque) It/Fra/Spain, 61
Raymond Pellegrin	*Venere Imperiale* (Castellani/Delannoy) It, 63
Janusz Zakrzenski	*Ashes* (Wajda) Pol, 65
Gyula Bodrogi	*Hary Jonos* (Szinetar) Hung, 65
Jock Livingstone	*Zero In The Universe* (Moorse) USA/Neth, 66
Vladislav Strzhelchik	*War And Peace* (Bondarchuk) USSR, 66–67
Giani Esposito	*The Sea Pirate* (Rowland) Fra/Spa/It, 67
Eli Wallach	*The Adventures Of Gerard* (Skolimowski) GB/It/Swi, 70
Rod Steiger	*Waterloo* (Bondarchuk) It/USSR, 71
Kenneth Haigh	*Eagle In A Cage* (Cook) GB, 71
James Tolkan	*Love And Death* (Woody Allen) USA, 75
Aldo Maccione	*The Loves And Times Of Scaramouche* (Castellari) It/Yug, 76
Ian Holm	*Time Bandits* (Gilliam) GB, 81
Daniel Harris	*Stuck On You!* (Herz/Weil) USA, 82
Patrice Chereau	*Adieu Bonaparte* (Chahine) Fra/Eg, 85
Armand Assante	*Napolean and Josephine* (Heffron) TVM/USA, 87

Note: There were over 100 silent portrayals of Napoleon on screen, the most famous being that of Albert Dieudonne in Abel Gance's 1927 French epic *Napoleon,* filmed in a revolutionary triple-screen process. Other silent portraits include those of Charles Barratt in *Madame Recamier* (GB, 23) and *Empress Josephine* (GB, 23), Charles Vanel in *Konigen Louise* (Ger, 27) and *Waterloo* (Ger, 29), Paul Muni in *Seven Faces* (USA, 29) and *The Valiant* (USA, 29) and Otto Matieson in *The Lady Of Victories* (USA, 27) and *Napoleon's Barber* (USA, 29).

Bond, James [F]

The secret agent of modern times, an indestructible operator licensed 'to kill for queen and country'. Something of a sadist in the novels of Ian Fleming, little more than a comic-strip hero in the later films in the series. Code number: 007. Favourite drink: vodka martini, very dry, shaken not stirred. First appeared in print in 'Casino Royale' in 1953. The definitive portrayal? Still that of Sean Connery who together with Roger Moore has played the role seven times.

Sean Connery	*Dr No* (Young) GB, 62
Sean Connery	*From Russia, With Love* (Young) GB, 63
Sean Connery	*Goldfinger* (Hamilton) GB, 64
Sean Connery	*Thunderball* (Young) GB, 65
Sean Connery	*You Only Live Twice* (Gilbert) GB, 67
George Lazenby	*On Her Majesty's Secret Service* (Hunt) GB, 69
Sean Connery	*Diamonds Are Forever* (Hamilton) GB, 71
Roger Moore	*Live And Let Die* (Hamilton) GB, 73
Roger Moore	*The Man With The Golden Gun* (Hamilton) GB, 74
Roger Moore	*The Spy Who Loved Me* (Gilbert) GB, 77
Roger Moore	*Moonraker* (Gilbert) GB, 79
Roger Moore	*For Your Eyes Only* (Glen) GB, 81
Roger Moore	*Octopussy* (Glen) GB, 83
Sean Connery	*Never Say Never Again* (Kershner) GB, 83
Roger Moore	*A View To A Kill* (Glen) GB, 85
Timothy Dalton	*The Living Daylights* (Glen) GB, 87

Note: In the 1967 spoof *Casino Royale* David Niven appeared as an ageing 007 and Woody Allen as his inept nephew Jimmy Bond. The very first actor to play James Bond was Barry Nelson who starred in the 1954 one hour TV version of *Casino Royale.* Directed by Robert E. Brandt, it was part of the CBS 'Climax' TV Drama series. CBS paid Ian Fleming 1000 dollars for the TV rights.

Bond's controller 'M' was played by Bernard Lee in the first 11 films; Robert Brown succeeded to the

Sean Connery in action in his 007 comeback film *Never Say Never Again,* a reworking of the earlier James Bond movie *Thunderball*

role in *For Your Eyes Only* (81) and has since played it in *Octopussy* (83), *A View To A Kill* (85) and *The Living Daylights* (87). John Huston brought eccentricity to the part in *Casino Royale* (67), Edward Fox added an aristocratic air in *Never Say Never Again* (83).

Bonney, Anne [R]

Seventeenth century woman pirate who operated in the Caribbean with all the ruthlessness of her male counterparts. Something of an early 'women's libber', she dressed as a man, wore close-cropped hair and eventually escaped with her life after a trial in Jamaica. Jean Peters (as Captain Providence) featured as Bonney in *Anne Of The Indies*.

Binnie Barnes	*The Spanish Main* (Borzage)	USA, 45
Hope Emerson	*Double Crossbones* (Barton)	USA, 50
Jean Peters	*Anne Of The Indies* (Tourneur)	USA, 51
Hillary Brooke	*Abbott And Costello Meet Captain Kidd* (Lamont)	USA, 52

Bonnie And Clyde [R]

Young gangster twosome (full names, Bonnie Parker and Clyde Barrow) who operated in the early 30s and robbed and murdered some 18 people in a three-year killing spree across the American Mid-west. Finally ambushed and shot by police in May, 1934. Romanticized out of all proportion in Arthur Penn's famous 1967 film but portrayed more realistically in William Witney's earlier 'cheapie', *The Bonnie Parker Story*.

Warren Beatty and Faye Dunaway as Clyde Barrow and Bonnie Parker, the two young Depression bank robbers who murdered their way across the American Mid-West in the early 30s. A scene from Arthur Penn's gangster classic, *Bonnie and Clyde*

Dorothy Provine and Jack Hogan	*The Bonnie Parker Story* (Witney) USA, 58
Faye Dunaway and Warren Beatty	*Bonnie And Clyde* (Penn) USA, 67

Note: Directors drew on the escapades of Parker and Barrow frequently during the 30s and 40s, most notably Joseph H. Lewis with his B movie *Gun Crazy* (49), a film scripted by MacKinlay Kantor and starring Peggy Cummins and John Dall. Fritz Lang's *You Only Live Once* (37) starring Henry Fonda and Sylvia Sidney, Nicholas Ray's *They Live By Night* (49) with Farley Granger and Cathy O'Donnell, plus Robert Altman's 1974 remake *Thieves Like Us* with Keith Carradine and Shelley Duvall, also derived from the exploits of the death and glory duo.

Booth, John Wilkes

(1839–65) Assassin of President Lincoln, an embittered Southerner who, in 1865, joined a conspiracy to avenge the defeat of the Confederates. The murder occurred on 14 April at Ford's Theatre in Washington. Lincoln was shot in the head and Booth escaped on horseback. A few days later, he was tracked to a barn in Virginia and shot. The event has been portrayed several times on film, in most detail in the 1977 film *The Lincoln Conspiracy*.

Ian Keith	*Abraham Lincoln* (Griffith) USA, 30
Francis McDonald	*The Prisoner Of Shark Island* (Ford) USA, 36
John Derek	*Prince Of Players* (Dunne) USA, 55
Bradford Dillman	*The Lincoln Conspiracy* (Conway) USA, 77

Note: Raoul Walsh in *Birth Of A Nation* (USA, 15) and William Moran in *Abraham Lincoln* (USA, 24) both featured as Booth in silent movies; Edwin Booth, the actor-brother of John, was played by Richard Burton in *Prince Of Players*.

Bill Gribble appeared as Lincoln's assassin in the 1980 TV film *The Ordeal Of Dr Mudd*.

Borgia, Cesare

(1475–1507) Italian prince, son of Pope Alexander VI, notorious for his ruthlessness in Renaissance Italy. He lived for only 32 years, but left behind him countless legends of cruelty and murder, including the killing of his own brother, and incest with his sister Lucrezia. Orson Welles relished in a brief cameo of sinister treachery in *Prince Of Foxes*, Lorenzo Berinizi in one of uncontrollable lust in Borowczyk's *Immoral Tales*.

Gabriel Gabrio	*Lucrezia Borgia* (Gance) Fra, 35
Macdonald Carey	*Bride Of Vengeance* (Leisen) USA, 49
Orson Welles	*Prince Of Foxes* (King) USA, 49
Pedro Armendariz	*Lucrezia Borgia* (Christian-Jaque) Fra, 52
Franco Fabrizi	*The Nights of Lucrezia Borgia* (Grieco) It/Fra, 59
Cameron Mitchell	*The Black Duke* (Mercanti) It/Spa, 63
Edmund Purdom	*The Man With The Golden Mask* (Corbucci) It/Fra, 65
Lou Castel	Lucrezia (Civirani) It/Aus, 68
Lorenzo Berinizi	*Immoral Tales* (Borowczyk) Fra, 74

Note: Enrico Piacentini in *The Power Of The Borgias* (It, 20), Conrad Veidt in *Lucrezia Borgia* (Ger, 22) and Warner Oland in *Don Juan* (USA, 26) were among the actors who contributed to Cesare's villainy on the silent screen.

Borgia, Lucrezia

(1480–1519) Sister of Cesare and, for many, the world's most infamous woman. Disappointingly, most of her legendary poisonings and incestuous relationships are untrue and although she worked her way through three husbands in her 39 years, she was a much respected woman and patron of many artists. But for moviemakers the motto has always been, 'film the legend, not the fact'.

Edwige Feuillere	*Lucrezia Borgia* (Gance) Fra, 35
Paulette Goddard	*Bride Of Vengeance* (Leisen) USA, 49
Martine Carol	*Lucrezia Borgia* (Christian-Jaque) Fra, 52
Belinda Lee	*The Nights Of Lucrezia Borgia* (Grieco) It/Fra, 59
Lisa Gastoni	*The Man With The Golden Mask* (Corbucci) It/Fra, 65
Olinka Berova	*Lucrezia* (Civirani) It/Aus, 68
Florence Bellamy	*Immoral Tales* (Borowczyk) Fra, 74

Note: Oda Alstrup (Den, 09), Stacia Napierkowska (Fra, 09), Maria Jacobini (It, 10), Diana Karenne (It, 17) and Liane Haid (Ger, 22) all played Lucrezia Borgia on the silent screen.

Boston Blackie F

Wise-cracking, girl-chasing ex-jewel thief who turns his attentions to the amateur detective business but never quite convinces the police that he's going straight for good. Numerous silent screen portrayals but best remembered for Chester Morris' B movie interpretations of the 40s. Appears in only one book – 'Boston Blackie', writted by Jack Boyle in 1919.

Chester Morris	*Meet Boston Blackie* (Florey) USA, 41
Chester Morris	*Confessions Of Boston Blackie* (Dmytryk) USA, 41
Chester Morris	*Alias Boston Blackie* (Landers) USA, 42
Chester Morris	*Boston Blackie Goes Hollywood* (Gordon) USA, 42
Chester Morris	*After Midnight With Boston Blackie* (Landers) USA, 43
Chester Morris	*The Chance Of A Lifetime* (Castle) USA, 43
Chester Morris	*One Mysterious Night* (Boetticher, Jr) USA, 44
Chester Morris	*Boston Blackie Booked On Suspicion* (Dreifuss) USA, 45
Chester Morris	*Boston Blackie's Rendezvous* (Dreifuss) USA, 45
Chester Morris	*A Close Call For Boston Blackie* (Landers) USA, 46
Chester Morris	*The Phantom Thief* (Lederman) USA, 46
Chester Morris	*Boston Blackie And The Law* (Lederman) USA, 46
Chester Morris	*Trapped by Boston Blackie* (Friedman) USA, 48
Chester Morris	*Boston Blackie's Chinese Venture* (Friedman) USA, 49

Note: The following actors also played Boston Blackie on the silent screen – Bert Lytell in *Boston Blackie's Little Pal* (18) and *Blackie's Redemption* (19), Lionel Barrymore in *The Face In The Fog* (22), David Powell in *Missing Millions* (22), William Russell in *Boston Blackie* (23), Forrest Stanley in *Through The Dark* (24) and Raymond Glenn in *The Return Of Boston Blackie* (27).

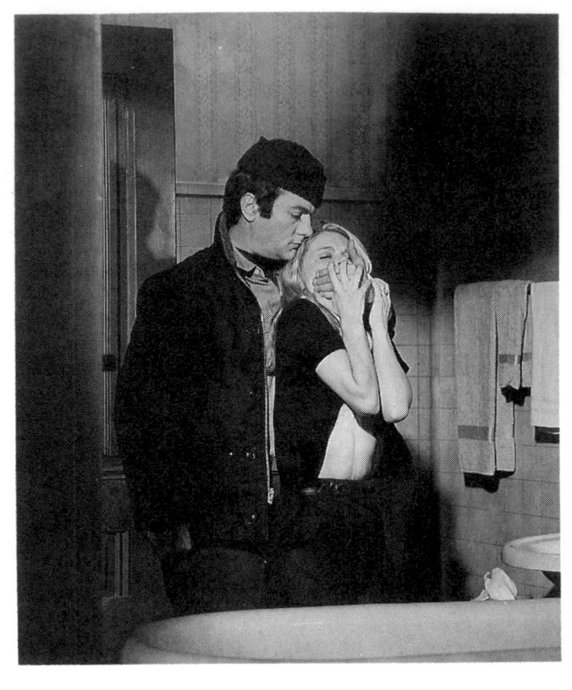

Tony Curtis in his most terrifying and unusual role—as the mass murderer Albert de Salvo in *The Boston Strangler*

Boston Strangler, The 

The notorious sex maniac whose activities terrified the female population of Massachussetts between June 1962 and January 1964 when he raped and murdered 13 women. A 34-year-old former mental patient (real name, Albert DeSalvo) he eventually confessed to the crimes and in 1967 was committed to a state mental institution. In 1973 he was found dead in his prison cell, stabbed through the heart. The film starring Tony Curtis was advertised with the words: 'Come In – He did, 13 times!'

Tony Curtis	*The Boston Strangler* (Fleischer) USA, 67

Bovary, Emma 

Young doctor's tragic wife whose discontent and thirst for romance lead her to adultery, disillusionment and ultimately suicide. The central character in 'Madame Bovary' (1857), Gustave Flaubert's classic novel of mid-nineteenth century provincial France, and a role much coveted by actresses over the years. Valentine Tessier's performance in

Renoir's 1934 version remains perhaps the most satisfying screen interpretation to date.

Lila Lee	*Unholy Love* (Ray)	USA, 32
Valentine Tessier	*Madame Bovary* (Renoir)	Fra, 34
Pola Negri	*Madame Bovary* (Lamprecht)	Ger, 37
Mecha Ortiz	*Madame Bovary* (Schlieper)	Arg, 47
Jennifer Jones	*Madame Bovary* (Minnelli)	USA, 49
Edwige Fenech	*Madame Bovary* (Scott)	W.Ger/It, 69
Jadwiga Janksowska-Cieslak	*Madame Bovary, That's Me* (Kaminski)	Pol, 77

Note: In the 1949 version by Vincente Minnelli, James Mason appeared as Flaubert. David Lean's *Ryan's Daughter* (70) has been described by the director as a loose adaptation 'of sorts' of Flaubert's novel. It starred Sarah Miles and was set in Ireland. On TV Nyree Dawn Porter (BBC, 64) and Francesca Annis (BBC, 75) have both played Emma Bovary in recent times.

Bowie, Jim R

(*c.* 1790–1836) Inventor of the deadly Bowie knife and, like Davy Crockett, a folk hero of the American West. In 1836 he died with Crockett and 180 other heroes defending the Alamo against the might of a Mexican army totalling 4000 men. Alan Ladd and Richard Widmark brought their star personal to the role; Sterling Hayden a more rugged realism in Frank Lloyd's *The Last Command*.

Robert Armstrong	*Man Of Conquest* (Nicholls, Jr)	USA, 39
Macdonald Carey	*Comanche Territory* (Sherman)	USA, 50
Alan Ladd	*The Iron Mistress* (Boetticher)	USA, 52
Stuart Randall	*The Man From The Alamo* (Boetticher)	USA, 53
Kenneth Tobey	*Davy Crockett, King Of The Wild Frontier* (Foster)	USA, 55
Sterling Hayden	*The Last Command* (Lloyd)	USA, 55
Jeff Morrow	*The First Texan* (Haskin)	USA, 56
Richard Widmark	*The Alamo* (Wayne)	USA, 60

Note: Scott Forbes starred as Bowie in a 1956–7 TV series *The Adventures Of Jim Bowie;* James Arness played the frontier knifeman in Burt Kennedy's three hour TV movie *The Alamo: 13 Days to Glory* (87).

Bowles, Sally

Amoral but forever optimistic cabaret singer whose adventures in pre-war Berlin during the rise to power of the Nazi party were first chronicled by Christopher Isherwood in his books 'Sally Bowles' (1937) and 'Goodbye To Berlin' (1939). Later, she went on to become both a stage and film heroine in *I Am A Camera* and *Cabaret*. For her performance in the latter movie Liza Minnelli won an Academy Award as the best actress of 1972.

Julie Harris	*I Am A Camera* (Cornelius)	GB, 55
Liza Minnelli	*Cabaret* (Fosse)	USA, 72

Bradley, General Omar N.

(1893–1981) American general of World War II, chosen by Eisenhower to command the US First Army

Liza Minnelli as Christopher Isherwood's bizarre heroine Sally Bowles, pictured here with Joel Grey's Master of Ceremonies in Bob Fosse's musical *Cabaret*

during the D-Day landings of June, 1944. A quiet, calm man, the very opposite to General Patton, with whom his career was closely linked during the war. Portrayed in most depth and with quiet effectiveness by Karl Malden in the Award-winning *Patton*.

Nicholas Stuart	*The Longest Day* (Marton/ Annakin/Wicki)	USA, 62
Glenn Ford	*Is Paris Burning?* (Clement)	Fra/USA, 66
Karl Malden	*Patton* (Schaffner)	USA, 70
Fred Stuthman	*MacArthur* (Sargent)	USA, 77

Braun, Wernher von [R]

(1912–77) German scientist who designed wartime rockets for Hitler, including the V-2 which could travel over a distance of 200 miles and land on target. He surrendered to the Americans in 1945 who used his knowledge and expertise in the development of their space programme. Von Braun's story was chronicled in the 1960 production, *I Aim At The Stars*.

Curt Jurgens	*I Aim At The Stars* (Lee Thompson)	USA, 60

Breck, Alan [F]

Jacobite adventurer who helps the young David Balfour secure his rightful inheritance in Robert Louis Stevenson's 'Kidnapped' (1886). On screen, usually no more than a straightforward swashbuckler, although Michael Caine provided a less than romantic portrait of a sometimes ruthless man dogged by weariness and disillusionment.

Warner Baxter	*Kidnapped* (Werker)	USA, 38
Daniel O'Herlihy	*Kidnapped* (Beaudine)	USA, 48
Peter Finch	*Kidnapped* (Stevenson)	GB, 60
Thomas Weisgerber	*Kidnapped* (Seemann)	E.Ger, 68
Michael Caine	*Kidnapped* (Delbert Mann)	GB, 71

Note: David Balfour has been played by Freddie Bartholomew (38), Roddy McDowall (48), James MacArthur (60), Werner Kanitz (68) and Lawrence Douglas (71).

Breckinridge, Myra [F]

The end result of a sex change operation, a shapely man-eater whom, sadly, 'no man can ever possess'. Before the change: a dedicated young film critic named Myron. Created by Gore Vidal in his 1968 novel and played before and after by Rex Reed and Raquel Welch, respectively.

Raquel Welch	*Myra Breckinridge* (Sarne)	USA, 70

Brice, Fanny [R]

(1891–1951) American singer-comedienne whose success on the Broadway stage contrasted sharply with the unhappiness of her private life, which included two tortuous marriages, to gambler Nick Arnstein and showman Billy Rose. A star in just a handful of movies, she remains best-known for her appearances for Ziegfeld and the introduction of the songs 'Second Hand Rose', 'My Man' and 'Rose Of Washington Square'. She appeared as herself in the 1936 bio-pic *The Great Ziegfeld* and has twice

An elegant Barbra Streisand in her second portrayal of the famous Broadway singer/comedienne Fanny Brice. A scene from the 1975 Herbert Ross production *Funny Lady*

been portrayed on screen by Barbra Streisand (one marriage per film), who won an Oscar for her performance in the first picture, *Funny Girl*.

Barbra Streisand	*Funny Girl* (Wyler)	USA, 68
Barbra Streisand	*Funny Lady* (Ross)	USA, 75
Catherine Jacoby	*Ziegfeld: The Man And His Women* (Kulik)	USA,TV, 78
Rosalind Harris	*The Cotton Club* (Coppola)	USA, 84

Note: The 1939 Fox musical *Rose Of Washington Square* starring Alice Faye (as Rose Sargent) and Tyrone Power as her handsome crook/lover was a fictionalized account of Fanny Brice's story. Fox denied Brice's claim that the film was based on her life but when Brice sued the studio quietly settled out of court.

Brontës, The

R

Three writers of genius who lived with their preacher father and alcoholic brother in their remote home on the Yorkshire moors and who released their inner emotions and frustrations in a series of brilliant novels that included *Wuthering Heights* and *Jane Eyre*. The novels have been rather more satisfactorily translated to the screen than the actual lives of the Brontës, Hollywood and France both failing miserably in their biographical efforts of the 40s and 70s. Only Julie Harris in the film of her one woman show *Brontë* managed to capture something of the true nature of the oldest sister, Charlotte. In an engrossing performance she played the writer when she was 33 years of age and

The Brontés, Hollywood style in Warner Brothers' *Devotion* (1944). From left to right (all of them too robust and well-dressed): Olivia de Havilland as Charlotte, Ida Lupino as Emily, and Nancy Coleman as Anne. Bette Davis and Miriam Hopkins were the actresses originally set to play Charlotte and Emily

remembering back with wistful melancholy to better times.

Charlotte (1816–55)

Olivia de Havilland	*Devotion* (Bernhardt)	USA, 44
Marie-France Pisier	*The Brontë Sisters* (Techine)	Fra, 79
Julie Harris	*Brontë* (Delbert Mann)	USA, 83

Anne (1820–49)

Nancy Coleman	*Devotion* (Bernhardt)	USA, 44
Isabelle Huppert	*The Brontë Sisters* (Techine)	Fra, 79

Emily (1818–48)

Ida Lupino	*Devotion* (Bernhardt)	USA, 44
Isabelle Adjani	*The Brontë Sisters* (Techine)	Fra, 79

Note: Brother Branwell was played by Arthur Kennedy in *Devotion* (44) and by Pascall Gregory in *The Brontë Sisters* (79); Sydney Greenstreet made an appearance as Thackeray in Curtis Bernhardt's 1944 film for Warners.

Broughton, Lady Diana Delves R

A much-married young beauty whose millionaire husband – Sir Jock Broughton – stood trial for (but was acquitted of) the murder of her lover, the philandering Earl of Erroll who was shot one dark night in Nairobi in 1941. The events leading up to the murder in Kenya's 'Happy Valley' of decadent expatriates were recreated by director Michael Radford in the 1988 film *White Mischief.* Just a few months earlier the same story was told in the BBC TV film *The Happy Valley.*

Amanda Hillwood	*The Happy Valley* (Devenish)	TVM,GB, 87
Greta Scacchi	*White Mischief* (Radford)	GB, 88

Note: Sir Jock Broughton was played by Denholm Elliott in the TV film and Joss Ackland in *White Mischief;* the murdered Earl of Erroll by Peter Sands (87) and Charles Dance (88).

Brown, Father F

The meekest of all amateur detectives, a gentle little Essex priest who detects crimes by using a psychological and humane approach to his mysteries. Frequently more interested in a criminal's redemption than his arrest. Most notable adversary: arch criminal Flambeau. The creation of G. K. Chesterton, he first appeared in print in the short story collection, 'The Innocence Of Father Brown' (1911).

Walter Connolly	*Father Brown, Detective* (Sedgwick)	USA, 34
Alec Guinness	*Father Brown* (Hamer)	GB, 54
Heinz Rühmann	*Das Schwarze Schaf* (Ashley)	W.Ger, 60
Heinz Rühmann	*Er Kanns Nicht Lassen* (Ambesser)	W.Ger, 62

Note: Barnard Hughes appeared as Father Brown in the 1980 TV movie *Sanctuary of Fear* (Moxey) which transported the little English cleric to New York City to solve a series of unmotivated murders. Six years earlier Kenneth More appeared in 26 50 minute episodes of *Father Brown* (74), all of them based on Chesterton's originals.

Browning, Lt General Frederick 'Boy' R

(1896–1966) British general who pioneered the use of airborne troops and commanded the First Airborne Corps at Arnhem during the ill-fated 'Operation Market Garden' of 1944. Given wide exposure on film in Richard Attenborough's Arnhem epic, *A Bridge Too Far.*

Dirk Bogarde	*A Bridge Too Far* (Attenborough)	GB, 77

Bruce, Lenny R

For some, a brilliantly inventive American comic who was one of the precursors of social upheaval and change; for others, a dangerous, obscene performer whose use of four-letter words and scathing material made him a figure to despise. Either way, a prominent figure on the night club circuit of the 60s and a man whose tortured, self-destructive life (which ended from a drug overdose in 1966) was recreated with great skill by Bob Fosse in his 1974 biography.

Dustin Hoffman	*Lenny* (Fosse)	USA, 74

Brummell, George Bryan ('Beau') R

(1778–1840) Handsome English dandy who won the friendship of the Prince of Wales in Regency England and led a colourful bachelor's life until his indiscretions with the ladies and eventual quarrel

A woman whom any man would kill—or get killed for! Greta Scacchi as the promiscuous Diana Broughton whose lover was murdered in his car in Africa in the early '40s and whose elderly husband was later accused but acquitted of the crime. Charles Dance co-starred as the philandering lover the Earl of Erroll and Joss Ackland as the middle aged aristocratic husband Jack Broughton. A scene from the Michael Radford 1988 production *White Mischief*

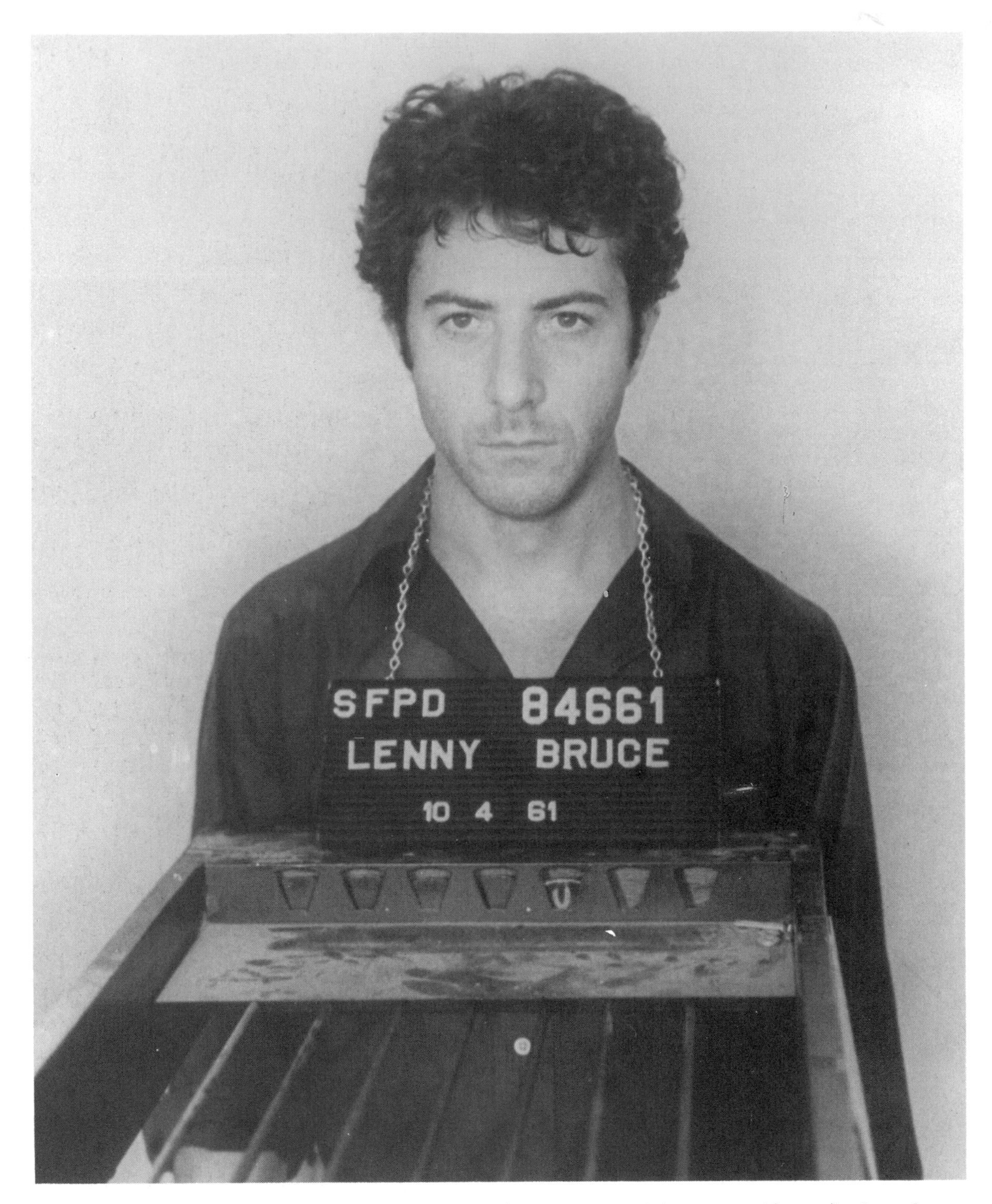

Dustin Hoffman, in trouble with the law in *Lenny,* Bob Fosse's dramatic account of the controversial comedian Lenny Bruce, produced by Marvin Worth in 1974

with the Prince led to his downfall. Forced to leave England to escape his creditors, he died in poverty in France. Two major interpretations on screen, one by John Barrymore in the silent era, one by Stewart Granger in MGM's swashbuckling period of the early 50s.

Barry Morse	*Mrs Fitzherbert* (Tully)	GB, 47
Stewart Granger	*Beau Brummell* (Bernhardt)	GB, 54

Note: John Barrymore appeared in Harry Beaumont's silent *Beau Brummell* in 1924.

Brutus R

(*c.* 85–42 BC) The last to plunge his sword into Caesar in Shakespeare's play of conspiracy and political power in Ancient Rome, 'Julius Caesar'. The 'noblest Roman of them all', he agonizes over the morality of the murder and eventually commits suicide after the battle of Philippi. Given a quiet sincerity and dignity by James Mason in the 1953 version of Shakespeare's play; only a minor figure in the two spectacles made about Cleopatra.

Arthur Hohl	*Cleopatra* (DeMille)	USA, 34
David Bradley	*Julius Caesar* (Bradley)	USA, 50
James Mason	*Julius Caesar* (Mankiewicz)	USA, 53
Kenneth Haigh	*Cleopatra* (Mankiewicz)	USA, 63
Jason Robards	*Julius Caesar* (Burge)	GB, 70

Note: Norman Wooland played the Brutus character in *An Honourable Murder* (GB, 60), a modern business drama based on Shakespeare's stage play; Murray Carrington featured as a silent Brutus in a 1911 British *Julius Caesar*.

Bullitt, Frank 

Honest San Francisco cop who outwits a politically ambitious D.A. as he investigates the details of an intricate Mafia plot. Arguably Steve McQueen's most famous role, although stunt co-ordinator Carey Loftin and driver Bud Ekins lent considerable assistance during the car chase sequence.

Steve McQueen	*Bullitt* (Yates)	USA, 68

Buntline, Ned 

(1823–86) Prolific American dime novelist who turned Buffalo Bill into a hero of legendary proportions with a long series of exaggerated adventure

Jason Robards as Brutus in Stuart Burge's 1970 adaptation of Shakespeare's *Julius Caesar.* Just assassinated: John Gielgud

John Gielgud as Cassius and MGM's James Mason as Brutus in the 1953 production of *Julius Caesar*

Honest cop and ambitious politician! Steve McQueen and Robert Vaughn at odds in Peter Yates' 1968 thriller *Bullit*

stories. Generally overlooked in films about Cody but allowed his proper place in Western mythology in movies by Wellman and Altman. Real name: Edward Zane Carroll Judson.

Dick Elliott	*Annie Oakley* (Stevens) USA, 35
Thomas Mitchell	*Buffalo Bill* (Wellman) USA, 44
Burt Lancaster	*Buffalo Bill And The Indians, Or Sitting Bull's History Lesson* (Altman) USA, 76

Burgess, Guy [R]

(–1963) Foreign office spy, notorious for his extrovert ways, homosexuality and alcoholic excesses, who defected to Russia with fellow spy Donald Maclean one famous Friday night in May, 1951. Not portrayed on the large or small screen until the late 70s/80s when three TV films were made of his exploits. Derek Jacobi featured as Burgess in the documentary-styled *Philby, Burgess and Maclean* (77), Alan Bates starred in John Schlesinger's *An Englishman Abroad* (83), an account of Burgess' meeting with actress Coral Browne during a culture exchange theatre visit in Moscow in 1958, and Anthony Hopkins appeared in the BBC production, *Blunt* (87), the story of Burgess' relationship with the distinguished art historian Anthony Blunt who helped form the famous Cambridge spy ring in the 30s.

Derek Jacobi	*Philby, Burgess and Maclean* (Flemyng) TV,GB, 77
Alan Bates	*An Englishman Abroad* (Schlesinger) TV,GB, 83
Anthony Hopkins	*Blunt* (Glenister) TV,GB, 87

Note: Burgess' colleague Donald Maclean was played by Michael Culver in *Philby, Burgess And*

Joel McCrea as William Frederick Cody and Thomas Mitchell as the dime novelist Ned Buntline in the 1944 Fox production of *Buffalo Bill*

Maclean and by Michael McStay in *Blunt.* Blunt himself was portrayed by Ian Richardson.

The other famous member of the group, Kim Philby, a Soviet agent for thirty years, was played by Anthony Bate in the 1977 film. Denis Potter's British agent Adrian Harris (played by John Le Mesurier in the 1971 TV play *Traitor*) and Graham Greene's Maurice Castle (portrayed by Nicol Williamson in the 1979 film *The Human Factor*) were both modelled on the character of Philby.

Burke And Hare R

A pair of nineteenth century scoundrels who enjoyed a lucrative grave-robbing career in Edinburgh in the 1820s, often providing corpses for the medical dissecting table just 24 hours after burial! Carried away by success, they finally overstepped the mark when they turned to murder and tried to up the rate of sale. Burke was hanged in 1829, Hare turned king's evidence and finished his days a blind beggar in London. All screen portrayals have been suitably black and enjoyable.

George Rose and Donald Pleasence	*The Flesh And The Fiends* (Gilling) GB, 60
Ivor Dean and Tony Calvin	*Dr Jekyll and Sister Hyde* (Baker) GB, 71
Derren Nesbitt and Glynn Edwards	*Burke And Hare* (Sewell) GB, 72

Note: The characters played by Boris Karloff and Bela Lugosi in Robert Wise's *The Body Snatcher* (USA, 45) and by Jonathan Pryce (as Robert Fallon) and Stephen Rea (as Timothy Broom) in *The Doctor And The Devils* (GB, 86) were modelled on Burke and Hare.

Byron, Lord George 

(1788–1824) English poet and satirist, the darling of early nineteenth century society, not only for his prose but also for his debauchery and dissipated life. A short, somewhat stout man who limped as a result of a club foot, he was turned, by cinema magic, into Richard Chamberlain in Robert Bolt's soap opera *Lady Caroline Lamb.* Noel Willman, in a minor role in *Beau Brummell,* has come the closest to a realistic screen interpretation. The most recent portrayals have all been in films dealing with the famous 1816 Byron/Shelley get-together at Lake Geneva when Shelley's wife Mary was first inspired to write the story of *Frankenstein.*

Gavin Gordon	*The Bride Of Frankenstein* (Whale) USA, 35
Malcolm Graham	*The Last Rose Of Summer* (Fitzpatrick) GB, 37
Dennis Price	*The Bad Lord Byron* (Macdonald) GB, 49
Noel Willman	*Beau Brummell* (Bernhardt) GB, 54
Richard Chamberlain	*Lady Caroline Lamb* (Bolt) GB/It, 72
Gabriel Byrne	*Gothic* (Russell) GB, 86
Eric Stoltz	*The Haunted Summer* (Passer) 88
Hugh Grant	*Rowing With the Wind* (Suarez) Spa, 88

Note: Howard Gaye in *A Prince Of Lovers* (GB, 22) and André de Beranger in *Beau Brummell* (USA, 24) both featured as Byron on the silent screen; Lady Caroline Lamb, who enjoyed a brief two month love affair with Byron, has been played by Mary Clare in *A Prince Of Lovers,* Joan Greenwood in *The Bad Lord Byron,* and Sarah Miles in *Lady Caroline Lamb.*

Lust, debauchery, drugs, orgies and decadent fantasies—to name but a few ingredients of Ken Russell's bizarre *Gothic,* the story of the famous haunted summer on Lake Geneva in 1816 when the poets Shelley and Byron, Dr Polidori and Mary Wollstonecraft Shelley spent their time dreaming up weird and fanciful ghost stories, the most fanciful of all being Mary Shelley's *Frankenstein.* In this scene: Gabriel Byrne as Byron and Timothy Spall as Dr Polidori

Caesar, Julius [R]

(101–44 BC) Roman general, statesman and dictator; one of the foremost orators of his age whose career changed the course of Roman history. Kubrick sketched in his youth via the performance of John Gavin in *Spartacus,* Claude Rains and Rex Harrison lingered with Cleopatra, and Louis Calhern and John Gielgud acted out Caesar's last days just prior to his assassination on the Ides of March.

Warren William	*Cleopatra*	(DeMille)	USA, 34
Claude Rains	*Caesar And Cleopatra*	(Pascal)	GB, 46
Harold Tasker	*Julius Caesar*	(Bradley)	USA, 50
Louis Calhern	*Julius Caesar*	(Mankiewicz)	USA, 53
William Lundigan	*Serpent Of The Nile*	(Castle)	USA, 53
Reginald Sheffield	*The Story Of Mankind*	(Allen)	USA, 57
John Gavin	*Spartacus*	(Kubrick)	USA, 60
Cameron Mitchell	*Caesar The Conqueror*	(Anton)	It, 62
Ivo Garrani	*Son Of Spartacus*	(Corbucci)	It, 62
Rex Harrison	*Cleopatra*	(Mankiewicz)	USA, 63
Kenneth Williams	*Carry On Cleo*	(Thomas)	GB, 75
John Gielgud	*Julius Caesar*	(Burge)	GB, 70

Assassination! Louis Calhern's Julius Caesar failing to beware 'The Ides Of March'. A scene from MGM's 1953 production *Julius Caesar*

Note: John Longden played the equivalent of the Caesar role in the modern updating of Shakespeare's play *An Honourable Murder* (GB, 60).

William V. Ranous (USA, 08), Charles Kent (USA, 08), Guy Rathbone (GB, 11) and Amleto Novelli (It, 14) all featured as Caesar on the silent screen; Maurice Denham (69) and Charles Gray (79) have both appeared in TV productions of Shakespeare's play.

Cagliostro, Count Alessandro Di [R]

(1743–95) A peasant criminal (real name, Giuseppe Balsamo) who rose from the poverty-stricken back streets of Palermo to become one of the most powerful men of the eighteenth century. His claim to the title of 'Count' and his boast that he possessed magic elixirs and miracle cures made him a favourite with the aristocracy and royal families of Europe who flocked to seek his advice. He was finally undone when he was imprisoned (ironically for a crime he did not commit) in the Bastille and the truth emerged about his fakery. He finished his days languishing in an Italian prison and died in poverty aged 52. Orson Welles played him with a flourish in the undistinguished *Black Magic;* Hans Stune starred in a German silent directed by Richard Oswald in 1929.

Hans Stune	*Cagliostro*	(Oswald)	Ger, 29
Ferdinand Marian	*Münchhausen*	(Von Baky)	Ger, 43
Orson Welles	*Black Magic*	(Ratoff)	USA, 49
Gino Cervi	*Versailles*	(Guitry)	Fra, 53
Bekim Fehmiu	*Cagliostro*	(Pettinari)	It, 75

Caligari, Dr [F]

After Dr Jekyll, the most famous doctor in movies, a frightening figure who creates a reign of terror in a German town by hypnotizing a somnambulist into committing a series of murders. At the final count, however, revealed to be a kindly doctor and no more than a figment of the insane narrator's imagination. In the 1962 remake, Caligari is a bearded sadist who subjects his patients to a series of tortures inside a mysterious mansion. Again, in the final scenes, he is revealed as a kindly specialist, and the narrator, a woman undergoing psychiatric treatment.

Werner Krauss	*The Cabinet of Dr Caligari* (Wiene) Ger, 19
Dan O'Herlihy	*The Cabinet Of Dr Caligari* (Kay) USA, 62

Caligula [R]

(AD 12–41) The most decadent and bloodthirsty of all the Roman emperors, adept at murder and assorted acts of madness and who ruled over Rome between AD 37–41. Portrayals mostly minor until Tinto Brass cast Malcolm McDowell in a semi-pornographic movie shot in Italy in 1980. On TV John Hurt's escapades were less explicit although he did have his moments, not least when he cut and then devoured his unborn child from the womb of his luckless wife!

Emlyn Williams	*I Claudius* (Von Sternberg – unfinished) GB, 37
Jay Robinson	*The Robe* (Koster) USA, 53
Jay Robinson	*Demetrius And The Gladiators* (Daves) USA, 54
Carlo Colombo	*Caligula's Hot Nights* (Montero) It, 77
Malcolm McDowell	*Caligula* (Brass) USA/It, 80
David Cain Haughton	*The Emperor Caligula – The Untold Story* (Hills) It, 81
John Turner	*Caligula And Messalina* (Pass) Fra, 82

Note: N. Carotenuto played Caligula in the 1923 Italian silent *Messalina;* on TV John Hurt in *I Claudius* (76) and John McEnery in *AD – Anno Domini* (85) both starred as the emperor.

Callahan, Harry [F]

Hard-hitting San Francisco cop (better known as 'Dirty Harry'), always under fire from his superiors

Decadent, bloodthirsty and insane! And a gift for any actor who can prevent himself from going over the top. Malcolm McDowell as the Roman Emperor *Caligula*

because of his rough justice methods, but constantly coming out ahead in his war against psychotic killers and revolutionary thugs. Too many fascist impulses for some, just right for others. An original screen creation (by Harry Julian Fink and Rita M. Fink) his best known phrase was uttered in his first film when he held a Magnum 44 to the temple of a nervous criminal: 'I know what you're thinking. Did he fire six shots or only five? .... Well, you've got to ask yourself one question. Do I feel lucky? Well, do ya punk?'

Clint Eastwood	*Dirty Harry* (Siegel)	USA, 71
Clint Eastwood	*Magnum Force* (Post)	USA, 73
Clint Eastwood	*The Enforcer* (Fargo)	USA, 76
Clint Eastwood	*Sudden Impact* (Eastwood)	USA, 83
Clint Eastwood	*The Deadly Pool* (Van Horn)	USA, 88

Camille [F]

Notorious courtesan of nineteenth century Paris, a tragic heroine who enjoys an idyllic interlude with a young lover before returning to her pleasure-

Clint Eastwood as 'Dirty Harry' Callahan in the second of the Dirty Harry thrillers, *Magnum Force*

seeking ways and a lingering death from consumption. Garbo's Camille, with her long death scene in the arms of Robert Taylor, is regarded by many as her finest achievement; Daniel Gaubert brought the melodramatics up-to-date in *Camille 2000* which incorporated drugs, sex and a background of modern day Rome. Dumas' novel 'La Dame aux Camelias' introduced Camille and was published in 1848.

Yvonne Printemps	*La Dame aux Camelias* (Rivers/Gance)	Fra, 34
Greta Garbo	*Camille* (Cukor)	USA, 36
Mecha Ortiz	*Margarita, Armando y su Padre* (Mugica)	Arg, 39
Leila Mourad	*Carmen* (Selim)	Egy, 41
Lina Montes	*La Dama de las Camelias* (Soria)	Mex, 44
Micheline Presle	*La Dame aux Camelias* (Bernard)	Fra, 52
Maria Felix	*Camelia* (Gavaldon)	Mex, 52
Zully Moreno	*La mujer de las Camellas* (Arancibia)	Arg, 53
Colpan Ilhan	*Kamelyali Kadin* (Sirmali)	Turk, 56
Sarita Montiel	*La Belle Lola, Une Dame aux Camelias* (Balcazar)	Spa/It/France, 62
Daniele Gaubert	*Camille 2000* (Metzger)	USA, 69
Carla Fracci	*The True Story Of Camille* (Bolognini)	It/Fra, 81
Greta Scacchi	*Camille* (Davis)	TVM/USA, 84

Note: In Bolognini's 1981 film Carla Fracci appeared only briefly as a 'stage' Camille being directed in turn-of-the-century Paris by Alexandre Dumas. The real Camille of the film was played by Isabelle Huppert who featured as the true-life model for Dumas' tragic heroine, one Alphonsine Plessis, a country girl who in Paris became a seamstress, a prostitute, a nobleman's wife and eventually a high class courtesan.

On the silent screen Camille was played by Oda Alstrup (Den, 07), Vittoria Lepanto (It, 09), Sarah Bernhardt (Fra, 11), Gertrude Shipman (USA, 12), Clara Kimball Young (USA, 15) Francesca Bertini (It, 15), Theda Bara (USA, 17), Erna Morena (Ger, 17), Pola Negri (Ger, 20), Nazimova (USA, 21), Tora Teje (Swe, 25) and Norma Talmadge (USA, 27).

Garbo in one of her most famous roles—the tragic courtesan Camille, filmed in 1936 by George Cukor at MGM. Sharing the scene: Henry Daniell

(Above) Paul Muni, the first actor to portray Chicago gangleader Al Capone on screen, in Howard Hawk's 1932 production *Scarface;* (top left) Jason Robards as Capone in *The St Valentine's Day Massacre* of 1967; (left) Capone 1987 style as portrayed by Robert De Niro in Brian De Palma's stylish version of *The Untouchables*

Cantor, Eddie [R]

(1892–1964) Eye-popping American comedian who rose to fame by playing the small man who always triumphs over adversity. His rags to riches story, from New York's Lower East Side to Broadway and then the movies, was related in Warners' biography of 1954. Cantor's films for Goldwyn, with whom he enjoyed a fruitful relationship in the early 30s, included *Palmy Days* (31), *The Kid From Spain* (32), *Roman Scandals* (33) and *Kid Millions* (34).

Buddy Doyle	*The Great Ziegfeld* (Leonard)	USA, 36
Keefe Brasselle	*The Eddie Cantor Story* (Green)	USA, 54

Note: Cantor appeared as himself in *Thank Your Lucky Stars* (43) and *Hollywood Canteen* (44); Jimmie Quinn played him on the silent screen in *Pretty Ladies* (USA, 25), Richard Shea in the TV movie *Ziegfeld: The Man And His Women* (78).

Capone, Al [R]

Two parallel scars on his left cheek earned this Italian-born gangster the name of Scarface; the deaths of a thousand people in Chicago's gang wars of the 20s established him as the undisputed 'Public Enemy Number One'. The statistics duly impressed Hollywood who began painting Capone's bloody career on celluloid as early as 1932, when Howard Hawks cast Paul Muni as *Scarface*. Since then the films and performances have ranged from the good to the indifferent. Tops in the former category: Rod Steiger in Richard Wilson's documentary-styled 1959 film *Al Capone*.

Paul Muni	*Scarface* (Hawks)	USA, 32
Rod Steiger	*Al Capone* (Wilson)	USA, 59
Neville Brand	*The Scarface Mob* (Karlson)	USA, 59
Neville Brand	*Spin Of A Coin* (Newman)	USA, 62
Jason Robards	*The St Valentine's Day Massacre* (Corman)	USA, 67
Ben Gazzara	*Capone* (Carver)	USA, 75
Robert De Niro	*The Untouchables* De Palma	USA, 87

Note: Capone was never convicted for any of his gangland crimes, not even the St Valentine's Day Massacre. Instead, he was arrested in 1931 for tax evasion and sentenced to 11 years imprisonment. He was paroled in 1939 for 'good behaviour' and died in 1947, aged 48, either of bronchial pneumonia or a brain haemorrhage or syphilis – or a bit of all three.

Captain Jack [R]

(*c.* 1840–73) Not one of the West's best-known figures but a man who was given some attention by director Delmer Daves in the 1954 Alan Ladd western *Drum Beat*. A Modoc leader, real name Keintpoos, who operated along the California/Oregon border with a small band of renegades in the 1860s, he was eventually captured and hung after taking part in the murder of some federal peace commissioners. The role was one of the first to help Charles Bronson (known as Charles Buchinsky in previous films) on the road to stardom.

Charles Bronson	*Drum Beat* (Daves)	USA, 55

Caravaggio, Michelangelo Merisi da [R]

(1569–1609) Post-Renaissance painter who caused controversy among artists of his time by introducing a powerful realism into his painting of biblical scenes, employing crude peasant types as models and dramatizing them by means of harsh light and violent contrasts. He later influenced such painters as George de la Tour, Velasquez and Rubens. Derek Jarman's flamboyant 1986 film looked at Caravaggio's tortured life in flashback, highlighting the painter's poverty and his involvement with pimps, prostitutes and street urchins, all of whom he used to depict sacred figures.

Nigel Terry and Dexter Fletcher (as the young Caravaggio)	*Caravaggio* (Jarman)	GB, 86

Carella, Steve [F]

The most prominent member of Ed McBain's famous eighty-seventh Precinct and among the best-known cops in modern fiction. Despite appearing in over 30 novels since 1956, his screen career has been spasmodic, ranging from the low budget *Cop Hater* in 1958 (in which he was renamed Carelli) to the semi-humorous *Fuzz* with Burt Reynolds. In 1978 Claude Chabrol turned his eyes in his direction with the thriller *Blood Relatives*, set in Montreal.

Robert Loggia	*Cop Hater* (Berke)	USA, 58

Jean-Louis Trintignant	*Without Apparent Motive* (Labro) Fra, 71
Burt Reynolds	*Fuzz* (Colla) USA, 72
Donald Sutherland	*Blood Relatives* (Chabrol) Can/Fra, 78

Note: *The Mugger* (58) was based on an 87th Precinct novel but did not feature Carella; Kurosawa's *High And Low* (63) was adapted from 'King's Ransom' and again did not feature the detective.

Robert Lansing played Carella in a 1961/2 TV series.

Carmen

F

Lustful gypsy tigress of Prosper Merimee, the ultimate femme fatale who wrecks the career of a young Spanish officer and eventually pays for her fickle ways with her life. Her amorous escapades inspired the Bizet opera of 1875 and also several films which have told her story, both in its original form and in updated versions. Rita Hayworth, at her peak in the 1948 film, *The Loves Of Carmen,* remains perhaps the most beautiful of screen Carmens; Dorothy Dandridge in an all black *Carmen Jones,* the most seductive.

Imperio Argentina	*Andalusische Nachte* (Maisch) Ger/Spa, 38
Viviane Romance	*Carmen* (Christian-Jaque) Fra, 43
Rita Hayworth	*The Loves Of Carmen* (Charles Vidor) USA, 48
Ana Esmeralda	*Carmen Prohibida* (Scotese) It/Spa, 52
Dorothy Dandridge	*Carmen Jones* (Preminger) USA, 54
Sara Montiel	*Carmen, de la Ronda* (Demicheli) Spa, 59

Harry Belafonte, having more than a little trouble with Dorothy Dandridge's *Carmen Jones,* in the all-black version of Bizet's opera, directed by Otto Preminger in 1954

Giovanna Ralli	*Carmen Di Trastevere* (Gallone) It, 62
Tina Aumont	*L'uomo, l'orgoglio, la vendetta* (Bazzoni) It/W.Ger, 67
Uta Levka	*Carmen, Baby* (Metzger) USA, 67
Laura Del Sol	*Carmen* (Saura) Spa, 83
Helene Delavault	*The Tragedy Of Carmen* (Brook) Fra, 83
Julia Migenes-Johnson	*Carmen* (Rosi) Fra/It, 84

Note: Grace Bumbry appeared in a Swiss film of Bizet's opera, directed by Herbert von Karajan in 1967; the following actresses all flirted successfully as Carmen on the silent screen: Kathlyn Williams (USA, 09), Regina Badet (Fra, 09), Vittorina Lepanto (It, 09), Florence La Badie (USA, 13), Marion Leonard (USA, 13), Marguerite Snow (USA, 13), Geraldine Farrar (USA, 15), Theda Bara (USA, 15), Pola Negri (Ger, 18), Annie Bos (Holl), Elvira Ortiz (Mex, 20), Raquel Meller (Fra, 26) and Dolores Del Rio (USA, 27).

Carter, Nick

F

Dime novel American detective who has figured in literally thousands of stories since making his debut in the 'New York Weekly' in 1886. In the late 30s appeared set for a flourishing career at MGM, but his traditional methods were found wanting when compared with the wily oriental talents of Charlie Chan, Mr Moto, etc. Resurrected briefly by Eddie Constantine in France in the 60s. First created by John R. Coryell.

Walter Pidgeon	*Nick Carter, Master Detective* (Tourneur) USA, 39
Walter Pidgeon	*Phantom Raiders* (Tourneur) USA, 40
Walter Pidgeon	*Sky Murder* (Seitz) USA, 40
Eddie Constantine	*Nick Carter Va Tout Casser* (Decoin) Fra, 64
Eddie Constantine	*Nick Carter Et Le Trefle Rouge* (Savignac) Fra, 66
Michael Docolomansky	*Nick Carter In Prague* (Lipsky) Czech, 77

Note: Lyle Talbot starred as the son of Nick Carter in the 15-episode Columbia serial, *Nick Carter, Detective* (46); Carter himself appeared on the silent screen in four French serials between 1909 and 1912 and was played by both Thomas Carrigan and Edmund Lowe in a series of short films in 1922.

Carton, Sydney

Dissolute, drunken lawyer who sacrifices his life for the woman he loves in Dickens' stirring novel of the French Revolution, 'A Tale Of Two Cities' (1859). An early anti-hero, famous for his 'Far, far better thing' speech as he meets his death on the guillotine, and incomparably played by Ronald Colman in the MGM production of 1935.

Ronald Colman	*A Tale Of Two Cities* (Conway) USA, 35
Dirk Bogarde	*A Tale Of Two Cities* (Thomas) GB, 58
Chris Sarandon	*A Tale Of Two Cities* (Goddard) TVM,GB, 80

Note: On the silent screen Carton was played by Maurice Costello (USA, 11), William Farnum (USA, 17) and John Martin Harvey in Herbert Wilcox's 1925 British production, *The Only Way*.

Other characters in Dickens' novel – the former prisoner of the Bastille Dr Manette, the revolutionaries Madame and Ernest Defarge and the ruthless aristocrat Marquis de St Evremonde — have been played on screen by the following actors:

Dr Manette

Henry B. Walthall	*A Tale Of Two Cities* (Conway) USA, 35
Stephen Murray	*A Tale Of Two Cities* (Thomas) GB, 58
Peter Cushing	*A Tale Of Two Cities* (Goddard) TVM,GB, 80

Silent: Charles Kent (USA, 11), Josef Swickard (USA, 17) and Fisher White (GB, 25).

Madame Defarge

Blanche Yurka	*A Tale Of Two Cities* (Conway) USA, 35
Rosalie Crutchley	*A Tale Of Two Cities* (Thomas) GB, 58
Billie Whitelaw	*A Tale Of Two Cities* (Goddard) TVM,GB, 80

Silent: Helen Gardiner (USA, 11), Rosita Marstini (USA, 17) and Jean Jay (GB, 25).

Ernest Defarge

Mitchell Lewis	*A Tale Of Two Cities* (Conway) USA, 35

Duncan Lamont	*A Tale Of Two Cities* (Thomas) GB, 58
Norman Jones	*A Tale Of Two Cities* (Goddard) TVM,GB, 80

Silent: Tefft Johnson (USA, 11), Herschel Mayall (USA, 17) and Gordon McLeod (GB, 25).

Marquis de St Evremonde

Basil Rathbone	*A Tale Of Two Cities* (Conway) USA, 35
Christopher Lee	*A Tale Of Two Cities* (Thomas) GB, 58
Barry Morse	*A Tale Of Two Cities* (Goddard) TVM,GB, 80

Silent: William Humphreys (USA, 11), Charles Clary (USA, 17) and Ben Webster (GB, 25).

Caruso, Enrico [R]

(1873–1921) One of the greatest operatic tenors of all time, born in Naples and especially famous for his lead roles in 'Aida', 'Pagliacci', 'La Bohème' and 'Tosca'. Mario Lanza reached star status with his portrayal of Caruso in MGM's 1951 biography: Caruso himself appeared in a few films just prior to his death in 1921 – *My Cousin, The Splendid Romance,* etc.

Mario Lanza	*The Great Caruso* ◐ (Thorpe) USA, 51
Ermanno Randi	*Enrico Caruso, Legend Of A Voice* (Gentilomo) It, 51
Howard Caine	*Pay Or Die* (Wilson) USA, 60
Milan Karpisek	*The Divine Emma* (Krejcik) Cze, 79

Note: Peter Edward Price played Caruso as a boy in *The Great Caruso;* Maurizio Di Nardo in *Enrico Caruso, Legend Of A Voice.*

Casanova, Giovanni [R]

(1725–98) Eighteenth century Italian profligate and ardent amorist whose lively career as a charlatan and lecher took him to all the capitals of Europe. A run-of-the-mill screen romantic, until Fellini's three-hour spectacular stripped away the glamour and presented Casanova's story as a pathetic saga of a wasted life and Casanova himself as an adventurer with a need to declare undying love to a succession of women.

Gustav Waldau	*Münchhausen* (von Baky) Ger, 43
Georges Guetary	*Les Adventures de Casanova* (Boyer) Fra, 46
Arturo de Cordova	*The Adventures Of Casanova* (Gavaldon) USA, 48
Gabriele Ferzetti	*Casanova* (Vanzina) It/Fra, 55
Marcello Mastroianni	*Casanova 70* (Monicelli) It/Fra, 65
Felix Le Breux	*Les Dernieres Roses De Casanova* (Krska) Czech, 66
Leonard Whiting	*The Youth, Vocation And Early Experiences Of Casanova, The Venetian* (Comencini) It, 69
Tony Curtis	*The Rise And Rise Of Casanova* (Legrand) Aus/It/Fra/W.Ger, 77
Donald Sutherland	*Fellini's Casanova* (Fellini) It, 77
Giulio Boseti	*The Return Of Casanova* (Campanile) It, 78

Note: Bob Hope appeared as a servant impersonator in *Casanova's Big Night* (USA, 54) and Ivan Mosjoukine starred in a 1928 French silent film directed by Alexander Volkoff. On TV Frank Finlay – in a six part 1971 BBC serial by Dennis Potter – and Richard Chamberlain in Simon Langton's three hour TV movie *Casanova* (87) have both appeared in the role.

Cassidy, Butch [R]

(1866–1908?) The last of the Western gang leaders; an engaging train robber who operated with his 'Wild Bunch' in Wyoming and Nevada before fleeing with the Sundance Kid to South America at the turn of the century. George Roy Hill's 1969 film had them both die at the hands of the Bolivian cavalry. Rumour has it, however, that Cassidy and possibly Sundance escaped and returned to live peacefully in America under assumed names.

John Doucette	*The Texas Rangers* (Karlson) USA, 51
Gene Evans	*Wyoming Renegades* (Sears) USA, 55
Howard Petrie	*The Maverick Queen* (Kane) USA, 56
Neville Brand	*The Three Outlaws* (Newfield) USA, 56

The most famous bicycle ride in movie history! Paul Newman as Butch Cassidy shows off for Katharine Ross in *Butch Cassidy and the Sundance Kid*

Neville Brand	*Badman's Country*	(Sears)	USA, 58
Arthur Hunnicutt	*Cat Ballou*	(Silverstein)	USA, 65
Tex Gates	*Ride A Wild Stud*	(Ekard)	USA, 69
Paul Newman	*Butch Cassidy And The Sundance Kid*	(Hill)	USA, 69
Tom Berenger	*Butch And Sundance – The Early Days*	(Lester)	USA, 79

Note: Paul Newman's famous bicycle ride was not a film invention. It happened in real life, even down to the bowler hat perched jauntily on the side of Newman's head.

Cassius [R]

The chief conspirator in the plot to kill Julius Caesar, the man with the 'lean and hungry look' who persuades the reluctant Brutus to join the assassination on the Ides of March. John Gielgud led the conspirators in Joe Mankiewicz's 1953 film and completed an unusual double 17 years later when he played Caesar and finished up on the receiving end of the assassins' swords!

Ian MacLaren	*Cleopatra*	(DeMille)	USA, 34
Grosvenor Glenn	*Julius Caesar*	(Bradley)	USA, 50
John Gielgud	*Julius Caesar*	(Mankiewicz)	USA, 53
John Hoyt	*Cleopatra*	(Mankiewicz)	USA, 63
Richard Johnson	*Julius Caesar*	(Burge)	GB, 70

Note: Douglas Wilmer played the equivalent of Cassius in the modern drama, *An Honourable Murder* (60); Eric Maxon featured in the role in a silent British version of 1911.

Catherine The Great [R]

(1729–96) German-born Russian empress whose 34-year reign was marked by great territorial expansion. Like Elizabeth I of England, she has attracted many distinguished screen actresses, including Bette Davis who offered a fiery cameo in *John Paul Jones*. None, however, has quite matched Marlene Dietrich stomping around the palace in hussar's outfit in *The Scarlet Empress,* a lavish Paramount extravaganza climaxed by horsemen charging the palace steps to the accompaniment of bells and 'The Ride Of The Valkyries' on the soundtrack.

Salka Steuermann	*Seven Faces* (Viertel)	USA, 29
Marlene Dietrich	*The Scarlet Empress* (von Sternberg)	USA, 34
Elisabeth Bergner	*Catherine The Great* (Czinner)	GB, 34
Suzy Prim	*Betrayal* (Ozep)	Fra, 37
Francoise Rosay	*The Devil Is An Empress* (Dreville)	Fra, 39
Brigitte Horney	*Münchhausen* (von Baky)	Ger, 43
Olga Zhizneva	*Christmas Slippers* (Shapiro and Kosheverova)	USSR, 44
Tallulah Bankhead	*A Royal Scandal* (Preminger)	USA, 45
Binnie Barnes	*Shadow Of The Eagle* (Salkow)	GB, 50
Olga Zhizneva	*Admiral Ushakov* (Romm)	USSR, 53
Viveca Lindfors	*Tempest* (Lattuada)	USA/It, 58
Bette Davis	*John Paul Jones* (Farrow)	USA, 59
Hildegarde Neff	*Catherine Of Russia* (Lenzi)	It/Fra, 62
Jeanne Moreau	*Great Catherine* (Flemyng)	GB, 68

Note: Pola Negri in Lubitsch's *Forbidden Paradise* (USA, 24) and Louise Dresser in *The Eagle* (USA, 25) both featured in the role on the silent screen.

Cavell, Nurse Edith 

(1865–1915) Just one of Anna Neagle's many true-life screen heroines (they ranged from Nell Gwynn to Queen Victoria, Florence Nightingale to Amy Johnson), a gallant English nurse who served in Belgium in World War I and was finally executed by the Germans for her part in the escape of Allied and Belgian prisoners.

Anna Neagle	*Nurse Edith Cavell* (Wilcox)	GB, 39

Note: Cora Lee, in *Nurse And Martyr* (GB, 15) and Sybil Thorndike in Wilcox's *Dawn* (GB, 28) played Edith Cavell on the silent screen.

Cervantes, Miguel de [R]

(1547–1616) Spanish author of 'Don Quixote' (1605), prior to his writing career as adventurous a swash-buckler as any created by Dumas or Sabatini – fighting the Moors in Spain, falling prisoner to Barbary pirates and being taken as a slave to Algiers. Horst Buchholz played the young Cervantes in a 1968 European co-production; Peter O'Toole doubled as Don Quixote and the ageing author in the musical *Man Of La Mancha*.

Horst Buchholz	*Cervantes* (Sherman)	Fra/It/Spa, 68
Peter O'Toole	*Man Of La Mancha* (Hiller)	It, 72

Challenger, Professor 

Explorer-scientist of Conan Doyle's 'The Lost World' (1912). In view of his adventures in South America where he discovers a prehistoric land of animals and ape-men, something of an under-exposed figure on screen, only two versions (one silent) having been made of 'The Lost World' to date.

Claude Rains	*The Lost World* (Allen)	USA, 60

Note: Challenger was played by Wallace Beery in the 1925 silent version, directed by Harry Hoyt.

Champion, Bob 

British steeplechase jockey who became a national hero in 1981 when he came back after a horrific fight against cancer and won the Grand National on another hero – the ageing Aldaniti – a horse that had broken down and people believed would never race again. John Hurt portrayed Champion in the 1984 film which exposed the jockey's suffering

John Hurt as Bob Champion, the steeplechase jockey who made a heroic comeback after triumphing over cancer

as he underwent chemotherapy treatment and illustrated his determination to ride again.

John Hurt	*Champions* (Irvin)	GB, 84

Note: Bob Champion's trainer Josh Gifford was played in the film by Edward Woodward.

Chan, Charlie 

Wily Chinese sleuth who became the screen's most prolific investigator of the 40s and 50s. Solved nearly 50 cases, making frequent use of aphorisms whenever the occasion demanded, i.e. 'Alibi, like dead fish, cannot stand test of time' and 'When player cannot see man who deal cards, much wiser to stay out of game'. Once wrapped up a scene with the words, 'Please inform me whenever any other incidents permit themselves the luxury of occurring'. Films usually second features of 65–70 minutes. Most famous interpreter: Warner Oland. First appeared in print in 'House Without A Key' (1925), a Saturday Evening Post serial by Earl Derr Biggers.

E. L. Park	*Behind That Curtain* (Cummings)	USA, 29
Warner Oland	*Charlie Chan Carries On* (MacFadden)	USA, 31
Warner Oland	*Black Camel* (MacFadden)	USA, 31
Warner Oland	*Charlie Chan's Chance* (Blystone)	USA, 32
Warner Oland	*Charlie Chan's Greatest Case* (MacFadden)	USA, 33
Warner Oland	*Charlie Chan's Courage* (Hadden/Forde)	USA, 34
Warner Oland	*Charlie Chan In London* (Forde)	USA, 34
Warner Oland	*Charlie Chan In Paris* (Seiler)	USA, 35
Warner Oland	*Charlie Chan In Egypt* (King)	USA, 35
Warner Oland	*Charlie Chan in Shanghai* (Tinling)	USA, 35
Warner Oland	*Charlie Chan's Secret* (Wiles)	USA, 36
Warner Oland	*Charlie Chan At The Circus* (Lachman)	USA, 36
Warner Oland	*Charlie Chan At The Racetrack* (Humberstone)	USA, 36
Warner Oland	*Charlie Chan At The Opera* (Humberstone)	USA, 36
Warner Oland	*Charlie Chan At The Olympics* (Humberstone)	USA, 37
Warner Oland	*Charlie Chan On Broadway* (Forde)	USA, 37
Warner Oland	*Charlie Chan At Monte Carlo* (Forde)	USA, 38
Sidney Toler	*Charlie Chan In Honolulu* (Humberstone)	USA, 38
Sidney Toler	*Charlie Chan In Reno* (Foster)	USA, 39
Sidney Toler	*Charlie Chan At Treasure Island* (Foster)	USA, 39
Sidney Toler	*Charlie Chan In The City Of Darkness* (Leeds)	USA, 39
Sidney Toler	*Charlie Chan In Panama* (Foster)	USA, 40
Sidney Toler	*Charlie Chan's Murder Cruise* (Forde)	USA, 40
Sidney Toler	*Charlie Chan At The Wax Museum* (Shores)	USA, 40
Sidney Toler	*Murder Over New York* (Lachman)	USA, 40
Sidney Toler	*Dead Men Tell* (Lachman)	USA, 41
Sidney Toler	*Charlie Chan In Rio* (Lachman)	USA, 41
Sidney Toler	*Castle In The Desert* (Lachman)	USA, 42

Sidney Toler — *Charlie Chan In The Secret Service* (Rosen) USA, 44
Sidney Toler — *The Chinese Cat* (Rosen) USA, 44
Sidney Toler — *Charlie Chan In Black Magic* (Rosen) USA, 44
Sidney Toler — *The Jade Mask* (Rosen) USA, 45
Sidney Toler — *The Scarlet Clue* (Rosen) USA, 45
Sidney Toler — *The Shanghai Cobra* (Karlson) USA, 45
Sidney Toler — *The Red Dragon* (Rosen) USA, 45
Sidney Toler — *Dark Alibi* (Karlson) USA, 46
Sidney Toler — *Shadows Over Chinatown* (Morse) USA, 46
Sidney Toler — *Dangerous Money* (Morse) USA, 46
Sidney Toler — *The Trap* (Bretherton) USA, 47
Roland Winters — *The Chinese Ring* (Beaudine) USA, 47
Roland Winters — *Docks Of New Orleans* (Abrahams) USA, 48
Roland Winters — *The Shanghai Chest* (Beaudine) USA, 48
Roland Winters — *The Mystery Of The Golden Eye* (Beaudine) USA, 48
Roland Winters — *The Feathered Serpent* (Beaudine) USA, 48
Roland Winters — *Sky Dragon* (Selander) USA, 49
Peter Ustinov — *Charlie Chan And The Curse Of The Dragon Queen* (Donner) USA, 81

Note: Both George Kuwa in the 1926 serial *The House Without A Key,* and Kamiyama Sojin in Paul Leni's *The Chinese Parrot* played Chan on the silent screen. Fox produced all the sound films up until *Castle In The Desert* (1942), thereafter they were made by Monogram. Warners were the studio responsible for the 1981 spoof travesty starring Peter Ustinov.

On TV J. Carrol Naish featured in a series of 39 half hour programmes titled *The New Adventures Of Charlie Chan* (57) and in 1971 Ross Martin appeared in *Charlie Chan: Happiness Is a Warm Clue* (71) an inept tale in which Chan emerges from retirement to solve some murders committed on a yacht.

Chanel, Gabrielle Bonheur [R]

(1883–1971) French fashion designer, who revolutionized women's fashions after World War I with the straight simple lines of the 'Chanel Look'. The subject of the 1969 Broadway musical *Coco* starring Katharine Hepburn (never filmed) and also a lush movie soap opera which covered the first 38 years of her life, focused on her love affairs and related her rags to riches story from orphanage to international fame and considerable fortune.

Marie-France Pisier — *Chanel Solitaire* (Kaczender) Fra/GB, 81

Chaney, Lon [R]

(1883–1930) American actor (the son of deaf mute parents) who scared a whole generation with his horror roles of the 20s; *The Miracle Man* (19), *The Hunchback Of Notre Dame* (23), *The Phantom Of The Opera* (25), etc. Known as 'The Man Of A Thousand Faces', he was responsible for his own make-up and often suffered extreme pain during the course of his roles. Died of throat cancer just as he was preparing to play the vampire Count Dracula and embark on a sound career. Cagney's bio-pic remains one of the most detailed of a film personality.

James Cagney — *Man Of A Thousand Faces* (Pevney) USA, 57

Channing, Margo

One of the cinema's legendary characters, a glamorous but ageing stage actress whose best days are behind her and who is eventually superseded as the toast of Broadway by her scheming understudy. Created by Mary Orr in her 1946 short story 'The Wisdom Of Eve' (in which she was named Margola Cranston) she was allowed such extravagant lines as 'Fasten your seatbelts, it's going to be a bumpy night' and became one of Bette Davis' most famous screen creations.

Bette Davis — *All About Eve* (Mankiewicz) USA, 50

Note: Joseph Mankiewicz's film was supposedly a fictionalized account of an incident in the career of the Austrian actress Elizabeth Bergner. Bette Davis was cast as Channing after Claudette Colbert pulled out at the last minute with a wrenched back. Both Marlene Dietrich and Gertrude Lawrence were considered for the part in the early casting stages. As an in-joke Mankiewicz listed the name of Margo

Bette Davis in one of her most famous roles—as the ageing Broadway actress Margo Channing in *All About Eve* (1950)

Channing in his subsequent film *Sleuth* (72), Margo being the often referred to but never seen wife of thriller writer Laurence Olivier.

Chapman, Eddie

[R]

British safecracker who performed one of the most difficult and dangerous acts of double espionage of World War II – pretending to spy for the Germans (under the name of Fritz Grauman) whilst all the time working for British Intelligence. Awarded the Iron Cross by Hitler and a full pardon by the Allies he was played in *Triple Cross* by Christopher Plummer who attempted to overcome the banalities of Terence Young's colourless film by portraying Chapman as a cynical opportunist anxious to finish the war on the winning side, no matter what the cost. The full account of Chapman's 'stranger than fiction' exploits was first published in 1953 under the title 'The Eddie Chapman Story'.

Christopher Plummer	*Triple Cross* (Young)	Fra/GB, 67

Charles I

[R]

(1600–49) Stuart king whose disputes with Parliament on finance, religion and foreign policy led to civil war, and also his own execution for treason. Alec Guinness' dandified yet stubborn and devious monarch in Ken Hughes' *Cromwell* is the only major screen portrait to date.

Hugh Miller	*The Vicar Of Bray* (Edwards)	GB, 37
Robert Rietty	*The Scarlet Blade* (Gilling)	GB, 63
Alec Guinness	*Cromwell* (Hughes)	GB, 70

Charles, Nick

[F]

The lazy half of the most refreshing husband and wife team ever to grace the detective scene, a wealthy San Francisco playboy who quipped his way through some hundred martinis and six Thin Man films during the 30s and 40s. Always ready with the throwaway wisecrack, both he and his wife Nora ignored the Depression and proved that wedded life – and crime – could be fun. William Powell and Myrna Loy featured in all the films; Asta, their wire-haired terrier was constantly in attendance. In the first film, adapted from Dashiell Hammett's novel of 1932, The Thin Man of the title was one of the subsidiary characters, an eccentric inventor who is finally murdered. Thereafter, he became the alias of Powell's reluctant private-eye.

William Powell	*The Thin Man* (Van Dyke II)	USA, 34
William Powell	*After The Thin Man* (Van Dyke II)	USA, 36
William Powell	*Another Thin Man* (Van Dyke II)	USA, 39
William Powell	*Shadow Of The Thin Man* (Van Dyke II)	USA, 41
William Powell	*The Thin Man Goes Home* (Thorpe)	USA, 44
William Powell	*Song Of The Thin Man* (Buzzell)	USA, 47

Note: Peter Lawford and Phyllis Kirk (transferred from San Francisco to New York) starred in the popular *Third Man* TV series of 1957/8; in Neil Simon's crime spoof *Murder by Death* (76) David Niven and Maggie Smith appeared as a Thin Man type couple Dick and Dora Charleston.

Charley's Aunt/Sir Fancourt Babberley F

The hero/heroine of Brandon Thomas' 1892 farce; an Oxford student who poses as his own maiden aunt in order to act as chaperon to two fellow students but then finds that the joke gets out of hand when he himself receives a proposal of marriage. A bit antiquated these days but a regular standby for film-makers over the years who have worked out numerous variations of the drag theme. Jack Benny played the role when he was trying unsuccessfully to get his film career off the ground in the early 40s; a decade later Roy Bolger starred in the musical *Where's Charley?*, a film version of the 1948 Broadway hit, the first to boast both words and music by Frank Loesser.

Charlie Ruggles	*Charley's Aunt* (Christie) USA, 30
Paul Kemp	*Charley's Tante* (Stemmle) Ger, 34
Lucien Baroux	*La Marraine de Charley* (Colombier) Fra, 35
Arthur Askey	*Charley's Big-Hearted Aunt* (Forde) GB, 39
Jack Benny	*Charley's Aunt* (Mayo) USA, 41
Erminio Macario	*La Zia di Carlo* (Guarini/Cassano) It, 42
Ray Bolger	*Where's Charley?* (Butler) GB, 52
Alfredo Barbieri	*La Tia de Carlitos* (Carreras) Arg, 53
Heinz Ruhmann	*Charley's Tante* (Quest) W.Ger, 56
Fernand Raynaud	*La Marraine de Charley* (P. Chevalier) Fra, 57
Dirch Passer	*Charles' Tante* (Barg) Den, 59
Peter Alexander	*Charley's Tante* (Cziffra) W.Ger, 63
Cassen	*La Tia de Carlos en Mini-falda* (Fenollar) Spa, 67

Note: Sid Chaplin (USA, 25) and Elis Ellis (Swe, 26) both played the role on the silent screen.

Charters And Caldicott F

Two of the most famous Englishmen in movies, a couple of ex-Public School gents who were first introduced to the screen in Hitchcock's *The Lady Vanishes* and who reacted to every crisis that came their way by enquiring about the latest cricket score in England. A typical example of their behaviour occurred in the subsequent *Night Train To Munich* when they warn old school chum Rex Harrison (posing as a Nazi) that he's been rumbled and slip him a message under a doughnut telling him that he's 'batting on a sticky wicket!'

Arthur Lowe and Ian Carmichael as the eccentric cricket-loving Englishmen Charters and Caldicott in the 1979 remake of Alfred Hitchcock's pre-war classic *The Lady Vanishes*

Basil Radford and Naunton Wayne	*The Lady Vanishes* (Hitchcock) GB, 38
Basil Radford and Naunton Wayne	*Night Train To Munich* (Reed) GB, 40
Basil Radford and Naunton Wayne	*Millions Like Us* (Launder/Gilliat) GB, 43
Arthur Lowe and Ian Carmichael	*The Lady Vanishes* (Page) GB, 79

Note: The characters did not appear in Ethel Lina White's novel 'The Wheel Spins' upon which Hitchcock's film was based. They were conceived first by screenwriter Sidney Gilliat who originally named them Charters and Spanswick, the latter being the name of his Wiltshire gardener. Robin Bailey and Michael Aldridge appeared as the cricket-obsessed duo in a six part BBC TV series in the 1980s.

Chessman, Caryl R

American sex offender, tried for rape and murder in 1948, who spent 12 years in the condemned cell, studying law and delaying his execution with a succession of appeals. In 1960 his luck ran out and he was put to death at San Quentin after eight stays of execution. His story, based on his own best-seller, was filmed in 1955 whilst he was still fighting for his life.

William Campbell — *Cell 2455, Death Row* (Sears) USA, 55

Note: The American TV movie *Kill Me If You Can,* directed by Buzz Kulik in 1977, featured Alan Alda as Chessman and was notable for its powerful anti-capital punishment sentiments and an unsparing gas chamber sequence.

Chetwynd-Hayes, R. R

(1919–)British writer of horror and supernatural tales who first turned his hand to blood curdling when he was in his 50s. Four of his stories were filmed in 1974 in *From Beyond The Grave;* seven years later he was portrayed on screen by John Carradine when he was bitten in the neck by vampire Vincent Price and led into *The Monster Club* a home from home he had first created in print in 1975.

John Carradine — *The Monster Club* (Ward Baker) GB, 81

Cheyney, Fay

A scheming lady Raffles who travels in British high society, her eager eyes always firmly fixed on the expensive jewellery worn by her vulnerable companions. A seemingly indestructible character, first created by Frederick Lonsdale in his 1926 London play 'The Last Of Mrs Cheyney' and still proving attractive to stage actresses in the 80s.

Norma Shearer — *The Last Of Mrs Cheyney* (Franklin) USA, 29

Joan Crawford — *The Last Of Mrs Cheyney* (Boleslawski) USA, 37

Greer Garson — *The Law And The Lady* (Knopf) USA, 51

Lilli Palmer — *Frau Cheney's Ende* (Josef Wild) W.Ger, 61

Chisum, John R

(1824–84) A powerful cattle baron (known as the 'Cattle King Of New Mexico') who became heavily involved in the Lincoln County War of 1878–9 and was responsible for turning Billy The Kid into an outlaw, paying him 500 dollars for his services as a gunman. To date, Andrew McLaglen's 1970 movie remains the only film to concentrate on Chisum's life. Unfortunately, it missed out on most of its opportunities and finished up as just another John Wayne western carrying such dialogue as: 'Did you bring some gold with you?' (Mexican rustler). 'No' (Wayne). 'Silver?' (rustler). 'No just lead' (Wayne). Gunfire!

John Wayne — *Chisum* (McLaglen) USA, 70

Chopin, Frederic R

(1810–49) Polish composer and master pianist whose brilliant career was marred by an ill-fated love affair with novelist George Sand and a losing fight against tuberculosis. Jose Iturbi played the nocturnes and preludes for Cornel Wilde in the extravagant *A Song To Remember;* Alexander Ford took a more respectful look at the composer's youth in the 1951 production, *The Young Chopin.*

Wolfgang Liebeneiner — *Abschiedswalzer* (Bolvary) Ger, 34

Cornel Wilde — *A Song To Remember* (Charles Vidor) USA, 45

Vaclay Voska — *Bohemian Rapture* (Krska) Czech, 48

Czeslaw Wollejko — *The Young Chopin* (Ford) Pol, 51

Alex Davion — *Song Without End* (Charles Vidor) USA, 60

Christopher Sandford — *Jutrzenka: A Winter In Majorca* (Camino) Spa, 71

Ken Colley — *Lisztomania* (Russell) GB, 75

Note: Conrad Veidt appeared as Chopin in the 1918 German silent, *Nocturno der Liebe.*

Christian, Fletcher

Leader of the mutineers on board HMS Bounty during the ill-fated voyage to Tahiti in 1787–9. A muscular, traditional hero in the Oscar winning 1935 version of the story, a fop in the controversial

Clark Gable as mutineer Fletcher Christian in the 1935 version of *Mutiny On The Bounty*; (above) the 1962 remake starring Marlon Brando (Fletcher Christian) and Trevor Howard (Captain Bligh); (opposite page) Mel Gibson's turn to mutiny! The 1984 version of *The Bounty* co-starring Anthony Hopkins as Captain Bligh

remake of 1962 and a more melancholy realistic figure in the 1984 version. The Flynn portrayal was in a little-known Australian production made before he began his Hollywood career.

Errol Flynn	*In The Wake Of The Bounty* (Chauvel) Austral, 33
Clark Gable	*Mutiny On The Bounty* (Lloyd) USA, 35
Marlon Brando	*Mutiny On The Bounty* (Milestone) USA, 62
Mel Gibson	*The Bounty* (Donaldson) GB, 84

Note: In Raymond Longford's silent Australian version of *The Mutiny On The Bounty* (16) Christian was played by Wilton Power.

Christie, Agatha R

(1891–1976) The most celebrated British mystery writer of the twentieth century. Many works filmed (*Witness For the Prosecution, Murder On The Orient Express, Death On The Nile,* etc.) and herself the central subject of a film thriller about her unexplained ten day disappearance in December, 1926. Also portrayed on TV by Peggy Ashcroft in an ingenious one hour drama about her meeting with Poirot who visits her when he discovers that he is about to be killed off in her next book!

Vanessa Redgrave	*Agatha* (Apted) GB, 79
Peggy Ashcroft	*Murder By The Book* (Evans) GB,TV, 86

Christie, Anna 

Waterfront tramp of Eugene O'Neill who returns home to her drunken father's river barge to find eventual happiness with an honest young sailor. The leading character in O'Neill's Pulitzer Prize-winning play of 1922; also Greta Garbo's first talking role in movies.

Greta Garbo	*Anna Christie* (Brown) USA, 30

Note: Blanche Sweet appeared in a 1923 silent version directed by John Griffith Wray.

Christie, John Reginald R

(1898–1953) Rapist-murderer, known as 'The Strangler Of Notting Hill', whose unsavoury activities at 10 Rillington Place created a sensation when brought to light in 1953. Christie's notorious career included the slaying of six women (among them his wife) whom he buried in various parts of his house. His story was told in clinical, almost documentary fashion by Richard Fleischer in 1971.

Richard Attenborough	*10 Rillington Place* (Fleischer) GB, 71

Note: Timothy Evans, a near mental defective who lodged in Christie's house and was hanged for the murder of his wife and baby daughter, was played by John Hurt in Fleischer's film. Later evidence revealed that both crimes were committed by Christie and Evans was granted a pardon.

Christina, Queen R

(1626–89) Seventeenth century Queen of Sweden (contrary to legend an unattractive woman with a deformed shoulder) who, in 1654, renounced her powerful Protestant kingdom to become a convert to the Catholic Church. Romanticized out of all proportion in the two films made about her life, the first with Garbo in which she indulges in a hopeless love affair with Spanish envoy John Gilbert, the second with Liv Ullmann in which she embraces

Richard Attenborough as the mass murderer John Reginald Christie and John Hurt as the innocent but executed Timothy Evans in the film of *10 Rillington Place*

Vanessa Redgrave as mystery writer Agatha Christie in Michael Apted's thriller *Agatha,* an account of what might have happened to Christie during her disappearance in 1926

not only catholicism but the flesh that goes with it, i.e. the handsome figure of Peter Finch's Cardinal Azzolino!

Greta Garbo	*Queen Christina* (Mamoulian)	USA, 33
Liv Ullmann	*The Abdication* (Harvey)	GB, 74

Churchill, Sir Winston R

(1874–1965) Ebullient English statesman and Prime Minister whose fighting spirit and eloquent speech-making did much to help Britain survive the darkest days of World War II. His role in the war has yet to be examined on screen, although his early life, from his schooldays to his military exploits in India and South Africa and his election to Parliament, were chronicled at length in the 157-minute biography, *Young Winston*.

Dudley Field Malone	*Mission To Moscow* (Curtiz)	USA, 43
Victor Stanitsine	*The Fall Of Berlin* (Chiaureli)	USSR, 49
Victor Stanitsine	*The Unforgettable Year: 1919* (Chiaureli)	USSR, 52
Jimmy Sangster	*The Siege Of Sidney Street* (Baker)	GB, 60
Patrick Wymark	*Operation Crossbow* (Anderson)	GB, 65
Yuri Durov	*The Great Battle* (Ozerov)	USSR/Pol/Yug/E.Ger/It, 69
Simon Ward	*Young Winston* (Attenborough)	GB, 72
Leigh Dilley	*The Eagle Has Landed* (Sturges)	GB, 77

Note: Patrick Wymark also voiced Churchill in the two documentaries, *The Finest Hours* (64) and *A King's Story* (65); Peter Sellers voiced the role in the spy thriller *The Man Who Never Was* (56).

In *Young Winston,* Russell Lewis played Churchill aged seven, Michael Anderson the 13-year-old Churchill.

The actors who have portrayed Churchill on television include Warren Clarke (as the young Winston) in *Jennie* (74), Richard Burton in *Walk With Destiny* (74), Timothy West in *Churchill And The Generals* (79), Wensley Pithey in *F.D.R. – The Last Year* (80), Robert Hardy in *Winston Churchill: The Wilderness Years* (81) and Howard Lang in *The Winds Of War* (83).

Cicero R

(1904–70) Code name for the Albanian spy Elyesa Bazna who served as valet to the British Ambassador in Ankara in World War II and sold 35 top secrets to the Germans, including the plans for the invasion of Europe. The Nazis, believing the plans to be false, failed to act on his information and paid him in forged bank notes. Bazna subsequently disappeared from the international scene and died in poverty. Rumour has it that he once turned up on the set of Mankiewicz's *Five Fingers* and, for a fee, offered his services to the production company!

James Mason	*Five Fingers* (Mankiewicz)	USA, 52

Cinderella F

Fairy tale girl heroine who finds romance and happiness with a handsome prince after losing her magic slipper at the ball. The story, which is assumed to be of Eastern origin and mentioned in sixteenth century German literature, has been animated by Disney, adapted into two glossy musicals by Charles Walters and Bryan Forbes, and even updated into a male fable of the 60s with Jerry Lewis.

Ilene Woods	*Cinderella* (Disney)	USA, 50
Leslie Caron	*The Glass Slipper* (Walters)	USA, 55
Jerry Lewis	*Cinderfella* (Tashlin)	USA, 60
Gemma Craven	*The Slipper And The Rose* (Forbes)	GB, 76

Note: Ilene Woods voiced the role in Disney's 1950 version; Laura Bayley appeared as Cinderella as far back as 1898 in the British film, *Cinderella And The Fairy Godmother.* Dolly Lupone (GB, 07), Louise Legrange (Fra, 09), Florence LaBadie (USA, 11), Fernanda Pouget (It, 13), Lillian Walker (USA, 13), Gertie Potter (GB, 13), Mary Pickford (USA, 14) and Helga Thomas (Ger, 23) were other silent actresses who featured in the part. In 1965 Lesley Ann Warren played the role in Rodgers and Hammerstein's TV musical *Cinderella.*

Claudius R

(10 BC–AD 54) Of all the Roman emperors easily the pick of the bunch, a lame but noble scholar who became emperor after the murder of Caligula, his predecessor and nephew. His biggest mistake was paying too much attention to his wife Agrippina

Simon Ward as the adventurous young war correspondent Winston Churchill in action in India in Richard Attenborough's biography *Young Winston*

Gemma Craven (in her film debut) and Richard Chamberlain in Bryan Forbes' 1976 musical adaptation of the Cinderella story, *The Slipper and the Rose,* music and lyrics by the Sherman Brothers

who persuaded him to set aside his own son, Britannicus, for the succession and opt instead for her son from a previous marriage. His name? Nero! Charles Laughton's performance in Von Sternberg's sadly uncompleted film of Robert Graves' *I Claudius* would undoubtedly have been the definitive screen portrayal; Derek Jacobi eventually essayed the role on TV some 40 years later.

Charles Laughton	*I Claudius* (Von Sternberg – uncompleted)	GB, 37
Barry Jones	*Demetrius And The Gladiators* (Daves)	USA, 54
Peter Damon	*The Fall Of The Roman Empire* (Mann)	USA, 64
Vittorio Caprioli	*Messalina, Messalina* (Corbucci)	It, 77
Giancarlo Badessi	*Caligula* (Brass)	USA/It, 80

Note: Fragments of Laughton's performance can be glimpsed in the 1965 documentary, *The Epic That Never Was;* On TV Derek Jacobi's performance was in the 1976 TV series of Herbert Wise. Richard Kiley also featured as Claudius in *AD–Anno Domini* (85).

Cleopatra [R]

(69–30 BC) Egyptian queen of great beauty whose years as mistress of both Caesar (whom she bore one son) and Antony, have been chronicled many times on screen. Vivien Leigh in Shaw's *Caesar And Cleopatra* and Hildegard Neil in Shakespeare's *Antony And Cleopatra* offered classical interpretations. Elizabeth Taylor a more earthy, sensual and controversial portrait. Miss Taylor's entry into Rome in the Mankiewicz production of 1963 remains one of the most spectacular moments in epic cinema.

Claudette Colbert	*Cleopatra* (DeMille)	USA, 34
Vivien Leigh	*Caesar and Cleopatra* (Pascal)	GB, 46
Rhonda Fleming	*Serpent Of The Nile* (Castle)	USA, 53
Sophia Loren	*Due Notti con Cleopatra* (Mattoli)	It, 54
Virginia Mayo	*The Story of Mankind* (Allen)	USA, 57
Linda Cristal	*Legions Of The Nile* (Cottafavi)	It/Spa/Fra, 59
Elizabeth Taylor	*Cleopatra* (Mankiewicz)	USA, 63
Amanda Barrie	*Carry On Cleo* (Thomas)	GB, 65
Hildegard Neil	*Antony And Cleopatra* (Heston)	Swi/Spa/GB, 72
Dena Ferrara	*The Devil in Miss Jones* (Pachard)	USA, 82
Starr Wood	*Irresistible* (Brown)	USA, 82

Note: Debra Paget appeared as *Cleopatra's Daughter* (Fra/It, 60); Florence Lawrence (USA, 08), Helen Gardner (USA, 13), Giovanna Terribili Gonzales (It, 13), Lydia Borelli (It, 16) and Theda Bara (USA, 17) all appeared as the Egyptian queen on the silent screen. TV portrayals include those of Janet Suzman (72) and Jane Lapotaire (81).

Cline, Patsy [R]

1950s country and western singer who achieved her childhood dream of success – to sing, earn money, have kids and live in a little house with yellow roses round the door – but missed out on the happiness she hoped would go with it. Killed, like so many singers of her generation in a plane crash at the height of her career, she was played in the 1985 bio-pic *Sweet Dreams* by Jessica Lange who lip-synched to Cline's original recordings. Reisz's stark and unsentimental film concentrated on Cline's stormy personal life and unhappy marriages; it featured nearly a dozen of the singer's chart songs including 'Sweet Dreams', 'I Fall To Pieces' and 'Lovesick Blues'.

Beverly D'Angelo	*Coal Miner's Daughter* (Apted)	USA, 80
Jessica Lange	*Sweet Dreams* (Reisz)	USA, 85

Clouseau, Inspector Jacques [F]

The most accident-prone policeman in screen history, a kind of Jacques Tati of the Paris Sureté, forever losing battles with revolving doors, swimming pools, vacuum cleaners, etc. and constantly ignoring the most obvious of clues but always managing to come up smiling. Not so his superior, Inspector Dreyfus, who teetered on the edge of insanity in several of the early films and went right over the edge in the later ones.

Peter Sellers	*The Pink Panther* (Edwards)	USA, 64
Peter Sellers	*A Shot In The Dark* (Edwards)	USA, 64
Alan Arkin	*Inspector Clouseau* (Yorkin)	GB, 68
Peter Sellers	*The Return Of The Pink Panther* (Edwards)	GB, 75
Peter Sellers	*The Pink Panther Strikes Again* (Edwards)	GB, 76

(Above) The humorous side of life in Ancient Rome. Sid James as Mark Antony and Amanda Barrie as a none too bright Cleopatra in *Carry on Cleo;* (right) Hildegard Neil as Cleopatra in the film version of Shakespeare's play *Antony and Cleopatra* directed by Charlton Heston

Peter Sellers	*Revenge Of The Pink Panther* (Edwards)	GB, 78
Peter Sellers	*The Trail Of The Pink Panther* (Edwards)	GB, 82
Roger Moore	*Curse Of The Pink Panther* (Edwards)	GB, 83

Note: With *The Trail Of The Pink Panther* Blake Edwards fashioned a new Clouseau film (despite the death of star Sellers) by combining previously unseen footage and slapstick sequences with linking material. *Curse Of The Pink Panther,* shot at the same time, featured Ted Wass as Clifton Sleigh, the New York equivalent to the missing Clouseau, who travels to Europe to search for his nemesis. When Clouseau is discovered at the end of the film he turns out to have undergone plastic surgery and emerges as Roger Moore! Herbert Lom's Inspector Dreyfus and Burt Kwouk's Cato (Clouseau's oriental manservant) appeared in all the Pink Panther films other than the very first and Bud Yorkin's movie of 1968.

Peter Sellers, in trouble as usual as Inspector Clouseau in *A Shot In The Dark.* Sharing his misfortune: George Sanders

Cochise R

(*c.* 1820–74) Chief of the Chiricahua Apaches whose long, full-scale war with the American government was finally resolved when frontiersman Tom Jeffords rode alone into the Indian camp and pleaded for a safe passage for mail riders through Apache territory. The relationship between Jeffords and Cochise was examined in Delmer Daves' classic western *Broken Arrow.* For his portrayal of Cochise, Jeff Chandler received a supporting Oscar nomination. He later played the role on two subsequent occasions.

Antonio Moreno	*Valley Of The Sun* (Marshall)	USA, 42
Miguel Inclan	*Fort Apache* (Ford)	USA, 48
Jeff Chandler	*Broken Arrow* (Daves)	USA, 50
Chief Yowlachie	*The Last Outpost* (Foster)	USA, 51
Jeff Chandler	*The Battle At Apache Pass* (Sherman)	USA, 52
John Hodiak	*Conquest Of Cochise* (Castle)	USA, 53
Jeff Chandler	*Taza, Son Of Cochise* (Sirk)	USA, 54
Michael Keep	*Forty Guns To Apache Pass* (Witney)	USA, 67

American actor Alan Arkin who also portrayed the accident-prone *Inspector Clouseau* (directed by Bud Yorkin in 1968)

Cody, William Frederick

R

(1846–1917) Heroic figure of the American West whose adventures as a Pony Express rider, Indian scout and buffalo hunter became legendary through the stories of dime novelist Ned Buntline. Only William Wellman's *Buffalo Bill* has dealt with his full career; many movies have preferred to concentrate on his later years when he founded his famous Wild West Show. Robert Altman's *Buffalo Bill And The Indians* starring Paul Newman portrayed Cody as no more than a hollow fake.

Douglas Dumbrille	*The World Changes* (LeRoy) USA, 33
Maroni Olsen	*Annie Oakley* (Stevens) USA, 35
James Ellison	*The Plainsman* (DeMille) USA, 37
Carlyle Moore	*Outlaw Express* (Waggner) USA, 38
Roy Rogers	*Young Buffalo Bill* (Kane) USA, 40
Joel McCrea	*Buffalo Bill* (Wellman) USA, 44
Richard Arlen	*Buffalo Bill Rides Again* (Ray) USA, 47
Monte Hale	*Law Of The Golden West* (Ford) USA, 49
Louis Calhern	*Annie Get Your Gun* (Sidney) USA, 50
Tex Cooper	*King Of The Bullwhip* (Ormond) USA, 50
Clayton Moore	*Buffalo Bill In Tomahawk Territory* (Ray) USA, 52
Charlton Heston	*Pony Express* (Hopper) USA, 53
Malcolm Atterbury	*Badman's Country* (Sears) USA, 58
James McMullan	*The Raiders* (Daugherty) USA, 64
Rick van Nutter	*Seven Hours Of Gunfire* (Marchent) Spa/It/W.Ger, 64
Gordon Scott	*Buffalo Bill* (Costa) It/W.Ger/Fra, 65
Guy Stockwell	*The Plainsman* (Rich) USA, 66
Michel Piccoli	*Touche Pas La Femme Blanche* (Ferreri) Fra, 74
Paul Newman	*Buffalo Bill And The Indians, Or Sitting Bull's History Lesson* (Altman) USA, 76
Ted Flicker	*Legend Of The Lone Ranger* (Fraker) USA, 81

Paul Newman as William Cody in *Buffalo Bill and the Indians, or Sitting Bull's History Lesson,* directed by Robert Altman in 1976

Note: George Waggner in *The Iron Horse* (USA, 24), John Fox, Jr in *The Pony Express* (USA, 25), Jack Hoxie in *The Last Frontier* (USA, 26) and William Fairbanks in *Wyoming* (USA, 27) were among the actors who appeared as Cody on the silent screen; Matt Clark in *That Was The West That Was* (74), R. L. Tolbert in *The Legend Of The Golden Gun* (79) and Ken Kercheval in *Calamity Jane* (84) have featured in the role on TV.

Cogburn, Rooster

F

John Wayne's most famous role and the one for which he won his Academy Award; a one-eyed, hard-drinking US Marshal who is hired by a 14-year-old ranch girl to track down the murderer of her father. In a subsequent screen adventure (not derived from Charles Portis' 1968 novel) he teamed with spinster missionary Katharine Hepburn in an 'African Queen' type adventure about the hunt for a band of outlaws who have hi-jacked a wagon-load of nitroglycerine.

John Wayne	*True Grit* (Hathaway)	USA, 69
John Wayne	*Rooster Cogburn* (Millar)	USA, 75

Note: In 1978 Warren Oates featured as Cogburn in the TV movie *True Grit: A Further Adventure,* directed by Richard T. Heffron.

Cohan, George M. [R]

(1878–1942) Multi-talented song and dance man whose dynamic showbiz career was celebrated (and told in flashback to President Roosevelt) in the Warner biography *Yankee Doodle Dandy.* James Cagney repeated his Oscar-winning portrayal in a guest spot in the subsequent Eddie Foy bio-pic *The Seven Little Foys.* Among Cohan's song compositions: 'Over There', 'The Yankee Doodle Boy' and 'Give My Regards To Broadway'.

James Cagney	*Yankee Doodle Dandy* (Curtiz)	USA, 42
James Cagney	*The Seven Little Foys* (Shavelson)	USA, 55
Mark Baker	*After The Ball* (Bennett)	GB, 57

Conan The Barbarian [F]

Powerful hero of pulp fiction who operates in the Hyborean Age, a mythical epoch some 8000 years after the sinking of Atlantis, and who avenges his people's senseless slaughter with a magic sword of steel. His adventures (debut 1932 in *The Phoenix On The Sword*) were first chronicled in the stories of Robert E. Howard and subsequently carried on by other writers and in Marvel Comics. He enjoyed a rebirth of popularity in the mid-60s when the stories were reissued in paperback. In 1982, some 50 years after first appearing in print, he was

Muscle-man Arnold Schwarzenegger as the sword-wielding warrior *Conan the Barbarian,* directed by John Milius in 1982. Schwarzenegger subsequently repeated the role in the sequel *Conan The Destroyer*

portrayed on screen by Austrian-born muscleman Arnold Schwarzenegger. Just two portrayals to date.

Arnold Schwarzenegger	*Conan The Barbarian* (Milius)	USA, 82
Arnold Schwarzenegger	*Conan The Destroyer* (Fleischer)	USA, 84

Connecticut Yankee In King Arthur's Court [F]

Mark Twain hero who is transported back from nineteenth century America to the court of King Arthur where he is branded a wizard because of his modern ingenuity and know-how. Twain's 1889 novel satirized the world of chivalry, king and church; Paramount's 1949 musical version was less ambitious and allowed Bing Crosby, William Bendix and Cedric Hardwicke to whoop it up 'Busily Doing Nothing!' The most recent version of the tale, an updated Walt Disney adaptation, starred Dennis Dugan as a robotics engineer who arrives in Camelot by way of a spacecraft travelling faster than the speed of light.

Will Rogers	*A Connecticut Yankee* (Butler)	USA, 31
Bing Crosby	*A Connecticut Yankee In King Arthur's Court* (Garnett)	USA, 49
Dennis Dugan	*The Spaceman And King Arthur* (Mayberry)	USA, 79

Note: Harry Myers starred in a 1921 silent production, directed by Emmett J. Flynn.

Corbett, James J. [R]

(1866–1933) Or, as he was better known, 'Gentleman Jim', the first official heavyweight champion under the Marquis of Queensbury rules. A boxer of style, he introduced 'science' into his sport and gained the title after a 21-round epic with John L. Sullivan in New Orleans in 1892. Errol Flynn's dashing portrait in Raoul Walsh's expert Warner film of 1942 was one of the actor's own favourite performances despite one critic commenting that his feet were decidedly more mobile than his features. Corbett's subsequent championship fight with Bob Fitzsimmons in Carson City in 1897 formed the springboard for Fox's 1953 western *City Of Bad Men.*

Errol Flynn	*Gentleman Jim* (Walsh)	USA, 42
John Day	*City Of Bad Men* (Jones)	USA, 53
Steve Oliver	*Tom Horn* (Wiard)	USA, 80

Corsican Brothers, The [F]

Siamese twin heroes of Alexandre Dumas, vastly different in character – one is a Parisian gentleman, the other a Corsican bandit – but both linked by their resolve to avenge the murder of their family. Engagingly played by Douglas Fairbanks Jr in Gregory Ratoff's 1942 swashbuckler; spoofed by Bud Yorkin in *Start The Revolution Without Me* (70) and even more unmercifully by raucous comedians Cheech and Chong in 1984. The original novel of Alexandre Dumas was first published in 1845.

Pierre Brasseur and Jacques Erwin	*The Corsican Brothers* (Kelber)	Fra, 38
Douglas Fairbanks Jr	*The Corsican Brothers* (Ratoff)	USA, 41
Richard Greene	*Return Of The Corsican Brothers* (Nazarro)	USA, 53
Antonio Vilar	*The Corsican Brothers* (Fleider)	Arg, 55

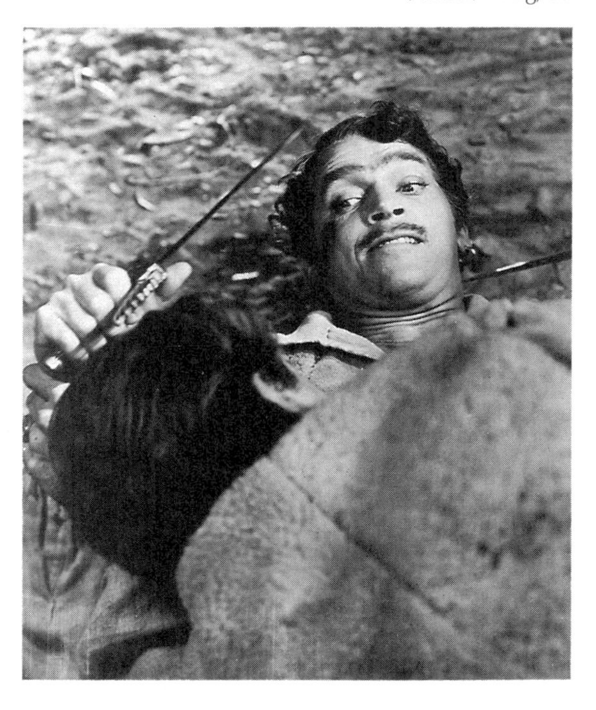

Douglas Fairbanks Jnr, following in the footsteps of his famous swashbuckling father in the 1941 swashbuckler, *The Corsican Brothers*

Geoffrey Horne	*The Corsican Brothers* (Majano) Fra/It, 60
Gene Wilder and Donald Sutherland	*Start The Revolution Without Me* (Yorkin) USA, 70
Cheech Marin and Thomas Chong	*Cheech & Chong's The Corsican Brothers* (Thomas Chong) USA, 84

Note: Trever Eve appeared in the most recent straight adaptation, a 1985 TV film directed by Ian Sharp; on the silent screen, King Baggot (USA, 15), Henry Krauss (Fra, 17) and Dustin Farnum (USA, 19) all featured in the dual role.

Count of Monte Cristo, The [F]

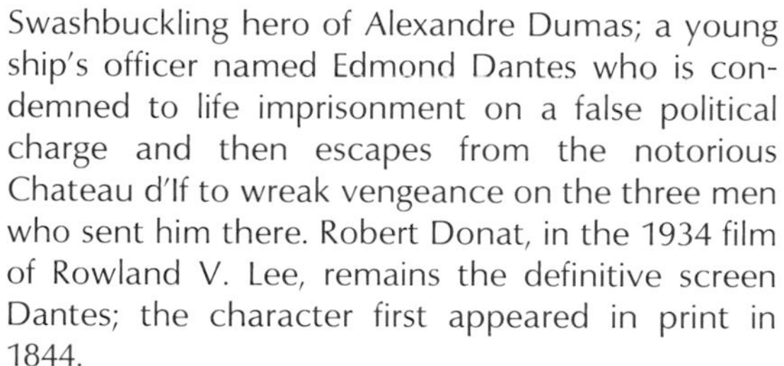

Swashbuckling hero of Alexandre Dumas; a young ship's officer named Edmond Dantes who is condemned to life imprisonment on a false political charge and then escapes from the notorious Chateau d'If to wreak vengeance on the three men who sent him there. Robert Donat, in the 1934 film of Rowland V. Lee, remains the definitive screen Dantes; the character first appeared in print in 1844.

Robert Donat	*The Count Of Monte Cristo* (Lee) USA, 34
Arturo de Cordova	*The Count Of Monte Cristo* (Urueta) Mex, 41
Pierre Richard-Willm	*The Count Of Monte Cristo* (Vernay/Cerio) Fra/It, 43
Ramon Delgado	*The Sword Of The Avenger* (Salkow) USA, 48
Jorge Mistral	*Le Testament de Monte Cristo* (Klimovski) Arg/Mex, 53
Jean Marais	*The Count Of Monte Cristo* (Vernay) Fra/It, 54
Louis Jourdan	*The Story Of The Count Of Monte Cristo*
Paul Barge	*The Count Of Monte Cristo* (Hunebelle) Fra/It, 68
Richard Chamberlain	*The Count Of Monte Cristo* (Greene) GB, 74

Note: *The Sword Of The Avenger* was a loose adaptation of the story with the names of the characters changed; the Count spawned several offspring, all of whom received the chance to swashbuckle like their illustrious father – Louis Hayward (son) in *The Son Of Monte Cristo* (USA, 40) and (grand-nephew) in *Monte Cristo's Revenge* (USA, 46), and Robert Clarke (son) in *Island Of Monte Cristo* (52). Lenore Aubert featured as *The Wife Of Monte Cristo* (46).

Umberto Mozzato (It, 09), Hobart Bosworth (USA, 12), James O'Neill (USA, 13), Leon Mathot (Fra, 17), Max Devrient (Aus, 21), John Gilbert (USA, 22) and Jean Angelo (Fra, 29) were among the silent actors who played the avenging count; Jacques Weber starred in the 205 minute TV version of Dumas' story, directed by Denys de la Patelliere in 1980.

Escaped prisoner Edmond Dantes (Richard Chamberlain) about to become *The Count of Monte Cristo* in the 1974 version of Dumas' famous tale

Coward, Noel 

(1899–1973) The most successful multi-talented artist in the history of the British theatre. A writer of operettas, revues and straight plays ('Bitter Sweet', 'Cavalcade', 'Blithe Spirit', etc.), he wrote and starred in several of his own films and was portrayed on celluloid in *Star!* as the young friend and confidant of British stage actress Gertrude Lawrence. Not yet the subject of a major screen biography.

Daniel Massey	*Star!* (Wise)	USA, 68

Crawford, Joan

R

(1904–77) One of the screen's great sufferers, a flamboyant Hollywood star whose wide-eyed histrionics embraced many MGM and Warner films of the 30s and 40s. Her private life, as revealed by her daughter Christina in the book *Mommie Dearest,* was something of a horror story, much of it transferred to the screen in the 1981 movie version which included such camp scenes as a demented Crawford trying to strangle her daughter, wreaking havoc with an axe in her rose garden and hacking off Christina's blonde curls in a manic rage. How much was truth and how much was fiction is difficult to ascertain but the performance of Faye Dunaway, made up to look remarkably like Crawford, often made it appear ludicrous.

Faye Dunaway	*Mommie Dearest* / (Perry)	USA, 81

Note: Diana Scarwid (adult) and Mara Hobel (child) featured as Christina in *Mommie Dearest.*

Crazy Horse

Sioux chief who, together with Sitting Bull, led the tribal uprising that culminated in the massacre of Custer's Seventh Cavalry at the Little Big Horn. His triumph was short lived, however. Shortly after the battle he was captured and bayoneted to death by the cavalry. Mostly a subsidiary character in westerns, although Universal afforded him a full-scale biography in 1955 with Victor Mature.

Anthony Quinn	*They Died With Their Boots On* (Walsh)	USA, 42
Iron Eyes Cody	*Sitting Bull* (Salkow)	USA, 54
Victor Mature	*Chief Crazy Horse* (Sherman)	USA, 55
Murray Alper	*The Outlaws Is Coming* (Maurer)	USA, 65
Iron Eyes Cody	*The Great Sioux Massacre* (Salkow)	USA, 65
Will Sampson	*The White Buffalo* (Lee Thompson)	USA, 77

Note: Crazy Horse was renamed Dull Knife and played by Kieron Moore in Siodmak's 1967 film, *Custer Of The West;* the Indian chief was portrayed by High Eagle in the 1936 serial, *Custer's Last Stand.*

Crime Doctor, The

F

American radio sleuth, equally popular when portrayed in the movies by Warner Baxter in the 40s. An ex-gangster turned criminologist, he is always a cut above his fellow detectives in that he solves most of his cases through psychiatry. Ray Collins created the role on radio in 1940; the first film appeared three years later. Creator: Max Marcin.

Warner Baxter	*Crime Doctor* (Gordon)	USA, 43
Warner Baxter	*Crime Doctor's Strangest Case* (Forde)	USA, 43
Warner Baxter	*Shadows In The Night* (Forde)	USA, 44
Warner Baxter	*Crime Doctor's Courage* (Sherman)	USA, 45
Warner Baxter	*Crime Doctor's Warning* (Castle)	USA, 45
Warner Baxter	*Crime Doctor's Man Hunt* (Castle)	USA, 46
Warner Baxter	*Just Before Dawn* (Castle)	USA, 46
Warner Baxter	*The Millerson Case* (Archainbaud)	USA, 47
Warner Baxter	*Crime Doctor's Gamble* (Castle)	USA, 47
Warner Baxter	*Crime Doctor's Diary* (Friedman)	USA, 49

Crippen, Dr

(1862–1910) Something of an enigma in the annals of crime. Either a mild-mannered little doctor driven to the murder of his overbearing wife because of his love for a young girl or, in the view of one noted criminologist, 'one of the most dangerous criminals of his century'. The 1962 film proffered the former view. The facts, however, remain. Mrs Crippen was poisoned, her body mutilated and buried in various parts of the cellar and Crippen arrested in Canada whilst trying to make his escape.

Rudolf Fernau	*Dr Crippen am Bord* (Engels)	Ger, 42
Donald Pleasence	*Dr Crippen* (Lynn)	GB, 62

Note: *The Suspect* (44) in which Charles Laughton played a middle-aged London shop-keeper who murders his intolerably spiteful wife for the love of a younger woman, had strong hints of the Crippen

Joan Crawford or Faye Dunaway? Answer: Miss Dunaway, made up to look remarkably like the great MGM and Warner star in the 1981 production *Mommie Dearest,* the story of Crawford's relationship with her adopted and abused daughter, Christina

case. Samantha Eggar played the young girl, Ethel Le Neve in the 1962 film, Ella Raines her equivalent in 1944.

Alfred Hitchcock's long desire to make a film of the case (he had wanted Alec Guinness for the leading role) came to nothing although he did subsequently make a movie with strong Crippen elements i.e. *Rear Window,* the story of a photographer confined to his wheelchair in his apartment who becomes convinced that a neighbour has murdered his wife and dismembered her corpse.

Crockett, Davy R

(1786–1836) American frontiersman, an expert rifleman and bear hunter who served as a scout for Andrew Jackson and was elected three times to Congress before dying a hero's death defending the Alamo. Fess Parker (who played the part twice for Disney) and John Wayne rate as the best-known screen Crocketts; grizzled character actor Arthur Hunnicutt as the most accurate.

Lane Chandler	*Heroes Of The Alamo* (Fraser) USA, 37
Robert Barrat	*Man Of Conquest* (Nichols, Jr.) USA, 39
George Montgomery	*Davy Crockett, Indian Scout* (Landers) USA, 49
Trevor Bardette	*The Man From The Alamo* (Boetticher) USA, 53
Arthur Hunnicutt	*The Last Command* (Lloyd) USA, 55
Fess Parker	*Davy Crockett, King Of The Wild Frontier* (Foster) USA, 55
Fess Parker	*Davy Crockett And The River Pirates* (Foster) USA, 56
Fess Parker	*Alias Jesse James* (McLeod) USA, 59
John Wayne	*The Alamo* (Wayne) USA, 60

Note: George Montgomery played a cousin of Davy Crockett in *Davy Crockett, Indian Scout* (49); Fess Parker's two screen performances were made up from five one-hour segments of Disney's TV series *Frontierland,* made in 1954 and 1955. The segments were titled *Davy Crockett, Indian Fighter, Davy Crockett Goes To Congress, Davy Crockett At The Alamo, Davy Crockett's Keelboat Race* and *Davy Crockett And The River Pirates.*

Dustin Farnum in *Davy Crockett* (USA, 16) and Cullen Landis in *Davy Crockett At The Fall Of The Alamo* (USA, 26) both featured in the role on the silent screen; Brian Keith played Crockett in Burt Kennedy's 1987 TV movie *The Alamo: 13 Days To Glory.*

Cromwell, Oliver

(1599–1658) Puritan squire and Member of Parliament who led England into a Civil War to rid her of injustice and oppression. Commanded the famous cavalry regiment known as the 'Ironsides' and reigned as Lord Protector of England from 1653 to 1658. Generally regarded in films as a ruthless tyrant. Not so in Ken Hughes' full-scale biography in which his rise from humble beginnings to a national hero caught up in political intrigue was movingly and realistically conveyed.

George Merritt	*The Vicar Of Bray* (Edwards) GB, 37
Edmund Willard	*Cardboard Cavalier* (Forde) GB, 49
John Le Mesurier	*The Moonraker* (MacDonald) GB, 58

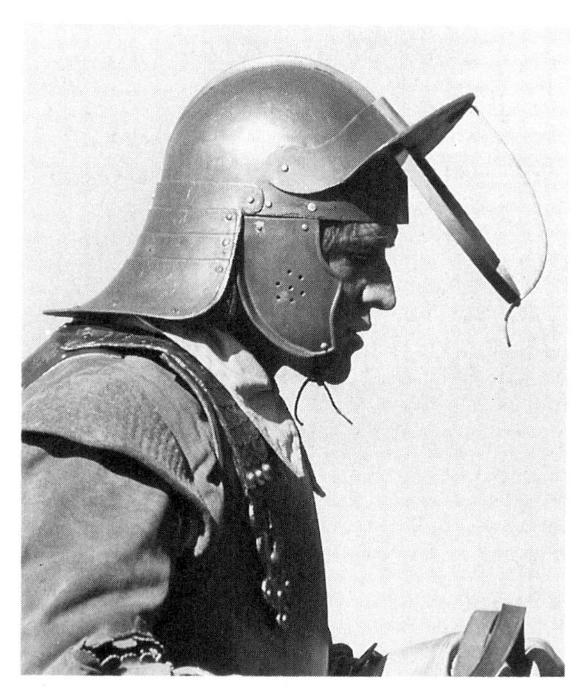

The Lord Protector of England from 1653 to 1658. Richard Harris as *Cromwell* in Ken Hughes' ambitious film biography of 1970

Patrick Wymark	*Witchfinder General* (Reeves) GB, 68
Richard Harris	*Cromwell* (Hughes) GB, 70

Note: Booth Conway in *The Tavern Knight* (GB, 20), Henry Ainley in *The Royal Oak* (GB, 23) and Frederick Burton in *The Fighting Blade* (USA, 23) all featured as Cromwell on the silent screen.

Cromwell, Thomas [R]

(1485–1540) Chief minister to Henry VIII who rose quickly to power after the fall from royal favour of Cardinal Wolsey and Sir Thomas More. A prominent figure during Henry's reign (but only recently on film), he advised on ecclesiastical matters and helped fake the evidence of adultery against Anne Boleyn. He eventually meddled once too often – in Henry's marriage to Anne Of Cleves – and was himself executed for treason. The scheming ambition and rough, peasant origins of the man were given full rein by Leo McKern in Zinnemann's *A Man For All Seasons*.

Leo McKern	*A Man For All Seasons* (Zinnemann) GB, 66
John Colicos	*Anne Of The Thousand Days* (Jarrott) GB, 69
Kenneth Williams	*Carry On Henry* (Thomas) GB, 71
Donald Pleasence	*Henry VIII And His Six Wives* (Hussein) GB, 72

Note: Reginald Owen appeared as Cromwell in a 1911 British silent film, *Henry VIII*.

Curie, Marie 

(1867–1934) Polish-born French physicist who worked with her husband Pierre on radioactivity and magnetism and, in 1903, made the vital discovery of radium. The first person to be awarded two Nobel Prizes, she was portrayed on screen by Greer Garson in a 1943 MGM film which, despite the usual glossy Hollywood production values, still managed to capture some of the zeal and integrity of the tireless woman scientist.

Greer Garson	*Madame Curie* (Le Roy) USA, 43

Custer, George Armstrong [R]

(1839–76) Vain, glory-seeking Cavalry officer (a general at 26) who tried to emulate his heroic feats of the Civil War in his subsequent campaigns against the Indians. His ambition to secure a place in the history books was satisfied when he and his 264 men of the Seventh Cavalry were massacred by the Sioux and Cheyenne at the Little Big Horn in June, 1876. The picture of him standing defiant, pistol raised, against hordes of charging Indians, remains one of the classic images of Hollywood westerns. Errol Flynn expressed Custer's gallantry, Robert Shaw his flamboyance, Henry Fonda his stubborness.

Clay Clement	*The World Changes* (LeRoy) USA, 33
John Miljan	*The Plainsman* (DeMille) USA, 37
Paul Kelly	*Wyoming* (Thorpe) USA, 40
Addison Richards	*Badlands Of Dakota* (Green) USA, 41
Ronald Reagan	*Santa Fe Trail* (Curtiz) USA, 40
Errol Flynn	*They Died With Their Boots On* (Walsh) USA, 42
James Millican	*Warpath* (Haskin) USA, 42
Sheb Wooley	*Bugles In The Afternoon* (Rowland) USA, 52
Douglas Kennedy	*Sitting Bull* (Salkow) USA, 54
Britt Lomond	*Tonka* (Foster) USA, 58
Philip Carey	*The Great Sioux Massacre* (Salkow) USA, 65
Leslie Nielsen	*The Plainsman* (Rich) USA, 66
Robert Shaw	*Custer Of The West* (Siodmak) USA/Spa, 67
Richard Mulligan	*Little Big Man* (Penn) USA, 70
Marcello Mastroianni	*Touche Pas La Femme Blanche* (Ferreri) Fra, 74
Keir Dullea	*The Legend Of The Golden Gun* (Levi) TVM,USA, 79
Lincoln Tate	*Legend Of The Lone Ranger* (Fraker) USA, 81

Note: Henry Fonda (as Colonel Thursday) in John Ford's *Fort Apache* (USA, 48) and Andrew Duggan (as General McCabe) in *The Glory Guys* (USA, 65) also appeared as the Custer character on screen; Dustin Farnum in *The Flaming Frontier* (USA, 26) and John Beck in *General Custer at the Little Big*

Even Errol Flynn couldn't win this one. One of the closing scenes from Raoul Walsh's *They Died With Their Boots On*

Horn (USA, 26) were among the silent actors who portrayed him. On TV Wayne Maunder featured as the legendary general in the 1967 western series *Custer.*

Cyrano de Bergerac F

Owner of the longest nose in literature, a soulful poet-swordsman of seventeenth century France whose flamboyant ways with a rapier somewhat overshadowed his wooing of the ladies. Jose Ferrer (Academy Award, 1950) has portrayed him twice; Edmond Rostand's play, based on a real-life French playwright, was first performed in 1897.

Claude Dauphin	*Cyrano de Bergerac* (Rivers)	Fra, 45
Jose Ferrer	*Cyrano de Bergerac* (Gordon)	USA, 50
Karel Hoger	*Münchhausen* (Zeman)	Czech, 61
Jose Ferrer	*Cyrano and D'Artagnan* (Gance)	Fra/It/Spa, 62

Note: In *Roxanne* (Schepisi, USA, 87) Steve Martin updated Rostand's play and cast himself as a long-nosed small-town fire chief named C.D. Bales, fighting his duels with a tennis racket instead of a sword and reciting nose jokes instead of Alexandrine couplets. On the silent screen Coquelin Aine (France, 1900), Henry Krauss in Capellani's French adaptation of 1909 and Pierre Magnier in a 1923 Italian version all featured as somewhat more orthodox Cyranos.

(Above) Steve Martin as Cyrano 'update' C. D. Bales—the long nosed fireman of a small American town who fights his duels with tennis rackets and longs for the lovely Darryl Hannah; (right) Jose Ferrer as the soulful poet-swordsman *Cyrano de Bergerac,* renowned for his long nose but always longing for the love of a beautiful woman. The central character in Edmond Rostand's play of 17th century Paris

Daddy Long Legs [F]

American millionaire who sponsors the education of an orphan girl on the condition that his identity never be revealed but then finds unexpected romantic complications setting in when his charge begins to fall in love with him. Created in 1912 by novelist Jean Webster (grand niece of Mark Twain), the character has been played on numerous occasions on screen, most notably by Fred Astaire in the 1955 CinemaScope musical which teamed him with Leslie Caron and included Johnny Mercer's Oscar nominated song 'Something's Gotta Give'. The 1935 movie *Curly Top,* in which Shirley Temple sang 'Animal Crackers In My Soup', was also a version of the story.

Warner Baxter	*Daddy Long Legs* (Santell) USA, 31
John Boles	*Curly Top* (Cummings) USA, 35
Fred Astaire	*Daddy Long Legs* (Negulesco) USA, 55

Note: On the silent screen Mahlon Hamilton played Daddy Long Legs in the 1919 film directed by Marshal Neilan; the young orphan has been played by Mary Pickford (19), Janet Gaynor (31), Shirley Temple (35) and Leslie Caron (55).

Danton, Georges Jacques [R]

(1759–94) One of the major figures of the French Revolution, a great orator and man of the people who together with Robespierre and others was prominent in overthrowing the monarchy and establishing the new republic. Like most of the revolutionaries he perished on the guillotine, instructing his executioner: 'Show my head to the people, it is worth it!' Emil Jannings starred in a silent biography and Fritz Kortner in the German production of 1931. The most recent portrayal was by Gerard Depardieu in Wajda's film *Danton,* based on the 1931 play 'The Danton Affair' by Stanlislawa Przybyszewska. Wajda's film centred on Danton's clash with Robespierre whom he accused of having forgotten the revolution's original purpose. The film closely paralleled the political situation in Poland today.

Richard Cramer	*Captain Of The Guard* (Robertson) USA, 30
Fritz Kortner	*Danton* (Behrendt) Ger, 31
Wade Crosby	*Reign Of Terror* (Mann) USA, 49
William Sabatier	*Valmy* (Gance) Fra, 67
Gerard Depardieu	*Danton* (Wajda) Pol/Fra, 82
Olivier de Kersauzon	*Liberty, Equality, Sauerkraut* (Yanne) Fra/It, 85

Note: Emil Jannings in Buchowetzki's *Danton* (Ger, 21), Monte Blue in Griffiths' *Orphans Of The Storm* (USA, 21) and George Siegmann in Rex Ingram's *Scaramouche* (USA, 23) were among the actors who portrayed Danton on the silent screen.

Dark, Mr [F]

The sinister owner of 'Dark's Pandemonium Shadow Show', a travelling carnival that offers to fulfill people's secret longings and desires in exchange for their souls. Trapped on one of his own devices – a carousel that ages or regresses depending on which direction it's moving – he finally turns into an old man and crumbles away. He was played by British actor Jonathan Pryce in Jack Clayton's 1983 film of Bradbury's novel 'Something Wicked This Way Comes'.

Jonathan Pryce	*Something Wicked This Way Comes* (Clayton) USA, 83

Note: Ray Bradbury's Gothic novel was published in 1962; it was first considered for filming from a 75-page outline by Gene Kelly in 1955. Sam Peckinpah, Mark Rydell, John Carpenter and Steven Spielberg were other film-makers who were interested in bringing the story to the screen.

Darrow, Clarence [R]

(1857–1938) American lawyer, famed for his liberal views and never ending crusade for the abolition of capital punishment. Two of his most famous cases – the defence of Leopold and Loeb and the schoolteacher accused of teaching Darwin's theory of evolution in a Tennessee school – were filmed in *Compulsion* and *Inherit The Wind,* respectively.

Have you seen these two boys? Ray Bradbury's frightening villain Dr Dark (Jonathan Pryce) seeks out the boys whose innocence is needed to fuel his carnival of evil. A scene from Jack Clayton's version of Bradbury's novel *Something Wicked This Way Comes*

Darrow was not named in either film, appearing as Jonathan Wilk in the Richard Fleischer movie and Henry Drummond in the Kramer production.

Orson Welles — *Compulsion* (Fleischer) USA, 59
Spencer Tracy — *Inherit The Wind* (Kramer) USA, 60

Darwin, Charles [R]

(1809–82) British naturalist who revolutionized nineteenth century thinking with his theory of the evolution of man and later authored the famous 'Origin Of The Species' (1859). Not the most entertaining subject for a film, although Jack Couffer's 1972 movie which included Darwin's journeys to South Africa and New Zealand, made an honest attempt to recreate his life and work.

Nicholas Clay — *The Darwin Adventure* (Couffer) GB, 72

King David [R]

(*c.* 1000–960 BC) Shepherd king, reputedly the author of many of the Psalms and whose adventures (including his slaying of the giant Goliath) belong with the most copious and vivid of the Old Testament. Film-makers have tried on several occasions to capture his life – especially his sinful love for the married Bathsheba – but despite an honourable and ambitious attempt by Bruce Beresford in 1986, none have so far succeeded. Gregory Peck, Jeff Chandler and Richard Gere have been the unlikely actors cast as movie Davids; Timothy Bottoms was an even more improbable King in the four-hour TV film *The Story Of David* (76).

Gregory Peck — *David And Bathsheba* (King) USA, 51

Gregory Peck and Susan Hayward as *David and Bathsheba* In Henry King's 1951 production for 20th Century Fox

Jeff Chandler	*A Story Of David* (McNaught)	GB, 60
Ivo Payer	*David And Goliath* (Pottier/Baldi)	It, 60
Gianni Garko	*Saul And David* (Baldi)	It/Spa, 65
Timothy Bottoms	*The Story Of David* (Rich)	TVM/USA, 76
Richard Gere	*King David* (Beresford)	USA, 86

Bathsheba was played by Susan Hayward in the 1951 film, Jane Seymour in the 1976 TV production and Alice Krige in Bruce Beresford's film.

Dean, Dizzy

R

(1911–) A baseball pitcher of the early 30s, christened Jay Hanna but dubbed 'Dizzy' by fans and sports writers alike, who hit the bottle after he seriously damaged his throwing arm when playing for the St Louis Cardinals. His early success and his second career as a colourful radio commentator was covered in the minor Fox biography, *The Pride of St Louis.* Herman J. Mankiewicz (*Citizen Kane, The Pride Of The Yankees*) scripted the film; Dan Dailey featured as Dean.

Dan Dailey	*The Pride Of St Louis* (Harmon Jones)	USA, 52

Demara, Ferdinand

R

Canadian imposter who conned his way across America disguised variously as a trappist monk, a psychologist, a deputy sheriff, a prison warden and an instructor of theology. His most extraordinary achievement was posing as a surgeon in the Korean War when he carried out cardiac surgery on many men including a soldier with a bullet near his heart. He later recalled: 'I had to keep one basic principle in mind. The less cutting you do, the less patching up you have to do afterwards'. Finally exposed when the navy insisted on publicizing his heroic work, he later reformed and settled down as a religious counsellor at a Californian hospital. In a much underrated film by Robert Mulligan, Tony Curtis featured as the extraordinary trickster.

Tony Curtis — *The Great Imposter* (Mulligan) USA, 60

DeSylva, Brown and Henderson

R

An unusual combination, a songwriting *trio* who wrote the scores for several Broadway musicals ('George White's Scandals', 'Good News', 'Flying High'), all of which reflected the madcap mood of the Jazz Age. Their rise from Tin Pan Alley to Hollywood was the subject of the 1956 biography by Michael Curtiz. Among their hit songs are 'The Birth Of The Blues', 'Button Up Your Overcoat', 'It All Depends On You', 'The Varsity Drag'.

Gordon MacRae (DeSylva) — *The Best Things In Life Are Free* (Curtiz) USA, 56
Ernest Borgnine (Brown)
Dan Dailey (Henderson)

Note: Buddy DeSylva (1895–1950) was also played by Eddie Marr in *Rhapsody In Blue* (45); Lew Brown died in 1958, aged 65, Ray Henderson in 1970, aged 74.

Devil, The

F

Satan, Beelzebub, Mephistopheles, Old Nick – call him what you will, but God's opposite number has positively thrived on the screen and even, on occasion, displayed a humorous side to his dark, forbidding nature. Walter Huston, Laird Cregar, Burgess Meredith and Peter Cook are among those who have chuckled with manic delight; in more recent times the Devil has been slightly more reticent about making personal appearances and been content to rest snugly within the frames of unsuspecting children, e.g. Linda Blair in *The Exorcist* and Harvey Stephens in *The Omen*.

Walter Huston — *All That Money Can Buy* (Dieterle) USA, 41
Alan Mowbray — *The Devil With Hitler* (Douglas) USA, 42
Jules Berry — Les Visiteurs du Soir (Carné) Fra, 42
Rex Ingram — *Cabin In The Sky* (Minnelli) USA, 43
Laird Cregar — *Heaven Can Wait* (Lubitsch) USA, 43
Emil Fjellstrom — *The Heavenly Play* (Sjöberg) Swe, 44
Claude Rains — *Angel On My Shoulder* (Mayo) USA, 46
Ray Milland — *Alias Nick Beal* (Farrow) USA, 49
Michel Simon — *La Beauté du Diable* (Clair) Fra, 49
Italo Tajo — *Faust And The Devil* (Gallone) It, 50
Stanley Holloway — *Meet Mr Lucifer* (Pelissier) GB, 53
Cedric Hardwicke — *Bait* (Haas) USA, 54
Yves Montand — *Marguerite Of The Night* (Autant-Lara) Fra, 56
Fernando Gomez — *Faustina* (de Heredia) Spa, 57
Mel Welles — *The Undead* (Corman) USA, 57
Vincent Price — *The Story Of Mankind* (Allen) USA, 57
Ray Walston — *Damn Yankees* (Donen) USA, 58
Jose Galvez — *Macario* (Gavaldon) Mex, 60
Gustaf Gruendgens — *Faust* (Gorski) W.Ger, 60
Stig Jarrel — *The Devil's Eye* (Bergman) Swe, 60
Georgiy Millyar — *A Night Before Christmas* (Rou) USSR, 61
Lon Chaney, Jr. — *The Devil's Messenger* (Strock) USA/Swe, 62
Roban Cody — *Faust* (Suman) USA, 64
Robert Helpmann — *The Soldier's Tale* (Birkett) GB, 64
Donald Pleasence — *The Greatest Story Ever Told* (Stevens) USA, 65
Vittorio Gassman — *The Devil In Love* (Scola) It, 66
Andreas Teuber — *Doctor Faustus* (Burton/Coghill) GB/It, 67
Peter Cook — *Bedazzled* (Donen) GB, 67
Burgess Meredith — *Torture Garden* (Francis) GB, 67
Jorj Voicu — *Faust* (Popescu-Gopo) Rum, 67

Five faces of Satan (this page, clockwise from top left) Ernest Borgnine, goat-like in *The Devil's Rain*; an impish Jack Nicholson in *The Witches Of Eastwick*; Tim Curry in Ridley Scott's *Legend*; a bearded Robert De Niro in *Angel Heart*; (opposite page) a young Harvey Stephens, up against Gregory Peck in the first of the three *Omen* films.

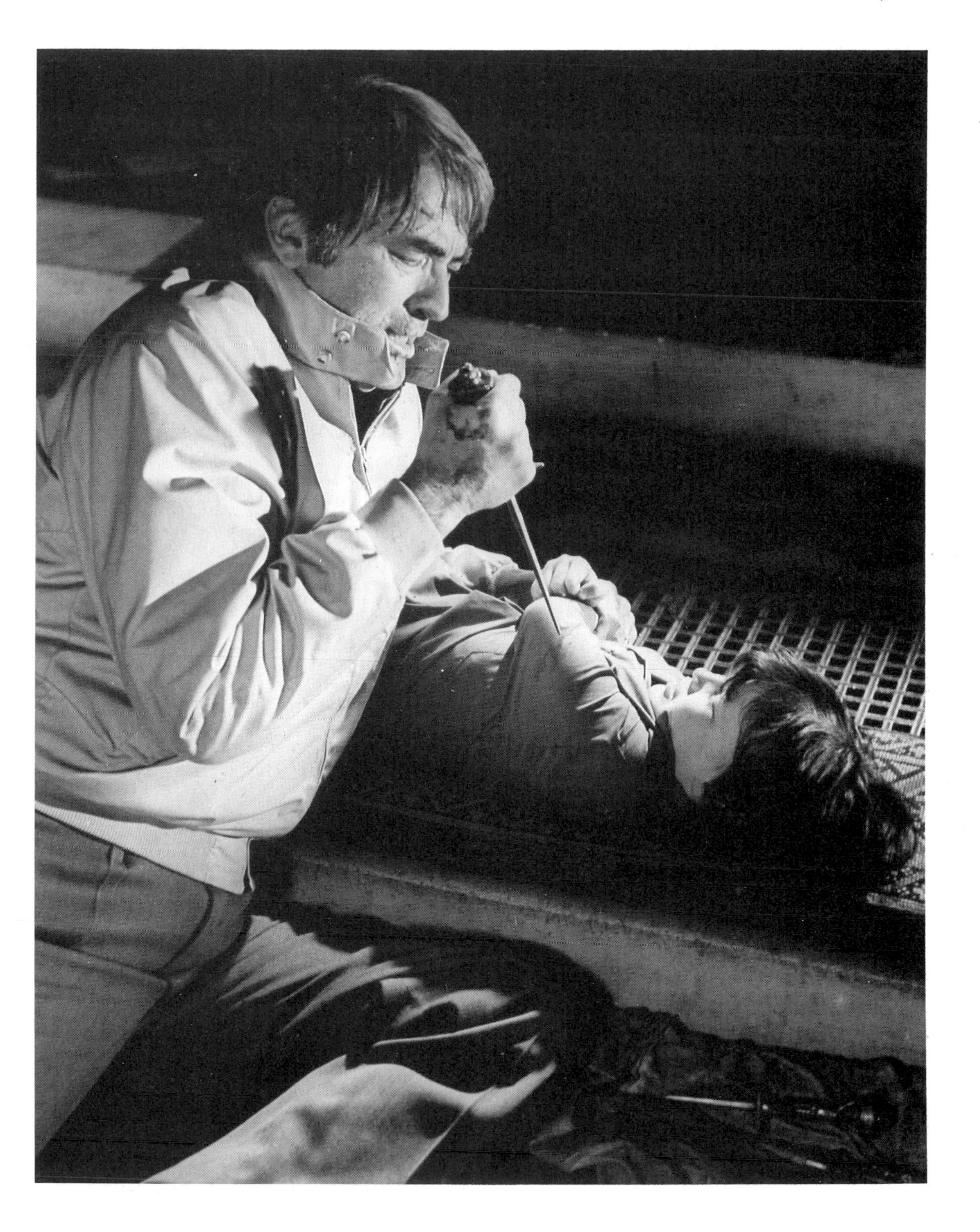

Pierre Clementi	*The Milky Way* (Bunuel) Fra/It, 69
Mio Domani	*Scratch Harry* (Matter) USA, 70
Christopher Stone	*The Joys Of Jezebel* (Stootsberry) USA, 70
Alain Cuny	*The Master & Margarita* (Petrovic) Yug/It, 72
Ralph Richardson	*Tales From The Crypt* (Francis) GB, 72
Linda Blair	*The Exorcist* (Friedkin) USA, 73
Juliet Mills	*The Devil Within Her* (Hellman) It, 74
Carla Gravina	*The Antichrist* (de Martino) It, 74
Ernest Borgnine	*The Devil's Rain* (Fuest) USA, 76
Harvey Stephens	*The Omen* (Donner) USA, 76
Burgesss Meredith	*The Sentinel* (Winner) USA, 77
Linda Blair	*Exorcist II: The Heretic* (Boorman) USA, 77
Simon Ward	*Holocaust 2000* (de Martino) It/GB, 78
Victor Buono	*The Evil* (Trikonis) USA, 78
Jonathan Scott-Taylor	*Damien: Omen II* (Taylor) USA, 78
Sam Neill	*The Final Conflict* (Baker) USA, 81
Army Archerd	*The Devil And Max Devlin* (Stern) USA, 81
David Warner	*Time Bandits* (Gilliam) GB, 81
Robert Prosky	*The Natural* (Levinson) USA, 84
Tim Curry	*Legend* (Scott) USA, 85
Charles Dance	*The Golden Child* (Ritchie) USA, 86
Robert DeNiro	*Angel Heart* (Parker) USA, 87
Jack Nicholson	*The Witches Of Eastwick* (Millar) USA, 87

Note: On the silent screen Satan was played by Leopold Kramer (Hung, 18), Eduard Verkada (Holl, 19), George Arliss (USA, 21), Emil Jannings (Ger, 25) and Alan Brooks (USA, 27).

Diamond, Jack 'Legs' [R]

(–1931) The gangster they couldn't kill – almost! A racketeer and bootlegger, he was riddled with bullets on at least three occasions and still managed to live to tell the tale. The only sure way to dispose of him was to murder him in his sleep which some unknown gangsters finally accomplished in December, 1931. Strictly an also ran compared with Dillinger, Capone and the rest, but vividly portrayed in Boetticher's *The Rise and Fall Of Legs Diamond.*

Ray Danton	*The Rise And Fall Of Legs Diamonds* (Boetticher) USA, 60
Ray Danton	*Portrait Of A Mobster* (Pevney) USA, 61

Dietrichson, Phyllis [F]

Not too many film bad girls come any more dangerous than this one; a gold-digging femme fatale who seduces a luckless insurance man into murdering her husband and then double-crosses him when the crime is complete. Brought vividly to life by Barbara Stanwyck in Billy Wilder's *Double Indemnity;* less effectively so by Samantha Eggar in the TV remake of 1973. Lawrence Kasdan's *Body Heat* (81) starring Kathleen Turner had no direct connections with Cain's original story (published in 1936) but the theme (wife persuades lawyer to bump off hubby) and the torrid sex scenes bore a very close resemblance to Cain's novel.

Barbara Stanwyck	*Double Indemnity* (Wilder) USA, 44
Samantha Eggar	*Double Indemnity* (Smight) TV USA, 73

Note: Cain's story was first published in 'Liberty' magazine, a nickel weekly that was famous for its gimmick of printing the reading time to the exact minute of each article and story it published. The reading time for *Double Indemnity* was two hours, 50 minutes and seven seconds. Because he didn't move his lips when reading Wilder got through it in 58 minutes and correctly assumed that a story about 'a dame who kills her husband for the insurance money' would make ideal film material.

Dillinger, John [R]

(1903–34) A Public Enemy Number One before being betrayed by a prostitute and shot down outside a Chicago movie theatre in July, 1934 – an event re-enacted many times on screen. Despite his reputation, Dillinger was not one of the most vicious American gangsters and seldom injured

Barbara Stanwyck as the scheming Phyllis Dietrichson about to ensnare unsuspecting insurance man Fred MacMurray in Billy Wilder's *Double Indemnity*, filmed at Paramount in 1944

people during his meticulously planned bank raids. Warren Oates' portrait in John Milius' 1973 film is the most efficient screen portrayal, although Lawrence Tierney's performance in the low-budget thriller of 1945 is not without merit.

Lawrence Tierney	*Dillinger* (Nosseck)	USA, 45
Leo Gordon	*Baby Face Nelson* (Siegel)	USA, 57
Scott Peters	*The FBI Story* (LeRoy)	USA, 59
Nick Adams	*Young Dillinger* (Morse)	USA, 65
Warren Oates	*Dillinger* (Milius)	USA, 73
Robert Conrad	*The Lady In Red* (Teague)	USA, 79

Note: William Jordan appeared as Dillinger in Dan Curtis' 1975 TV movie *The Kansas City Massacre;* the prostitute (known as 'The Lady In Red') who helped the FBI was named Anna Sage. She was played by Ann Jeffreys in the 1945 film, Cloris Leachman in the Milius adaptation and Louise Fletcher in 1979.

Disraeli, Benjamin [R]

(1804–81) British statesman and Prime Minister (1868 and 1874–80), responsible for acquiring the Suez Canal and proclaiming Queen Victoria Empress of India. Portrayed on screen more than any other British premier with George Arliss appearing twice in the role – once on the silent screen, once in the early years of sound – and Alec Guinness rendering the definitive portrait of Disraeli as a wily opportunist in the underrated *The Mudlark*.

George Arliss	*Disraeli* (Green)	USA, 29

Warren Oates as Public Enemy Number One, John Dillinger (popular with the ladies and the American public) in John Milius' film biography of 1973

Derrick de Marney & Hugh Miller	*Victoria The Great* (Wilcox)	GB, 37
Derrick de Marney	*Sixty Glorious Years* (Wilcox)	GB, 38
Miles Mander	*Suez* (Dwan)	USA, 38
John Gielgud	*The Prime Minister* (Dickinson)	GB, 41
Abraham Sofaer	*The Ghosts of Berkeley Square* (Sewell)	GB, 47
Alec Guinness	*The Mudlark* (Negulesco)	GB, 50

Note: Arliss first played the role in the 1921 silent film, *Disraeli* (USA); Dennis Eadie in *Disraeli* (GB, 16) and Douglas Munro in *The Life Story Of Lloyd George* (GB, 18) also featured in the part.

Dith Pran [R]

Cambodian guide and interpreter who helped New York Times correspondent Sydney Schanberg escape execution at the hands of the Khmer Rouge but only by jeopardizing his own life. His subsequent experiences as a slave labourer and his long trek to safety to the borders of Thailand were recounted in Roland Joffe's *The Killing Fields*. Pran was played by the non-professional actor Haing S. Ngor (in real life a Cambodian doctor) who won a supporting actor Oscar for his performance; Schanberg, who wrote a series of articles on Pran's heroism and was later reunited with him in Thailand, was played by Sam Waterston.

Haing S. Ngor	*The Killing Fields* (Joffe)	GB, 84

Dolly Sisters, The 

Dancing headliners who began in US vaudeville and then scored their first Broadway hit in the 1911 production 'Ziegfeld Follies'. Subsequently became 'the toast of two continents' with their famous sister act. In the 1945 film biography Jennie (1892–1941) was played by Betty Grable, and Rosie (1892–1970) by June Haver.

Betty Grable and June Haver	*The Dolly Sisters* (Cummings)	USA, 45

The story of a remarkable friendship. Haing S. Ngor as Cambodian guide and interpreter Dith Pran and Sam Waterston as war correspondent Sydney Schanberg in *The Killing Fields*

Dominici, Gaston

R

Patriarchal French farmer who belongs in the annals of crime as one of the 'was he innocent' variety. His confessions, retractions, counter-accusations and attempted suicide when charged with the murder of the British Drummond family in the south of France in 1952, led to confusion and doubt. Eventually convicted, he was sentenced to life imprisonment but released in 1960. He died five years later, aged 88. Jean Gabin, in one of his final screen roles, portrayed him on screen in 1973.

Jean Gabin	*L'Affaire Dominici* (Bernard-Aubert) Fra, 73

Don Juan

Legendary rake whose dissolute life in seventeenth century Spain attracted two major Hollywood stars, Douglas Fairbanks and Errol Flynn, during their final swashbuckling years. His romantic escapades were also the subject of the 1926 John Barrymore costumer, *Don Juan,* the first movie to incorporate sound effects – bells, the clashing of swords, etc. – onto a synchronized soundtrack.

John Barrymore	*Don Juan* (Crosland) USA, 26
Douglas Fairbanks	*The Private Life Of Don Juan* (Korda) GB, 34
Adriano Rimoldi	*The Loves Of Don Juan* (Falconi) It, 48
Errol Flynn	*The Adventures Of Don Juan* (Sherman) USA, 49
Antonio Vilar	*The Loves Of Don Juan* (de Heredia) Spa, 50
Jean-Marie Amato	*Men Think Only Of That* (Robert) Fra, 54
Erno Crisa	*Don Juan* (Berry) Fra/It, 56
Jarl Kulle	*The Devil's Eye* (Bergman) Swe, 60
Brigitte Bardot	*Don Juan or If Don Juan Were A Woman* (Vadim) Fra/It, 73

Note: In John Berry's 1956 film, Fernandel (as the servant of Don Juan who impersonates his master) had the starring role; Vadim's picture revamped the legend and centred on Don Juan reincarnated as a woman.

Don Quixote

Gallant sixteenth century knight of novelist Cervantes, an idealistic hero who takes to the road with his squire Sancho Panza in an attempt to restore the age of chivalry. The Russian version with Nikolai Cherkassov remains one of the most assured screen adaptations of a classic novel; *Man Of La Mancha,* the musical version with Peter O'Toole doubling as both Cervantes and Quixote, ranks as one of the most dismal.

Feodor Chaliapin	*Don Quixote* (Pabst) GB, 33
Rafael Rivelles	*Don Quixote* (Gil) Spa, 47
Nikolai Cherkassov	*Don Quixote* (Kozintsev) USSR, 57
Peter O'Toole	*Man Of La Mancha* (Hiller) It, 72
Pino Micol	*Don Quixote* (Scaparro) It, 84

Note: Claude Garry (Fra, 13), De Wolf Hopper (USA, 16), Jerrold Robertshaw (GB, 24) and Carl Schenstrom (Den, 26) all played Quixote on the silent screen; George Robey (24) and (33), Harald Madsen (26),

Man of la Mancha! Peter O'Toole as Don Quixote and James Coco as Sancho Panza in the 1972 film of Dale Wasserman's musical version of Cervantes tale

Juan Calvo (47), Yuri Tolubeyev (57), Folco Lulli in *Dulcinea* (62), James Coco (72) and Peppe Barra (84) are the actors who have featured as Sancho Panza.

Don Quixote was seen in only one brief sequence (on his death bed and photographed from behind) in the Spanish production of *Dulcinea.* On TV Rex Harrison appeared as Don Quixote and Frank Finlay as Sancho Panza in a 1972 BBC production, and Alec Guinnes and Leo McKern starred in *Monsignor Quixote,* (85), Graham Greene's reworking of Cervantes' tale.

Orson Welles' unfinished modern adaptation (at one time titled *Don Quixote's Trip To The Moon*) was begun in 1955 and remained unedited into a final form at the time of Welles' death. It featured Francisco Rieguera as Quixote and Akim Tamiroff as Panza.

Dolittle, Dr

F

Eccentric English country physician whose knowledge of over 500 different dialects (taught him by his parrot Polynesia) leads him into innumerable escapades. Created by Hugh Lofting (an American writer born in Britain) he featured in more than a dozen books and was eventually brought to the screen in the musical *Doctor Dolittle* which dealt with the doctor's home life in the village of Puddleby-On-The-Marsh and with his obsessive search for the Giant Pink Sea Snail. Rex Harrison brought Dolittle to screen life, voicing the year's Oscar-winning song 'Talk To The Animals'. He replaced Christopher Plummer who had originally been cast in the role. Dolittle first appeared in print in 1920 in 'The Story Of Dr Dolittle'.

The man who could talk to the animals. Rex Harrison as Hugh Lofting's famous Doctor Dolittle, created by the author in 1920 and brought to the screen in a lavish Fox musical in 1967

Rex Harrison	*Doctor Dolittle*	(Fleischer)	USA, 67

Doolittle, Eliza

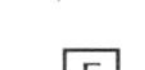

George Bernard Shaw's cockney flower girl, turned into an elegant lady of society by a teacher of phonetics. The 'straight' screen Eliza was played by Wendy Hiller in 1938, the musical fair lady by Audrey Hepburn whose songs – 'I Could Have Danced All Night', 'Show Me', 'Wouldn't It Be Luverly' — were dubbed by Marni Nixon. Two earlier screen versions of 'Pygmalion' were produced in Germany and Holland. Shaw's play originally opened in London in 1913.

Jenny Jugo	*Pygmalion*	(Engel)	Ger, 35
Lily Bouwmeester	*Pygmalion*	(Berger)	Hol, 36
Wendy Hiller	*Pygmalion*	(Pascal)	GB, 38
Audrey Hepburn	*My Fair Lady*	(Cukor)	USA, 64

Note: Henry Higgins, the conceited, chauvinistic professor of dialects has been played by Gustaf Grundgens (35), Johan de Meester (36), Leslie Howard (38) and Rex Harrison (64). Harrison played the stage role on Broadway (56) and in London (58) and won an Academy Award for best screen actor of 1964.

In 1984 Margot Kidder starred as Eliza and Peter O'Toole as Higgins in a Canadian/American TV movie version of *Pygmalion,* directed by Dan Redler.

Doolittle, Lt General James

(1896–) American general, famous for leading the 1942 bomber raid on Japan in which squadrons of B-25s were launched from aircraft carriers, bombed the Japanese capital and then landed on airfields in China. The events leading up to the raid and the raid itself were described in meticulous, often semi-documentary fashion in Mervyn LeRoy's film of 1944.

Spencer Tracy	*Thirty Seconds Over Tokyo*	(LeRoy)	USA, 44

'Why can't the English teach their children how to speak? Phonetics teacher Rex Harrison ponders the question as he surveys cockney flower-girl Eliza Doolittle in the film version of the musical *My Fair Lady*. Audrey Hepburn played Eliza in the Warner Bros film which was directed by George Cukor and won eight Academy Awards

Doone, Lorna

F

Heroine of R. D. Blackmore's novel of seventeenth century Devonshire, the kidnapped daughter of a Scottish nobleman who is raised by the Doone outlaw clan on the wilds of Exmoor. Somewhat out of screen favour in recent years, no version of her story having been made since Phil Karlson's low budget production of 1951. More popular in the less demanding silent era.

Victoria Hopper	*Lorna Doone*	(Dean)	GB, 35
Barbara Hale	*Lorna Doone*	(Karlson)	USA, 51

Note: Silent performances were given by Dorothy Bellew (GB, 12), Bertie Gordon (GB, 20) and Madge Bellamy (USA, 22).

Dorrit, William

F

The 'Father of the Marshalsea'; a selfish, defeated debtor who languishes in the Marshalsea Prison for 25 years, finds himself the heir to a fortune but then loses it and ruins his family afresh through speculating with the crooked financier Merdle. Memorably played by Alec Guinness in Christine Edzard's two part (each of three hours) 1987 adaptation; only one other sound portrayal, that of Gustav Waldau in the 1934 German production *Klein Dorrit.* Dickens' 'Little Dorrit' was first published in 1855–7.

Gustav Waldau	*Klein Dorrit*	(Lamac)	Ger, 34
Alec Guinness	*Little Dorrit*	(Edzard)	GB, 87

Note: Arthur Lennard (GB, 20) and Frederik Jensen (Den, 24) played William Dorrit on the silent screen.

Other notable figures in Dickens' dark and complex novel include the devoted daughter Amy Dorrit, the gentle dreamer Arthur Clennam, his invalid mother and her sinister servant Jeremiah Flintwich, and the shady financier Merdle. Screen portrayals have been as follows:

Amy (Little) Dorrit

Anny Ondra	*Klein Dorrit*	(Lamač)	Ger, 34
Sarah Pickering	*Little Dorrit*	(Edzard)	GB, 87

Silent: Joan Morgan (GB, 20) and Karina Bell (Den, 24).

Arthur Clennam

Mathias Wieman	*Klein Dorrit*	(Lamač)	Ger, 34
Derek Jacobi	*Little Dorrit*	(Edzard)	GB, 87

Silent: Langhorne Burton (GB, 20) and Gunnar Tocnaes (Den, 24).

Mrs Clennam

Antonie Jackel	*Klein Dorrit*	(Lamač)	Ger, 34
Joan Greenwood	*Little Dorrit*	(Edzard)	GB, 87

Silent: Lady Tree (GB, 20) and Ingeborg Pehrson (Den, 24).

Jeremiah Flintwich

Fritz Rasp	*Klein Dorrit*	(Lamač)	Ger, 34
Max Wall	*Little Dorrit*	(Edzard)	GB, 87

Silent: Arthur Walcott (GB, 20) and Carl Hinz (Den, 24).

Mr Merdle

Otto Stockel	*Klein Dorrit*	(Lamač)	Ger, 34
Michael Elphick	*Little Dorrit*	(Edzard)	GB, 87

Silent: George Foley (GB, 20).

Dorsey, Jimmy

R

(1904–57) Saxophone player/band leader of the 30s and 40s who made several screen appearances with his orchestra – *The Fleet's In, I Dood It, Four Jills And A Jeep, Hollywood Canteen* – before achieving the unique distinction of portraying himself in the 1947 biography, *The Fabulous Dorseys.*

As himself	*The Fabulous Dorseys*	(Green)	USA, 47
Ray Anthony	*The Five Pennies*	(Shavelson)	USA, 59

Dorsey, Tommy

R

(1905–56) Like his brother, a top bandleader of the pre-war and war periods, featuring with his trombone and orchestra in several top movies at MGM – *Du Barry Was A Lady, Presenting Lily Mars, Girl Crazy, Broadway Rhythm.* Played himself in *The Fabulous Dorseys,* a minor, uninspired little biography redeemed by several of the Dorseys' most popular hits i.e. 'Green Eyes', 'Marie', 'Never Say Never', 'The Object Of My Affections'.

As himself	*The Fabulous Dorseys*	(Green)	USA, 47
Bobby Troup	*Drum Crazy*	(Weis)	USA, 59

Dostoevsky, Feodor Mikhailovich

R

(1821–81) Russian novelist who authored such brilliant works as *The Brothers Karamazov, The Idiot* and *Crime And Punishment* and whose acute psychological perceptions and analyses amazed later experts in psychology, including Freud. Anatoly Solonitsyn appeared as the tormented writer in the Soviet production *26 Days In The Life Of*

Arguably the most ambitious of all the Dickens screen adaptations – Christine Edzard's six-hour 2-part version of *Little Dorrit* with (right) Sarah Pickering in the title role, (above right) Alec Guinness as William Dorrit, inmate of the debtor's prison, the Marshalsea, and (above left) Derek Jacobi as the lonely, middle aged Arthur Clennam

Dostoevsky, a film which looked at the period when he was nearing completion of *Crime And Punishment* but was forced to dictate (in just 26 days to a stenographer) the novel *The Gambler* to help pay off his own gambling debts.

Anatoly Solonitsyn — *26 Days In The Life Of Dostoevsky* (Zarkhi) USSR, 81

Dowding, Air Chief Marshal Sir Hugh [R]

(1882–1970) The leader of RAF Fighter Command during the critical months of July, August and September 1940, when the Luftwaffe made a massive air assault on the British Isles. A man of single-minded determination and rather humourless character, played with quiet authority by Olivier in Guy Hamilton's *Battle Of Britain.*

Charles Carson — *Reach For The Sky* (Gilbert) GB, 56

Laurence Olivier — *Battle Of Britain* (Hamilton) GB, 69

Doyle, Jimmy 'Popeye' [R]

Fanatical American cop, a member of the New York narcotics squad, obsessed with tracking down a French dope syndicate smuggling heroin into the USA. A 'Lock 'em up and throw away the key' personality, a shabby determination, and a better than average skill behind the wheel of a car, eventually see him through, although it takes him two movies to nail criminal kingpin Fernando Rey. Gene Hackman won an Oscar for the first of his two characterizations.

Gene Hackman — *The French Connection* (Friedkin) USA, 71

Gene Hackman — *The French Connection II* (Frankenheimer) USA, 75

Dracula [F]

The most enduring horror figure in all cinema, a Transylvanian count who sleeps in a coffin by day and drinks human blood to sustain him in working hours. Bela Lugosi brought Dracula worldwide fame in Tod Browning's 1931 film; Christopher Lee enhanced the vampire's popularity still further in the post-war years. Bram Stoker's novel was published in 1897 and derived from the unsavoury activities of a certain Vlad Dracula who operated in the Carpathian mountains in the fifteenth century. A checklist of the major screen Draculas is shown below:

Detective 'Popeye' Doyle (Gene Hackman) checks a switchblade knife found during a raid. A scene from William Friedkin's 1971 thriller *The French Connection*

Bela Lugosi — *Dracula* (Browning) USA, 31

Carlos Villarias — *Dracula* (Melford) Mex, 31

Lon Chaney, Jr — *Son Of Dracula* (Siodmak) USA, 43

John Carradine — *House Of Frankenstein* (Kenton) USA, 44

John Carradine — *House Of Dracula* (Kenton) USA, 45

Bela Lugosi — *Abbott & Costello Meet Frankenstein* (Barton) USA, 48

Atif Kaptan — *Drakula Istanbulda* (Muhtat) Turk, 53

German Robles — *El Castillo de los monstruos* (Soler) Mex, 57

Jerry Blaine — *Blood Of Dracula* (Strock) USA, 57

Francis Lederer — *The Return of Dracula* (Landres) USA, 58

Christopher Lee — *Dracula* (Fisher) GB, 58

Christopher Lee	*Tempi duri per i vampiri* (Steno) It, 59
David Peel	*Brides Of Dracula* (Fisher) GB, 60
Yechoon Lee	*Ahkea Khots* (Lee) S.Korea, 61
John Carradine	*Billy The Kid vs Dracula* (Beaudine) USA, 66
Christopher Lee	*Dracula – Prince Of Darkness* (Fisher) GB, 66
Pluto Fleix	*The Worst Crime Of All!* (Lamb) USA, 66
Mitch Evans	*Dr Terror's Gallery Of Horrors* (Hewitt) USA, 67
Christopher Lee	*Dracula Has Risen From The Grave* (Francis) GB, 68
Aldo Monti	*El Vampiro y el Sexo* (Cardona) Mex, 68
Alex d'Arcy	*The Blood Of Dracula's Castle* (Adamson/Hewitt) USA, 69
Vince Kelly	*Dracula (The Dirty Old Man)* (Edwards) USA, 69
Christopher Lee	*The Magic Christian* (McGrath) GB, 69
Des Roberts	*Guess What Happened To Count Dracula* (Merrick) USA, 70
Dennis Price	*Vampyros Lesbos* (Franco) Spa,W.Ger., 70
Christopher Lee	*The Scars Of Dracula* (Baker) GB, 70
Christopher Lee	*Taste The Blood Of Dracula* (Sasdy) GB, 70
Christopher Lee	*El Conde Dracula* (Franco) Spa, 70
Paul Albert Krumm	*Jonathan, Vampire Sterben Nicht* (Gissendorfer) W.Ger, 70
Zandor Vorkov	*Blood Of Frankenstein* (Adamson) USA, 70
Howard Vernon	*Dracula Contra El Doctor Frankenstein* (Franco) Spa, 71
Christopher Lee	*Dracula AD 1972* (Gibson) GB, 72
Mori Kishida	*Lake Of Dracula* (Yamamoto) Jap, 72
Paul Naschy	*Count Dracula's Great Love* (Aguirre) Spa, 72
Howard Vernon	*La Hija De Dracula* (Franco) Spa, 72
Charles Macaulay	*Blacula* (Crain) USA, 72
William Marshall	*Blacula* (Crain) USA, 72
Narcisso Ibanez Menta	*La Saga de los Draculas* (Klimovsky) Spa, 73
Paul Naschy	*El Gran amor del Conde Dracula* (Aguirre) Spa, 73
Christopher Lee	*The Satanic Rites Of Dracula* (Gibson) GB, 73
Udo Kier	*Blood For Dracula* (Morrissey) USA, 74
John Forbes Robertson	*The Legend Of The Seven Golden Vampires* (Baker) GB/Hong Kong, 74
David Niven	*Vampira* (Donner) GB, 75
Christopher Lee	*Dracula, Pere Et Fils* (Molinaro) Fra, 76
Michael Pataki	*Zoltan: Hound Of Dracula* (Band) USA, 77
Klaus Kinski	*Nosferatu, The Vampyre* (Herzog) W.Ger, 79
Frank Langella	*Dracula* (Badham) USA, 79
George Hamilton	*Love At First Bite* © (Dragoti) USA, 79
John Carradine	*Nocturna* (Tampa) USA, 79
Stefan Sileanu	*The True Life Of Dracula* (Nastase) Rum, 79
Gerald Fielding	*Dracula's Last Rites* (Paris) USA, 80
Kostas Soumas	*Dracula Tan Exarchia* (Gre, 83

Note: Gloria Holden appeared as *Dracula's Daughter* in 1936, Ingrid Pitt as the *Countess Dracula* in 1970, Evelyne Kraft in *Lady Dracula* in 1977 and Louise Fletcher as *Mama Dracula* in 1980. Bela Lugosi (as Armand Tesla) in *The Return Of The Vampire* (USA, 43) and David Peel (as Baron Meinster) in *Brides Of Dracula* (GB, 60) both featured as the Dracula character under another name. The 1979 Rumanian production *The True Life Of Dracula* was based on the historical Dracula, Vlad The Impaler.

Max Schreck (as Count Orlock) appeared for F. W. Murneau in the German silent production, *Nosferatu* (22). On TV Denholm Elliott (71), Jack Palance (74), Louis Jourdan (77), Judd Hirsch (79) and Richard Lynch (79) have all portrayed the vampire count.

Drake, Sir Francis [R]

(1540–96) English naval adventurer who sailed as a privateer against the ships of Spain and helped defeat the Armada in 1588. An under-exposed figure on screen despite being portrayed by Matheson Lang in a little-known British biography of the

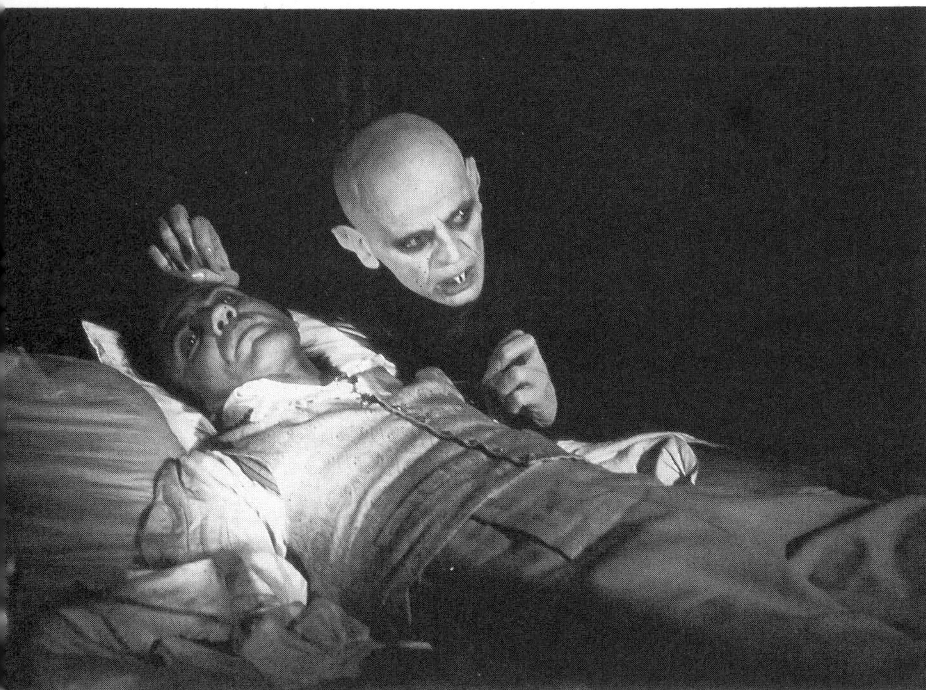

Faces of terror! Some of the most notable of the many screen Draculas: (clockwise from top left) Bela Lugosi in the first sound version of Bram Stoker's story; Frank Langella in John Badham's 1979 production; William Marshall as *Blacula*; Christopher Lee; Klaus Kinski in *Nosferatu, The Vampyre* and (opposite page) George Hamilton (with Arte Johnson) in the satirical *Love At First Bite*

30s and Rod Taylor (as a heroic swashbuckler) in *Seven Seas To Calais*.

Matheson Lang	*Drake Of England* (Woods)	GB, 35
Rod Taylor	*Seven Seas To Calais* (Mate)	It/USA, 62
Philip Stearns	*Winstanley* (Brownlow/Mollo)	GB, 76

Note: Hay Plumb appeared in the role in the British silent production, *Drake's Love Story* (13).

Dresser, Paul [R]

(1857–1906) Relatively minor American songwriter who flourished briefly in the 1890s with such sentimental ballads as 'On The Banks Of The Wabash Far Away' and 'Just Tell Them That You Saw Me' and was afforded a lavish Technicolor Fox biography in 1942. A somewhat unlikely Victor Mature played Dresser, the lovely Rita Hayworth appeared as the fictional singer who helps him to the top. Not illustrated in the film was the fact that Dresser was ultimately something of a tragic figure, losing his songwriting touch in the early 1900s and finishing his life in near obscurity, living with his sister in Brooklyn.

Victor Mature	*My Gal Sal* (Cummings)	USA, 42

Note: Dresser was the older brother of the novelist Theodore Dreiser who was seen as a young boy in the film and played by Barry Downing. Dreiser himself wrote the original story for the film entitled 'My Brother Paul'. The story was reworked by Helen Richardson (uncredited) and then turned into a finished screenplay by three of the studio's top writers – Seton I. Miller, Darryl Ware and Karl Tunberg.

Dreyfus, Alfred [R]

(1859–1935) Jewish officer of the French artillery who was unjustly accused of betraying military secrets and, in 1894, sentenced to life imprisonment on Devil's Island. Only through the untiring efforts of novelist Emile Zola who uncovered anti-semitism and corruption in the establishment in his letter 'J'Accuse', was he eventually pardoned. The case has been the subject of four different films. Joseph Schildkraut won a supporting actor Academy Award for his performance in *The Life Of Emile Zola*.

Fritz Kortner	*The Dreyfus Case* (Oswald)	Ger, 30
Cedric Hardwicke	*Dreyfus* (Kraemer/Rosmer)	GB, 31
Joseph Schildkraut	*The Life Of Emile Zola* (Dieterle)	USA, 37
Jose Ferrer	*I Accuse!* (Jose Ferrer)	GB, 58

Drummond, Bulldog [F]

On the printed page an ex-World War I officer who is little more than an upper-class fascist thug seeking an outlet for his latent violence. On screen the epitome of the gallant English adventurer, especially when portrayed by Ronald Colman in his two films for Goldwyn. Unsatisfactorily updated in the 60s to become a womanizing super-hero. First appeared in print in 1920 in H. C. McNeile's 'Bulldog Drummond'.

Ronald Colman	*Bulldog Drummond* (Jones)	USA, 29
Kenneth MacKenna	*Temple Tower* (Gallagher)	USA, 30
Ralph Richardson	*The Return Of Bulldog Drummond* (Summers)	GB, 34
Ronald Colman	*Bulldog Drummond Strikes Back* (Del Ruth)	USA, 34
Athol Fleming	*Bulldog Jack* (Forde)	GB, 35
John Lodge	*Bulldog Drummond At Bay* (Lee)	GB, 37
Ray Milland	*Bulldog Drummond Escapes* (Hogan)	USA, 37
John Howard	*Bulldog Drummond Comes Back* (Louis King)	USA, 37
John Howard	*Bulldog Drummond's Revenge* (Louis King)	USA, 37
John Howard	*Bulldog Drummond's Peril* (Hogan)	USA, 38
John Howard	*Bulldog Drummond In Africa* (Louis King)	USA, 38
John Howard	*Arrest Bulldog Drummond* (Hogan)	USA, 38
John Howard	*Bulldog Drummond's Secret Police* (Hogan)	USA, 39
John Howard	*Bulldog Drummond's Bride* (Hogan)	USA, 39
Ron Randell	*Bulldog Drummond At Bay* (Salkow)	USA, 47
Ron Randell	*Bulldog Drummond Strikes Back* (McDonald)	USA, 47

Tom Conway	*The Challenge* (Yarbrough) USA, 48
Tom Conway	*Thirteen Lead Soldiers* (McDonald) USA, 48
Walter Pidgeon	*Calling Bulldog Drummond* (Saville) GB, 51
Richard Johnson	*Deadlier Than The Male* (Thomas) GB, 67
Richard Johnson	*Some Girls Do* (Thomas) GB, 69

Note: Carlyle Blackwell in Oscar Apfel's *Bulldog Drummond* (22) and Jack Buchanan in *Bulldog Drummond's Third Round* (25) both played the role on the British silent screen.

Du Barry, Madame

R

(1743–93) A former shop girl (real name Mari Jeanne Becu) who became one of France's most famous courtesans and eventually made it to the bed of King Louis XV as his last mistress. None of which did her much good for, like so many others of the period, she finished up headless on the guillotine. A great favourite with glamorous actresses of the silent and sound eras she has been afforded any number of movie biographies, the most notable being the 1919 film of Ernst Lubitsch which contained a memorable Du Barry from Polish actress Pola Negri.

Norma Talmadge	*Du Barry, Woman Of Passion* (Taylor) USA, 30
Dolores Del Rio	*Madame Du Barry* (Dieterle) USA, 34
Simone Renant	*The Pearls Of The Crown* (Guitry/Jaque) Fra, 37
Liane Pathe	*Champs-Elysées* (Guitry) Fra, 38
Gladys George	*Marie-Antoinette* (Van Dyke) USA, 38
Lucille Ball	*DuBarry Was A Lady* (Del Ruth) USA, 43
Martine Carol	*Mistress Du Barry* (Christian-Jaque) Fra/It, 54

Note: the 1943 portrayal by Lucille Ball was a musical interpretation set in a long flashback dream sequence; on the silent screen Du Barry was played by Mrs Leslie Carter (USA, 15), Theda Bara (USA, 17) and Pola Negri (Ger, 19). A French film of her adventures was released in 1913.

Duchin, Eddy

R

(1909–51) Boston pianist-bandleader, a society favourite of the 30s, whose show-biz career and ill-fated private life were sentimentally recounted by George Sidney in Columbia's 1956 biography. Duchin and his band appeared on screen in person in *Mr. Broadway* (32), *Coronado* (35), *1937 Hit Parade* (37).

Tyrone Power	*The Eddy Duchin Story*  (Sidney) USA, 56

Note: Carmen Cavallaro played the piano music for Power in Sidney's film.

Duncan, Isadora

R

(1878–1927) San Francisco-born dancer who created 'headlines' wherever she went, both in her scandalous private life and through her revolutionary interpretations of classical Greek dancing. Scarves were frequently used to bring expression to her dances; ironically, it was a scarf that caused her untimely end, catching in the wheel of her fast moving car and choking her to death. Vanessa Redgrave starred for Karel Reisz in his detailed 138-minute biography, based on Duncan's 'Life' and the memoirs by Sewell Stokes.

Vanessa Redgrave	*Isadora* (Reisz) GB, 69

Note: Three years prior to Karel Reisz' feature film Ken Russell filmed an exhuberant BBC TV production starring Vivian Pickles as the legendary dancer. Also entitled *Isadora,* it was shot in black and white.

Eagels, Jeanne [R]

(1849–1929) One of Hollywood's most unhappy figures, a high-living, tempestuous Broadway actress who rose quickly to the top in the 20s and then became a victim of alcohol and narcotics. Her rise and fall were the subject of a 1957 biography by George Sidney. Film appearances in *The World And The Woman* (16), *Under False Colours* (17), *Man, Woman And Sin* (27), *The Letter* (29), *Jealousy* (29).

Kim Novak — *Jeanne Eagels* (Sidney) / USA, 57

Earp, Wyatt [R]

(1848–1929) The most famous lawman of the American West, not, in reality, a 'whiter than white' good guy but an often merciless character equally as tough as some of the gunmen he disposed of in Wichita and Dodge City. Best known for his part in the Gunfight At The O.K. Corral (1881) when, along with his brothers Virgil and Morgan and Doc Holliday, he wiped out the Clanton gang. Romanticized, lengthy portrayals by Fonda and Lancaster; more three-dimensional portraits by James Garner and Harris Yulin.

Randolph Scott — *Frontier Marshal* (Dwan) USA, 39
Richard Dix — *Tombstone, The Town Too Tough To Die* (McGann) USA, 42
Henry Fonda — *My Darling Clementine* (Ford) USA, 46
Will Geer — *Winchester 73* (Anthony Mann) USA, 50
James Millican — *Gun Belt* (Nazarro) USA, 53
Bruce Cowling — *Masterson Of Kansas* (Castle) USA, 54
Joel McCrea — *Wichita* (Tourneur) USA, 55
Burt Lancaster — *Gunfight At The O K Corral* (Sturges) USA, 57
Buster Crabbe — *Badman's Country* (Sears) USA, 58
Hugh O'Brian — *Alias Jesse James* (McLeod) USA, 59
James Stewart — *Cheyenne Autumn* (Ford) USA, 64
Guy Madison — *Gunmen Of The Rio Grande* (DeMicheli) Fra/It/Spa, 65
Bill Camfield — *The Outlaws Is Coming* (Maurer) USA, 65
James Garner — *Hour Of The Gun* (Sturges) USA, 67
Harris Yulin — *Doc* (Perry) USA, 71

Note: Walter Huston (as Frame Johnson) featured as the Wyatt Earp character in Edward L. Cahn's 1932 production *Law And Order.*

On TV Bruce Boxleitner appeared as the lawman in Michael O'Herlihy's 1983 TV movie *I Married Wyatt Earp,* the story of Earp's relationship with Old West singer Josephine Marcus who met up with Earp in Tombstone and settled down with him for 47 years. O'Herlihy's film was based on Marcus' memoirs and co-starred Marie Osmond.

Edison, Thomas A. [R]

(1847–1931) In real life, the inventive genius of the incandescent electric lamp, microphone, phonograph and over a thousand other inventions. On screen a man who changed from Mickey Rooney into Spencer Tracy in the course of one year. Between inventions took time out to describe genius as '2% inspiration, 98% perspiration'.

Mickey Rooney — *Young Tom Edison* (Taurog) USA, 40
Spencer Tracy — *Edison, The Man* (Brown) USA, 40

Note: Frank Glendon featured as Edison in the 1925 silent production, *Lights Of Old Broadway.*

Ehrlich, Dr Paul [R]

(1854–1915) German scientist, 1908 Nobel prizewinner, who discovered one of the first cures for syphilis and forced an unwilling medical profession to take notice of the disease. Portrayed by Edward G. Robinson in one of the last of William Dieterle's biographies for Warner Bros.

Edward G. Robinson — *Dr Ehrlich's Magic Bullet* (Dieterle) USA, 40

Eichmann, Adolf [R]

(1906–62) Nazi war criminal, condemned to death and executed in Israel for his part in the extermination of six million Jews. His reign of terror and post-war life were recreated in the 1961 film *Operation Eichmann;* his capture by Israeli agents in Argentina, in the 1979 TV film *The House On Garibaldi Street,* based on the book by the former head of Israeli Intelligence Isser Harel.

Werner Klemperer	*Operation Eichmann* (Springsteen)	USA, 61
Walter Czaschke	*Death Is My Trade* (Kotulla)	W.Ger, 77
Alfred Burke	*The House On Garibaldi Street* (Collinson)	TVM/USA, 79

El Cid

R

(*c.*1043–99) Spanish warrior (real name Rodrigo Diaz de Vivar), famous for his heroic exploits against the Moors in eleventh century Spain. Earned the name 'Cid' or 'Cid Campeador' (Lord or Lord Conqueror) and achieved his greatest success when capturing Valencia in 1094. A major figure in Spanish history, given due legendary status in Anthony Mann's superior epic of 1961.

Charlton Heston	*El Cid* (Mann)	USA, 61
Sandro Moretti	*La Spada del Cid* (Iglesias)	It/Spa, 62

Note: Amleto Palermi featured as El Cid in an Italian silent production of 1910.

Elephant Man, The

R

A Victorian freak, real name John Merrick, whose head and body were so grotesquely deformed that he could only exist as a sideshow exhibit. He was eventually rescued by a dedicated young surgeon who cared for him in the London Hospital and discovered that behind the appalling disfigurement lay an intelligent and sensitive human being. After enjoying a brief career as a minor celebrity in London in the 1880s Merrick suffocated in his sleep while still a young man. John Hurt, who spent hours daily in the makeup chair, played Merrick in David Lynch's 1980 film; Anthony Hopkins featured as the surgeon Frederick Treves who helped make his later years bearable.

John Hurt	*The Elephant Man* (Lynch)	USA, 80

Note: In 1981 a TV version of Bernard Pomerance's Broadway play (also titled *The Elephant Man*) was transmitted on US television. Philip Anglim mimed Merrick's deformity, Kevin Conway featured as Treves.

Elizabeth I

R

(1533–1603) Powerful British monarch, daughter of Henry VIII and Anne Boleyn, whose often ruthless personality and ill-fated love affairs have attracted actresses of the calibre of Bette Davis, Glenda Jackson and Flora Robson. Davis provided portraits of a middle-aged Elizabeth in love with first Essex and then Raleigh; Glenda Jackson's performance centred on the queen's feud with Mary, Queen of Scots, whom she executed for her complicity in a Catholic plot to seize the throne. Elizabeth's reign lasted for 45 years and heralded the beginning of Britain's great colonial empire.

Athene Seyler	*Drake Of England* (Woods)	GB, 35
Florence Eldridge	*Mary Of Scotland* (Ford)	USA, 36
Yvette Pienne	*The Pearls Of The Crown* (Guitry/Jaque)	Fra, 37
Flora Robson	*Fire Over England* (Howard)	GB, 37
Bette Davis	*The Private Lives Of Elizabeth And Essex* (Curtiz)	USA, 39
Maria Koppenhofer	*Heart Of A Queen* (Froelich)	Ger, 40
Flora Robson	*The Sea Hawk* (Curtiz)	USA, 40
Jean Simmons	*Young Bess* (Sidney)	USA, 53
Bette Davis	*The Virgin Queen* (Koster)	USA, 55
Agnes Moorehead	*The Story Of Mankind* (Allen)	USA, 57
Irene Worth	*Seven Seas To Calais* (Mate)	It, 62
Catherine Lacey	*The Fighting Prince Of Donegal* (O'Herlihy)	GB, 66
Glenda Jackson	*Mary, Queen Of Scots* (Jarrott)	GB, 71
Lalla Ward	*The Prince And The Pauper* (Fleischer)	GB, 77
Jenny Runacre	*Jubilee* (Jarman)	GB, 77

Note: The following actresses played Elizabeth in silent movies: Sarah Bernhardt in *Queen Elizabeth* (Fra, 12), Miriam Nesbitt in *Mary Stuart* (USA, 13), Lady Diana Manners in *The Virgin Queen* (GB, 23), and Ellen Compton in *Loves Of Mary, Queen Of Scots* (GB, 23).

John Hurt as the hideously deformed John Merrick 'The Elephant Man', a Victorian freak who was saved from his pathetic existence as a carnival attraction by Frederick Treves, a surgeon who cared for him at the London Hospital

Two of the many screen portrayals of the British Monarch, Elizabeth I—(above) Glenda Jackson as an aged Elizabeth in *Mary Queen of Scots* and (left) a young Jean Simmons in George Sidney's 1953 version of *Young Bess*

Ellis, Ruth R

The last woman to be hanged in Britain, a 28-year-old West End hostess who pumped six bullets into her playboy lover outside a pub in Hampstead one April evening in 1955! Mike Newell's *Dance With A Stranger* (scripted by Shelagh Delaney) looked closely at the oppressive, class-bound British society of the early 50s and closed with Ellis committing the crime of murder. An earlier, more compassionate film *Yield To The Night*, was closely modelled on the life of Ellis, centring on the agonies of her final days in prison and covering her story in flashback.

Diana Dors (as Mary Hilton) — *Yield To The Night* (Lee Thompson) GB, 56
Miranda Richardson — *Dance With A Stranger* (Newell) GB, 85

Erickson, Eric 

A real-life World War II spy, a Swedish-American businessman who in the early years of the conflict traded in oil with the Nazis and was then induced by Allied Intelligence to feed them with vital information after he had toured German oil plants.

William Holden as World War II spy Eric Erickson under surveillance by the Nazi Youth in *The Counterfeit Traitor*

Exposed by members of the Hitler Youth, he subsequently escaped via the German underground, first into Denmark and then into Sweden. His often harrowing experiences were recounted in the 1958 book of Alexander Klein, later filmed on authentic European locations by George Seaton.

William Holden — *The Counterfeit Traitor* (Seaton) USA, 62

Etting, Ruth 

(1896–1978) Actress-singer who rose from humble beginnings in the chorus of a Chicago revue to starring roles in the Ziegfeld Follies and several Hollywood movies. Made famous such songs as 'Ten Cents A Dance', 'Shine On Harvest Moon' and 'Love Me Or Leave Me', the last named being used as the title for the 1955 biography with Doris Day as Etting and James Cagney as Martin Snyder, the racketeer whose influence helped her to the top.

Doris Day — *Love Me Or Leave Me* (Charles Vidor) USA, 55

Everdene, Bathsheba 

Wessex heroine of Thomas Hardy whose lusty, headstrong ways enrapture three men – the faithful Gabriel Oak who becomes the bailiff of her farm, the dashing adventurer Sergeant Troy and the wealthy landowner William Boldwood who is destroyed by his all-consuming passion. Julie Christie (too modern an actress for some) played the independent Bathsheba in John Schlesinger's 1967 film; Florence Turner appeared in a 1915 silent production.

Julie Christie — *Far From The Madding Crowd* (Schlesinger) GB, 67

Note: 'Far From The Madding Crowd' was Hardy's fourth novel. It was first published in Cornhill Magazine between January and December 1874 and launched the author's career as a major novelist.

Eyre, Jane 

Charlotte Brontë's young orphan girl who takes up a post of governess in the mysterious household of Thornfield where she experiences fear, love and ultimately the only real happiness in her young life. A shy, intense heroine whose early experiences at a harsh Yorkshire orphanage are vividly created,

(Above) Miranda Richardson as Ruth Ellis with Ian Holm in *Dance With A Stranger,* the story of the last months in the life of the night club hostess who killed her young aristocratic lover and became the last woman in Britain to be executed; (right Diana Dors as Ellis in *Yield to the Night* – an account of her last months in prison before her execution

both in print and in the numerous screen versions of her story.

Virginia Bruce	*Jane Eyre*	(Cabanne)	USA, 34
Joan Fontaine	*Jane Eyre*	(Stevenson)	USA, 44
Susannah York	*Jane Eyre*	(Delbert Mann)	GB, 71

Note: The 1943 horror picture *I Walked With A Zombie* was an updated version of the 'Jane Eyre' story, transferred to a West Indies setting. Frances Dee featured in the Eyre role.

At least eight silent versions of the story were produced, including a little-known Hungarian production, *The Orphan Of Lowood* (20). Irma Taylor (10), Ethel Grandin (14), Minnie Maddern Fiske (15), Louise Vale (15), Alice Brady (18) and Mabel Ballin (21) were among the American silent actresses who appeared in the role; Evelyn Holt featured in Kurt Bernhardt's 1926 German version.

Fagin

One of Charles Dickens' most memorable creations, a villainous old Jewish fence who trains a gang of youthful thieves (including the runaway workhouse orphan Oliver Twist) in the art of pickpocketing in the slums of nineteenth century London. Little more than a merry old gentleman in Lionel Bart's musical *Oliver!* but a grasping figure, full of cruelty and malice, in Alec Guinness' brilliant portrait of 1948. Features in Dickens' 1837–39 novel 'Oliver Twist'.

Irving Pichel	*Oliver Twist*	(Cowen)	USA, 33
Alec Guinness	*Oliver Twist*	(Lean)	GB, 48
Ron Moody	*Oliver!*	(Reed)	GB, 68
George C. Scott	*Oliver Twist*	(Donner)	GB, 83

Note: John McMahon (GB, 12), Nat C. Goodwin (USA, 12), Tully Marshall (USA, 16) and Lon Chaney (USA, 22) all starred as Fagin in silent productions; Wilson Hummell appeared in a modernized 1921 adaptation *Oliver Twist Jr.* A Hungarian version of the novel, directed by Marton Garas, was released in 1919.

The young Oliver, the brutal housebreaker Bill Sikes and his sluttish mistress Nancy, the pickpocket the Artful Dodger and workhouse beadle Mr. Bumble are other memorable figures in Dickens' novel. Screen portraits have been as follows:

Oliver Twist

Dickie Moore	*Oliver Twist*	(Cowen)	USA, 33
John Howard Davies	*Oliver Twist*	(Lean)	GB, 48
Mark Lester	*Oliver!*	(Reed)	GB, 68
Richard Charles	*Oliver Twist*	(Donner)	GB, 83

Silent: Ivy Millais (GB, 12), Miss Vinnie Burns (USA, 12), Marie Doro (USA, 16) and Jackie Coogan (USA, 22). Harold Goodwin featured in the 1921 modernized version *Oliver Twist Jr.*

Bill Sikes

William Boyd	*Oliver Twist*	(Cowen)	USA, 33
Robert Newton	*Oliver Twist*	(Lean)	GB, 48
Oliver Reed	*Oliver!*	(Reed)	GB, 68
Tim Curry	*Oliver Twist*	(Donner)	GB, 83

Silent: Harry Royston (GB, 12), Mortimer Martine (USA, 12), Hobart Bosworth (USA, 16) and George Siegmann (USA, 22). G. Raymond Nye featured in the 1921 modernized version *Oliver Twist Jr.*

Nancy

Doris Lloyd	*Oliver Twist*	(Cowen)	USA, 33
Kay Walsh	*Oliver Twist*	(Lean)	GB, 48
Shani Wallis	*Oliver!*	(Reed)	GB, 68
Cherie Lunghi	*Oliver Twist*	(Donner)	GB, 83

Silent: Alma Taylor (GB, 12), Elsie Jane Wilson (USA, 16) and Gladys Brockwell (USA, 22). Irene Hunt appeared in the 1921 modernized version *Oliver Twist Jr.*

The Artful Dodger

Sonny Ray	*Oliver Twist*	(Cowen)	USA, 33
Anthony Newley	*Oliver Twist*	(Lean)	GB, 48
Jack Wild	*Oliver!*	(Reed)	GB, 68
Martin Tempest	*Oliver Twist*	(Donner)	GB, 83

Silent: Willie West (GB, 12), Charles Rogers (USA, 12), Raymond Hatton (USA, 16) and Edouard Trebaol (USA, 22). Scott McKee featured in the 1921 modernized version, *Oliver Twist Jr.*

Mr Bumble

Lionel Belmore	*Oliver Twist*	(Cowen)	USA, 33
Francis L. Sullivan	*Oliver Twist*	(Lean)	GB, 48
Harry Secombe	*Oliver!*	(Reed)	GB, 68
Timothy West	*Oliver Twist*	(Donner)	GB, 83

Silent: Harry Ruttenberg (USA, 16) and James Marcus (USA, 22).

Falcon, The

Another suave detective adventurer of the 40s; most at home 'in society' with champagne and a bevy of witty girls, but invariably drawn out on a case by the distress signals of a beautiful female. Net result: 65 minutes of RKO crime. The third movie in the series, *The Falcon Takes Over,* is an adaptation of Chandler's 'Farewell My Lovely'.

George Sanders	*The Gay Falcon*	(Reis)	USA, 41
George Sanders	*A Date With The Falcon*	(Reis)	USA, 41
George Sanders	*The Falcon Takes Over*	(Reis)	USA, 42
George Sanders	*The Falcon's Brother*	(Logan)	USA, 42
Tom Conway	*The Falcon Strikes Back*	(Dmytryk)	USA, 43
Tom Conway	*The Falcon And The Co-Eds*	(Clemens)	USA, 43

Charles Dickens' Fagin! (Above) Alec Guinness, with Robert Newton (as Bill Sikes) and Kay Walsh (as Nancy) in David Lean's classic *Oliver Twist*; (left) Ron Moody, with and without make-up, in the musical *Oliver!,* and (right) George C. Scott in Clive Donner's 1983 version of the Dickens' story

ROVISION MERCHANTS
AGENTS AND BROKERS
Quality

Tom Conway	*The Falcon In Danger* (Clemens)	USA, 43
Tom Conway	*The Falcon In Hollywood* (Douglas)	USA, 44
Tom Conway	*The Falcon In Mexico* (Berke)	USA, 44
Tom Conway	*The Falcon Out West* (Clemens)	USA, 44
Tom Conway	*The Falcon In San Francisco* (Lewis)	USA, 45
Tom Conway	*The Falcon's Alibi* (McCarrey)	USA, 46
Tom Conway	*The Falcon's Adventure* (Berke)	USA, 46
John Calvert	*The Devil's Cargo* (Link)	USA, 48
John Calvert	*Appointment With Murder* (Bernhard)	USA, 48
John Calvert	*Search For Danger* (Martin)	USA, 49

Falstaff, Sir John F

Shakespeare's portly, lecherous lover of life, invariably to be found in the company of his fellow scoundrels, Bardolph, Pistol and company, at the tavern of Mistress Quickly. Orson Welles' *Chimes At Midnight*, which included scenes from 'Henry IV Parts I & II', 'Henry V' and 'The Merry Wives Of Windsor', centred on Falstaff's friendship with the young Prince Hal and his rejection when the prince becomes King Henry V of England.

Leo Slezak	*The Merry Wives Of Windsor* (Hoffmann)	Ger, 35
George Robey	*Henry V* (Olivier)	GB, 45
Paul Esser	*The Merry Wives Of Windsor* (Wildhagen)	E.Ger, 50
Orson Welles	*Chimes At Midnight* (Welles)	Spa/Swi, 66

Fanny F

A central figure in Marcel Pagnol's delightful trilogy of life in the old port of Marseilles; a young fish seller who is deserted by her adventurous lover, marries an elderly sailmaker to provide a father for her unborn child and is finally reunited with her lover after the death of her husband. The characters who surround her in Marseilles – Cesar, the proprietor of the quayside bistro, Panisse, the warmhearted widower she marries, and Marius, her seafaring lover – helped turn the three films made in France in the early 30s into minor classics. The three stories were subsequently combined into one film, first in *Port Of Seven Seas* and then in *Fanny*.

Fanny

Orane Demazis	*Marius* (Korda)	Fra, 31
Orane Demazis	*Fanny* (Allégret)	Fra, 32
Orane Demazis	*Cesar* (Pagnol)	Fra, 36
Maureen O'Sullivan	*Port Of Seven Seas* (Whale)	USA, 38
Leslie Caron	*Fanny* (Logan)	USA, 61

Marius

Pierre Fresnay	*Marius* (Korda)	Fra, 31
Pierre Fresnay	*Fanny* (Allégret)	Fra, 32
Pierre Fresnay	*Cesar* (Pagnol)	Fra, 36
John Beal	*Port Of Seven Seas* (Whale)	USA, 38
Horst Buchholz	*Fanny* (Logan)	USA, 61

Cesar

Raimu	*Marius* (Korda)	Fra, 31
Raimu	*Fanny* (Allégret)	Fra, 32
Raimu	*Cesar* (Pagnol)	Fra, 36
Wallace Beery	*Port Of Seven Seas* (Whale)	USA, 38
Charles Boyer	*Fanny* (Logan)	USA, 61

Panisse

Fernand Charpin	*Marius* (Korda)	Fra, 31
Fernand Charpin	*Fanny* (Allégret)	Fra, 32
Fernand Charpin	*Cesar* (Pagnol)	Fra, 36
Frank Morgan	*Port Of Seven Seas* (Whale)	USA, 38
Maurice Chevalier	*Fanny* (Logan)	USA, 61

Farmer, Frances R

(1914–70) Thirties actress whose rebellious and self-destructive views and clashes with Hollywood big shots led to alcoholism, mental breakdown and an early end to her career. Forced into an early retirement in 1942 she made just 15 movies, none of them especially memorable. Director William Wyler who directed her in *Come And Get It* (36) said of her: 'The nicest thing I can say about Frances Farmer is that she is unbearable'. In the 80s film-makers took a somewhat less harsh view when three films (including a Made For TV Movie) portrayed her as a victim although all highlighted the actress' outspokenness and radical views. She died of cancer at the age of 57.

Jessica Lange	*Frances* (Clifford)O	USA, 82
Susan Blakely	*Will There Really Be A Morning?* (Cook)	TVM USA, 83

Laughter, drink and not too much work in the old port of Marseilles in the 1930s. Featuring in this scene from Joshua Logan's 1961 production of *Fanny:* Lionel Jeffries, Baccaloni, Maurice Chevalier as the old sailmaker Panisse and Charles Boyer as Cesar, proprietor of the local bistro

Sheila McLaughlin	*Committed* (McLaughlin/ Tillman) USA, 84

Note: Playwright Clifford Odets, Farmer's cultural idol and mentor and in whose *Golden Boy* she appeared in New York, was played by Jeffrey DeMunn (82), John Heard (TV, 83) and Lee Breuer (84).

Faust

F

Legendary figure who sells his soul to the Devil in exchange for all knowledge and experience. Based on a fifteenth century necromancer named George Faust, he was developed by Goethe (1808) and has been revamped many times on screen, appearing as a New Hampshire farmer in *All That Money Can Buy,* an ambitious politician in *Alias Nick Beal,* a young baseball player in *Damn Yankees* and even a hamburger chef in *Bedazzled.*

James Craig	*All That Money Can Buy* (Dieterle) USA, 41
Thomas Mitchell	*Alias Nick Beal* (Farrow) USA, 49
Gerard Philipe and Michel Simon	*La Beaute du Diable* (Clair) Fra, 49
Gino Mattera	*Faust The Devil* (Gallone) It, 50
Jean Francois Calve and Louis Seigner	*Marguerite Of The Night* (Autant-Lara) Fra, 56
Will Quadflieg	*Faust* (Gorski) Ger, 56
Maria Felix	*Faustina* (de Heredia) Spa, 57
Tab Hunter	*Damn Yankees* (Donen) USA, 58

The downfall of a movie star, Jessica Lange in a violent scene from the 1982 film *Frances,* the tragic story of the rebellious and self-destructive film actress Frances Farmer who was forced into an early retirement after she had made just a handful of movies

Robert Towner	*Faust* (Suman)	USA, 64
Emil Botta	*Faust* (Popescu-Gopo)	Rum, 67
Dudley Moore	*Bedazzled* (Donen)	GB, 67
Richard Burton	*Doctor Faustus* (Burton/ Coghill)	GB/It, 67

Note: Michel Simon played the ageing Faust (and also Mephistopheles) and Gerard Philipe the young Faust in Rene Clair's *La Beaute du Diable.* Louis Seigner (old) and Jean-Francois Calve (young) also divided the role in *Marguerite Of The Night.* Maria Felix is the only female Faust to appear on screen.

Gosta Ekmann appeared for F. W. Murnau in the silent German *Faust* of 1926.

Feversham, Harry

F

'The Four Feathers' hero; a young British officer who is branded a coward by his fiancée then sets out for the Sudan to perform fantastic feats of endurance in order to prove his courage. If ever a movie hero seems passé it is this one, yet, as recently as 1978, a film has been made about his exploits. Somehow, against all the odds, he seems to have survived such lunatic ravings as 'You're a Feversham and the army expects every Feversham to be a hero!' John Clements starred in the definitive screen version of 1939; A. E. W. Mason's novel was first published in 1902.

Richard Arlen	*The Four Feathers* (Cooper/ Schoedsack/Mendes)	USA, 29
John Clements	*The Four Feathers* (Zoltan Korda)	GB, 39
Anthony Steel	*Storm Over The Nile* (Young/ Zoltan Korda)	GB, 55

Beau Bridges *The Four Feathers* (Sharp) GB, 78

Note: Francis X. Bushman (USA, 15) and Harry Ham (GB, 21) both starred as Feversham on the silent screen.

Fields, W. C.

R

(1879–1946) Bulbous-nosed, rasping ex-vaudevillian who played swindlers, pool hustlers, card sharks and salesmen in over 40 films, endowing each with an acid sense of humour. A sample: 'If at first you don't succeed, try, try again. Then quit. No use being a damn fool about it'. The author of many of his own scripts, he brought about his own self-destruction through an excess in just about everything, especially alcohol.

Rod Steiger *W. C. Fields And Me* (Hiller) USA, 76

Note: Chuck McCann appeared as Fields in the 1982 TV biography of *Mae West* starring Ann Jillian.

Finn, Huckleberry

F

Orphan boy hero of Mark Twain's 1884 classic, 'The Adventures of Huckleberry Finn'. A carefree, pipe-smoking rebel, he lives on the river banks of the Old South, enjoying the company of fellow adventurer Tom Sawyer and the runaway slave Jim, with whom he adventures on a raft down the Mississippi. Many times played on screen, Jeff East appearing in the two musicals of the 70s, *Tom Sawyer* and *Huckleberry Finn*.

Junior Durkin *Tom Sawyer* (Cromwell USA, 30

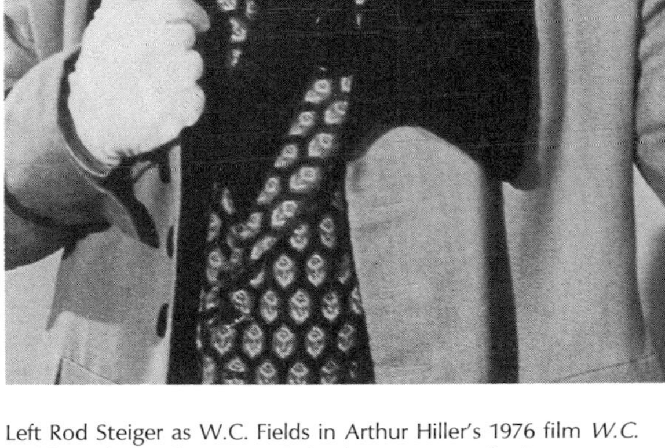

Left Rod Steiger as W.C. Fields in Arthur Hiller's 1976 film *W.C. Fields and Me,* the story of the famous comedian's romance with Carlotta Monti. (Right) Fields as he appeared on screen for Universal in the 40s

Jeff East enjoying an idyllic life on the banks of the Mississippi in Arthur P. Jacob's version of Mark Twain's classic *Huckleberry Finn*. Paul Winfield co-starred in the film as the runaway black slave Jim; Harvey Korman and David Wayne featured as the two conmen, 'The King' and 'The Duke', Huck meets on his adventures

Junior Durkin	*Huckleberry Finn*	(Taurog)	USA, 31
Kolya Katsowitch	*Tom Soyer*	(Frenkel)	USSR, 36
Jackie Moran	*The Adventures Of Tom Sawyer*	(Taurog)	USA, 38
Donald O'Connor	*Tom Sawyer, Detective*	(Louis King)	USA, 38
Mickey Rooney	*The Adventures Of Huckleberry Finn*	(Thorpe)	USA, 39
Eddie Hodges	*The Adventures Of Huckleberry Finn*	(Curtiz)	USA, 60
Marc Dinapoli	*Tom Sawyer*	(Iacob)	Fra/Rum, 69
Jeff East	*Tom Sawyer*	(Taylor)	USA, 73
Jeff East	*Huckleberry Finn*	(Lee-Thompson)	USA, 74
Roman Madianov	*Huckleberry Finn*	(Daniela)	USSR, 74

Note: Robert Gordon in *Tom Sawyer* (USA, 17) and *Huck And Tom* (USA, 18) and Lewis Sargent in *Huckleberry Finn* (USA, 20) featured as Huck on the silent screen; on TV he has been played by Jeff Tyler in *Tom Sawyer* (73), Ron Howard in *Huckleberry Finn* (75), Kurt Ida in *The Adventures Of Huckleberry Finn* (81) and Patrick Day in Peter Hunt's 4 hour TV Movie *The Adventures Of Huckleberry Finn* (86).

The runaway slave Jim has been played by Clarence Muse (31), Rex Ingram (39), ex-boxing champ Archie Moore (60), Paul Winfield (74) and on TV by Antonio Fargas (75), Brock Peters (81) and Samm-Art Williams (86).

Fitzgerald, F. Scott [R]

(1896–1940) Distinguished American author who enjoyed phenomenal success with a series of novels about the jazz age, then declined into obscurity in Hollywood during the 30s. Gregory Peck played him on screen in *Beloved Infidel,* which concentrated on the final months of Fitzgerald's life when he embarked on a turbulent romance with gossip columnist Sheilah Graham (played by Deborah Kerr).

Gregory Peck	*Beloved Infidel*	(Henry King)	USA, 59

Note: Fitzgerald has been played twice on TV. In 1974 Richard Chamberlain starred in *F. Scott Fitzgerald And The Last Of The Belles* which interweaved the real lives of Fitzgerald and his wife Zelda with his writing of the story 'The Last Of The Belles'; and in 1976 Jason Miller appeared in *F. Scott Fitzgerald In Hollywood* which centred on the writer when he was on the downward slope and had become an alcoholic.

Fitzgerald's ill-fated wife Zelda was played by Blythe Danner in 1974 and Tuesday Weld in 1976. Julia Foster appeared as Sheilah Graham in the 1976 production.

Flashman, Harry [F]

The cheating 'bounder' from Thomas Hughes' 'Tom Brown's Schooldays' (1857) and a character who has continued to thrive, thanks to the best selling novels of George MacDonald Fraser who has taken Flashman into young adulthood and turned him into a popular anti-hero. Only one screen version to date of Flashman's latter-day activities – as a captain in the 11th Hussars in *Royal Flash* – but several of him in his younger days as chief bully at Rugby school.

Billy Halop	*Tom Brown's Schooldays*	(Stevenson)	USA, 40
John Forrest	*Tom Brown's Schooldays*	(Parry)	GB, 51
Malcolm McDowell	*Royal Flash*	(Lester)	GB, 75

Note: Laurie Leslie played Flashman in a British silent version of *Tom Brown's Schooldays* (16).

Floyd, Charles 'Pretty Boy' [R]

Oklahoma farm boy turned gangster who earned himself a prominent place on the FBI's wanted list when he committed a series of bank robberies in the early 30s. Different from his fellow gangsters in that he only robbed the rich, he also brought a new term into the English language when he shouted at the FBI, 'Don't shoot, G-men!' One detailed film biography with John Ericson.

Doug Wilson	*Guns Don't Argue*	(Karn/Kahn)	USA, 55
John Ericson	*Pretty Boy Floyd*	(Leder)	USA, 59
Robert Conrad	*Young Dillinger*	(Morse)	USA, 64
Fabian Forte	*A Bullet For Pretty Boy*	(Buchanan)	USA, 71
Steve Kanaly	*Dillinger*	(Milius)	USA, 73

Note: Bo Hopkins appeared as Floyd in Dan Curtis' TV film *The Kansas City Massacre* (75).

Fogg, Phileas F

Intrepid, never-say-die English gentleman who wagers £20 000 with members of the Reform Club that he can journey round the world in eighty days. Eventually succeeds in his aim after experiencing numerous hazardous adventures with his French servant Passepartout. The gallant, elegant hero of Verne's 1873 novel 'Around The World In Eighty Days'.

David Niven — *Around The World In 80 Days* (Anderson) USA, 56

Note: Conrad Veidt portrayed Fogg in Richard Oswald's silent German version of 1919.

Ford, Bob R

(–1893) Cousin and assassin of Jesse James, notorious for shooting the famous outlaw in the back when he was straightening a picture on the wall in his home. Subsequently became a wanderer and stage actor, appearing in 'The Outlaws Of Missouri' in which he related (incorrectly) how he had shot down his outlaw chief. He was finally killed in a bar-room fight but not, as shown in *The Return Of Frank James,* by the vengeful Frank.

John Carradine	*Jesse James* (Henry King)	USA, 39
John Carradine	*The Return Of Frank James* (Fritz Lang)	USA, 40
John Ireland	*I Shot Jesse James* (Fuller)	USA, 49
Clifton Young	*The Return Of Jesse James* (Hilton)	USA, 50
Whit Bissell	*The Great Missouri Raid* (Douglas)	USA, 51
Jim Bannon	*The Great Jesse James Raid* (Le Borg)	USA, 53
Rory Mallinson	*Jesse James v The Daltons* (Castle)	USA, 54
Carl Thayler	*The True Story Of Jesse James* (Ray)	USA, 56
Robert Vaughn	*Hell's Crossroads* (Andreon)	USA, 57
Nicholas Guest	*The Long Riders* (Hill)	USA, 80

Note: Harry Woods played the role in a 1927 version of *Jesse James,* directed by Lloyd Ingraham; Darrell Wilks featured as the assassin in the TV movie *The Last Days Of Frank and Jesse James* (Graham, 86).

Fosse, Bob R

(1927–87) Dynamic American choreographer/director who brought a slick, erotic and razzle dazzle style to the American film and stage musical in the 1970s. His award-winning *All That Jazz* recounted a period in his own life when he suffered a massive heart attack whilst working simultaneously on his film of *Lenny* and his Broadway show *Chicago.* Roy Scheider portrayed the surrogate Fosse figure (renamed Joe Gideon for the film) ending up dead of overwork, a fate that eventually befell Fosse some eight years later when he suffered a second heart attack in a Washington street. Among Fosse's films: *Sweet Charity* (69), *Cabaret* (72), *Lenny* (74), *All That Jazz* (79) and *Star 80* (83).

Roy Scheider — *All That Jazz* (Fosse) USA, 79

Fossey, Dian 

Naturalist who, for 18 years, devoted her life to studying and protecting the dwindling population of long haired gorillas in Africa and who met a tragic end when she was found hacked to death

Writer-director Bob Fosse who cast a self-indulgent look at his show-biz life in the autobiographical musical *All That Jazz*

at a remote camp on the slopes of Mount Visoke in Rwanda. Her life among the gorillas and her controversial death were the subject of Michael Apted's 1988 film *Gorillas In The Mist.*

Sigourney Weaver	*Gorillas In The Mist* (Apted)	USA, 88

Foy, Eddie R

(1854–1928) The subject of one of Bob Hope's more serious performances of the 50s, an American vaudeville comic and dancer who trained his large family to join him on stage in an act which became famous as 'Eddie Foy And The Seven Little Foys'. Eddie Foy, Jr, later went on to portray his father several times on screen e.g. in *Lillian Russell* (40), *Yankee Doodle Dandy* (42), *Wilson* (44).

Bob Hope	*The Seven Little Foys* (Shavelson)	USA, 55

Francis Of Assisi 

(1181–1226) Thirteenth century Italian monk who devoted himself to the sick and poor and founded the monastic order of the Franciscans. Hollywood thought him a suitable case for screen treatment in the 60s; so too did the Italian cinema with Liliana Cavani's controversial production of 1966. Predictably, Hollywood lost and Italy won!

Jose Luis Jiminez	*St Francis Of Assisi* (Gout)	Mex, 47
Bradford Dillman	*Francis Of Assisi* (Curtiz)	USA, 61
Lou Castel	*Francis Of Assisi* (Cavani)	It, 66
Graham Faulkner	*Brother Sun, Sister Moon* (Zeffirelli)	It/GB, 72

Note: Alberto Pasquali played Francis in an Italian silent production of 1926.

Frank, Anne 

(1929–45) German Jewish girl who hid with her family and four other people in an Amsterdam attic in a futile attempt to escape the Nazi holocaust of World War II. Her deeply moving diary, discovered after her death in Belsen and published in 1947, records the daily lives of the hideaways from 1942 until August 1944 when they were eventually betrayed. George Stevens' film was an adaptation of the stage play by Frances Goodrich and Albert Hackett which, in turn, was based on the diary.

Millie Perkins	*The Diary Of Anne Frank* (Stevens)	USA, 59

Note: In Boris Sagal's 1980 Made-For-TV movie Anne was portrayed by Melissa Gilbert; Anne Frank's father Otto, who discovered the diary after the war, was played by Joseph Schildkraut in the Stevens film and by Maximilian Schell in 1980.

Frankenstein, Baron 

The longest-serving mad scientist in the business, dating back over 160 years to when he first startled an unprepared reading public by making a monster from the organs of dead bodies. Mary Shelley's novel (published in 1818) has been filmed by James Whale in 1931, Terence Fisher in 1957 and Jack Smight in 1974, but ever since Karloff escaped from the burning mill in *Bride Of Frankenstein,* a host of the baron's relatives – sons, nephews, grandsons, etc – have been trying to emulate their illustrious predecessor by creating bigger and better monsters. In the 30s, Colin Clive was the best known Baron Frankenstein; for post-war audiences no-one can hold a scalpel to Peter Cushing!

Colin Clive	*Frankenstein* (Whale)	USA, 31
Colin Clive	*Bride Of Frankenstein* (Whale)	USA, 35
Basil Rathbone	*Son Of Frankenstein* (Lee)	USA, 39
Cedric Hardwicke	*The Ghost Of Frankenstein* (Kenton)	USA, 42
Ilona Massey	*Frankenstein Meets The Wolf Man* (Neill)	USA, 43
Boris Karloff	*House Of Frankenstein* (Kenton)	USA, 44
Peter Cushing	*The Curse Of Frankenstein* (Fisher)	GB, 57
Whit Bissell	*I Was A Teenage Frankenstein* (Strock)	USA, 57
Peter Cushing	*The Revenge Of Frankenstein* (Fisher)	USA, 58
Boris Karloff	*Frankenstein – 1970* (Koch)	USA, 58
Peter Cushing	*The Evil Of Frankenstein* (Francis)	GB, 64
Robert Reilly	*Frankenstein Meets The Space Monster* (Gaffney)	USA, 66
Peter Cushing	*Frankenstein Created Woman* (Fisher)	GB, 67

Peter Cushing (as the scientist with brains) and Christopher Lee (as the monster with none) in Terence Fisher's *The Curse Of Frankenstein,* the 1957 film that began the long series of Hammer horror films. Lee played the monster but once, Cushing repeated the role of Baron Frankenstein on several occasions in the 60s and 70s

Peter Cushing	*Frankenstein Must Be Destroyed* (Fisher) GB, 69
Robin Ward	*Dr Frankenstein On Campus* (Taylor) Can, 70
J. Carrol Naish	*Blood Of Frankenstein* (Adamson) USA, 70
Ralph Bates	*The Horror Of Frankenstein* (Sangster) GB, 70
Joseph Cotten	*Lady Frankenstein* (Mel Welles) It, 71
Peter Cushing	*Frankenstein And The Monster From Hell* (Fisher) GB, 73
Gene Wilder	*Young Frankenstein* (Mel Brooks) USA, 74
Leonard Whiting	*Frankenstein: The True Story* (Smight) USA, 74
Leon Vitali	*Victor Frankenstein* (Floyd) Swe/Ire, 77
Gianrico Tedeschi	*Frankenstein – Italian Style* (Crispino) It, 77
Richard Cox	*Frankenstein 88/The Vindicator* ((Jean-Claude Lord) Can, 84
Donald Pleasence	*Frankenstein's Great Aunt Tillie* (Gold) Mex, 85
Sting	*The Bride* (Roddam) GB, 85
Joseph Bologna	*Transylvania 6,500* (DeLuca) USA, 85

Note: Narda Onyx and Steven Geray played the grandchildren of Frankenstein in *Jesse James Meets Frankenstein's Daughter* (USA, 66); Boris Karloff remains the only actor to play both Frankenstein and his monster on screen.

On TV Robert Foxworth starred as Shelley's scientist in Glenn Jordan's 1973 production, *Frankenstein.*

Frankenstein's Monster F

Still the most chilling monster of them all, if only because his creation appears to be a distinct medical possibility in this modern age of transplants. Karloff lumbered to stardom in three Universal pictures of the 30s, Christopher Lee did the same at Hammer in 1957; Michael Sarrazin rang the changes in 1974 by appearing as a monster more handsome than his creator.

Boris Karloff	*Frankenstein* (Whale)	USA, 31
Boris Karloff	*Bride Of Frankenstein* (Whale)	USA, 35
Elsa Lanchester	*Bride Of Frankenstein* (Whale)	USA, 35
Boris Karloff	*Son Of Frankenstein* (Lee)	USA, 39
Lon Chaney, Jr	*The Ghost Of Frankenstein* (Kenton)	USA, 42
Bela Lugosi	*Frankenstein Meets The Wolf Man* (Neill)	USA, 43
Glenn Strange	*House Of Frankenstein* (Kenton)	USA, 44
Glenn Strange	*House Of Dracula* (Kenton)	USA, 45
Glenn Strange	*Abbott and Costello Meet Frankenstein* (Barton)	USA, 48
Christopher Lee	*The Curse Of Frankenstein* (Fisher)	GB, 57
Gary Conway	*I Was A Teenage Frankenstein* (Strock)	USA, 57
Michael Gwynn	*The Revenge Of Frankenstein* (Fisher)	GB, 58
Mike Lane	*Frankenstein – 1970* (Koch)	USA, 58
Sandra Knight	*Frankenstein's Daughter* (Cunha)	USA, 58
Kiwi Kingston	*The Evil Of Frankenstein* (Francis)	GB, 64
Cal Bolder	*Jesse James Meets Frankenstein's Daughter* (Beaudine)	USA, 66
Susan Denberg	*Frankenstein Created Woman* (Fisher)	GB, 67
Freddie Jones	*Frankenstein Must Be Destroyed* (Fisher)	GB, 69
Dave Prowse	*The Horror Of Frankenstein* (Sangster)	GB, 70
John Bloom	*Blood Of Frankenstein* (Adamson)	USA, 70
Dave Prowse	*Frankenstein And The Monster From Hell* (Fisher)	GB, 73
Michael Sarrazin	*Frankenstein: The True Story* (Smight)	USA, 74
Peter Boyle	*Young Frankenstein* (Mel Brooks)	USA, 74
Per Oscarsson	*Victor Frankenstein* (Floyd)	Swe/Ire, 77
Aldo Maccione	*Frankenstein – Italian Style* (Crispino)	It, 77
Clancy Brown	*The Bride* (Roddam)	GB, 85
Jennifer Beals	*The Bride* (Roddam)	GB, 85
Petar Buntic	*Transylvania 6500* (DeLuca)	USA, 85

Note: Charles Ogle appeared as Frankenstein's Monster in Edison's 1910 production of Mary Shelley's story; Bo Svenson featured in the 1973 TV production by Glenn Jordan, Rosella Olson played The Bride Monster in the same film.

Freud, Sigmund R

(1856–1939) Famed Austrian pioneer of psychoanalysis; the subject of John Huston's 140-minute biography, *Freud,* a serious, restrained account of the psychiatrist's early struggles for recognition, and also the fictional *The Seven-Per-Cent Solution* in which Freud probes into the broken mind of Sherlock Holmes and then joins him in a thrilling adventure across Europe. The comedy *Lovesick* (with Alec Guinness as the shade of Freud) and the equally unfunny *The Secret Diary Of Sigmund Freud* were somewhat less ambitious attempts to portray the psychiatrist on screen.

Montgomery Clift	*Freud* (Huston)	USA, 62
Alan Arkin	*The Seven-Per-Cent Solution* (Ross)	GB, 76
Alec Guinness	*Lovesick* (Brickman)	USA, 83
Bud Cort	*The Secret Diary Of Sigmund Freud* (Greene)	USA, 84
Frank Finlay (voice only)	*Nineteen, Nineteen* (Brody)	GB, 85

Note: *Sigmund Freud's Dora* (82), a 35 minute short featuring Joel Kovel as Freud, recounted a conversation concerning psychoanalysis between a man and a women and at the same time provided a chronology of the years 1882–1905 in Freud's life. David Suchet played the psychiatrist in the six part TV series of 1984.

Friar Tuck F

Plump, jovial friar whose rotund frame invariably provides the humorous incidents in Robin Hood's

(Above) Montgomery Clift as Sigmund Freud in John Huston's 1962 film about the young psychiatrist's early struggles for acceptance and (right) Alan Arkin as Freud in the Sherlock Holmes adventure *The Seven Per Cent Solution*

screen adventures. Despite his bulky appearance, a swordsman of some distinction who joins the outlaws after a memorable duel with Robin Hood in midstream. No definitive screen portrayal, although Eugene Pallette endowed him with an engaging gruffness, shortness of temper and large appetite in Warners' classic of 1938.

Eugene Pallette	*The Adventures Of Robin Hood* (Curtiz/Keighley) USA, 38
Edgar Buchanan	*The Bandit Of Sherwood Forest* (Sherman/Levin) USA, 46
Billy House	*Rogues Of Sherwood Forest* (Douglas) USA, 50
Ben Welden	*Tales Of Robin Hood* (Tinling) USA, 51
James Hayter	*The Story Of Robin Hood And His Merrie Men* (Annakin) GB, 52
Reginald Beckwith	*Men Of Sherwood Forest* (Guest) GB, 54
Niall MacGinnis	*Sword Of Sherwood Forest* (Fisher) GB, 60
James Hayter	*A Challenge For Robin Hood* (Pennington Richards) GB, 67
Kenneth Gilbert	*Wolfshead: The Legend Of Robin Hood* (Hough) GB, 73
Ronnie Barker	*Robin And Marian* (Lester) USA, 76
Roy Kinnear	*The Zany Adventures Of Robin Hood* (Austin) TVM/USA, 84

Note: Andy Devine voiced Friar Tuck in Walt Disney's 1973 feature cartoon *Robin Hood;* M. Hannafly (USA, 12), H. Holles (USA, 13), Ernest Redding (USA, 14) and Willard Louis (USA, 22) were among the actors who played the role in the silent days. On TV Phil Rose featured in the 1984–6 series *Robin Of Sherwood.*

Friese-Greene, William [R]

(1855–1921) British motion picture pioneer who, in 1889, demonstrated his first celluloid film in public – supposedly to a startled policeman in Hyde Park – and later experimented with both three dimensional and colour photography. Died penniless just a few years after D. W. Griffith had demonstrated in America the enormous potential of film with his classic *Birth of a Nation* (1915).

Robert Donat	*The Magic Box* (John Boulting) GB, 51

Robert Donat as William Friese-Greene, the Bristol-born pioneer of the movie camera, in John Boulting's 1951 biography *The Magic Box*

Froman, Jane [R]

(1910–) American radio and stage singer, severely crippled in a plane crash in 1943, who struggled to recovery after a leg amputation and sang to US Forces in combat zones in World War II. Her gallantry was admirably conveyed on screen by an Oscar-nominated Susan Hayward who mimed to such Froman soundtracks as 'Blue Moon', 'I'll Walk Alone' and 'Get Happy'.

Susan Hayward	*With A Song In My Heart* (Walter Lang) USA, 52

Fu Manchu 

Chinese master criminal of Sax Rohmer, not unlike Ian Fleming's subsequent Dr No in that he is cultured, wealthy, intelligent — and deadly! Main aim in life: to destroy the entire white race and become emperor of the world. Sidelines: inventing unpatented tortures and depriving his henchmen of their will-power by cutting into their brains and removing their frontal lobes. First appeared in print in a short

Master criminal Fu Manchu captured here by famed caricaturist Hirschfeld and portrayed in 1980 by Peter Sellers in *The Fiendish Plot of Dr Fu Manchu*

story in 1911, then in the novel 'The Mystery Of Fu Manchu' in 1913. Screen career of variable quality, but a notable portrayal by Boris Karloff in Charles Brabin's film of 1932.

Warner Oland	*The Mysterious Dr Fu Manchu* (Lee) USA, 29
Warner Oland	*The Return Of Dr Fu Manchu* (Lee) USA, 30
Warner Oland	*Daughter Of The Dragon* (Corrigan) USA, 31
Boris Karloff	*The Mask Of Fu Manchu* (Brabin) USA, 32
Henry Brandon	*Drums Of Fu Manchu* (Witney/English) USA, 40
Manuel Requena	*The Other Fu Manchu* (Barreiro) Spa, 45
Christopher Lee	*The Face Of Fu Manchu* (Sharp) GB, 65
Christopher Lee	*The Brides Of Fu Manchu* (Sharp) GB, 66
Christopher Lee	*The Vengeance Of Fu Manchu* (Summers) GB, 67
Christopher Lee	*The Castle Of Fu Manchu* (Franco) W.Ger/Spa/It/GB, 68
Christopher Lee	*The Blood Of Fu Manchu* (Franco) W.Ger/Spa/USA/GB, 68
Peter Sellers	*The Fiendish Plot Of Dr Fu Manchu* (Haggard) USA, 80

Note: Harry Agar Lyons appeared as Fu Manchu in two British silent serials: the 15-episode *The Mystery Of Dr Fu Manchu* (23) and the 8-episode *The Further Mysteries Of Dr Fu Manchu* (24). Henry Brandon's portrayal in 1940 was another serial performance – in 15 episodes.

Gable, Clark

R

(1901–60) The 'king' of Hollywood and a man who reigned for nearly 30 years as one of the most personable movie stars on the American screen. Almost impossible to imitate on celluloid, although James Brolin was given the opportunity in Furie's *Gable And Lombard*. The jug handle ears, bootlace moustache and impudent grin were there; the personality, not surprisingly, was missing.

James Brolin	*Gable And Lombard* (Furie)	USA, 76

Galileo, Galilei

R

(1564–1642) Italian mathematician and astronomer who changed the course of civilization with his revolutionary ideas about the planetary system and mankind's place in the universe. His battles with the hierarchy of the Catholic Church would hardly rank as 'popcorn entertainment', but two little known films have examined his life with some success. Joseph Losey's 1974 film was based on the play by Bertolt Brecht.

Cyril Cusack	*Galileo* (Cavani)	It/Bul, 68
Topol	*Galileo* (Losey)	GB/Can, 74

The imitation and the real thing! (Left) James Brolin and Jill Clayburgh in Sidney Furie's fictionalized account of the offscreen romance between *Gable and Lombard*. (Right) The two stars photographed together in Hollywood in the early 40s

Gandhi, Mahatma [R]

(1869–1948) For many, the greatest figure of the twentieth century, a Hindu nationalist leader and the architect of Indian independence and self rule. Portrayed on screen by Ben Kingsley who earned an Oscar for his performance which required him to age 60 years from when he played Gandhi as a young attorney experiencing at first hand South African *apartheid*, through his acclaim as a spiritual leader in India and his passive resistance against the British, to his assassination in 1948!

J. S. Casshyap	*Nine Hours To Rama* (Robson)	USA/GB, 63
Ben Kingsley	*Gandhi* (Attenborough)	GB/Ind, 82

Note: Many top actors – Anthony Hopkins and John Hurt among them – were considered for the role before Richard Attenborough settled on Ben Kingsley who had appeared only twice before on screen, on both occasions in minor roles. The 1963 film *Nine Hours To Rama* concentrated not on the life of Gandhi but on that of his assassin, Naturam Godse (played by Horst Buchholtz); Sam Dastor featured as Gandhi in the 1986 TV series *Mountbatten: The Last Viceroy*.

Gantry, Elmer [F]

Whoring, whisky-drinking salesman who joins up with a tent pitching revivalist group in the Midwest and, through his talent for rabble rousing, turns the enterprise into big business. A brazen opportunist, he figures in Sinclair Lewis' controversial novel of 1927 and was played on screen in vigorous Oscar-winning style by Burt Lancaster.

Burt Lancaster	*Elmer Gantry* (Brooks)	USA, 60

Garrett, Pat [R]

(1854?–1908) A man who earned himself a place in the record books of the American West by shooting down Billy The Kid (in the back and in a darkened room) in New Mexico in July 1881. A former colleague of Bonney, he found that his fame as the killer of the West's most notorious outlaw was short-lived and he eventually went into the ranching and cattle business before meeting a violent death himself at the hands of a fellow rancher. Not always in evidence in films about Billy The Kid, but strikingly played by John Dehner in Arthur Penn's *The Left-Handed Gun* and James Coburn in Peckinpah's *Pat Garrett And Billy The Kid.*

Wallace Beery	*Billy The Kid* (King Vidor)	USA, 30
Wade Boteler	*Billy The Kid Returns* (Kane)	USA, 38
Thomas Mitchell	*The Outlaw* (Hughes)	USA, 43
Charles Bickford	*Four Faces West* (Green)	USA, 48
Robert Lowrey	*I Shot Billy The Kid* (Berke)	USA, 50
Frank Wilcox	*Texas Kid Outlaw* (Neumann)	USA, 50
James Griffith	*The Law vs Billy The Kid* (Castle)	USA, 54
James Craig	*Last Of The Desperadoes* (Newfield)	USA, 55
John Dehner	*The Left-Handed Gun* (Penn)	USA, 58
George Montgomery	*Badman's Country* (Sears)	USA, 58
Fausto Tozzi	*The Man Who Killed Billy The Kid* (Buchs)	Spa/It, 67
Glenn Corbett	*Chisum* (McLaglen)	USA, 70
James Coburn	*Pat Garrett And Billy The Kid* (Peckinpah)	USA, 73

Gatsby, Jay  

Perhaps the most tragic figure in all Scott Fitzgerald's novels of the 20s, a mysterious ex-bootlegger who lives in a luxurious Long Island mansion to be near the woman he once loved and lost. Despite the glamorous performance of Robert Redford in Jack Clayton's 1974 film, it is Alan Ladd who comes closest to Fitzgerald's original conception in Elliott Nugent's flat, but curiously effective adaptation of 1949. Paramount has filmed all three versions of the novel to date.

Alan Ladd	*The Great Gatsby* (Nugent)	USA, 49
Robert Redford	*The Great Gatsby* (Clayton)	USA, 74

Note: Warner Baxter featured as Gatsby in Herbert Brenon's silent version of 1926.

Gauguin, Paul 

(1843–1903) French post-impressionist who abandoned his wife and family, and his career as a

(Right) Horst Bucholtz as the assassin of Gandhi in the 1963 thriller *Nine Hours To Rama*; (below) Martin Sheen as the newspaperman Walker and Ben Kingsley as Gandhi in the role that earned the latter an Academy Award as best actor of the year

Alan Ladd (pictured here with Betty Field) in the first talking version of Scott Fitzgerald's *The Great Gatsby,* produced by Paramount in 1949

A slightly more handsome portrayal of the same bootlegger! Robert Redford as Gatsby in the 1974 film (also produced by Paramount) of Jack Clayton

stockbroker in Paris, to concentrate on his art in the islands of Tahiti. Anthony Quinn's Oscar-winning performance in Minnelli's *Lust For Life* covered Gauguin's period with Van Gogh at Arles; Donald Sutherland's more recent portrayal centered on his hapless years in Paris in the 1890s when he returned from Tahiti with just four francs in his pocket and hoped to conquer the art world with his paintings of his South Seas paradise. George Sanders portrayal in *The Moon And Sixpence* (Somerset Maugham's fictional account of Gauguin's life in which the artist was named Charles Strickland) incorporated most of his later years.

George Sanders	*The Moon And Sixpence* (Lewin) USA, 42
Anthony Quinn	*Lust For Life* (Minnelli) USA, 56
Donald Sutherland	*Wolf At The Door* (Carlsen) Fra/Den, 86

Note: David Carradine appeared as Gauguin in Fielder Cook's 1980 TV movie *Gauguin The Savage.*

Gawain

F

One of the noblest of King Arthur's knights, frequently referred to as the flower of chivalrous knighthood. A secondary figure in most Arthurian films until Stephen Weeks cast Murray Head in *Gawain And The Green Knight,* the story of how Gawain accepts the challenge of a huge, bearded stranger to find and defeat him within one year or forfeit his own life. Miles O'Keefe featured in the same director's less impressive remake *Sword Of The Valiant;* Liam Neeson appeared as a somewhat maudlin and drunken Gawain in John Boorman's *Excalibur,* a version of Thomas Malory's 'Le Morte D'Arthur'.

Sterling Hayden	*Prince Valiant* (Hathaway) USA, 54
Robert Urquhart	*Knights Of The Round Table* (Thorpe) GB, 54
George Baker	*Lancelot And Guinevere* (Wilde) GB, 63
Murray Head	*Gawain And The Green Knight* (Weeks) GB, 73
Humbert Balsan	*Lancelot du Lac* (Bresson) Fra/It, 74
John Le Mesurier	*The Spaceman And King Arthur* (Mayberry) GB, 79
Liam Neeson	*Excalibur* (Boorman) USA, 81

Miles O'Keefe — *Sword Of The Valiant: The Legend Of Gawain And The Green Knight* (Weeks) GB, 85

Note: *Gawain And The Green Knight* derived from a fourteenth century poem, the authorship of which remains unknown; Patrick Ryecart featured as Gawain in Clive Donner's 1983 TV movie *Arthur The King*.

Gehrig, Lou [R]

(1903–41) One of the legends of American baseball, a renowned hitter who joined the New York Yankees in 1925 and made regular appearances for the next 14 years, playing in a record 2130 games in succession and earning himself the nickname of 'Iron Horse' because of his stamina. The Goldwyn movie of 1942 concentrated on Gehrig's final years when he was struck down at the early age of 38 by a rare form of multiple sclerosis. Gary Cooper featured in the starring role having to learn to throw left-handed in order to undertake the part.

Gary Cooper — *Pride Of The Yankees* (Wood) USA, 42

Note: Fielder Cook's 1977 TV Movie *A Love Affair: The Eleanor And Lou Gehrig Story* retold the story of the baseball immortal from his wife's viewpoint. Edward Herrman played Gehrig, Blythe Danner his wife. In Goldwyn's 1942 movie Teresa Wright featured as Eleanor Gehrig.

Genghis Khan

(1162–1227) Twelfth century Mongol Emperor who invaded vast areas of Northern China, Iran and Russia with his barbarous hordes. Film accounts of his ruthless exploits have generally been undistinguished, and, in the case of John Wayne's *The Conqueror* ('You're bewdiful in your wrath') unbelievable!

Marvin Miller — *The Golden Horde* (Sherman) USA, 51
Manuel Conde — *Genghis Khan* (Salvador) Philippines, 52
John Wayne — *The Conqueror* (Powell) USA, 56
Roldano Lupi — *The Mongols* (DeToth/Savona) Fra/It, 60
Omar Sharif — *Genghis Khan* (Levin) USA/GB/W.Ger, 65

Geronimo [R]

(1829–1909) The most ferocious of all the Apaches, a renegade who refused to accept the peace treaty of Cochise and operated with a small band of Indians on both sides of the Mexican border. For a man with such a ruthless nature he survived a remarkable 80 years. Two films have centred on his activities, the first with real-life Cherokee Chief Thundercloud, the second with Chuck Connors.

Chief White Horse — *Stagecoach* (Ford) USA, 39
Chief Thundercloud — *Geronimo!* (Sloane) USA, 39
Tom Tyler — *Valley Of The Sun* (Marshall) USA, 42
Chief Thundercloud — *I Killed Geronimo* (Hoffman) USA, 50
Jay Silverheels — *The Battle At Apache Pass* (Sherman) USA, 52
Ian MacDonald — *Taza, Son Of Cochise* (Sirk) USA, 54
Monte Blue — *Apache* (Aldrich) USA, 54
Jay Silverheels — *Walk The Proud Land* (Hibbs) USA, 56
Chuck Connors — *Geronimo* (Laven) USA, 62

Note: Enrique Lucero featured as Geronimo in the TV movie *Mr Horn* (79).

Gershwin, George

(1898–1937) American composer who brought his genius to bear on many different aspects of American music in the 20s and 30s – revue, musical comedy, folk opera ('Porgy And Bess'), even concert works ('Rhapsody In Blue'). The Warner Bros biography of 1945, despite the familiar shortcomings, did on occasion capture some of Gershwin's infectious enthusiasm for his work. Among the Gershwin stage shows: 'Lady Be Good', 'Funny Face', 'Strike Up The Band'. Among his songs: 'Fascinating Rhythm', 'S'Wonderful', 'Embrace You'.

Robert Alda — *Rhapsody In Blue* (Rapper) USA, 45

Note: Gershwin's brother, Ira, was played by Herbert Rudley in the above film.

Gervaise

The tragic heroine of Emile Zola's 1877 novel 'L'Assommoir', a young girl who struggles against her environment in the slums of mid-nineteenth century Paris then finally succumbs to the sordid life style of her alcoholic husband. The mother of the prostitute Nana whose escapades Zola chronicled in a subsequent novel. Memorably played by Maria Schell in Rene Clement's masterpiece of 1956.

Line Noro	*L'Assommoir* (Roudes)	Fra, 33
Maria Schell	*Gervaise* (Clément)	Fra, 56

Note: Silent portrayals of Gervaise included those by Catherine Foneteney in a 1909 French film by Albert Capellani, Emilie Sannom (Den, 08), Pauline Polaire (Fra, 13), Irene Browne in the British production *Drink* (17) and Louise Sforza in *L'Assommoir* (Fra, 21).

Geste, Beau F

'Boy's Own Paper' hero of P. C. Wren; one of three brothers who takes the blame for his aunt's theft of a priceless diamond then flees to the Foreign Legion to do battle with the arab hordes and a despotic regimental sergeant. Marty Feldman spoofed the whole thing in his 1977 film with Michael York; Ronald Colman remains the definitive 'let me be the first to die' hero in Herbert Brenon's silent film for Paramount. Wren's novel was first published in 1924.

Ronald Colman	*Beau Geste* (Brenon)	USA, 26
Gary Cooper	*Beau Geste* (Wellman)	USA, 39
Guy Stockwell	*Beau Geste* (Heyes)	USA, 66
Michael York	*The Last Remake Of Beau Geste* (Feldman)	USA, 77

Gigi F

Fifteen-year-old Parisian schoolgirl who suddenly grows into a beautiful young woman and enslaves the bored rake who has known her since childhood. Created by Colette in her 1945 novel and portrayed twice on film, first in straight drama then in Vincente Minnelli's Oscar-winning musical.

Daniele Delorme	*Gigi* (Audry)	Fra, 48
Leslie Caron	*Gigi* (Minnelli) /	USA, 58

Gilbert, W. S. and Sullivan, Arthur R

Nineteenth century English composers of a series of comic operas – 'HMS Pinafore', 'The Pirates of Penzance', 'The Mikado', 'The Gondoliers' – which satirized aspects of Victorian life. The story of their turbulent 18-year partnership which produced 13 operas – and a much publicised quarrel – was related in the Launder/Gilliat biography, *The Story Of Gilbert And Sullivan.*

Nigel Bruce (Gilbert) Claud Allister (Sullivan)	*Lillian Russell* (Cummings)	USA, 40
Robert Morley (Gilbert) Maurice Evans (Sullivan)	*The Story Of Gilbert and Sullivan* (Launder/Gilliat)	GB, 53

Note: In *The Magic Box,* the 1951 Festival of Britain film, conductor-arranger Muir Matheson guested briefly as composer Arthur Sullivan.

Gilda R

Only a Christian name, but enough to describe this alluring torch singer who, in 1946, girated her body within a strapless black evening gown 'down South America way'. Marriage to Nazi-styled despot George Macready brought dark tinges to her sensuality; a neat line in wisecracks ('If I'd have been a ranch they would have called me the Bar Nothing') revealed a more appealing side to her nature.

Rita Hayworth	*Gilda* (Charles Vidor)	USA, 46

Note: Hayworth's famous song 'Put The Blame On Mame Boys' was mimed and sung in the movie by Anita Ellis.

Gilmore, Gary R

(1941–77) Controversial American murderer (of a petrol station attendant and motel manager) who made headlines across the world by insisting that his lawyers should not appeal for clemency and that he should be executed by firing squad. After prolonged legal battles his wish was granted, making him the first person to be executed in more than a decade in the United States. Tommy Lee Jones played Gilmore in a TV movie version of Norman Mailer's Pulitzer Prize-winning book (which Mailer himself adapted) and which probed deeply and with insight into the psyche of Gilmore.

Tommy Lee Jones	*The Executioner's Song* (Schiller)	TVM/USA, 82

Note: Tommy Lee Jones earned an Emmy award for his portrayal of Gilmore; the 240 minute TV movie was later released in a shortened cinema version in Europe in 1983.

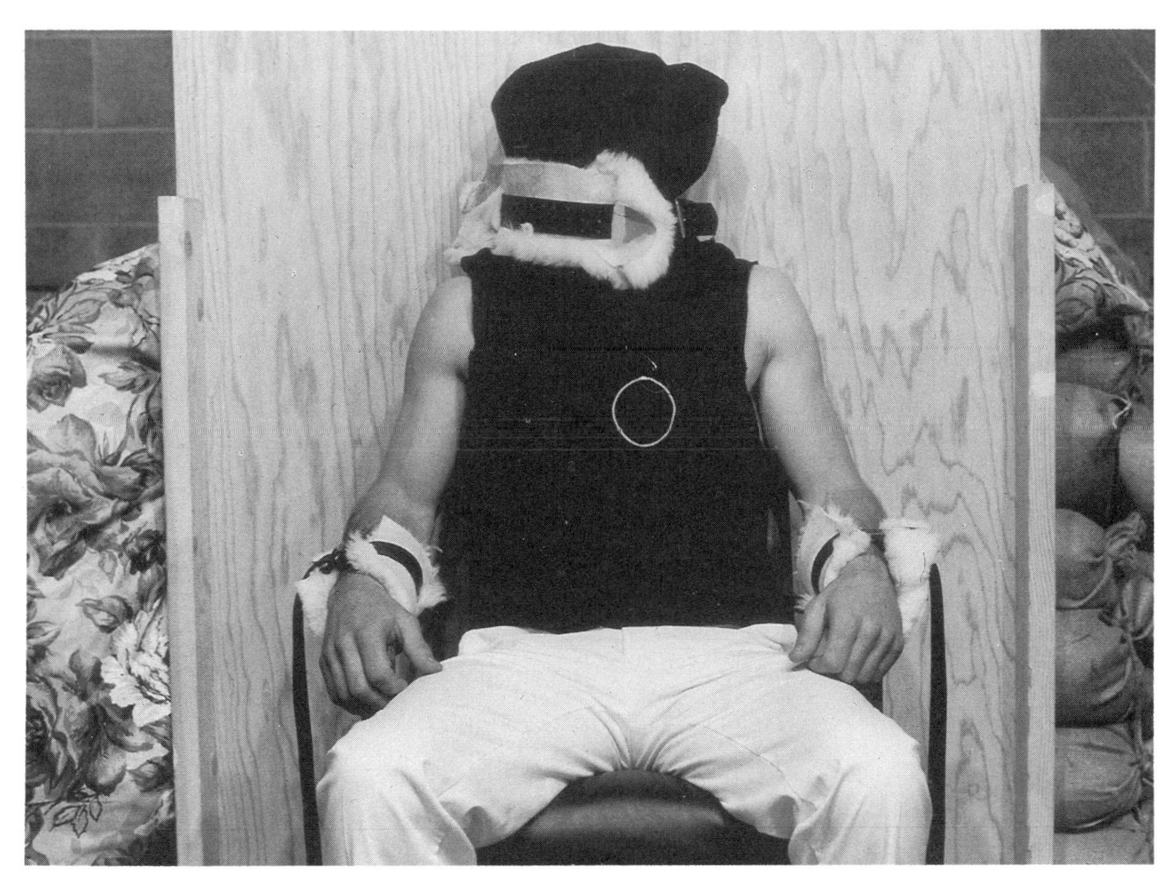

The end for Gary Gilmore, a psychopathic killer who made world headlines when he appealed against his sentence of life imprisonment and asked that the state of Utah execute him for his crimes. Tommy Lee Jones won an Emmy for his portrayal of Gilmore in the film *The Executioner's Song*

Glinka, Mikhail

R

(1804–57) Russian composer, a former civil servant, who travelled widely throughout his country in search of the true Russian musical idiom. He introduced a national element into his operas e.g. 'A Life For The Tsar' (1836) and pioneered the style of the Russian national school of composers. Two major screen biographies, both Russian.

Boris Chirkov	*The Great Glinka* (Arnstam)	USSR, 46
B. Smirnov	*Glinka* (Alexandrov)	USSR, 52

The Godfather

F

One of the cinema's best-known family men; a former Sicilian peasant (real name Don Vito Corleone) who rules as the omnipotent chieftain of a violent empire of Italian-American crime and presides over the five families who control the Mafia in post-war New York. A fictional character but as portrayed in Mario Puzo's bestseller, one of the most awesome villains of recent times. Francis Ford Coppola filmed his activities in two masterly films: the first tracing Corleone's final years and the accession to his throne of his son Michael, the second revealing Corleone's early life in flashback and Michael's steady and ruthless rise to power.

Marlon Brando	*The Godfather* O (Coppola)	USA, 72
Robert De Niro and (as a boy) Oreste Baldini	*The Godfather Part II* O (Coppola	USA, 74

Marlon Brando as Don Vito Corleone in *The Godfather*—directed by Francis Ford Coppola in 1972. Robert de Niro played the role subsequently in the *The Godfather Part II*

Note: The character of Corleone was said to be an amalgam of several real-life Mafia figures but was most closely modelled on Carlo Gambino, one of the most cunning of the post-war gangsters and who propelled the Anastasia family to the foremost position in organized crime. In true 'Godfather' style he went out not in a hail of bullets but of a heart attack, aged 74!

Golden Marie (Casque D'Or) [F]

Arguably Simone Signoret's most effective screen role, a Parisian prostitute who embarks on a tragic romance with a young suburban carpenter, drives him twice to murder and then watches him die on the guillotine. Signoret's sensual performance and Jacques Becker's evocation of the Paris underworld of the 1890s helped make the film one of the greatest in the history of the French cinema.

Simone Signoret — *Casque D'Or* (Becker) Fra, 52

Golightly, Holly [F]

Among the most loved of all movie kooks, an amoral teenager from the Texas backwoods who is kept in luxury in a New York apartment by a notorious racketeer and poses as one of the most sophisticated girls about town. Based on a character Truman Capote knew when he lived in an old brownstone building in New York in the 40s, she first appeared in print in the 1958 novella 'Breakfast At Tiffany's'. Audrey Hepburn made the part all her own in Blake Edwards' 1961 adaptation even though the role had originally been set for Marilyn Monroe.

Audrey Hepburn — *Breakfast At Tiffany's* (Edwards) USA, 61

Goodman, Benny [R]

(1909–86) The legendary 'King of Swing' and one of the most important figures in the history of American jazz. Following the box-office success of *The Glenn Miller Story* his life was filmed by Universal in 1955, but despite an electrifying climax at the famous Carnegie Hall concert, the film failed to find the same sympathetic audience. Goodman himself recorded the film's soundtrack and ghosted the clarinet for Steve Allen.

Steve Allen — *The Benny Goodman Story* (Davies) USA, 55

Note: Goodman and his orchestra appeared as themselves in several Hollywood movies of the 40s e.g. *Syncopation* (42), *Stage Door Canteen* (43), *The Gang's All Here* (43), *Sweet And Lowdown* (44), *A Song Is Born* (48).

Gordon, General Charles 

(1833–85) One of Britain's most popular military figures of the nineteenth century, an officer of the Royal Engineers who distinguished himself in China and the Sudan before being killed by Arab tribesmen at Khartoum. Basil Dearden's 1966 film explored the motives and character of Gordon in some depth; Charlton Heston's strikingly intelligent performance quelled all doubts about the ability of an American actor to portray an English hero convincingly on screen.

Laidman Browne — *Sixty Glorious Years* (Wilcox) GB, 38

Charlton Heston — *Khartoum* (Dearden) GB, 66

Gordon, Flash 

All-American astronaut permanently at odds with super villain Ming The Merciless, emperor of the planet Mongo and would be ruler of the Universe. Cartoonist-artist Alex Raymond brought him to life in a comic strip of 1934 and 'Buster' Crabbe played him in three prewar serials of Universal, all of which pitted him against not only Ming but also Shark Men, Death Rays, Zebra-striped Bears, etc. Sam Jones appeared in the role in the lavish Dino De Laurentiis production of 1980.

'Buster' Crabbe	*Flash Gordon* (Stephani)	USA, 36
'Buster' Crabbe	*Flash Gordon's Trip To Mars* (Beebe/Hill)	USA, 38
'Buster' Crabbe	*Flash Gordon Conquers The Universe* (Beebe/Taylor)	USA, 40
Sam Jones	*Flash Gordon* (Hodges)	GB, 80

Note: Charles Middleton starred as the despot Ming in the Universal serials; Max Von Sydow played the power-crazed Emperor in the 1980 version.

Gorki, Maxim

R

(1868–1936) The first great writer to emerge from the poverty of the lower classes in Tsarist Russia. A pedlar, dishwasher, gardener and dock hand before turning to writing, he wrote socially realistic novels and dramas ('The Lower Depths') and contributed much of his earnings to the Marxist revolutionary movement. His autobiographical trilogy, written from 1913–23, was filmed over a period of three years by Mark Donskoi. The films dealt with Gorki's boyhood in provincial Russia and his life as a young man.

Alexei Lyarski	*The Childhood Of Maxim Gorki* (Donskoi)	USSR, 38
Alexei Lyarski	*My Childhood* (Donskoi)	USSR, 39
Y. Valbert	*My Universities* (Donskoi)	USSR, 40

Goya y Lucientes, Francisco de

R

(1746–1828) Spanish painter, famous for his portraits, religious canvasses and realistic scenes of war, and also the 'Maja Nude' which aroused considerable speculation when it was first unveiled to the public. Henry Koster's 1959 Hollywood film revolved around the romance between Goya and the Duchess of Albany (Ava Gardner), supposedly the model for the portrait; the 1971 Spanish biography invited more serious study.

Anthony Franciosa	*The Naked Maja* (Koster)	USA, 59
Francisco Rabal	*Goya* (Vedo)	Spa, 71

Note: In the five and a half hour Spanish TV movie *Goya* (directed by Jose Ramon Larraz in 1985) Enric Majo featured as the painter and Laura Morante as the Duchess Of Albany.

Graham, Barbara

R

33-year-old American, known as 'Bloody Babs', who was found guilty of murdering an elderly woman during a house burglary in Burbank in 1953. Not a major figure in the history of American crime, but important in that she may, quite possibly, have been innocent, and had to endure a living hell right up until her death in the gas chamber in San Quentin in 1955. Robert Wise's film of her life and trial cast strong doubts about her guilt; Susan Hayward's acting won her an 1958 Academy Award.

Susan Hayward	*I Want To Live* (Wise)	USA, 58

Note: Lindsay Wagner appeared as Graham in a routine TV movie (also titled *I Want To Live*) directed by David Lowell Rich in 1983.

Gray, Dorian

A man who sells his soul for eternal youth, remaining young while only his portrait reveals the stigma of age and corruption. The central figure in Oscar Wilde's famous morality tale, most ably characterized on screen by Hurd Hatfield in Albert Lewin's definitive film version of 1945. Wilde's novel was first published in 1891.

Hurd Hatfield	*The Picture Of Dorian Gray* (Lewin)	USA, 45
Helmut Berger	*Dorian Gray* (Dallamano)	It/W.Ger, 70

Note: Adam Poulsen (Den, 10), Wallace Reid (USA, 13), Charles Victor (GB, 16), Bernd Aldor (Ger, 17) and Norbert Dan (Hung, 18) all featured as Dorian Gray in silent screen versions of the story; Lord Henry Wotton, the cynical aristocrat whose evil influence is responsible for Gray embarking on his decadent ways, has been played by Phillips Smalley (13), Jack Jordan (16), Bela Lugosi (18), George Sanders (45) and Herbert Lom (70).

On TV Shane Briant (Gray) and Nigel Davenport (Wotton) appeared in a 1973 American production

Barbara Graham—was she guilty or innocent of murder? Robert Wise's 1958 film *I Want To Live* hinted strongly at the latter as it followed her trial and charted the final months of her life as she awaited execution in the gas chamber of San Quentin. Susan Hayward earned an Academy Award as best actress of 1958 for her portrayal of 'Bloody Babs'

directed by Glenn Jordan, and Peter Firth (Gray) and John Gielgud (Wotton) in a 1976 BBC version. A more recent – and ludicrous – TV update, *The Sins Of Dorian Gray* (83) cast Dorian as a woman (Barbara Bauer), a fashion model whose perfect video test grows old while she stays young. Anthony Perkins played the evil 'influence'.

Graziano, Rocky [R]

(1922–) New York adolescent who descended into delinquency and crime before boxing his way out of trouble and winning the middleweight championship of the world. Paul Newman's screen portrayal turned him into a major star, in many ways a lucky break, as the role had originally been scheduled for James Dean.

Paul Newman — *Somebody Up There Likes Me* (Wise) USA, 56

Greco, El [R]

(1541–1614) Greek-born Spanish painter whose intense, deeply religious portraits inspired a 1964 film biography. Instead of compiling a serious film dedicated to the work of a great artist, the producers opted instead for soap opera, i.e. El Greco's unrequited love for an aristocratic lady and his subsequent inquisition for witchcraft and heresy. Mel Ferrer competed with and lost to the lovely Spanish locations of Toledo.

Mel Ferrer — *El Greco* (Salce) It/Fra, 64

Lady Jane Grey [R]

(1537–54) The Queen of England for just nine days when the Earl of Northumberland (her father-in-law and Protector of Edward VI) persuaded the dying boy king to settle the crown on Jane and bypass the claims of Mary and Elizabeth. The plan failed and Jane and her husband were later executed after her short reign was brought to an end when Mary defeated the forces of Northumberland. Only two films have concentrated on the tragic events although, as a character, Lady Jane has frequently popped up in supporting roles in the versions of Mark Twain's *The Prince And The Pauper* story.

Nova Pilbeam — *Tudor Rose* (Stevenson) GB, 36

Ann Howard — *The Prince And The Pauper* (Keighley) USA, 37

Jane Asher — *The Prince And The Pauper* (Chaffey) GB, 62

Felicity Dean — *The Prince And The Pauper* (Fleischer) Panama, 77

Helena Bonham Carter — *Lady Jane* (Nunn) GB, 86

Grieg, Edvard [R]

(1843–1907) Norwegian composer who reflected the landscapes and history of his homeland in his music. A composer of operas, choral works and concertos, and best-known for his 'Peer Gynt', he was played by Toralv Maurstad in the 140-minute biography directed by Andrew Stone. The film was based on the stage musical first performed on the New York stage in 1944.

Toralv Maurstad — *Song Of Norway* (Stone) USA, 70

Griffith, Corinne 

(1894–1979) Silent screen actress (known as 'The Orchid Lady' because of her delicate beauty) who took up writing when she retired from films in 1933. Her most popular book – 'Papa's Delicate Condition' – recalled her childhood in turn-of-the-century Texas where her hard-drinking, railroad supervisor father was given to such extravagant gestures as buying a bankrupt circus in order to get a pony for his daughter and purchasing a drug store so that he and his cronies could drink on Sundays. Linda Bruhl played the six-year-old Corinne and Jackie Gleason her inebriated father in George Marshall's 1963 film.

Linda Bruhl — *Papa's Delicate Condition* (Marshall) USA, 63

Note: Corinne Griffith made 60 films in the silent period including *The Common Law* and *The Divine Lady*. 'Papa's Delicate Condition' was first published in 1952.

Griffith, D. W. 

(1875–1948) The single most important figure in the history of American film and through *The Birth Of A Nation, Intolerance* and other silent classics, the man who was most influential in the development of cinema as an art. His tragic fall from the heights to a bitter obscurity (his last film was *The Struggle* in 1931) and a lonely death in a Hollywood hotel room would make for a moving screen biography.

Charles Dance as the American film director D.W. Griffith pictured during the filming of his epic *Intolerance* in the Taviani brothers' *Good Morning Babylon*

As yet, however, he has been played only once by British actor Charles Dance in *Good Morning Babylon,* a romantic portrait of early Hollywood where two Italian craftsmen enter the employ of Griffith and help him build the sets for *Intolerance*.

Charles Dance	*Good Morning Babylon* (Paolo & Vittorio Taviani) It/Fra/USA, 87

Note: Griffith was also glimpsed briefly in the final sequence of Peter Bogdanovich's *Nickleodeon* (76) when he is seen acknowledging the applause of the audience at the premiere of *The Clansman* (later renamed *The Birth Of A Nation*) in 1915.

Brothers Grimm

R

The famed German writers of fairy tales – Wilhelm (1785–1863) and Jacob (1786–1859) – whose lives, fantasies and stories were combined in the early Cinerama production *The Wonderful World Of The Brothers Grimm.* The three stories re-enacted in the film were 'The Cobbler And The Elves', 'The Dancing Princess' and 'The Singing Bone'.

Laurence Harvey (Wilhelm Grimm) Karl Boehm (Jacob Grimm)	*The Wonderful World Of The Brothers Grimm* (Levin) USA, 62

Guevara, Ernesto ('Che')

R

(1928–67) Argentine-born revolutionary, popularly known as 'El Che' or 'Che Guevara', who played an important part in the Cuban revolution of 1959 and later served in government posts under Castro. In 1965 he left Cuba to become a guerilla leader in South America and was subsequently captured and killed by government troops in Bolivia. A martyr in popular mythology, he deserves rather better treatment than he has so far received on screen.

Francisco Rabal	*El 'Che' Guevara* (Heusch) It, 68
Omar Sharif	*Che!* (Fleischer) USA, 69

Guinan, Texas

(1884–1933) A night club hostess, well known in several notorious New York speakeasies in the 20s. Her trademark was to greet her patrons from her high stool at the door with the phrase, 'Hello, suckers!' About an hour later the patrons discovered what she meant when they were presented with bills of 50 dollars upwards for an evening's entertainment. The only screen biography was made in 1945 to accommodate the talents of the then popular Betty Hutton. The film skirted around most of the unsavoury facts about Guinan's life but was helped along by such old-time songs as 'Ragtime Cowboy Joe', 'It Had To Be You' and 'Darktown Strutters' Ball'.

Betty Hutton	*Incendiary Blonde* (Marshall) USA, 45

Guinevere, Queen

Wife of King Arthur and one of those beautiful heroines forever being abducted and in need of rescue. Her passion for Arthur's favourite knight, Sir Lancelot, is the focal point for most screen characterizations. Ava Gardner played her with controlled twentieth century sensuality in *Knights Of The Round Table,* Vanessa Redgrave with charm and abandon in the Lerner and Loewe musical *Camelot,* and Cherie Lunghi with a certain degree of attractive nudity in John Boorman's *Excalibur.*

Ava Gardner	*Knights Of The Round Table* (Thorpe) GB, 54
Jean Lodge	*The Black Knight* (Garnett) GB, 54
Jarma Lewis	*Prince Valiant* (Hathaway) USA, 54
Jean Wallace	*Lancelot And Guinevere* (Wilde) GB, 63
Vanessa Redgrave	*Camelot* (Logan) USA, 67
Laura Duke Condominas	*Lancelot du Lac* (Bresson) Fra/It, 74
Marie Christine Barrault	*Perceval Le Gallois* (Rohmer) Fra, 78
Cherie Lunghi	*Excalibur* (Boorman) USA, 81
Pat Tallman	*Stuck On You* (Herz/Weil) USA, 82

Note: Rosalyn Landor appeared as Guinevere in the 1983 TV movie, *Arthur The King.*

Gulliver, Lemuel

F

The creation of Jonathan Swift; an eighteenth century doctor who encounters strange adventures when he is shipwrecked, first on the island of Lilliput where the people are no more than six inches high, and then in Brobdingnag where the situation is reversed and it is he who is the midget in a land of giants. Richard Harris starred opposite cartoon characters in the most recent version of Swift's satirical tale; other screen adaptations have included a feature length cartoon made by Max and Dave Fleischer in 1939 and a 1960 spectacular dominated by an assortment of Ray Harryhausen creations.

V. Konstantinov	*The New Gulliver* (Ptuschko) USSR, 34
Sam Parker (voice only)	*Gulliver's Travels* (Fleischer) USA, 39
Kerwin Matthews	*The Three Worlds Of Gulliver* (Sher) USA/GB/Spa, 60
Richard Harris	*Gulliver's Travels* (Hunt) GB, 76

Note: Silent versions of the story included a 1902 Georges Melies production entitled *Gulliver's Travels Among The Lilliputians* and the animated/model adaptation *Gulliver In Lilliput,* released in France in 1923. The 1934 Russian film was a modern Soviet version of the Lilliputian incident with puppets voiced by members of the Kamerny Theatre.

Gunga Din

?

Hindu water carrier who saves a British Indian regiment at the cost of his life; immortalized in Rudyard Kipling's poem ('You're A Better Man Than I, Gunga Din') which appeared in the author's 1892 collection 'Barrack Room Ballads'.

Sam Jaffe	*Gunga Din* (Stevens) USA, 39

Note: A western version of the story with Gunga Din recast as a freed slave (Sammy Davis Jr) was filmed as *Sergeants 3* in 1962.

Guthrie, Woody

(1912–67) American folk singer and composer who became a spokesman for the migrant workers of the Depression years. Wrote over 1000 songs including 'So Long It's Been Good To Know Yuh', 'This Land Is Your Land' and 'Union Maid'. Portrayed as a young man during the 30s by David Carradine in Hal Ashby's *Bound For Glory,* based on Guthrie's own autobiography.

Joseph Boley	*Alice's Restaurant* (Penn) USA, 69
David Carradine	*Bound For Glory* (Ashby) USA, 76

Gutman, Casper

As personified by Sydney Greenstreet in Huston's *The Maltese Falcon,* the most menacing of all fat screen villains, a mocking, effeminate leader of a small band of international crooks seeking the whereabouts of a priceless statuette. Created by Dashiell Hammett in his private-eye novel of 1930, the character also appeared in an earlier film version of the story, i.e. in 1931 when he was portrayed by Dudley Digges. In the 1936 adaptation, *Satan Met A Lady,* Gutman was renamed Madame Barabbas and resexed by actress Alison Skipworth.

Dudley Digges	*The Maltese Falcon* (Del Ruth) USA, 31
Sydney Greenstreet	*The Maltese Falcon* (Huston) USA, 41

Gwyn, Nell

(1650–87) English comedy actress and mistress of Charles II. Reputedly sold oranges before selling herself and bearing the king two sons between engagements on the London stage. Anna Neagle

Woody Guthrie (played by David Carradine) defends himself against unfriendly migrants in *Bound for Glory,* Hal Ashby's biography of the famous folk singer/composer. Ashby's film concentrated on the 1936–40 period when Guthrie travelled America fighting and singing for the victims of the Great Depression

romped good-naturedly with Cedric Hardwicke in the Herbert Wilcox biography of 1934, Margaret Lockwood explored the realms of slapstick in the Sid Field comedy *Cardboard Cavalier.*

Anna Neagle	*Nell Gwyn* (Wilcox)	GB, 34
Virginia Field	*Hudson's Bay* (Pichel)	USA, 41
Margaret Lockwood	*Cardboard Cavalier* (Forde)	GB, 49
Anna Neagle	*Lilacs In The Spring* (Wilcox)	GB, 54

Note: Dorothy Gish featured as Nell in an earlier, silent Wilcox production of 1926; Lois Sturt featured in a minor role in the 1922 film, *The Glorious Adventure* (GB/USA).

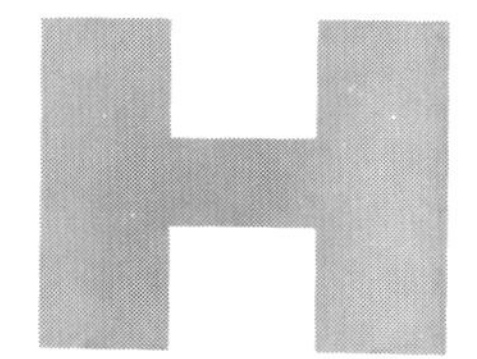

Haarmann, Fritz [R]

Possibly the most horrific mass murderer of all time, a meat trader who lured teenage boys to their doom in post-World War I Germany and subsequently sold their bodies for meat. A homosexual who was also an epileptic, he admitted surprise when charged with only 27 murders in 1924; he calculated the number to be nearer 40. He was beheaded in the same year, aged 45. Kurt Raab starred as Haarmann in the 1973 German film of Ulli Lommel.

Kurt Raab — *Tenderness Of The Wolves* (Lommel) W.Ger, 73

Haigh, John George [R]

(1910–49) A lethal 'charmer' who murdered once too often when he disposed of a wealthy 69-year-old widow in an acid bath after shooting her in the head. Eventually arrested because a denture of the victim was identified by her dentist, Haigh eventually owned up to a further eight acid bath murders, even claiming that he had drunk the blood of his victims. Haigh's case has not been officially documented on the screen although by a curious coincidence a 1949 film called *Obsession* bore a close resemblance to the real life events. Robert Newton featured as a Harley Street doctor who chains up his wife's lover in a cellar and then plans to murder him by disposing of his body in a bath filled with acid. Luckily, unlike Haigh, his plans came to nothing.

Robert Newton (as Dr Clive Riordan) — *Obsession* (Dmytryk) GB, 49

Note: The film's release was delayed for four months because of the Haigh case. On the morning of its press show the critics emerged from a Leicester Square cinema to see the newspaper hoarding: 'Haigh To Hang'.

Halsey, Vice-Admiral William F. [R]

(1882–1959) Flamboyant, quick-tempered Commander of the Allied Fleets in the South Pacific in World War II. His doggedness in battle earned him the nickname of 'Bull' Halsey and helped bring about several notable victories over the Japanese near Guadalcanal. One detailed screen portrait by James Cagney in *The Gallant Hours*.

James Cagney	*The Gallant Hours* (Montgomery)	USA, 60
James Whitmore	*Tora! Tora! Tora!* (Fleischer)	USA, 70
Robert Mitchum	*Midway* (Smight)	USA, 76
Kenneth Tobey	*MacArthur* (Sargent)	USA, 77

Hamilton, Emma [R]

(*c.* 1765–1815) Mistress of Lord Nelson, lowly-bred but of great beauty, who attained popularity and influence at the court of Naples (as the wife of Sir William Hamilton) before enslaving England's most popular hero. After Nelson's death she sank swiftly into debt, suffered imprisonment and died in poverty in France. Vivien Leigh's performance in *Lady Hamilton* is overtly romantic, Glenda Jackson's portrayal in *Bequest To The Nation,* too vulgar. The truth lies somewhere in between.

Corinne Griffith	*The Divine Lady* (Lloyd)	USA, 29
Vivien Leigh	*Lady Hamilton* (Korda)	GB, 41
Michele Mercier	*Lady Hamilton* (Christian-Jaque)	Ger/It/Fra/USA, 69
Glenda Jackson	*Bequest To The Nation* (Jones)	GB, 73

Note: Malvina Longfellow in *Nelson* (GB, 18) and *The Romance Of Lady Hamilton* (GB, 19), Liane Haid in *The Affairs Of Lady Hamilton* (Ger, 21) and Gertrude McCoy in *Nelson* (GB, 26) all featured as Emma Hamilton in silent productions.

Hamlet [F]

Shakespeare's tragic young Danish prince who resolves to avenge the murder of his father when he learns from his father's ghost that his mother has married the assassin. Arguably, the best-known character in the best-known play in the entire Shakespeare canon. Olivier, Burton and Nicol Williamson have all reflected different aspects of the mournful prince; Maximilian Schell starred in a West German adaptation of 1960. The revenge theme has also been adapted into a western, *Johnny Hamlet,* in 1972.

Sohrab Modi	*Hamlet* (Modi)	Ind, 35
Laurence Olivier	*Hamlet* (Olivier)	GB, 48
Erminio Macario	*Moi, Hamlet* (Simonelli)	It, 52
Kishore Sahu	*Hamlet* (Sahu)	Ind, 54
Hardy Kruger	*Der Rest ist Schweigen* (Käutner)	W.Ger, 59
Maximilian Schell	*Hamlet* (Wirth)	W.Ger, 60
Innokenti Smoktunovski	*Hamlet* (Kozintsev)	USSR, 64
Richard Burton	*Hamlet* (Gielgud)	USA, 64
Kofi Middleton-Mends	*Hamile* (Bishop)	Ghana, 65
Nicol Williamson	*Hamlet* (Richardson)	GB, 69

Note: George Melies produced a version of *Hamlet* in 1907; Sarah Bernhardt (Fra, 1900), Hacques Gretillat (Fra, 08), Mounet-Sulley (Fra, 09), Dante Capelli (It, 10), Amleto Palermi (It, 10), Alwin Neuss (Den, 10), Charles Raymond (GB, 10), Maurice Costello (USA, 13), James Young (USA, 14), Sir Johnston Forbes-Robertson (GB, 13), A. Hamilton Revelle (It, 14), Ruggoro Ruggeri (It, 17) and Asta Nielsen (Ger, 20) all starred in silent adaptations. The Shakespearean western, *Johnny Hamlet,* was produced in Italy in 1972 and starred Chip Corman.

TV portrayals have included those of Richard Chamberlain (70), Ian McKellen (72) and Derek Jacobi (80).

Olivier as *Hamlet* in his own Academy Award winning production of 1948. The film was the first British picture to be named best of the year by the American Oscar Academy and was the second of Olivier's four Shakespearean films. Others: *Henry V* (1945), *Richard III* (1955), and *Othello* (1965)

An updated Mike Hammer! Armand Assante as Mickey Spillane's rough tough private-eye in Richard T. Heffron's 1982 version of *I, the Jury*

Hammer, Mike [F]

Private-eye 'hero' of a series of violent and very sexy novels by Mickey Spillane. Devoid of any of the moral virtues of Chandler's Philip Marlowe, he is able to take care of himself in the toughest of situations and is motivated by the theory that the ends justify the means – no matter what! First appeared in print in 'I, The Jury' (1947). Deadliest foes: the commies! Screen career undistinguished except for Aldrich's *Kiss Me Deadly*, a near classic of its kind.

Biff Elliot	*I, The Jury* (Essex)	USA, 53
Ralph Meeker	*Kiss Me Deadly* (Aldrich)	USA, 55
Robert Bray	*My Gun Is Quick* (Victor)	USA, 57
Mickey Spillane	*The Girl Hunters* (Rowland)	USA, 63
Armand Assante	*I, The Jury* (Heffron)	USA, 82

Note: Richard T. Heffron's updated remake of *I, The Jury* had Hammer avenging the murder of an old Vietnam war buddy; on TV Darren McGavin appeared in *Mickey Spillane's Mike Hammer* (56–58), Kevin Dobson in *Mickey Spillane's Margin For Murder* (81), and Stacy Keach in Gary Nelson's *Murder Me, Murder You* (83), a TV movie which preceeded Keach's subsequent TV series *Mike Hammer*.

Hammett, Dashiell [R]

(1894–1961) Creator of Sam Spade in *The Maltese Falcon* and Nick Charles in *The Thin Man*, this American writer was responsible for the rise of the hard-boiled private-eye in contemporary fiction and was himself an operator for the famous Pinkerton Detective Agency before turning to writing. His only portrayals on screen have been in *Julia*, set during the 30s when he lived in semi alcoholic retirement with playwright Lillian Hellman, and *Hammett* which was not a biography but an ingenious *film noir* which placed the author in a wholly fictional situation and involved him with his ex-Pinkerton partner in a complex tale of murder and blackmail.

Jason Robards	*Julia* (Zinnemann)	USA, 77
Frederic Forrest	*Hammett* (Wenders)	USA, 83

Note: *Hammett* was the first American film of German director Wim Wenders; for his performance in *Julia* Jason Robards won an Oscar as best supporting actor of the year.

Handel, George Frederick [R]

(1685–1759) German composer of operas and oratorios; the subject of just one screen biography to date, a 1942 British production which focused on the years when Handel, deprived of Royal patronage and plagued by debtors, wrote his masterpiece, 'The Messiah' (1742).

Wilfrid Lawson	*The Great Mr Handel* (Walker)	GB, 42

Handy, W. C. 

(1873–1958) 'Father of the blues', the man whose compositions expressed the feelings of the Negro and gave America a national music. The son of a former slave turned preacher, he wrote down for the first time many of the Negro spirituals that had been sung over the years. Played on screen by Nat King Cole in the 1958 biography by Allen Reisner.

Nat King Cole	*St Louis Blues* (Reisner)	USA, 58

Note: Billy Preston featured as the boy Handy in the above film.

(Above) Oscar-winning Jason Robards as crime novelist Dashiell Hammett, portrayed in Fred Zinnemann's *Julia* (1977) after Hammett had retired from writing and was living with protegée Lillian Hellman; (right) Frederic Forrest as the famed athor in Wim Wender's intriguing American thriller *Hammett,* released in 1983

Hanff, Helene

R

A now celebrated New Yorker whose long-distance love affair with antique books, literary London and above all, the staff of a London bookshop, was turned first into a best-selling volume of letters and then into successful TV and stage plays. The most recent adaptation of her story was the screen version scripted by Hugh Whitemore and directed by David Jones. Anne Bancroft starred as Hanff and Anthony Hopkins as Frank Doel, the bookshop manager with whom she corresponded for over twenty years but was never destined to meet because of his death shortly before her first visit to London in 1969.

Anne Bancroft — *84 Charing Cross Road* (Jones) USA, 87

Note: The British TV adaptation (75) was also adapted by Whitemore. Anne Jackson featured as Hanff and Frank Finlay as Frank Doel.

Hannay, Richard

F

Heroic adventurer of novelist John Buchan; a young South African mining engineer who finds himself enmeshed in murder and espionage and being hunted across the Scottish countryside in the days preceding World War I. A three-time screen hero in *The Thirty Nine Steps* (first published in 1915), he has only once been portrayed in the correct period, i.e. in the most recent version starring Robert Powell.

Robert Donat — *The Thirty Nine Steps* (Hitchcock) GB, 35

Kenneth More — *The Thirty Nine Steps* (Thomas) GB, 59

John Buchan's Richard Hannay (Robert Powell) clinging to the clock hands of Big Ben in order to stop the detonation of a bomb. This 1978 film, directed by Don Sharp, was the third version of *The Thirty-Nine Steps* and the first to be set in the correct pre-World War I period of Buchan's novel

Robert Powell	*The Thirty Nine Steps* (Sharp)	GB, 78

Note: Hannay is also the central character of two other Buchan novels, 'Greenmantle' (1916) and 'The Three Hostages' (1924), the latter having been filmed (with Barry Foster as Hannay) as a British TV movie by Clive Donner in 1977. Robert Powell also featured in the 1988 TV series *Hannay*.

Hannibal R

(247–183 BC) Carthaginian general who spent his life fighting against the Romans and gained fame by invading his enemies after crossing the Alps with a team of elephants. Unfortunately, all the heroic effort proved futile for he lost anyway. Victor Mature provided a one-dimensional Hannibal in 1960; earlier, in the musical *Jupiter's Darling* (based on Robert Sherwood's 'The Road To Rome'), Howard Keel dallied too long with Esther Williams and missed his chance to invade.

Camillo Pilotto	*Scipione Africano* (Gallone)	It, 37
Howard Keel	*Jupiter's Darling* (Sidney)	USA, 55
Victor Mature	*Hannibal* (Ulmer/Bragaglia)	It/USA, 60

Harlow, Jean R

(1911–37) MGM's most glamorous sex symbol of the 30s, a 'blonde bombshell' who co-starred with many of the studio's leading actors, especially Gable, before meeting a tragically early death at the age of 26. Neither of the screen biographies produced during the 60s was satisfactory, although the opening scenes of studio activity in Gordon Douglas' film remain some of the most realistic ever put on celluloid.

Carol Lynley	*Harlow* (Segal) /	USA, 65
Carroll Baker	*Harlow* (Douglas)	USA, 65

Note: Carroll Baker's Rina Marlowe in *The Carpetbaggers* (64) was also fashioned after Harlow.

Paul Bern, Harlow's husband who committed suicide shortly after their marriage, was played by Hurd Hatfield in the Alex Segal film and by Peter Lawford in the Douglas movie.

Harper, Lew F

In many ways, Philip Marlowe updated to the 60s, better dressed and more tanned in the handsome personage of Paul Newman, but still retaining the snap, crackle and pop dialogue. Two screen cases to date, one involving a millionaire kidnap victim in Los Angeles, the other set in the steaming swamplands and colonial mansions of Louisiana. A hip Newman wins out both times. Harper is the creation of novelist Ross MacDonald who wrote over 20 thrillers about the private-eye. In the novels he is known as Lew Archer.

Paul Newman	*The Moving Target* (Smight)	USA, 66
Paul Newman	*The Drowning Pool* (Rosenberg)	USA, 75

Note: in 1975 Brian Keith starred in seven episodes of an American TV series; the pilot for the series was *The Underground Man* (Wendkos, 74) in which Archer (played by Peter Graves) becomes involved in the search for the kidnapped son of an old girl friend.

Harris, Andrew 'Crocker' F

Terence Rattigan's supreme creation, a lonely middle-aged schoolmaster whose life both as a teacher and husband has been a failure and whose ill-health causes his premature retirement from the school in which he has taught for twenty years. Michael Redgrave's performance in Anthony Asquith's film touched the heights and was rewarded with a best actor award at the Cannes Film Festival.

Michael Redgrave	*The Browning Version* (Asquith)	GB, 51

Harris, Frank R

(1856–1931) American author, journalist and editor (and according to those who knew him well a notorious liar when recounting his sexual escapades) whose autobiography 'My Life And Loves' was banned in America and Britain because of its many erotic passages. Delmer Daves' *Cowboy* (in which Jack Lemmon starred as Harris) derived from the 'On The Trail' section of his memoirs i.e. when a tenderfoot Harris, fed up with city life as a Chicago hotel clerk, decided to learn the cowboy life the hard way on a cattle drive to Mexico. Harris' varied sexual experiences (from childhood to old age) remain, as yet unfilmed.

Jack Lemmon	*Cowboy* (Daves)	USA, 58

One role, two films! (right) Carroll Baker, pictured with Peter Lawford as film executive Paul Bern, as MGM's glamorous 30s sex symbol *Harlow;* and (above) as the fictional 'Rina Marlowe', a character fashioned after Harlow in *The Carpetbaggers,* the film version of the best selling novel by Harold Robbins

Hart, Lorenz

R

(1895–1943) American lyricist noted for his bitter-sweet wit and originality of theme. The epitome of the undisciplined genius, he died of alcoholism at the early age of 48, after collaborating with Richard Rodgers on a long series of innovative Broadway musicals. Among their hit songs together: 'Lover', 'Isn't It Romantic', 'Manhattan', 'The Lady Is A Tramp'.

Mickey Rooney — *Words And Music* (Taurog) USA, 48

Hart, Moss

R

(1904–61) Among the most talented of American playwrights, many years in collaboration with George S. Kaufman ('Once In A Lifetime', 'You Can't Take It With You', 'The Man Who Came To Dinner') and later as a screenwriter in Hollywood (*Gentleman's Agreement, A Star Is Born*). His autobiography, 'Act One' (1959), described his early struggles and tentative beginnings on Broadway and was turned into a film by Dore Schary. George Hamilton featured as the young Hart, Jason Robards as the eccentric Kaufman.

George Hamilton — *Act One* (Schary) USA, 63

Havisham, Miss

F

Perhaps the most famous recluse in literature, an elderly man-hater who lives alone in a decaying house in Rochester, still dressed in the bridal gown she was wearing when jilted on her wedding eve. A key figure in Dickens' 'Great Expectations' (1860–61), she adopts the young Estella and uses her to wreak vengeance on the male sex. Definitive screen portrait: Martita Hunt in Lean's masterpiece of 1946.

Florence Reed — *Great Expectations* (Walker) USA, 34
Martita Hunt — *Great Expectations* (Lean) GB, 46
Margaret Leighton — *Great Expectations* (Hardy) GB, 75

Note: Grace Barton (USA, 16) and Marie Dinesen (Den, 22) both played Miss Havisham on the silent screen.

The other major characters in 'Great Expectations' i.e. Estella, the young Pip who narrates the novel, the convict Magwitch whom he encounters on the marshes, the blacksmith Joe Gargery and the lawyer Jaggers have been played by the following:

Estella (as a girl)
Ann Howard — *Great Expectations* (Walker) USA, 34
Jean Simmons — *Great Expectations* (Lean) GB, 46
Sarah Miles — *Great Expectations* (Hardy) GB, 75

(As a woman)
Jane Wyatt — *Great Expectations* (Walker) USA, 34
Valerie Hobson — *Great Expectations* (Lean) GB, 46
Sarah Miles — *Great Expectations* (Hardy) GB, 75

Silent: Louise Huff (USA, 16) and Olga D'Org (Den, 22)

Pip (as a boy)
George Breakston — *Great Expectations* (Walker) USA, 34
Anthony Wager — *Great Expectations* (Lean) GB, 46
Simon Gipps-Kent — *Great Expectations* (Hardy) GB, 75

(As a man)
Phillips Holmes — *Great Expectations* (Walker) USA, 34
John Mills — *Great Expectations* (Lean) GB, 46
Michael York — *Great Expectations* (Hardy) GB, 75

Silent: Jack Pickford (USA, 16); Martin Herzberg (as a boy) and Harry Komdrup (as a man) in Sandburg's Danish film of 1922.

Magwitch
Henry Hull — *Great Expectations* (Walker) USA, 34
Finlay Currie — *Great Expectations* (Lean) GB, 46
James Mason — *Great Expectations* (Hardy) GB, 75

Silent: Frank Losee (USA, 16) and Emil Helsengren (Den, 22).

Joe Gargery
Alan Hale — *Great Expectations* (Walker) USA, 34

(Above) Charles Dickens' famous recluse, Miss Havisham portrayed in David Lean's 1946 *Great Expectations* by Martita Hunt with Jean Simmons as Estella and Anthony Wager as the young Pip; (right) Miss Havisham played by Margaret Leighton in the 1975 version

Bernard Miles	*Great Expectations*	(Lean)	GB, 46
Joss Ackland	*Great Expectations*	(Hardy)	GB, 75

Silent: W. W. Black (USA, 16) and Gerhard Jessen (Den, 22).

Jaggers

Francis L. Sullivan	*Great Expectations*	(Walker)	USA, 34
Francis L. Sullivan	*Great Expectations*	(Lean)	GB, 46
Anthony Quayle	*Great Expectations*	(Hardy)	GB, 75

Silent: Herbert Prior (USA, 16) and Egill Rostrup (Den, 22).

Note: Tim Burstall's six hour TV film *Great Expectations: The Untold Story* (87) related the adventures of Magwitch 'down under' and how he made a fortune and became the young Pip's benefactor.

Hayes, Billy R

A young American student whose attempt to smuggle two kilos of hashish out of Turkey in 1970 resulted in a hideous four-year sentence in Istanbul's Sagamilcar prison. His personal degradation, struggle for survival under torture and spectacular escape were recounted in the award-winning *Midnight Express*.

Brad Davis	*Midnight Express*	(Parker)	GB, 78

Hearst, William Randolph 

(1863–1951) American press baron whose career formed the basis of Orson Welles' classic *Citizen Kane* (even though Welles denied it for many years) and who threatened to take legal action against RKO if they released the film. He also offered to reimburse the studio the total production cost — estimated at 842,000 dollars – if they would destroy the negative. Luckily they refused.

Orson Welles	*Citizen Kane*	(Welles)	USA, 41

Note: The 1985 TV Movie *The Hearst And Davies Affair* (directed by David Lowell Rich) concentrated on the publishing magnate's relationship with Marion Davies, the former Ziegfeld girl he turned into a star. Robert Mitchum featured as Hearst, Virginia Madsen as Davies. In *Citizen Kane* Davies was recast as an aspiring singer (renamed Susan Alexander) and played by Dorothy Comingore.

Heathcliff 

Passionate, almost demonic lover of Catherine Earnshaw in Emily Brontë's brooding romance 'Wuthering Heights'. A tragic figure, drawn on an heroic scale, he has been played four times on the sound screen, although only Olivier has truly captured his wildness, mystery and self-destructive power. The novel, set on the lonely Yorkshire moors, was first published in 1847.

Laurence Olivier	*Wuthering Heights*	(Wyler)	USA, 39
Jorge Mistral	*Wuthering Heights*	(Bunuel)	Mex, 53
Timothy Dalton	*Wuthering Heights*	(Fuest)	GB, 71
Lucas Belvaux	*Wuthering Heights*	(Rivette)	Fra, 85

Note: Jacques Rivette's recent film version of the novel was updated to the French countryside of the 30s with Heathcliff renamed Roch. Milton Rosmer starred as Heathcliff in a 1920 silent film, directed in England by A. V. Bramble; Cathy has been played by Anne Trevor (20), Merle Oberon (39), Eva Irasema Dilian (53), Anna Calder-Marshall (71) and Fabienne Babe (85).

Helen of Troy 

According to Greek legend, the most beautiful woman of her time, possessor of a face that launched a thousand ships and caused the Trojan War. Physically well-endowed young actresses have revelled in the role; a more mature but no less attractive Irene Papas featured in Cacoyannis' version of the play by Euripides.

Hedy Lamarr	*The Face That Launched A Thousand Ships*	(Allegret)	It, 54
Rossana Podesta	*Helen Of Troy*	(Wise)	USA, 55
Dani Crayne	*The Story Of Mankind*	(Allen)	USA, 57
Hedy Vessel	*The Trojan Horse*	(Ferroni)	Fra/It, 61
Elizabeth Taylor	*Doctor Faustus*	(Burton/Coghill)	GB/It, 67
Irene Papas	*The Trojan Women*	(Cacoyannis)	USA, 71

Note: Edy Darclea (Ger, 23) and Maria Corda in *The Private Life Of Helen Of Troy* (USA, 27) both appeared as Helen on the silent screen.

Laurence Olivier as Heathcliff and Merle Oberon as the doomed Cathy in William Wyler's 1939 version of Emily Brontë's *Wuthering Heights.* The film was notable for Gregg Toland's atmospheric black-and-white photography and for establishing Olivier as a major Hollywood star

Hellman, Lillian [R]

(1905–84) American dramatist noted for her plays of psychological conflict, many of which have been filmed, e.g. *The Children's Hour* (twice by Wyler), *The Little Foxes, Watch On The Rhine, Toys In The Attic.* Jane Fonda portrayed her on screen at the time of her life when she was endeavouring to write her first Broadway play.

Jane Fonda	*Julia* (Zinnemann)	USA, 77

Helm, Matt 

America's answer to James Bond, a happy-go-lucky cheesecake photographer who enjoys a double life as a secret service agent for ICE (Organization For Intelligence And Counter Espionage). Curves, rather than patriotism, inevitably motivate his actions. Features in over 15 novels by Donald Hamilton and in four glossy movies.

Dean Martin	*The Silencers* (Karlson)	USA, 66
Dean Martin	*Murderer's Row* (Levin)	USA, 66
Dean Martin	*The Ambushers* (Levin)	USA, 67
Dean Martin	*The Wrecking Crew* (Karlson)	USA, 69

Hemingway, Ernest 

(1899–1961) Celebrated American novelist and short story writer whose terse, economical style influenced a generation of writers across the world. Many novels and stories filmed (*A Farewell To Arms, For Whom The Bell Tolls, The Killers*) but no major film biography until 1988 when two TV series devoted themselves to his life–one based on the

Jane Fonda in one of her most striking roles—as playwright Lillian Hellman whose early career, love affair with playwright Dashiell Hammett and long association with her childhood friend *Julia* were charted by director Fred Zinnemann in his award winning film of 1977. The picture earned Fonda an Oscar nomination as best actress although it was the supporting players—Jason Robards as Hammett and Vanessa Redgrave as Julia—who emerged the Oscar winners

biography by Carlos Baker and starring Stacy Keach, the other featuring Victor Garber.

Stacy Keach	*Hemingway* (Sinkel)	TVM/W.Ger/It, 88
Victor Garber	*Hem – The Legendary Life Of Ernest Hemingway*	TVM/Yug/It, 88

Note: The only vague large screen rendering of Hemingway's life was by George C. Scott in *Islands In The Stream* (USA, 77), based on Hemingway's posthumous novel about an expatriate sculptor living in the Bahamas during World War II and whose life is distracted by the visits of his wife and sons.

Henry II

R

(1138–89) English king, responsible during his reign for many legal reforms, an achievement overlooked in films which have concentrated more on his colourful – and violent – clashes with the Archbishop of Canterbury (*Becket*) and his fiery wife, Eleanor of Aquitaine (*The Lion In Winter*). Peter O'Toole's portrait of Henry as a petulant, frightened neurotic, earned him two Oscar nominations in the 60s, but he lost on both occasions.

Alexander Gauge	*Murder In The Cathedral* (Hoellering)	GB, 51
Peter O'Toole	*Becket* (Glenville)	GB, 64
Peter O'Toole	*The Lion in Winter* (Harvey)	GB, 68

Note: Pamela Brown in *Becket* and Katharine Hepburn in *The Lion In Winter* have both featured as Eleanor Of Aquitaine, the latter winning an Academy Award as best actress of 1968.

Henry V

R

(1387–1422) Warrior king of England who gained a famous victory at Agincourt in 1415 and became Regent Of France. A stirring, heroic figure in Laurence Olivier's version of Shakespeare's 'Henry V'; mostly a subsidiary character in other movies. Olivier's performance earned him an Oscar nomination and was the first of his four Shakespearean screen roles.

Laurence Olivier	*Henry V* (Olivier)	GB, 45
Dan O'Herlihy	*The Black Shield Of Falworth* (Mate)	USA, 54
Keith Baxter	*Chimes At Midnight* (Welles)	Spa/Swi, 66

Note: Both O'Herlihy and Baxter appeared as Henry before he became king – as the young prince Hal.

On TV Robert Hardy (60), Douglas Rain (66) and David Gwillim (79) have all appeared in adaptations of 'Henry V'.

Henry VIII

R

(1491–1547) Sixteenth century British monarch who has coughed, spluttered and died on screen more times than any other British king. Portrayed in Oscar-winning style by Charles Laughton in 1933 and by such distinguished actors as Robert Shaw, Richard Burton and Keith Michell, each of whom elaborated on different aspects of Henry's ebullient personality. The six wives have appeared together in only one film (in 1972); Charles Laughton worked his way through five in *The Private Life Of Henry VIII.*

Charles Laughton	*The Private Life Of Henry VIII* (Korda)	GB, 33
Frank Cellier	*Tudor Rose* (Stevenson)	GB, 36
Montagu Love	*The Prince And The Pauper* (Keighley)	USA, 37
Lyn Harding	*The Pearls Of The Crown* (Guitry-Jaque)	Fra, 37
Alexandre Rignault	*François Ist* (Christian-Jaque)	Fra, 37
Iouri Toloubieiev	*The Prince And The Pauper* (Garine/Lokchina)	USSR, 43
James Robertson Justice	*The Sword And The Rose* (Annakin)	GB, 53
Charles Laughton	*Young Bess* (Sidney)	USA, 53
Paul Rogers	*The Prince And The Pauper* (Chaffey)	GB, 62
Robert Shaw	*A Man For All Seasons* (Zinnemann)	GB, 66
Richard Burton	*Anne Of The Thousand Days* (Jarrott)	GB, 69
Sidney James	*Carry On Henry* (Thomas)	GB, 71
Keith Michell	*Henry VIII And His Six Wives* (Hussein)	GB, 72
Charlton Heston	*The Prince And The Pauper* (Fleischer)	GB, 77

Note: Emil Jannings played Henry on the silent screen in Lubitsch's *Anna Boleyn* (Ger, 20). Other actors who appeared as the monarch include Arthur Bourchier in *Henry VIII* (GB, 11), Tefft Johnson in *Cardinal Wolsey* (USA, 12), Robert Broderick in *The Prince And The Pauper* (USA, 15) and Lyn Harding in *When Knighthood Was In Flower* (USA, 22).

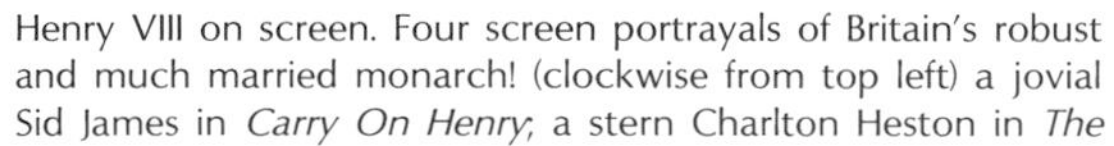

Henry VIII on screen. Four screen portrayals of Britain's robust and much married monarch! (clockwise from top left) a jovial Sid James in *Carry On Henry*; a stern Charlton Heston in *The Prince And The Pauper*; James Robertson Justice in *The Sword And The Rose*; and Richard Burton, courting Anne Boleyn (Genevieve Bujold) in *Anne Of The Thousand Days*

Herbert, Victor

R

(1859–1924) Irish-American composer of some thirty operettas ('Naughty Marietta', 'Sweethearts', etc.) who dominated the Broadway musical stage during the first years of the twentieth century. His romantic and stirring melodies, which included 'March Of The Toys' and 'Ah, Sweet Mystery Of Life', helped maintain the tradition of Viennese operettas, a tradition carried on after his death by Sigmund Romberg. Andrew Stone's 1939 bio-pic centred on Herbert's life in New York at the turn of the century.

Walter Connolly	*The Great Victor Herbert* (Stone) USA, 39
Paul Maxey	*Till The Clouds Roll By* (Whorf) USA, 46

Herod Antipas

R

(Died after AD 40) The son of Herod the Great; a man who enjoyed an incestuous marriage to Herodias, leered over Salome, executed the prophet John the Baptist and sent Jesus to Pontius Pilate for trial. Charles Laughton, Jose Ferrer and Christopher Plummer are among the actors who have indulged in his debauchery on screen.

Harry Baur	*Golgotha* (Duvivier) Fra, 35
Charles Laughton	*Salome* (Dieterle) USA, 53
Herbert Lom	*The Big Fisherman* (Borzage) USA, 59
Frank Thring	*King Of Kings* (Ray) USA, 61
Francesco Leonetti	*The Gospel According To St Matthew* (Pasolini) Fra/It, 64
Jose Ferrer	*The Greatest Story Ever Told* (Stevens) USA, 65
Carlos Casaravilla	*The Redeemer* (Breen) USA/Spa, 65
Christopher Plummer	*Jesus Of Nazareth* (Zeffirelli) GB, 77
	Jesus (Sykes/Krish) USA, 79
Jonathan Pryce	*The Day Christ Died* (Manulis) TVM,USA, 80
Tomas Milian	*Salome* (d'Anna) Fra/It, 86
Stratford Johns	*Salome* (Russell) GB, 88

Note: G. Raymond Nye (USA, 18), Mitchell Lewis (USA, 22) and Vincent Coleman (USA, 23) appeared as Antipas in three silent versions of *Salome*.

Herodias has been played by Judith Anderson in *Salome* (53), Martha Hyer in *The Big Fisherman* (59), Rita Gam in *King Of Kings* (61), Franca Cupane in *The Gospel According to St Matthew* (64), Marian Seldes in *The Greatest Story Ever Told* (65), Valentina Cortese in *Jesus Of Nazareth* (77), Pamela Salem in *Salome* (86) and Glenda Jackson in *Salome* (88).

Herod The Great

R

(73–45 BC) The King of Judea who ordered the slaughter of the male children of Bethlehem in an attempt to rid himself of the threat of the child Jesus, born in the last year of his reign. Usually only a minor figure in films about Christ, although Claude Rains produced a chilling portrait of near madness in George Stevens' *The Greatest Story Ever Told.*

Edmund Purdom	*Herod The Great* (Genoino) It/Fra, 59
Gregoire Aslan	*King Of Kings* (Ray) USA, 61
Amerigo Bevilacqua	*The Gospel According To St Matthew* (Pasolini) It/Fra, 64
Claude Rains	*The Greatest Story Ever Told* (Stevens) USA, 65
Peter Ustinov	*Jesus Of Nazareth* (Zeffirelli) GB, 77

Note: *Jesus Of Nazareth* was made for television.

Herriot, James

Self-effacing young vet whose amusing, often tender experiences with animals in Yorkshire in the days preceding World War II have been the subject of several best-selling books and a popular TV series starring Christopher Timothy. Two cinema versions of his exploits were filmed prior to the TV series.

Simon Ward	*All Creatures Great And Small* (Whatham) GB, 74
John Alderton	*It Shouldn't Happen To A Vet* (Till) GB, 76

Note: Siegfried Farnon, Herriot's bluff partner, was played by Anthony Hopkins in *All Creatures Great And Small,* and by Colin Blakely in *It Shouldn't Happen To A Vet.*

Heydrich, Reinhard [R]

(1904–42) The man who created a reign of terror as Nazi 'Protector' of occupied Czechoslovakia in World War II. Second only to Himmler in his total inhumanity, Heydrich was also in charge of the extermination squads that murdered thousands of Jews in the early years of the conflict. His tyrannical career was brought to an abrupt close when he was assassinated by a team of Czech agents in 1942, an event often celebrated on screen, notably in Lang's *Hangmen Also Die*.

Hans V. Twardowski	*Hangmen Also Die* (Fritz Lang) USA, 43
John Carradine	*Hitler's Madman* (Sirk) USA, 43
Anton Diffring	*Operation Daybreak* (Gilbert) GB, 76
David Warner	*Hitler's SS: Portrait In Evil* (Goddard) GB, 85
Dietrich Mattausch	*The Wannsee Conference* (Schirk) W.Ger, 87

Note: David Warner also portrayed Heydrich in Marvin Chomsky's nine-part TV mini series *Holocaust* (78); *the Wannsee Conference* was first released on German and Austrian TV in 1984 and told the true story of how a conclave of 15 leading Nazis decided to proceed with and implement the horrific 'Final Solution of the Jewish Question'.

Hickok, Wild Bill [R]

(1837–76) A legendary hero of the American West but, in reality, a gun-happy gambler who served as a scout in the Civil War, helped clean up Abilene as a town marshal and frequented the saloons

Violence in the old West. Dustin Hoffman (left) and Jeff Corey as a realistic Wild Bill Hickok, fighting off intruders in Arthur Penn's 1970 western *Little Big Man*

and whorehouses of Deadwood. Enjoyed a brief acquaintance with Calamity Jane before having his brains blown out by two-bit gambler Jack McCall. The screen has generally followed the legend in portraying him romantically, e.g. Gary Cooper in *The Plainsman,* although two recent performances by Jeff Corey and Charles Bronson have come closer to the truth. Real name: James Butler.

Gary Cooper	*The Plainsman* (DeMille) USA, 37
George Houston	*Frontier Scout* (Newfield) USA, 38
Roy Rogers	*Young Bill Hickok* (Kane) USA, 40
Richard Dix	*Badlands Of Dakota* (Green) USA, 41
Bruce Cabot	*Wild Bill Hickok Rides* (Enright) USA, 42
Reed Hadley	*Dallas* (Heisler) USA, 50
Robert 'Bob' Anderson	*The Lawless Breed* (Walsh) USA, 53
Ewing Brown	*Son Of The Renegade* (Brown) USA, 53
Douglas Kennedy	*Jack McCall, Desperado* (Salkow) USA, 53
Forrest Tucker	*Pony Express* (Hopper) USA, 53
Howard Keel	*Calamity Jane* (Butler) USA, 53
Tom Brown	*I Killed Wild Bill Hickok* (Talmadge) USA, 56
Robert Culp	*The Raiders* (Daugherty) USA, 64
Adrian Hoven	*Seven Hours Of Gunfire* (Marchent) Spa/It/W./Ger 64
Paul Shannon	*The Outlaws Is Coming* (Maurer) USA, 65
Robert Dix	*Deadwood '76* (Landis) USA, 65
Don Murray	*The Plainsman* (Rich) USA, 66
Jeff Corey	*Little Big Man* (Penn) USA, 70
Charles Bronson	*The White Buffalo* (Lee Thompson) USA, 77
Richard Farnsworth	*Legend Of The Lone Ranger* (Fraker) USA, 81

Note: On the silent screen William S. Hart in *Wild Bill Hickok* (23), John Padjan in *The Iron Horse* (24) and J. Farrell MacDonald in *The Last Frontier* (26) all featured as Hickok; Ben Murphy in *That Was The West That Was* (74) and Frederic Forrest in *Calamity Jane* (84) have played him on TV.

Hitler, Adolf [R]

(1889–1945) Nazi dictator and Führer of the Third Reich who rose to prominence in the 1930s and brought about the Second World War with his invasion of Poland in 1939. Apart from Stuart Heisler's 1962 biography with Richard Basehart, the most detailed screen portrayals of Hitler have been centred on his last few days in the Berlin bunker where he eventually committed suicide with his mistress Eva Braun, i.e. those of Albin Skoda in Pabst's *Ten Days To Die* and Alec Guinness in *Hitler: The Last Ten Days.*

Charles Chaplin	*The Great Dictator* (Chaplin) USA, 40
Bobby Watson	*The Devil With Hitler* (Douglas) USA, 42
Bobby Watson	*Hitler–Dead Or Alive* (Grinde) USA, 43
Bobby Watson	*The Nazty Nuisance* (Tryon) USA, 43
Ludwig Donath	*The Strange Death Of Adolf Hitler* (Hogan) USA, 43
Bobby Watson	*The Hitler Gang* (Farrow) USA, 44
Bobby Watson	*The Miracle Of Morgan's Creek* (Sturges) USA, 44
V. Savelyov	*The Fall Of Berlin* (Chiaureli) USSR, 49
M. Astangov	*The Battle Of Stalingrad* (Petrov) USSR, 50
Luther Adler	*The Desert Fox* (Hathaway) USA, 51
Luther Adler	*The Magic Face* (Tuttle) USA, 51
Albin Skoda	*Ten Days To Die* (Pabst) Aus, 55
Bobby Watson	*The Story Of Mankind* (Allen) USA, 57
Kenneth Griffith	*The Two-Headed Spy* (de Toth) GB, 58
Bobby Watson	*On The Double* (Shavelson) USA, 61
Richard Basehart	*Hitler* (Heisler) USA, 62
Billy Frick	*Is Paris Burning?* (Clemont) USA/Fra, 66
Rolf Stiefel	*Battle Of Britain* (Ozerov) USSR/Pol/Yug/E.Ger/It, 69
Fritz Diez	*The Great Battle* (Ozerov) GB, 69

Charles Chaplin (as Adenoid Hynkel of Tomania) spoofs Hitler in his first talkie—made some 13 years after the introduction of sound!

Sidney Miller	*Which Way To The Front?* (Lewis) USA, 70
Alec Guinness	*Hitler: The Last Ten Days* (De Concini) GB/It, 73
Gunnar Moller	*Day Of Betrayal* (Vavra) Czech, 74
Peter Sellers	*Soft Beds, Hard Battles* (Roy Boulting) GB, 74
Helmut Qualtinger	*Ice-Age* (Zadek) Ger/Nor, 75
Kurt Raab	*Adolf And Marlene* (Lommel) Ger, 77
Doug McGrath	*The Return Of Captain Invincible* (Mora) Austral, 82
Roy Goldman	*To Be Or Not To Be* (Brooks) USA, 83
Colin Jeavons	*Hitler's SS: Portrait In Evil* (Goddard) GB, 85

Note: Charles Chaplin gave a satirical portrayal of Hitler in his first sound film, *The Great Dictator*. The Führer was renamed Adenoid Hynkel.

On TV the following actors have all appeared as Hitler: Anthony Hopkins in *The Bunker* (81), Derek Jacobi in *Inside The Third Reich* (82), Gunter Meisner in *The Winds Of War* (83), Gunnar Moeller in *Mussolini: The Untold Story* (85) and Kurt Raab in *Mussolini And I* (85).

Hoffa, James Riddle [R]

(1913–?) Aggressive and ruthless labour leader who became the boss of the Teamsters' Union and turned it into the most powerful union in the States. Subsequently accused of corruption and involvement with underground figures he was investigated by Robert Kennedy and sent to jail. In July 1975 he was kidnapped outside a restaurant in a suburb of Detroit and never seen again. Kennedy's legal battles with Hoffa in the early 60s formed the basis of Mike Newell's TV movie *Blood Feud*; Norman Jewison's epic *F.I.S.T.* was closely modelled on the political career of Hoffa, renaming him Johnny Kovak.

Sylvester Stallone (as Johnny Kovak)	*F.I.S.T.* (Jewison) USA, 78
Robert Blake	*Blood Feud* (Newell) TVM, USA, 83

Hogan, Ben [R]

(1912–) Ace American golfer who came back to win the American Open after being seriously injured in a car crash in 1949. The accident and the events

Diana Ross in her film debut, as Billie Holiday the legendary jazz singer whose life was ruined by drug addiction. A scene from the 1972 biography, *Lady Sings the Blues*

Trade union boss Jimmy Hoffa was the model for Sylvester Stallone's Johnny Kovak in the 1978 Norman Jewison film *F.I.S.T.* Stallone played the leader of the Federation of Interstate Truckers, a man corrupted by power and eventually assassinated

that followed were depicted in *Follow The Sun,* the only major feature film to look closely at the career of a top-ranking golf star.

Glenn Ford — *Follow The Sun* (Lanfield) USA, 51

Holiday, Billie [R]

(1915–59) A streetwalker at 13 and a victim of drugs and alcohol (a combination that finally killed her), this black singer remains one of the greatest exponents of jazz singing in the history of popular music. Influenced early in her career by Bessie Smith and Louis Armstrong, she once described her singing as 'trying to make my voice behave like an instrument in the hands of a jazz musician'. Her tragic life was portrayed in detail in *Lady Sings The Blues.*

Diana Ross — *Lady Sings The Blues* (Furie) USA, 72

Hollander, Xaviera [R]

Danish call-girl who took her physical charms and sharp business acumen to the United States where she laid her way to the top and became the madam of one of the most famous bordellos in New York. Several screen portraits in the 70s, although her own performance as a promiscuous movie star in *My Pleasure Is My Business* rated higher than any of the biographical interpretations.

Samantha McClearn — *The Life And Times Of Xaviera Hollander* (Spangler) USA, 74

Lynn Redgrave — *The Happy Hooker* (Sgarro) USA, 75

Joey Heatherton — *The Happy Hooker Goes To Washington* (Levey) USA, 77

The alcoholic dentist Doc Holliday, one of the legendary heroes of the famous gun battle at the OK Corral. (Above) Stacey Keach with Faye Dunaway in Frank Perry's *Doc*; (left) Jason Robards as Holliday in John Sturges' *Hour Of The Gun*; (below) Kirk Douglas (Holliday) and Burt Lancaster (Earp) in *Gunfight At The OK Corral*

Holliday, Doc R

(1849–85) Professional poker player and dentist friend of Wyatt Earp. A familiar figure in Tombstone in the early 1880s, he joined the Earps in their triumphant gunfight at the O.K. Corral but died of consumption in Colorado four years later. A fair-haired, very small man, usually seen in an overcoat, he was totally unlike any of the actors who have portrayed him on the screen. Jason Robards in John Sturges' historically accurate *Hour Of The Gun* has given the most in-depth performance to date.

Actor	Film	Director	Country, year
Cesar Romero	*Frontier Marshal*	(Dwan)	USA, 39
Kent Taylor	*Tombstone, The Town Too Tough To Die*	(McGann)	USA, 42
Walter Huston	*The Outlaw*	(Hughes)	USA, 43
Victor Mature	*My Darling Clementine*	(Ford)	USA, 46
James Griffith	*Masterson Of Kansas*	(Castle)	USA, 54
Kirk Douglas	*Gunfight At The O K Corral*	(Sturges)	USA, 57
Arthur Kennedy	*Cheyenne Autumn*	(Ford)	USA, 64
Jason Robards	*Hour Of The Gun*	(Sturges)	USA, 67
Stacy Keach	*Doc*	(Perry)	USA, 71

Note: Harry Carey (as Ed Brant) featured as the Doc Holliday character in Edward L. Cahn's *Law And Order* (32); Jeffrey De Munn starred in the 1983 TV film *I Married Wyatt Earp*.

Holly, Buddy 

(1936–59) 'Tex-Mex'-style pop singer, enormously popular in the late 50s just prior to his death in a plane crash. His style has been described as a bridge between the harsh rock n' roll of the early innovators and the teen-beat sound of such singers as Frankie Avalon and Ricky Nelson. He enjoyed his first hit, 'Peggy Sue' in 1957 and was the subject of an acclaimed 1978 biography starring Gary Busey who won a best actor Oscar nomination for his performance.

Actor	Film	Director	Country, year
Gary Busey	*The Buddy Holly Story*	(Rash)	USA, 78

Holmes, Sherlock 

The most brilliant detective in English fiction, created in 1887 by Conan Doyle in his novel 'A Study In Scarlet'. Essential requirements when at work on a case: a pipe, a magnifying glass and a deerstalker. Essential requirements for relaxation at 221B Baker Street: tobacco, a violin and a seven-per-cent solution of cocaine. No one film actor has yet captured his lonely, introverted personality or the complexities of his brilliant mind. Devotees of pre-war cinema hold Arthur Wontner's performances in high regard, but for most it is Basil Rathbone who most closely fits the bill with his gaunt frame, lack of humour and abrupt manner.

Gary Busey as the legendary young musician Buddy Holly, a grass roots Texan who became a pioneer in rock and roll. A scene from the 1978 bio-pic *The Buddy Holly Story*

Actor	Film	Director	Country, year
Clive Brook	*The Return Of Sherlock Holmes*	(Dean/Brook)	USA, 29
Arthur Wontner	*The Sleeping Cardinal*	(Hiscott)	GB, 31
Raymond Massey	*The Speckled Band*	(Raymond)	GB, 31
Robert Rendel	*The Hound Of The Baskervilles*	(Gundrey)	GB, 32
Arthur Wontner	*The Missing Rembrandt*	(Hiscott)	GB, 32
Arthur Wontner	*The Sign Of Four*	(Cutts)	GB, 32
Clive Brook	*Sherlock Holmes*	(Howard)	USA, 32

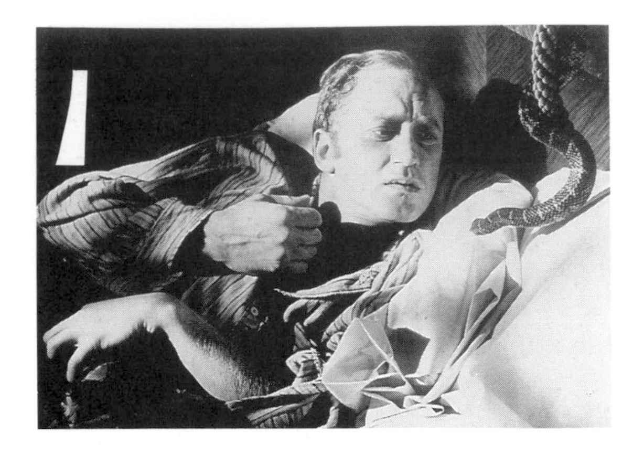

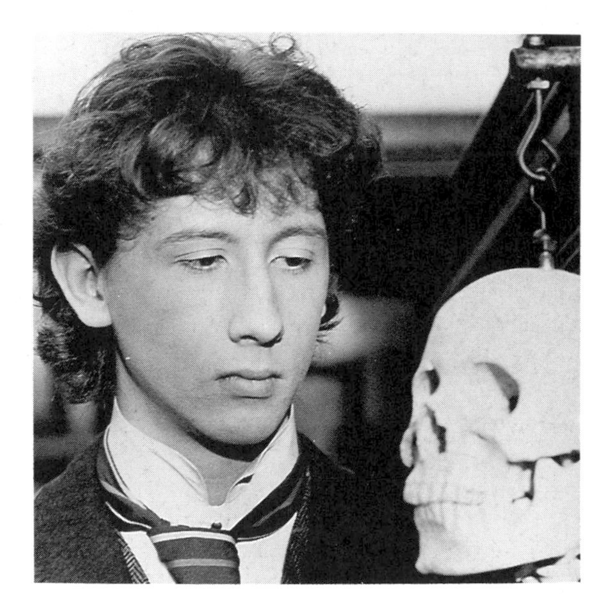

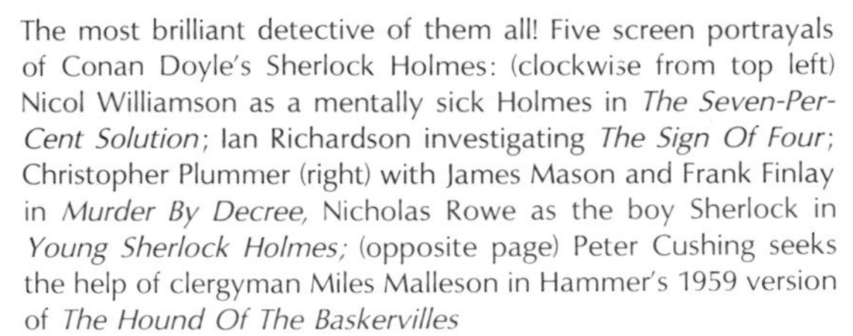

The most brilliant detective of them all! Five screen portrayals of Conan Doyle's Sherlock Holmes: (clockwise from top left) Nicol Williamson as a mentally sick Holmes in *The Seven-Per-Cent Solution*; Ian Richardson investigating *The Sign Of Four*; Christopher Plummer (right) with James Mason and Frank Finlay in *Murder By Decree,* Nicholas Rowe as the boy Sherlock in *Young Sherlock Holmes;* (opposite page) Peter Cushing seeks the help of clergyman Miles Malleson in Hammer's 1959 version of *The Hound Of The Baskervilles*

Martin Fric	*Lelicek In The Service Of Sherlock Holmes* (Lamač) Czech, 32
Reginald Owen	*A Study In Scarlet* (Marin) USA, 33
Arthur Wontner	*The Triumph Of Sherlock Holmes* (Hiscott) GB, 35
Bruno Guttner	*Der Hund Von Baskerville* (Lamač) Ger, 37
Hermann Speelmans	*Sherlock Holmes: The Gray Lady* (Engels) Ger, 37
Arthur Wontner	*Silver Blaze* (Bentley) GB, 37
Hans Albers	*The Man Who Was Sherlock Holmes* (Hart) Ger, 37
Basil Rathbone	*The Hound Of The Baskervilles* (Lanfield) USA, 39
Basil Rathbone	*The Adventures Of Sherlock Holmes* (Werker) USA, 39
Basil Rathbone	*Sherlock Holmes And The Voice Of Terror* (Rawlins) USA, 42
Basil Rathbone	*Sherlock Holmes And The Secret Weapon* (Neill) USA, 42
Basil Rathbone	*Sherlock Holmes In Washington* (Neill) USA 43
Basil Rathbone	*Sherlock Holmes Faces Death* (Neill) USA, 43
Basil Rathbone	*Spider Woman* (Neil) USA, 44
Basil Rathbone	*The Scarlet Claw* (Neil) USA, 44
Basil Rathbone	*The Pearl Of Death* (Neill) USA, 44
Basil Rathbone	*The House Of Fear* (Neill) USA, 45
Basil Rathbone	*The Woman In Green* (Neill) USA, 45
Basil Rathbone	*Pursuit To Algiers* (Neill) USA, 45
Basil Rathbone	*Terror By Night* (Neill) USA, 46
Basil Rathbone	*Dressed To Kill* (Neill) USA, 46
John Longden	*The Man With The Twisted Lip* (Grey) GB, 51
Peter Cushing	*The Hound Of The Baskervilles* (Fisher) GB, 59
Christopher Lee	*Sherlock Holmes And The Deadly Necklace* (Fisher) W.Ger, 62
John Neville	*A Study In Terror* (Hill) GB, 65
Robert Stephens	*The Private Life Of Sherlock Holmes* (Billy Wilder) GB, 70
Radovan Lukavsky	*Sherlock Holmes' Desire* (Skalsky) Czech, 71
Douglas Wilmer	*The Adventures Of Sherlock Holmes' Smarter Brother* (Gene Wilder) GB, 70
Nicol Williamson	*The Seven-Per-Cent Solution* (Ross) USA, 76
Peter Cook	*The Hound Of The Baskervilles* (Morrissey) GB, 78
Christopher Plummer	*Murder By Decree* (Clark) GB, 79
Ian Richardson	*The Sign Of Four* (Davis) GB, 83
Ian Richardson	*The Hound Of The Baskervilles* (Hickox) GB, 83
Nicholas Rowe	*Young Sherlock Holmes* (Levinson) USA, 85

Note: Peter O'Toole voiced Holmes in a series of Australian 50 minute animated films in the early 80s – *Sherlock Holmes And The Baskerville Curse, The Sign Of Four, A Study In Scarlet, A Valley Of Fear* (each 81); Barrie Ingham voiced Basil Of Baker Street in Disney's *The Great Mouse Detective* (86), a cartoon feature loosely derived from the Holmes stories.

More than 60 silent films featured Sherlock Holmes. Among the leading portrayals: Alwin Neuss in *The Hound Of The Baskervilles* (Ger, 15), H.A. Sainsbury in *The Valley Of Fear* (GB, 16), John Barrymore in *Sherlock Holmes* (USA, 22), Eille Norwood in three series of short films for Stoll (GB, 22–4) and Carlyle Blackwell in Richard Oswald's *Der Hund Von Baskerville* (Ger, 29).

Stewart Granger appeared as Holmes in the TV film *The Hound Of The Baskervilles* (72) as did Roger Moore in *Sherlock Holmes In New York* (77), Frank Langella in *Sherlock Holmes* (81) and Peter Cushing in *The Masks Of Death* (84). Alan Wheatley (51), Douglas Wilmer (65), Peter Cushing (68) and, more recently, Jeremy Brett (84–8) all starred in TV series adapted from Doyle's short stories. Michael Caine featured in the 1988 TV spoof *Sherlock and Me*.

Holmes, Mycroft F

The elder brother of Sherlock, by all accounts no less brilliant, but something of a mysterious figure in that he appears only fleetingly in Conan Doyle's stories. Of more interest in recent years to film-makers, who have begun to dig deeper into his private life at the Diogenese Club and with Her Majesty's government in Whitehall, Christopher Lee, who played Mycroft in Billy Wilder's *The Private Life Of Sherlock Holmes,* is the only actor to have played both Sherlock and Mycroft on the screen.

Robert Morley	*A Study In Terror* (Hill)	GB, 65
Christopher Lee	*The Private Life Of Sherlock Holmes* (Wilder)	GB, 70
Charles Gray	*The Seven-Per-Cent Solution* (Ross)	GB, 76

Note: Charles Gray repeated his performance as Mycroft in the 1985 TV episode of *The Greek Interpreter;* Ronald Adam played the role in the 1968 version of the same story (featuring Peter Cushing) and Derek Francis essayed the part in *The Bruce Partington Plans* (65) starring Douglas Wilmer as Holmes.

Holmes, Oliver Wendell R

(1809–94) One of the great judicial figures in American history, a High Court Judge who became known as the 'great dissenter' because of his frequent disagreements with other judges over the rights and problems of the ordinary people. Louis Calhern earned a best actor Oscar nomination for his portrayal in John Sturges' little known screen biography of 1950.

Louis Calhern	*The Magnificent Yankee* (Sturges)	USA, 50

Hoover, J. Edgar R

(1895–1972) Until recently, a shadowy behind-the-scenes character on screen, just as he was in real life during his 48-year term as Director of the FBI. Larry Cohen's film biography, which covered his life in office from the gang-busting days of the 30s to the behind-closed-doors activities of the 60s, changed all that, and presented Hoover as a repressed figure who remained blind to his own abuse of power. Treat Williams featured as the FBI man in the 1987 TV biography *J. Edgar Hoover.*

Erwin Fuller	*Lepke* (Golan)	USA, 75
Broderick Crawford	*The Private Files Of J. Edgar Hoover* (Cohen)	USA, 78
Sheldon Leonard	*The Brink's Job* (Friedkin)	USA, 78
Treat Williams	*J. Edgar Hoover* (Collins)	TVM/USA, 87

Note: James Wainwright played the young Hoover in Cohen's film; the FBI chief appeared briefly as himself in Mervyn LeRoy's *The FBI Story* (59). Other TV performances have been by Harris Yulin in *The FBI versus Alvin Karpis, Public Enemy Number One* (74), Dolph Sweet in *King* (78), Ernest Borgnine in *Blood Feud* (83), Vincent Gardenia in *Kennedy* (83) and Ned Beatty in *Robert Kennedy And His Times* (85).

Horn, Tom R

(1861–1903) A western figure usually overlooked by film-makers; a legendary bounty hunter who shot and killed a 14-year-old boy whilst out searching for rustlers and who was later hanged for the crime. Regarded as either a brave and loyal scout or a skilled butcher who 'drygulched' his victims, he was played by Steve McQueen as a Peckinpah-styled character out of touch with his time and resigned to his fate.

Steve McQueen	*Tom Horn* (Wiard)	USA, 80

Note: *Tom Horn* was once a Robert Redford project and covered only the final two years of the bounty hunter's life. The TV film *Mr Horn* (Starrett, 79) which starred David Carradine and was scripted by William Goldman, covered Horn's colourful career in more detail–from when he was an Indian scout and captured Geronimo to when he became a Pinkerton agent and a range detective in the Wyoming Cattle Wars.

US Deputy Marshal Joe Le Fors, the man who trapped Horn into a drunken confession, was played by Billy Green Bush in the McQueen film (in which he was named Joe Belle) and by John Durren in the 79 TV movie.

Hornblower, Horatio 

Heroic British naval captain and adventurer during the wars against Napoleon. Created in a long series of C. S. Forester novels which trace his career from midshipman to admiral, but has appeared on screen only once, a somewhat surprising statistic considering that the solitary film about his exploits was a resounding success. Raoul Walsh's 1951 film was adapted from the novels 'Hornblower And The Atropos', 'The Happy Return' and 'A Ship Of The Line'.

Gregory Peck — *Captain Horatio Hornblower* (Walsh) GB, 51

Horrocks, General Sir Brian

R

(1895–1985) One of the best-liked British Corps Commanders of World War II. Took part in the Battle of Normandy, the advance to Brussels, the drive through Germany and the tragic Operation Market Garden, code name for the attempt to seize a bridgehead over the Rhine in 1944. Portrayed sympathetically and with style by Edward Fox (*A Bridge Too Far*), during his involvement with the latter mission.

Edward Fox — *A Bridge Too Far* (Attenborough) GB, 77

Houdini, Harry

(1874–1926) An escape artist of unsurpassed skill who could free himself from any kind of container. George Marshall's 1953 biography sketched in a number of his remarkable escapes from handcuffs, straitjackets, safes, prison cells, etc. The film also revealed how he died—from the onset of appendicitis while trying to break loose from a head-down position in a glass tank full of water. Houdini apeared in several movies late in his career, among them *Terror Island* (20), *The Soul Of Bronze* (20), *The Man From Beyond* (22). His real name was Erich Weiss.

Tony Curtis — *Houdini* (Marshall) USA, 53
Jeff Demunn — *Ragtime* (Forman) USA, 81

Note: Paul Michael Glaser starred as Houdini in Melville Shavelson's *The Great Houdinis,* a TV movie made in 1976.

Hudson, Mrs

Sherlock Holmes' housekeeper, constantly flitting in and out of Conan Doyle's short stories, complete with hot breakfasts and complaints about Holmes' irregular hours and pipe smoking. Eventually came into her own in 'The Empty House' when, by moving the bust of Holmes in a lighted window, she helped bring about the downfall of the murderous Colonel Moran. Numerous character actresses have found her to be a rewarding minor role on screen; Irene Handl imbued her with a personality all her own in Wilder's *The Private Life Of Sherlock Holmes.*

Minnie Rayner — *The Sleeping Cardinal* (Hiscott) GB, 31
Marie Ault — *The Speckled Band* (Raymond) GB, 31
Minnie Rayner — *The Missing Rembrandt* (Hiscott) GB, 32
Clare Greet — *The Sign Of Four* (Cutts) GB, 32
Tempe Pigott — *A Study In Scarlet* (Marin) USA, 33
Minnie Rayner — *The Triumph Of Sherlock Holmes* (Hiscott) GB, 35
Gertrud Wolle — *Der Hund Von Baskerville* (Lamač) Ger, 37
Minnie Rayner — *Silver Blaze* (Bentley) GB, 37
Mary Gordon — *The Adventures Of Sherlock Holmes* (Werker) USA, 39
Mary Gordon — *Sherlock Holmes And The Voice Of Terror* (Rawlins) USA, 42
Mary Gordon — *Sherlock Holmes And The Secret Weapon* (Neill) USA, 42
Mary Gordon — *Spider Woman* (Neill) USA, 44
Mary Gordon — *Pearl Of Death* (Neill) USA, 44
Mary Gordon — *Woman In Green* (Neill) USA, 45
Mary Gordon — *Dressed To Kill* (Neill) USA, 46
Edith Schultze-Westrum — *Sherlock Holmes And The Deadly Necklace* (Fisher) W.Ger, 62
Barbara Leake — *A Study In Terror* (Hill) GB, 65
Irene Handl — *The Private Life Of Sherlock Holmes* (Wilder) GB, 70
Alison Leggatt — *The Seven-Per-Cent Solution* (Ross) GB, 76

Betty Woolfe — *Murder By Decree* (Clark) GB, 79

Note: Mme d'Esterre featured as Mrs Hudson in the silent films of Eille Norwood (21–23) comprising of 45 short pictures and a version of *The Sign Of Four* (23); on TV Marjorie Bennett in *Sherlock Holmes In New York* (76) and Jenny Laird in *The Masks Of Death* (84) have both appeared in the role. Iris Vandeleur (51), Enid Lindsey (65), Grace Arnold (68) and Rosalie Williams (84–88) above all played Mrs Hudson in TV series based on the Conan Doyle stories.

Hughes, Howard [R]

(1905–76) One of the most controversial figures of the twentieth century; an oil millionaire, aviator and movie producer who ended his life as the world's most famous recluse. The only full-length treatment of his life has been the four hour TV film *The Amazing Howard Hughes* starring Tommy Lee Jones although the cinema did offer a ten minute cameo in *Melvin And Howard,* the bizarre tale of a young man who supposedly gave Hughes a late night lift to Las Vegas and was later bequeathed the bulk of Hughes' million dollar estate. Sadly for him he never collected and the will was thrown out of court in 1968.

Recluse—a man of mystery—multi-millionaire! Jason Robards as tycoon Howard Hughes in Jonathan Demme's bittersweet fable, *Melvin and Howard* (1980)

Tommy Lee Jones — *The Amazing Howard Hughes* (Graham) TVM,USA, 77

Victor Holchak — *Hughes and Harlow: Angels in Hell* (Buchanan) USA, 78

Jason Robards — *Melvin And Howard* (Demme) USA, 80

Note: The proposed biography by Warren Beatty has yet to materialize; the oil tycoon/film producer Jonas Cord in *The Carpetbaggers* (64) was closely modelled on Hughes who asked to view the film at the time of its release but took no action. His chief attorney said with disgust: 'Any day in the life of Howard Hughes is more exciting than the whole fucking film'.

Hugo, Adele [R]

(1830–1915) The younger daughter of French novelist and poet Victor Hugo, a woman whose relentless persuit of her former lover to Nova Scotia and Barbados brought about her degradation and insanity. François Truffaut's chronicle of these events resulted in a major French film of the late 70s.

Isabelle Adjani — *The Story Of Adele H* (Truffaut) Fra, 76

Note: Hugo himself has not done so well by the screen, the only portrait of any note coming from Victor Varconi in Allan Dwan's *Suez* (38).

Hulot, Monsieur

One of society's most lovable outsiders, a pipe-smoking, accident-prone Frenchman, whose well meaning endeavours invariably make things worse rather than better. During his screen career constantly at odds with all things modern – the mechanics of contemporary living, scientific progress and machinery of all description. First created by Jacques Tati in *Monsieur Hulot's Holiday*.

Jacques Tati — *Monsieur Hulot's Holiday* (Tati) Fra, 53
Jacques Tati — *Mon Oncle* (Tati) Fra, 58
Jacques Tati — *Playtime* (Tati) Fra, 67
Jacques Tati — *Traffic* (Tati) Fra/It, 71

The incomparable Jacques Tati trying his hand at tennis in *Monsieur Hulot's Holiday,* the first of four films in which he starred as the accident prone but always optimistic Frenchman who enjoys the simple life but cannot come to terms with the scientific miracles of modern living

Hunchback of Notre Dame, The

F

The grotesque bellringer, Quasimodo, of Victor Hugo's masterpiece (1831), a man deafened by the bells he tolls day and night and whose unrequited love for a beautiful gypsy girl leads ultimately to tragedy and death. Generally regarded as a figure of horror, but beneath the hideous surface a character of pathos and sympathy. Chaney's 1923 performance brought out the horror, Laughton's 1939 portrayal ensured the sympathy.

Charles Laughton	*The Hunchback Of Notre Dame* (Dieterle)	USA, 39
Ulhas	*Badshah* (Chakrabarty)	Ind, 54
Anthony Quinn	*The Hunchback Of Notre Dame* (Delannoy)	Fra/It, 57

Note: Lon Chaney's famous silent interpretation in Wallace Worsley's film of 1923 was preceded by those of Henry Vorins in Alice Guy's *Esmeralda* (Fra, 06), Henry Krauss in Albert Capellani's *Notre Dame de Paris* (Fra, 11) and Glen White who starred in *The Darling Of Paris,* directed by J. Gordon Edwards in America in 1917. Anthony Hopkins appeared as Quasimodo in Michael Tuchner's 150 minute TV movie of 1982 (GB).

Hustler, The

F

Cynical young pool shark (named Eddie Felson) who sets out to become number one by beating the reigning champ Minnesota Fats but only succeeds in his aim after suffering physical pain and an agonizing personal loss. Paul Newman has assayed him twice on screen – in Robert Rossen's 1961 film

(Above) an unrecognizable Anthony Hopkins, made up as the hunchbacked Quasimodo in the 1982 Made-for-TV version of *The Hunchback of Notre Dame*. The only British version of Victor Hugo's classic, it followed earlier adaptations starring Lon Chaney, Charles Laughton and Anthony Quinn

The Hustler and then again 25 years later in *The Colour Of Money* which looked at Felson when he has become cynical and world-weary and comes face to face with a young braggart who is the image of him in his younger days.

Paul Newman	*The Hustler* (Rossen)	USA, 61
Paul Newman	*The Colour Of Money*	(Scorsese) USA, 86

Note: Paul Newman won an Oscar for his portrayal in *The Colour Of Money*; Walter Tevis' novel upon which the first movie was based was first published in 1959.

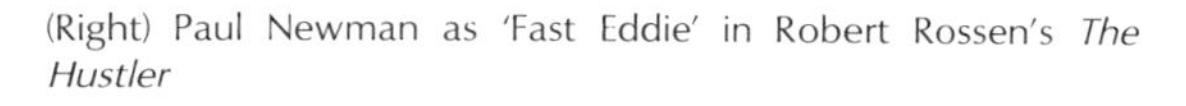

(Right) Paul Newman as 'Fast Eddie' in Robert Rossen's *The Hustler*

Iago

The epitome of malicious evil; an arch villain whose scheming destroys the Moorish General Othello in Shakespeare's tragedy of jealousy and revenge in fifteenth century Italy. Michael MacLiammoir's screen Iago suffered more than most, being hauled up to the castle battlements and left in a cage to be pecked to death by vultures!

Sebastian Cabot	*Othello* (Mackane)	GB, 46
Michael MacLiammoir	*Othello* (Welles)	Morocco, 52
Andrei Popov	*Othello* (Yutkevich)	USSR, 55
Frank Finlay	*Othello* (Burge)	GB, 65

Note: Hector Dion (USA, 08), Cesare Dondine (It, 09), Ricardo Tolentino (It, 14) and Werner Krauss (Ger, 22) were among the actors who appeared as Iago on the silent screen. More recently, Bob Hoskins featured as Iago in Jonathan Miller's 1981 TV adaptation.

Rod Steiger, as a sadistic cowhand, schemed his way through the western variation *Jubal* (56), Patrick McGoohan featured as an Iago type jazz drummer in *All Night Long* (62), and Lance LeGault appeared in the rock musical *Catch My Soul* (73)

Illustrated Man, The

One of Ray Bradbury's most celebrated creations, a luckless and rather frightening mystery man who has been seduced by a time-travelling tattoo lady who has covered his body with magical images which come alive when he tells stories. Ray Bradbury's 1951 book contained 18 different tales; in the 1969 film starring Rod Steiger director Jack Smight used three — 'The Veldt' in which two children conjure up on their nursery wall an African plateau where their parents are eaten by lions, 'The Long Rain' about the experiences of a rocketship crew on a rain-drenched planet, and 'The Last Night Of The World' in which a World Forum decides that all children must be put to sleep to escape the imminent ordeal of the world's end.

A lethal Ray Bradbury villain! Rod Steiger as the mysterious, tattooed story teller *The Illustrated Man* in Jack Smight's fantasy film of 1969

Rod Steiger	*The Illustrated Man* (Smight)	USA, 69

Note: It took nine men ten hours to cover Steiger's torso with the many coloured and intricate tattoos. It took another entire day to tattoo Steiger's lower body and hands and legs. 50 separate silk screen designs were used to tattoo the torso.

Incredible Shrinking Man, The

The central character in Richard Matheson's remarkable sci-fi novel 'The Shrinking Man' (56), a luckless American who is accidentally infected by a radioactive cloud while holidaying on a small cruiser and then diminishes at the rate of an inch a week until he is no larger than an atom. Grant Williams was the name of the actor who, on the way down, had to contend with all kinds of problems including a giant spider and a prowling cat. The role did not

(Above) Grant Williams in big trouble as Richard Matheson's *The Incredible Shrinking Man* (1957) and (right) Lily Tomlin in the spoot follow-up *The Incredible Shrinking Woman* (1981), the story of an American housewife who falls victim to 20th century technology!

make him a star. He died in 1985, aged 54, after an uneventful career in movies and on TV.

Grant Williams	*The Incredible Shrinking Man* (Arnold) USA, 57

Note: Housewife Lily Tomlin also shrank in size in the 1981 satirical comedy *The Incredible Shrinking Woman*.

Invisible Man, The [F]

H. G. Wells' megalomaniac doctor who succeeds in rendering himself invisible while experimenting with an Indian drug called monocaine. Destroyed on screen when his tell-tale footprints betray him in the snow, he still spawned several descendants at Universal in the 40s, and even had the dubious privilege of meeting up with Abbott and Costello. 44-year-old Claude Rains made his film debut in James Whale's film of 1933, still the only movie to have been adapted from Wells' original novel, published in 1897.

Claude Rains	*The Invisible Man* (Whale) USA, 33
Vincent Price	*The Invisible Man Returns* (May) USA, 40
Virginia Bruce	*The Invisible Woman* (Sutherland) USA, 41
Jon Hall	*Invisible Agent* (Marin) USA, 42
Jon Hall	*The Invisible Man's Revenge* (Beebe) USA, 44
Arthur Franz	*Abbott And Costello Meet The Invisible Man* (Lamont) USA, 51
Turan Seyfioglu	*Gorunmiyen Adam Istanbulda* (Akad) Tur, 56
Arturo de Cordova	*El Hombre Que Legre Ser Invisible* (Crevenna) Mex, 60

Irvine, Lucy [R]

A former Inland Revenue clerk who realized the ambition of thousands when she answered a magazine advertisement that read: 'One year on a deserted tropical island. Wife 20–30 needed to accompany man 35+. Write to Box 775 with details and evening phone number'. Her subsequent experiences and Robinson Crusoe/Girl Friday existence resulted in a turbulent 12 months and the bestseller 'Castaway', later turned into a film by Nicolas Roeg. Amanda Donohue featured as the adventurous Lucy, Oliver Reed as the randy teacher looking for sex and sand.

Amanda Donohue	*Castaway* (Roeg) GB, 86

Iscariot, Judas [R]

The most infamous man in history, a disciple of Christ who betrayed his leader to the Jewish priests for thirty pieces of silver. Difficult to play on screen without descending into darkest melodrama, although both David McCallum and Ian McShane gave thoughtful, intelligent performances for directors George Stevens and Franco Zeffirelli. In 1961 John Drew Barrymore achieved a unique double, appearing as both Judas and Christ in *Pontius Pilate*.

James Griffith	*The Day Of Triumph* (Pichel/Coyle) USA, 54
John Drew Barrymore	*Ponzio Pilato* (Callegari) Fra/It/USA, 61
Rip Torn	*King Of Kings* (Ray) USA, 61
Otello Sestili	*The Gospel According To St Matthew* (Pasolini) It/Fra, 64
Manuel Monroy	*The Redeemer* (Breen) USA/Spa, 65
David McCallum	*The Greatest Story Ever Told* (Stevens) USA, 65
Thomas Leventhal	*The Gospel Road* (Elfstrom) USA, 73
Scott Wilson	*The Passover Plot* (Campus) Israel/USA, 76
Ian McShane	*Jesus Of Nazareth* (Zeffirelli) GB, 77
Eli Danker	*Jesus* (Sykes/Krish) USA, 79
Barrie Houghton	*The Day Christ Died* (Manulis) TVM,USA, 80
Harvey Keitel	*The Passion* (Scorsese) USA, 88

Note: The Zeffirelli film of 1977 was made for TV; the rock musical *Jesus Christ, Superstar* (73) featured Carl Anderson as a black Judas.

The following actors appeared as Judas in silent productions – Robert Vignola in *From The Manger To The Cross* (USA, 12), Monsieur Jacquinet in *Behold The Man* (USA/Fra, 21), Alexander Granach in *I.N.R.I. A Portrayal Of The Life Of Christ* (Ger, 23) and Joseph Schildkraut in *King Of Kings* (USA, 27).

Amanda Donohue as former Inland Revenue clerk Lucy Irvine coming to terms with life on a desert island in Nicolas Roeg's 1986 film *Castaway*

Ivanhoe

[F]

Famed Saxon knight of novelist Sir Walter Scott, an adventurer in late twelfth century England when Prince John was attempting to usurp the throne of his brother Richard, taken prisoner on his return from the Crusades. Just two sound screen portrayals to date – one by Robert Taylor in MGM's lavish 1952 swashbuckler, the other by Anthony Andrews in Douglas Camfield's robust TV movie of 1982. Full name, Wilfred Of Ivanhoe; Scott's novel was first published in 1819.

Robert Taylor	*Ivanhoe*	(Thorpe)	USA, 52
Anthony Andrews	*Ivanhoe*	(Camfield)	TVM,USA, 82

Note: Earle Williams appeared as Ivanhoe in an American silent of 1910; two British silent versions of Scott's novel were released in 1913, the first starring Lauderdale Maitland, the second King Baggot.

Ivan The Terrible

[R]

(1530–84) Grand Duke of Moscow and the first to assume the title of Tsar, a mercilessly cruel man who embarked on a reign of terror when he sensed treachery in those serving him. He eventually died, heartbroken after slaying his own son in a fit of rage. The Russian director Sergei Eisenstein planned a screen trilogy on Ivan's life, but completed only two films before his death, both remarkable for their grandiose style and the performances of Nikolai Cherkassov.

Nikolai Cherkassov	*Ivan The Terrible*	(Eisenstein)	USSR, 44
Nikolai Cherkassov	*The Boyars Plot*	(Eisenstein)	USSR, 46

Note: Alfred Abel (Ger, 23) and Conrad Veidt as an insane Ivan in Paul Leni's three-episode German silent film, *Waxworks* (24) both featured as the Tsar on the silent screen.

The two Taylors—Elizabeth and Robert—in MGM's lavish British made version of Sir Walter Scott's *Ivanhoe,* directed by Richard Thorpe in 1952

Jackson, Andrew R

(1767–1845) An Indian fighter, a Tennessee backwoods lawyer and an army general, before becoming the seventh President of the United States in 1829. Sometimes known as 'Old Hickory', he was the subject of scandal over his romance with a married woman, a scandal that refused to die and was later used against him by his political enemies. Jackson's stormy private life was recounted in *The President's Lady*; his more vigorous activities at the Battle of New Orleans were highlighted in *The Buccaneer.* Charlton Heston played the President on both occasions.

Lionel Barrymore	*The Gorgeous Hussy* (Brown)	USA, 36
Hugh Sothern	*The Buccaneer* (DeMille)	USA, 38
Edward Ellis	*Man Of Conquest* (Nicholls, Jr)	USA, 39
Brian Donlevy	*The Remarkable Andrew* (Heisler)	USA, 42
Lionel Barrymore	*Lone Star* (Sherman)	USA, 52
Charlton Heston	*The President's Lady* (Levin)	USA, 53
Basil Ruysdael	*Davy Crockett, King Of The Wild Frontier* (Foster)	USA, 55
Carl Benton Reid	*The First Texan* (Haskin)	USA, 56
Charlton Heston	*The Buccaneer* (Quinn)	USA, 58

Note: F.C. Earle appeared as Jackson in *My Own United States* (USA, 18), George Irving in Frank Lloyd's *The Eagle Of The Sea* (USA, 26) and Russell Simpson in *The Frontiersman* (USA, 27).

Jack The Ripper 

Perhaps the most notorious murderer of all time, if only for the fact that his identity remains a secret to this day. A favourite character in the movies (he killed and mutilated at least five prostitutes with a knife), he has been variously portrayed as a fanatical woman hater, a surgeon, an escaped lunatic, even a member of the Royal Family. A fictional Sherlock Holmes has tracked him down twice on screen. Not so the real-life detectives of Scotland Yard whose investigations in London's East End during the late autumn of 1888 came to nothing.

Ivor Novello	*The Lodger* (Elvey)	GB, 32
Laird Cregar	*The Lodger* (Brahm)	USA, 44
Valentine Dyall	*Room To Let* (Grayson)	GB, 50
Jack Palance	*Man In The Attic* (Fregonese)	USA, 53
Ewen Solon	*Jack The Ripper* (Baker)	GB, 59
John Fraser	*A Study In Terror* (Hill)	GB, 65
Klaus Kinski	*Jack The Ripper* (Franco)	W.Ger./Swi, 76
Peter Jonfield	*Murder By Decree* (Clark)	GB, 79
David Warner	*Time After Time* (Meyer)	USA, 79

Note: Novello also played the Ripper in Hitchcock's silent version of *The Lodger* (26); Werner Krauss in *Waxworks* (24) and Gustav Diessl in *Pandora's Box* (29) – both German – were other silent actors who featured as the mass killer.

James, Frank 

(1843–1915) Older brother of outlaw Jesse James who rode with Quantrill and then his brother's gang before surrendering in 1882, the year of Jesse's death. Early in the twentieth century appeared for a time in a Wild West Show then finished his life peacefully as a starter for a racetrack. Generally portrayed on screen as the more restrained, less flamboyant of the two brothers, notably by Henry Fonda in Fox's two large scale westerns of 39–40.

Michael Worth	*Days Of Jesse James* (Kane)	USA, 39
Henry Fonda	*Jesse James* (Henry King)	USA, 39
Henry Fonda	*The Return Of Frank James* (Fritz Lang)	USA, 40
Tom Tyler	*Badman's Territory* (Whelan)	USA, 46
Tom Tyler	*I Shot Jesse James* (Fuller)	USA, 49
Richard Long	*Kansas Raiders* (Enright)	USA, 50
Don Barry	*Gunfire* (Berke)	USA, 50
Reed Hadley	*The Return Of Jesse James* (Hilton)	USA, 50

The Whitehall murderer Jack The Ripper as played by Laird Cregar (right) in the 1944 film *The Lodger;* and (above) by David Warner, threatening Mary Steenburgen, in the 1979 fantasy thriller *Time After Time*

Wendell Corey	*The Great Missouri Raid* (Douglas) USA, 51
Tom Tyler	*Best Of The Badmen* (Russell) USA, 51
James Brown	*Woman They Almost Lynched* (Dwan) USA, 53
Jack Buetel	*Jesse James' Women* (Barry) USA, 54
Jeffrey Hunter	*The True Story Of Jesse James* (Ray) USA, 56
Douglas Kennedy	*Hell's Crossroads* (Andreon) USA, 57
Jim Davis	*Alias Jesse James* (McLeod) USA, 59
Robert Dix	*Young Jesse James* (Claxton) USA, 60
John Pearce	*The Great Northfield Minnesota Raid* (Kaufman) USA, 72
Stacy Keach	*The Long Riders* (Hill) USA, 80

Note: James Pierce featured as Frank in Lloyd Ingraham's 1927 silent production, *Jesse James*; Johnny Cash appeared in the role in William A Graham's TV movie *The Last Days Of Frank And Jesse James* (86).

James, Jesse R

(1847–82) Leader of the most notorious outlaw gang of the Wild West, a Missouri-born bank and train robber, who, like Billy The Kid, became a legend in his own lifetime. The beginning of the end occurred in 1876 when his gang was virtually destroyed during the Northfield bank raid; the end of the end came six years later when he was shot in the back by his cousin, Bob Ford. The handsome features of Tyrone Power and Robert Wagner helped Hollywood perpetuate the legend: an unkempt Robert

The most unusual aspect of *The Long Riders* was that real-life brothers portrayed the outlaw brothers of the Jesse James gang. Pictured here are James and Stacy Keach as Jesse and Frank: other acting brothers—the Carradines, the Quaids, and the Guests portrayed the Youngers, Millers and Fords. Walter Hill directed in 1980

Duvall in *The Great Northfield Minnesota Raid* destroyed all illusions.

Tyrone Power	*Jesse James* (Henry King)	USA, 39
Roy Rogers	*Days Of Jesse James* (Kane)	USA, 39
Roy Rogers	*Jesse James At Bay* (Kane)	USA, 41
Alan Baxter	*Bad Men Of Missouri* (Enright)	USA, 41
Rod Cameron	*The Remarkable Andrew* (Heisler)	USA, 42
Lawrence Tierney	*Badman's Territory* (Whelan)	USA, 46
Dale Robertson	*Fighting Man Of The Plains* (Marin)	USA, 49
Reed Hadley	*I Shot Jesse James* (Fuller)	USA, 49
Audie Murphy	*Kansas Raiders* (Enright)	USA, 50
Macdonald Carey	*The Great Missouri Raid* (Douglas)	USA, 51
Lawrence Tierney	*Best Of The Badmen* (Russell)	USA, 51
Ben Cooper	*Woman They Almost Lynched* (Dwan)	USA, 53
Willard Parker	*The Great Jesse James Raid* (Le Borg)	USA, 53
Don Barry	*Jesse James' Women* (Barry)	USA, 54
Robert Wagner	*The True Story Of Jesse James* (Ray)	USA, 56
Henry Brandon	*Hell's Crossroads* (Andreon)	USA, 57
Wendell Corey	*Alias Jesse James* (McLeod)	USA, 58
Ray Stricklyn	*Young Jesse James* (Claxton)	USA, 60
Wayne Mack	*The Outlaws Is Coming* (Maurer)	USA, 65
John Lupton	*Jesse James Meets Frankenstein's Daughter* (Beaudine)	USA, 66
Audie Murphy	*A Time For Dying* (Boetticher)	USA, 69
Robert Duvall	*The Great Northfield Minnesota Raid* (Kaufman)	USA, 72
James Keach	*The Long Riders* (Hill)	USA, 80

Note: Jesse James, Jr in *Jesse James Under The Black Flag* (21) and *Jesse James As The Outlaw* (21), and Fred Thomson in *Jesse James* (27) both appeared in the role on the silent screen.

Clayton Moore featured as James in the serials, *Jesse James Rides Again* (47) and *The Adventures Of Frank and Jesse James* (48), Keith Richards in *The James Brothers Of Missouri* (50); Kris Kristofferson starred as Jesse in William A Graham's 1986 TV movie *The Last Days Of Frank and Jesse James*.

Jane, Calamity [R]

The most famous woman associated with the Old West and not a bit like Doris Day! A one-time mule-skinner who wore men's clothing, she swore, drank and chewed tobacco with the best of them. Once won a 50 dollar bet for shooting a hole in the top of a hat hanging in the rear of a saloon. Supposedly the lover of Wild Bill Hickok, she drifted into drunken obscurity after his murder in Deadwood and died on 20 August, 1903, the twenty-seventh anniversary of Hickok's death. Real name: Martha Jane Burke or Cannary.

Louise Dresser	*Caught* (Sloman)	USA, 31
Jean Arthur	*The Plainsman* (DeMille)	USA, 37
Sally Payne	*Young Bill Hickok* (Kane)	USA, 40
Frances Farmer	*Badlands Of Dakota* (Green)	USA, 41
Jane Russell	*The Paleface* (McLeod)	USA, 48
Yvonne De Carlo	*Calamity Jane And Sam Bass* (Sherman)	USA, 49
Evelyn Ankers	*The Texan Meets Calamity Jane* (Lamb)	USA, 50
Doris Day	*Calamity Jane* (Butler)	USA, 53
Judi Meredith	*The Raiders* (Daugherty)	USA, 64
Gloria Milland	*Seven Hours Of Gunfire* (Marchent)	It/W.Ger/Spa, 64
Abby Dalton	*The Plainsman* (Rich)	USA, 66

Note: Ethel Grey Terry played Calamity Jane in the 1923 silent production *Wild Bill Hickok*; Kim Darby in *That Was The West That Was* (74) and Jane Alexander in James Goldstone's *Calamity Jane* (84) have portrayed her on TV. Goldstone's film was far removed from the high jinks of Doris Day's 1953 musical and revealed the character of Jane from letters she supposedly wrote but never sent to her daughter about her relationship with Hickok.

Javert, Inspector

F

The police inspector who relentlessly pursues escaped convict Jean Valjean in *Les Misérables*. Unyielding and pitiless, he is basically a tragic figure in that his obsession with the law is due to the fact that he himself was born in prison, the son of a gypsy mother and a criminal father hanged on the gallows. Ultimately commits suicide in the River Seine. A memorable creation of Victor Hugo and one of the 'plum' heavy roles in all cinema. Most famous portrayal: Charles Laughton in Fox's lavish production of 1935.

Charles Vanel	*Les Misérables*	(Bernard)	Fra, 34
Charles Laughton	*Les Misérables*	(Boleslawski)	USA, 35
Antonio Bravo	*Les Misérables*	(Rivero)	Mex, 44
John Hinrich	*Les Misérables*	(Freda)	It, 46
Javar Seetharaman	*Ezhai Padum Padu*	(Ramanath)	Ind, 50
Robert Newton	*Les Misérables*	(Milestone)	USA, 52
Ulhas	*Kundan*	(Modi)	Ind, 55
Bernard Blier	*Les Misérables*	(Le Chanois)	Fra/It, 58
Anthony Perkins	*Les Misérables*	(Glenn Jordan)	GB, 79
Michel Bouquet	*Les Misérables*	(Hossein)	Fra, 82

Note: There were at least five silent versions of *Les Misérables*. France released a 1909 adaptation; Vitagraph produced a 4-reel adaptation in 1910;

Anthony Perkins (left) as the pitiless Inspector Javert who rigidly upholds the letter of the law and pursues an escaped convict, not for months but for years. One of the most relentless figures in all literature, he features in Victor Hugo's *Les Misérables* and has been played on screen by such actors as Charles Laughton, Charles Vanel and Robert Newton

J. P. Etievant was Javert in the 1913 French Film of Albert Capellani; Hardee Kirkland played the inspector in Frank Lloyd's 1917 production; and Jean Toulout in the 1925 film of Henri Fescourt.

Dr Jekyll And Mr Hyde F

Victorian doctor who tampers with the laws of nature and experiments with a potion that transforms him from good to evil (the bestial Mr Hyde) in a matter of seconds. A serious challenge for any actor, whether he be required to turn into a hairy creature of monstrous strength as in Mamoulian's 1932 film, or a more subtle but equally malignant sadist in Victor Fleming's remake. Robert Louis Stevenson's story, based, not surprisingly, on a nightmare, was published in 1886.

Fredric March	*Dr Jekyll And Mr Hyde* (Mamoulian) USA, 32
Spencer Tracy	*Dr Jekyll And Mr Hyde* (Fleming) USA, 41
Louis Hayward	*Son Of Dr Jekyll* (Friedman) USA, 51
Mario Soffici	*El Extraneo Caso Del Hombre Y La Bestia* (Soffici) Argentina, 51
Boris Karloff	*Abbott and Costello Meet Dr Jekyll And Mr Hyde* (Lamont) USA, 53
Gloria Talbot	*Daughter Of Dr Jekyll* (Ulmer) USA, 57
Jean-Louis Barrault	*Le Testament du Dr Cordelier* (Renoir) TV/Fra, 59
Paul Massie	*Two Faces Of Dr Jekyll* (Fisher) GB, 60
Christopher Lee	*I Monster* (Weeks) GB, 70
Ralph Bates & Martine Beswick	*Dr Jekyll And Sister Hyde* (Baker) GB, 71
Bernie Casey	*Dr Black, Mr Hyde* (Crain) USA, 76
Oliver Reed	*Dr Heckyl And Mr Hype* (Griffith) USA, 80
Udo Kier	*The Blood Of Dr Jekyll* (Borowczyk) Fra, 81
Mark Blankfield	*Jekyll And Hyde . . . Together Again* (Belson) USA, 82
Innokenti Smoktunovsky (Jekyll) & Alexander Feklistovh (Hyde)	*The Strange Case Of Dr Jekyll and Mr Hyde* (Orlov) USSR, 87

Note: In 1963 Jerry Lewis starred in *The Nutty Professor* (USA), a modern updating of Stevenson's story, with Lewis as a campus college professor who turns into a ladykilling hero; the 1970 film with Christopher Lee renamed the characters Dr Marlowe and Edward Blake, and in *Dr Jekyll And Sister Hyde,* Ralph Bates achieved the ultimate personality change by becoming Martine Beswick.

Silent actors who appeared in the dual role included Hobart Bosworth (USA, 08), Frank Oakes Rose (USA, 08), Alwin Neuss (Den, 10) and (Ger, 14), King Baggot (USA, 13), Sheldon Lewis (USA, 20), John Barrymore (USA, 20) and Conrad Veidt (20) who starred in a German variation of the theme, *Janus-Faced,* directed by F. W. Murnau. In a 1912 version, directed by Lucius Henderson, James Cruze played Jekyll and Harry Benham appeared as Hyde.

David Hemmings appeared in the role in a 1981 production for TV.

Jesus Christ 

(Born between 4 and 6 BC and crucified about AD28) The Messiah predicted by the Old Testament prophets and arguably the most dangerous role for any actor to attempt on screen. Few have been successful, not, surprisingly, because of vulgarization but because of an over pious attitude towards the part. Max Von Sydow and Robert Powell both resembled the conventional image of Christ, although the most convincing portrait remains that of Enrique Irazoqui in Pasolini's *The Gospel According To St Matthew.* In the 1976 film *The Passover Plot,* Christ was portrayed as a political revolutionary who contrives his own crucifixion as a plot against the Roman establishment.

Robert Le Vigan	*Golgotha* (Duvivier) Fra, 35
Robert Wilson	*The Day Of Triumph* (Pichel/Coyle) USA, 54
Claude Heater	*Ben-Hur* (Wyler) USA, 59
Jeffrey Hunter	*King Of Kings* (Ray) USA, 61
John Drew Barrymore	*Ponzio Pilato* (Callegari) It/Fra, 61
Roy Mangano	*Barabbas* (Fleischer) It, 62
Enrique Irazoqui	*The Gospel According To St Matthew* (Pasolini) It/Fra, 64

An unrecognizable Fredric March as the bestial Edward Hyde in the first sound version of Robert Louis Stevenson's chilling tale of good and evil *Dr Jekyll and Mr Hyde*. Rouben Mamoulian's film earned March an Academy Award as the best actor of 1932. The Hyde make-up was described by one critic as 'a triumph of realized nightmare'

(Right) Swedish actor Max Von Sydow as Christ in George Stevens' *The Greatest Story Ever Told;* (above) Ted Neeley in the rock musical *Jesus Christ Superstar*

Luis Alvarez	*The Redeemer* (Breen) USA/Spa, 65
Max Von Sydow	*The Greatest Story Ever Told* (Stevens) USA, 65
Bernard Verley	*The Milky Way* (Buñuel) Fra/It, 69
Radomir Reljic	*The Master And Margarita* (Petrovic) Yug/It, 72
Robert Elfstrom	*The Gospel Road* (Elfstrom) USA, 73
Zalman King	*The Passover Plot* (Campus) Israel/USA, 76
Robert Powell	*Jesus Of Nazareth* (Zeffirelli) GB, 77
Brian Deacon	*Jesus* (Sykes/Krish) USA, 79
Chris Sarendon	*The Day Christ Died* (Manulis) TVM,USA, 80
John Hurt	*History Of The World Part I* (Brooks) USA, 81
Willem Dafoe	*The Passion* (Scorsese) USA, 88

Note: Macdonald Carey dubbed the voice of Christ for the American version of *The Redeemer;* Ted Neeley appeared in the rock musical, *Jesus Christ, Superstar* (73).

There were many silent portrayals of Christ, among them Howard Gaye in *Intolerance* (USA, 16), George Fisher in *Civilization* (USA, 16), Alberto Pasquali in *Christus* (It, 17), Grigori Khmara (Ger, 23) and H.B. Warner in DeMille's *King Of Kings* (27).

Joan Of Arc

R

(1412–31) French peasant girl who was inspired by saintly voices to lead the French armies against the British and then, later, tried and burned as a heretic. Falconetti's silent performance apart, a role that has generally proved beyond even the most accomplished of actresses. Best to opt for the ridiculous rather than the sublime, e.g. Hedy Lamarr's Maid in Irwin Allen's historical pageant, *The Story Of Mankind.*

Simone Genevois	*Saint Joan – The Maid* (Gastyne) Fra, 29
Angela Salloker	*Das Madchen Johanna* (Ucicky) Ger, 35
Ingrid Bergman	*Joan Of Arc* (Fleming) USA, 48
Michele Morgan	*Destinees* (Delannoy) Fra, 53
Jean Seberg	*Saint Joan* (Preminger) GB, 57
Hedy Lamarr	*The Story Of Mankind* (Allen) USA, 57
Florence Carrez	*The Trial Of Joan Of Arc* (Bresson) Fra, 62

Note: Michele Morgan's performance in the three-part film *Destinees (Love, Soldiers And Women)* was in the episode *Jeanne;* Maria Jacobini (It, 13), Geraldine Farrar in DeMille's *Joan The Woman* (17) and Falconetti in Dreyer's *The Passion Of Joan Of Arc* (28) were among the silent actresses to appear as Joan.

John, Prince

(1167–1216) The youngest son of Henry II and Eleanor of Aquitaine who succeeded his brother Richard to the throne and was forced to sign the Magna Carta (1215) by English barons, which decreed that the king's power should be limited by law. In movies, usually the sly, cunning heavy in the Robin Hood adventures. Claude Rains retains the crown as the softest spoken but most menacing of all the screen Prince Johns.

Ramsay Hill	*The Crusades* (DeMille) USA, 35
Claude Rains	*The Adventures Of Robin Hood* (Curtiz/Keighley) USA, 38
George Macready	*Rogues Of Sherwood Forest* (Douglas) USA, 50
Guy Rolfe	*Ivanhoe* (Thorpe) GB, 52
Hubert Gregg	*The Story Of Robin Hood And His Merrie Men* (Annakin) GB, 52
Nigel Terry	*The Lion In Winter* (Harvey) GB, 68
Peter Ustinov (voice only)	*Robin Hood* (Disney) USA, 73

Johnson, Jack

R

(1878–1946) The first black boxer to win the heavyweight championship of the world, a controversial figure who shocked an already outraged American public by taking up with a divorced white woman and living as a playboy. He eventually lost his title in 1915 when he supposedly threw his fight with Jess Willard in Havana, Cuba and ended his career making personal appearances in carnivals and vaudeville houses. On screen he was played by James Earl Jones in Martin Ritt's version of *The Great White Hope* (in which he was renamed Jack

James Earl Jones with Jane Alexander in *The Great White Hope,* Martin Ritt's 1970 screen version of the Broadway stage success. Jones' portrayal of Jack Jefferson, a famed heavyweight champion with a white mistress, was based on real-life heavyweight champion Jack Johnson

Jefferson), a version of the Howard Sackler play first performed in 1967.

James Earl Jones	*The Great White Hope* (Ritt)	USA, 70

Note: The documentary *Jack Johnson* (1971) told the life story of the boxer by using stills and clips from old newsreels. It was narrated by Brock Peters and contained a jazz score by Miles Davis.

John The Baptist [R]

The forerunner of Christ who preached in the wilderness about the coming of the Messiah and eventually lost his head when he denounced Herod's incestuous marriage to Herodias. Robert Ryan roared his defiant warnings for director Nicholas Ray, Charlton Heston for George Stevens and Michael York for Franco Zeffirelli.

Alan Badel	*Salome* (Dieterle)	USA, 53
Jay Barney	*The Big Fisherman* (Borzage)	USA, 59
Robert Ryan	*King Of Kings* (Ray)	USA, 61
Mario Socrate	*The Gospel According To St Matthew* (Pasolini)	It/Fra, 64
Charlton Heston	*The Greatest Story Ever Told* (Stevens)	USA, 65
Larry Lee	*The Gospel Road* (Elfstrom)	USA, 73
Harry Andrews	*The Passover Plot* (Campus)	Israel/USA, 76
Michael York	*Jesus Of Nazareth* (Zeffirelli)	GB, 77
Eli Cohen	*Jesus* (Sykes/Krish)	USA, 79

Note: Albert Roscoe (USA, 18) and Nigel de Brulier (USA, 22) both appeared as John The Baptist in silent versions of *Salome*.

Johnson, Amy [R]

(1903–41) English woman aviator who made the first solo flight from England to Australia in 1930. Herbert Wilcox's 1942 biography with Anna Neagle was released just a year after Johnson's death. She was a pilot in the Air Transport Auxiliary, and drowned after baling out over the Thames estuary.

Anna Neagle	*They Flew Alone* (Wilcox)	GB, 42

Johnson, Andrew 

(1808–75) Vice-president of America at the time of Lincoln's assassination and the man who tried to carry through Lincoln's policy of reconciliation with the South at the end of the Civil War. His subsequent conflicts with Congress resulted in his near-impeachment. His turbulent Presidential career was recounted in William Dieterle's *Tennessee Johnson* in 1942.

Van Heflin	*Tennessee Johnson* (Dieterle)	USA, 42

Note: Bill Hindman appeared as Johnson in the 1980 TV movie *The Ordeal Of Dr Mudd*.

Johnson, Lyndon Baines 

(1908–73) Texas born American president who was sworn in just a few shattered hours after Kennedy's assassination in Dallas. Large screen portrayals have been only minor although Donald Moffat offered a somewhat broad caricature of LBJ's activities in Philip Kaufman's astronaut movie *The Right Stuff*. Randy Quaid's TV portrait in *L.B.J.: The Early Years* covered Johnson's life from 1934 to the time he took office in 1963 as the thirty-sixth President of the United States.

Donald Moffatt as Vice-President Lyndon B. Johnson in *The Right Stuff*, the story of the birth of America's space programme and the first astronauts

Ivan Triesault	*How To Succeed In Business With Really Trying* (Swift) USA, 67
Andrew Duggan	*The Private Files Of J. Edgar Hoover* (Cohen) USA, 77
Donald Moffat	*The Right Stuff* (Kaufman) USA, 83
Randy Quaid	*L.B.J.: The Early Years* (Werner) TVM/USA, 87

Note: Other TV portrayals of Johnson have included Warren Kemmerling in *King* (78), Nesbitt Blaisdell in *Kennedy* (83), Forrest Tucker in *Blood Feud* (83), Kenneth Mars in *Prince Jack* (84), G.D. Spradlin in *Robert Kennedy And His Times* (85) and Rip Torn in *J. Edgar Hoover* (87).

Jolson, Al

R

(1886–1950) Star of the first talkie, *The Jazz Singer* (27), a brash vaudeville performer who sang and knelt his way to the top with a large repertoire of hit songs — 'Mammy', 'Swannee', 'April Showers'. Known as the Minstrel of Broadway and the star of several movies, he declined in popularity during the 30s but enjoyed a rebirth when Columbia filmed his life story in 1946.

Larry Parks	*The Jolson Story* (Green) USA, 46
Larry Parks	*Jolson Sings Again* (Levin) USA, 49
Norman Brooks	*The Best Things In Life Are Free* (Curtiz) USA, 56
Buddy Lewis	*Harlow* (Segal) USA, 65

Note: Jolson sang all the songs on the soundtracks of both film biographies. In the second film he actually meets on screen his film impersonator, Larry Parks.

Jones, Indiana

Archaeologist hero derived from the serial adventures of the 1930s and turned by director Steven Spielberg and the laconic Harrison Ford into perhaps the most popular screen original of modern times. Short with words, strong on action and effective with women (but not so hot with snakes) he has to date starred in two cliff-hanging spectaculars with the promise of many more to come. Has so far defeated Nazis in search of the lost ark of the covenant, Chinese gangsters and a thuggee cult offering up human sacrifice in an underground temple!

'You Ain't Heard Nothing Yet!' Larry Parks as the legendary entertainer Al Jolson in the 1946 Columbia production, *The Jolson Story*

Harrison Ford	*Raiders Of The Lost Ark* (Spielberg) USA, 81
Harrison Ford	*Indiana Jones And The Temple Of Doom* (Spielberg) USA, 84

Jones, John Paul

(1747–92) Scottish-born American naval officer, famed for his exploits in the Revolutionary War and founder of the US Navy. Afforded a lavish Warner biography in 1959 by director John Farrow who, along with Raoul Walsh, was never happier than when his cameras were focused on ships at sea.

Robert Stack	*John Paul Jones* (Farrow) USA, 59

Jones, Tom

Rumbustious hero of one of the masterpieces of English literature, a wild, lusty country boy who wenches his way across the West Country to London in eighteenth century England and nearly

The most popular movie hero of modern times! Harrison Ford as the laconic, globe-trotting Indiana Jones, seen here coming face to face with a pitful of snakes in the first of his screen adventures, *Raiders of the Lost Ark*

pays for his philandering on the gallows. The novel was written by Henry Fielding in 1749; the definitive screen portrayal given by Albert Finney in the Oscar-winning film of Tony Richardson.

Albert Finney	*Tom Jones* (Richardson)	GB, 63
Nicky Henson	*The Bawdy Adventures Of Tom Jones* (Owen)	GB, 76

Note: Langhorne Burton played the role in Edwin Collins' British silent film of 1917.

Joplin, Scott [R]

(1868–1917) Black ragtime pianist-composer, famous for his celebrated 'Maple Leaf Rag' and also 'The Entertainer' which was used so effectively on the soundtrack of the Oscar-winning *The Sting*. His life, a tragic one ruined by syphilis, was the subject of a realistic, often harrowing film made in 1977.

Billy Dee Williams	*Scott Joplin* (Kagan)	USA, 77

Juarez, Benito Pablo [R]

(1806–72) Zapotec Indian who became President of Mexico in 1857 and fought and defeated the French-supported regime of Maximilian. In 1939 William Dieterle told his story in 132 absorbing minutes and drew from Paul Muni one of the most authoritative performances of his distinguished career.

Paul Muni	*Juarez* (Dieterle)	USA, 39
Jason Robards, Sr	*The Mad Empress* (Torres)	Mex, 40
Fausto Tozzi	*Der Schatz der Azteken* (Siodmak)	W.Ger/Fra/It/Yug, 65

Robert Stack as *John Paul Jones,* the man who founded the US Navy in the 18th century. Sam Bronston's 1959 epic was directed by John Farrow and also starred Bette Davis (in a cameo role) as Catherine The Great

castle administered by mysterious unseen forces, has been filmed twice in recent years.

Anthony Perkins	*The Trial* (Welles)	Fra/Ger/It, 62
Maximilian Schell	*The Castle* (Noëlte)	Swit/W.Ger, 69
Carl-Kristian Rundman	*The Castle* (Pakkasvirta)	Fin, 86

K., Joseph [F]

Helpless victim of Franz Kafka's nightmarish novel 'The Trial' (1925), a nameless young bank clerk who is awakened at night by the police and placed under arrest for a crime of which he knows nothing. The country is nameless, the crime never explained; the whole piece reflects the desperate confrontation of the individual against a mindless bureaucracy. The story was filmed in a suitably bizarre fashion by Orson Welles who made use of the urban wasteland of Zagreb and the deserted Gare D'Orsay railway station in Paris in his 1962 production. Kafka's subsequent novel 'The Castle' in which K is a land surveyor unable to gain entrance into a

A bewildered Anthony Perkins as Joseph K, a clerk who is arrested for a crime that is never explained to him in Orson Welles' version of Kafka's *The Trial*

Kahn, Gus [R]

(1886–1941) German-born lyricist of pop songs who first hit the big time in Tin Pan Alley and then moved on to even greater success on Broadway and in Hollywood. Most of his song hits (among them 'Makin' Whoopee', 'Pretty Baby', 'The Man I Love', 'It Had To Be You') were performed by Doris Day in the 1952 biography which starred Danny Thomas as Kahn and featured Frank Lovejoy as his most frequent composer/collaborator Walter Donaldson.

Danny Thomas	*I'll See You In My Dreams* (Curtiz)	USA, 52

Note: In the 30s Kahn worked on the films *Flying Down To Rio* (33), *Kid Millions* (34), *Thanks A Million* (35), *A Day At The Races* (37), *Girl Of The Golden West* (38), *Lillian Russell* (40) and *Ziegfeld Girl* (41). He collaborated with such composers as Vincent Youmans, Arthur Johnston, Bronislau Kaper, Sigmund Romberg and Nacio Herb Brown.

Kalmar and Ruby 

American songwriting team responsible for numerous Broadway shows and Marx Brothers movie scripts during the 20s and 30s. The story of their often turbulent relationship was related in MGM's biography of 1950. Among their movies: *Animal Crackers* (30), *Horse Feathers* (32), *Duck Soup* (33). Among their song hits: 'Three Little Words', 'I Loved You So Much', 'Nevertheless', 'Who's Sorry Now?'.

Fred Astaire and Red Skelton	*Three Little Words* (Thorpe)	USA, 50

Note: Bert Kalmar was born in 1884 and died in 1947; Harry Ruby (1895–1974) survived him by 27 years.

Karenina, Anna 

This most tragic of Tolstoy's heroines, a tortured passionate woman who flouts the conventions of nineteenth century Russian society by abandoning

Greta Garbo as Tolstoy's tragic heroine *Anna Karenina*, a lonely Russian woman languishing in a loveless marriage who flouts the rigid, hypocritical conventions of Russian society by embarking on an affair with a young army officer. Garbo played the role twice—first on the silent screen in *Love* opposite John Gilbert—then in 1935 with Fredric March (pictured above)

her husband and son and embarking on an ill-fated romance with a young army officer. A titanic part for any actress, yet one that has never quite been satisfactorily interpreted on screen, despite the fact that Garbo (twice) and Vivien Leigh both made ambitious attempts.

Greta Garbo	*Anna Karenina*	(Brown)	USA, 35
Vivien Leigh	*Anna Karenina*	(Duvivier)	GB, 48
Zully Moreno	*Amor Prohibido*	(Amadori)	Arg, 58
Tatiana Samoilova	*Anna Karenina*	(Zarkhi)	USSR, 67

Note: Garbo also played the role in MGM's 1927 silent *Love*. Earlier Annas were played by M. Sorokhtina (11) and M. Guermanova (14) in Russian adaptations and by Jeanne Delvair (Fra, 11), Theda Bara (USA, 15), Bianca Stagno Bellincioni (It, 17), Maria Melato (It, 17), Iren Varsanyi (Hung, 18) and Lya Mara (Ger, 20).

Actresses who have played the tormented Anna on TV include Nicola Pagett (BBC, 78) and Jacqueline Bisset who starred in the most recent version of the novel, directed by Hugh Benson for Columbia in 1985.

Keaton, Buster [R]

(1895–1966) Silent screen comedian (referred to by one critic as 'the supreme clown poet') who rivalled Chaplin as the king of slapstick comedy during the 20s, with a series of classic features: *Sherlock Junior* (24), *The Navigator* (24), *The General* (27). Known as the great stoneface because of his doleful expression, he declined rapidly in the 30s due to alcoholism and his inability to transfer his style of humour to the sound medium. Featured in only minor roles in some 30 movies until his death in 1966.

Donald O'Connor	*The Buster Keaton Story*	(Sheldon)	USA, 57

Keller, Helen [R]

(1880–1968) Struck deaf and blind when she was just 19 months old, this remarkable American lecturer/writer was taught to speak at the age of seven by her equally remarkable teacher, Annie Sullivan. The arduous months of Keller's agonizing education – she was taught to read with her fingers, and hear by feeling the vibrations of the throat – were related in Arthur Penn's *The Miracle Worker* based on the 1959 stage play by William Gibson. Both Patty Duke and Anne Bancroft (as Annie Sullivan) received Academy Awards for their performances.

Patty Duke	*The Miracle Worker*	(Penn)	USA, 62

Note: In Paul Aaron's 1979 TV remake Patty Duke (then Patty Duke Astin) switched roles and played Annie Sullivan. Melissa Gilbert featured as Helen Keller.

Kellerman, Annette [R]

(1888–1975) Australian swimming star who achieved prominence and notoriety in the early part of the century by swimming into the record books and wearing a brief, revolutionary one piece bathing suit. Hollywood beckoned and she subsequently appeared in several movies for Universal and Fox: *Neptune's Daughter* (14), *A Daughter Of The Gods* (16), *Queen Of The Sea* (18) etc. The 1952 screen biography proved to be the most substantial role of Esther Williams' aquatic career.

Esther Williams	*Million Dollar Mermaid*	(LeRoy)	USA, 52

Kelly, Ned [R]

(1855–80) Legendary Irish-born outlaw and horse thief who plagued the Australian authorities with his bushranging activities in Victoria and New South Wales during the 1870s. Eventually hanged for murder at the ripe old age of 25, he has been played on numerous occasions by Australian actors over the years but most controversially by pop star Mick Jagger in Tony Richardson's biopic of 1970.

Hay Simpson	*When The Kellys Rode*	(Southwell)	Austral, 34
Bob Chitty	*The Glenrowan Affair*	(Kathner)	Austral, 51
Mick Jagger	*Ned Kelly*	(Richardson)	GB, 70

Note: Frank Mills in *The Story Of The Kelly Gang* (06) and Godfrey Cass in *The Kelly Gang* (20) and *When The Kellys Were Out* (23), both featured as the outlaw on the silent screen.

Kennedy, President John F. [R]

(1917–63) The youngest man ever to be elected to the American Presidency, assassinated by Lee Harvey Oswald in Dallas, Texas, in November 1963. To date, only his war experiences (as the commander of a PT Boat in the South Pacific) have

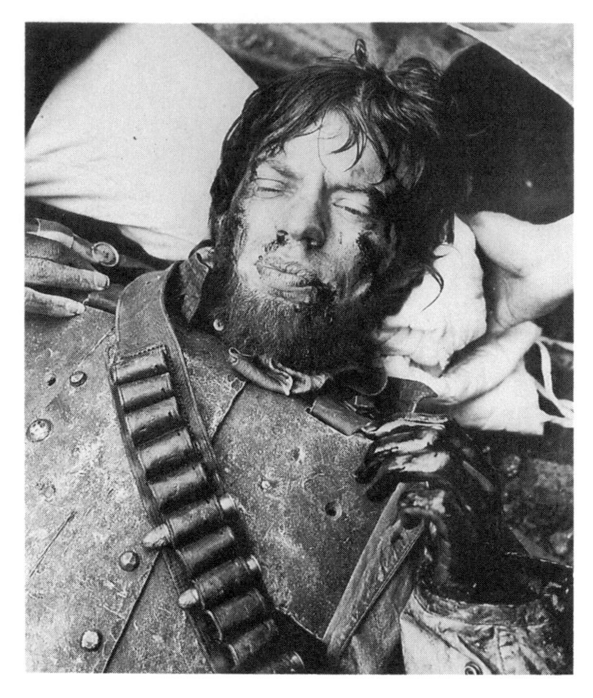

British rock star Mick Jagger as the legendary Australian outlaw Ned Kelly, an audacious piece of casting not much appreciated by the Aussies when Tony Richardson filmed Kelly's story in 1970

been recounted on the big screen and he has been served best by TV, notably Jim Goddard's 1983 biography *Kennedy* starring Martin Sheen. The earlier, *Johnny We Hardly Knew Ye* (Cates, 77) starring Paul Rudd, focused on Kennedy's first run for office as he sought a Congressional seat in 1946.

Cliff Robertson — *PT 109* (Martinson) USA, 63
William Jordan — *The Private Files Of J. Edgar Hoover* (Cohen) USA, 78

Note: The big screen documentary *John F. Kennedy: Years Of Lightning, Days Of Drums* covered Kennedy's two year ten month term of office and was released in 1964; other performers who have played Kennedy on TV include William Jordan in *King* (78), James Franciscus in *Jacqueline Bouvier Kennedy* (81), Sam Groom in *Blood Feud* (83), Cliff DeYoung in *Robert Kennedy And His Times* (85) and Charles Frank in *L.B.J.: The Early Years* (87).

Kenny, Sister Elizabeth [R]

(1886–1954) Australian bush nurse who gained international prominence for her methods of treating the crippling disease of polio. The one film about her career traces her life from her early days in the Australian bush to her constant battles with the world's medical boards over her controversial treatment. Rosalind Russell's portrayal was honoured with a best actress Oscar nomination.

Rosalind Russell — *Sister Kenny* (Nichols) USA, 46

Kern, Jerome [R]

(1885–1945) The father of the modern musical theatre, a composer whose music greatly influenced the later work of Gershwin, Youmans and Richard Rodgers. Nearly 40 Broadway shows including 'Sally', 'Show Boat' and 'Roberta'; several movies, *Swing Time, High Wide And Handsome, Cover Girl,* etc. and innumerable hit songs of exceptional tenderness – 'All The Things You Are', 'They Didn't Believe Me', 'The Last Time I Saw Paris'. The subject of a lavish MGM biography in 1946.

Robert Walker — *Till The Clouds Roll By* (Whorf) USA, 46

Kidd, Captain William [R]

(*c.* 1645–1701) Scottish-born sea captain and officer who turned pirate in 1699 and for two years plundered the Caribbean, earning a reputation for cruelty and torture. He surrendered on the promise of a pardon but nevertheless was promptly arrested in Boston and hanged at Execution Dock, London. Now something of a legendary figure, he was played by Charles Laughton in a minor biography of 1945.

Charles Laughton — *Captain Kidd* (Lee) USA, 45
Alan Napier — *Double Crossbones* (Barton) USA, 50
Charles Laughton — *Abbott And Costello Meet Captain Kidd* (Lamont) USA, 52
Robert Warwick — *Against All Flags* (Sherman) USA, 52
Anthony Dexter — *Captain Kidd And The Slave Girl* (Landers) USA, 54

Killers, The [F]

Not just any old bunch of thugs but the two sharp-talking American assassins of Hemingway's classic 1927 short story. Portrayed twice on screen, first in 1946 in a faithful recreation of the story with the two gunmen waiting in a small roadside diner to kill an ex-prizefighter, then again in a modernized Technicolor version in 1964.

Charles McGraw and William Conrad — *The Killers* (Siodmak) USA, 46
Lee Marvin and Clu Gulager — *The Killers* (Siegel) USA, 64

Note: Burt Lancaster made his screen debut as the prizefighter (Ole 'The Swede' Anderson) in the 1946 movie, John Cassavettes featured as the victim in the remake. Plans for a third version of the story, to be called *The Happy Death Of Johnny Blue Eyes,* a western set in Montana about two gunslingers waiting to kill an Apache half-breed, never materialized.

Kimmel, Admiral Husband

R

(1882–1968) Commander-in-chief of the US Pacific Fleet during the Japanese attack on Pearl Harbour on 7 December 1941. He was removed from command just ten days after the attack and took no further part in the war. Martin Balsam's portrayal in *Tora! Tora! Tora!* covers the few days prior to and during Pearl Harbour.

Martin Balsam — *Tora! Tora! Tora!* (Fleischer) USA/Japan, 70

Kipling, Rudyard

R

(1865–1936) British author of numerous stories of nineteenth century imperialist India ('Kim', 'Soldiers Three', 'Wee Willie Winkie'); portrayed on screen as part of his own story 'The Man Who Would Be King', a wry, witty and sobering tale of two British army sergeants adventuring in Kafiristan in the 1880s. Also seen briefly writing his poem 'Gunga Din' in George Stevens' 1939 spectacular for RKO.

Reginald Sheffield — *Gunga Din* (Stevens) USA, 39
Christopher Plummer — *The Man Who Would Be King* (Huston) USA, 75

Kipps, Arthur

F

H. G. Wells' 'simple soul', an Edwardian draper's assistant who comes into a fortune, tastes the fruits of high society then retreats back into his own less ambitious world and happiness. Michael Redgrave's portrait in Carol Reed's 1941 film remains the definitive portrayal; Tommy Steele's exuberant performance in the musical version includes the songs 'Half A Sixpence' and 'What A Picture'.

Michael Redgrave — *Kipps* (Reed) GB, 41
Tommy Steele — *Half A Sixpence* (Sidney) GB, 68

Note: George K. Arthur played the role in Harold Shaw's British silent version of 1921.

Knievel, Evel

R

Spectacular motor cycle stuntman who has successfully flirted with death for many years and become something of a legend in his own lifetime. He has featured in two movies, the first a biography starring George Hamilton, the second a crime thriller in which he appeared as himself. Most famous stunt: bike jumping from a ramp over a line of twenty adjacent cars.

George Hamilton — *Evel Knievel* (Chomsky) USA, 72
As himself — *Viva Knievel* (Douglas) USA, 77

Krupa, Gene

R

(1909–73) Arguably the most accomplished white jazz drummer of all time, at his best when improvising in small groups, but also inventive when contributing to the big bands of Red Nichols, Benny Goodman, Tommy Dorsey. Sal Mineo's performance in *Drum Crazy* covered 15 years of Krupa's life, following his rise to the top, his downfall when arrested for carrying marijuana, and his subsequent comeback.

Sal Mineo — *Drum Crazy* (Weis) USA, 59

Kurten, Peter

R

The frightening model for Peter Lorre's haunted child murderer in Fritz Lang's *M.* A mild-looking, middle-aged German factory worker, he created a reign of terror in Düsseldorf when he committed nine sexual murders between 1929 and 1930. He was eventually guillotined in 1931, after a plea of insanity had been rejected. The locale of Joseph Losey's remake was changed to Los Angeles.

Peter Lorre — *M* (Fritz Lang) Ger, 31
David Wayne — *M* (Losey) USA, 51
Robert Hossein — *The Vampire Of Dusseldorf* (Hossein) Fra, 64

Hunted! A terrified Peter Lorre being hounded by police and criminals alike in Fritz Lang's first sound movie, *M*, a German crime thriller derived from the gruesome activities of Peter Kurten, a child murderer known as 'The Vampire of Dusseldorf'

Lafitte, Jean [R]

(*c.* 1780–1854) French-born pirate whose band of smugglers and buccaneers came to the aid of Andrew Jackson against the British in the War of 1812. This bizarre association, culminating in the Battle of New Orleans, has been depicted twice on celluloid—in 1938 by Cecil B. DeMille and 20 years later in Anthony Quinn's remake. After the war, Lafitte returned to smuggling and piracy but eventually settled for respectability and a quiet life as a wealthy married merchant.

Fredric March	*The Buccaneer* (DeMille) USA, 38
Paul Henreid	*Last Of The Buccaneers* (Landers) USA, 50
Yul Brynner	*The Buccaneer* (Quinn) USA, 58

Note: Ricardo Cortez featured as Lafitte in Frank Lloyd's 1926 silent film *The Eagle Of The Sea.*

La Motta, Jake 

Rough, tough American boxer, raised on New York's Lower East Side, who reigned as middleweight champion of the world from June 1949 to February 1951. His violent career (both in and out of the ring) and his intense jealousy over his beautiful wife was recreated by Martin Scorsese in the ferocious *Raging Bull.* The film revealed how La Motta was eventually imprisoned on a morals charge involving a 14-year-old prostitute, became penniless and then started a new career as a stand-up comedian.

Robert De Niro	*Raging Bull* (Scorsese) USA, 80

Note: Scorsese came across La Motta when the ex-boxer was working as a bouncer in a New York strip joint. He later described his film as a 'straight, simple story of a guy attaining something, losing everything and then redeeming himself spiritually'. The searing boxing scenes occupied only 12 minutes of the film which was photographed in black and white.

Lampton, Joe 

The 'determined to make it in one bounce' working class hero of novelist John Braine. The antithesis of Osborne's Jimmy Porter, he sets his sights on the top and succeeds in his aim by seducing the daughter of a wealthy industrialist. Lives unhappily – but in comfort – ever after. First created in the novel 'Room At The Top', later a popular character on TV.

Laurence Harvey	*Room At The Top* (Clayton) GB, 59
Laurence Harvey	*Life At The Top* (Kotcheff) GB, 66
Kenneth Haigh	*Man At The Top* (Vardy) GB, 73

Lancelot 

The most valiant of the knights of King Arthur's Round Table. More often than not a simple cut and thrust swashbuckler on screen although Franco Nero's performance in *Camelot* conveyed much of his tragic passion for Queen Guinevere, a passion which destroyed his friendship with Arthur and led to the break up of the Order Of The Round Table. John Cleese in *Monty Python And The Holy Grail* remains the unlikeliest Lancelot to date; Nicholas Clay the most realistic and least romanticized.

Henry Wilcoxon	*A Connecticut Yankee In King Arthur's Court* (Garnett) USA, 49
Robert Taylor	*Knights Of The Round Table* (Thorpe) GB, 54
Don Megowan	*Prince Valiant* (Hathaway) USA, 54
Cornel Wilde	*Lancelot And Guinevere* (Wilde) GB, 63
Franco Nero	*Camelot* (Logan) USA, 67
Luc Simon	*Lancelot du lac* (Bresson) Fra/It, 74
John Cleese	*Monty Python And The Holy Grail* (Gilliam/Jones) GB, 75
Nicholas Clay	*Excalibur* (Boorman) USA, 81

Note: Wilfred McDonald played Lancelot in the silent version of *A Connecticut Yankee In King Arthur's Court*; on TV Rupert Everett featured as the knight in Clive Donner's *Arthur The King* (83).

The face of a Raging Bull—Robert De Niro as middleweight boxing champion Jake La Motta in Martin Scorsese's harrowing account of La Motta's life in and out of the ring. The film marked the peak of the De Niro/Scorsese collaborations. Only 12 of its 129 minutes were set inside the ring. For his later scenes when La Motta had descended to earning a living as a sleazy nightclub entertainer De Niro gained 60lbs in four months!

Chivalrous knight and lover of Queen Guinevere! Robert Taylor as Sir Lancelot in MGM's British-filmed CinemaScope epic *Knights of the Round Table*

Landru, Henri-Desire [R]

France's infamous 'Bluebeard', a bald, unprepossessing little family man who delighted in growing roses and dealing in antiques. Unfortunately, he also dabbled in murder, disposing of ten rich widows between 1915 and 1919, the motive on each occasion being money. When brought to trial he denied all charges but was eventually guillotined in February, 1922. Claude Chabrol's 1962 film is the definitive screen biography, its only fault bèing that the lovely Danielle Darrieux, Hildegarde Neff and Michele Morgan rank among the victims.

George Sanders — *Bluebeard's Ten Honeymoons* (Lee Wilder) GB, 60
Charles Denner — *Landru* (Chabrol) Fra, 62

Note: Chaplin's *Monsieur Verdoux* (USA, 47) about an elegant French murderer of rich widows, was closely modelled on the career of Landru.

Langsdorff, Captain Hans [R]

(1890–1939) One of the honourable figures of 'the phoney war', the German commander of the pocket battleship 'Graf Spee' which sank several ships before being trapped by three British cruisers – 'Ajax', 'Exeter' and 'Achilles' – near Montevideo harbour. Realizing escape was impossible, Langsdorff landed his crew and prisoners of war before scuttling his ship and committing suicide.

Peter Finch — *The Battle Of The River Plate* (Powell/Pressburger) GB, 56

Lao, Dr [F]

A mysterious Chinese showman who arrives in a small Arizona town on a yellow jackass, erects a single ragged tent he calls a circus and then teaches the inhabitants a series of moral lessons, changing his appearance with each story he has to tell. In George Pal's 1964 film Tony Randall underwent seven make-up changes, appearing as Lao, a giant serpent, the Abominable Snowman, Medusa, Merlin The Magician, Pan and Apollonius of Tyana. Charles Finney's book upon which the film was based was first published in 1935; Peter Sellers was first choice for the role of Lao but had not then played Inspector Clouseau and was not regarded as an international star.

Tony Randall — *The 7 Faces Of Dr Lao* (Pal) USA, 64

Larsen, Wolf [F]

Nietzschean figure, created by Jack London in his powerful novel 'The Sea Wolf' (1904). A ruthless yet educated captain of the schooner 'Ghost', he is finally destroyed by his mutinous crew and his own manic depression which finally gives way to blindness and madness. The 1950 version of the story, *Barricade,* was adapted into a western with Larsen recast as the owner of a gold mine utilizing slave labour.

Milton Sills — *The Sea Wolf* (Santell) USA, 30
Edward G. Robinson — *The Sea Wolf*  (Curtiz) USA, 41
Raymond Massey — *Barricade* (Godfrey) USA, 50
Barry Sullivan — *Wolf Larsen* (Jones) USA, 58
Chuck Connors — *Larsen, Wolf Of The Seven Seas* (Vari) It/USA, 74

Note: Hobart Bosworth (13), Noah Beery (20) and Ralph Ince (26) all appeared in silent versions of the role.

Lawrence, D.H.

R

(1885–1930) English novelist, short story writer and poet who created a furore in the 1920s with his highly charged novels, all of which frankly discussed sex, often with a liberal amount of four letter words. Several of his novels have been filmed, e.g. *Sons And Lovers, Lady Chatterley's Lover, Women In Love,* but only in recent times have film-makers explored Lawrence's own life in any detail. Christopher Miles, *Priest Of Love* concentrated on the author's life between 1915 and 1930 when he travelled extensively in Italy, Mexico and France and struggled against the debilitating effects of tuberculosis, and Tim Burstall's *Kangeroo* centred on his brief flirtation with Fascism during a trip to Australia.

Ian McKellen — *Priest Of Love* (Miles) GB, 81

Colin Friels (as Richard Somers) — *Kangeroo* (Burstall) Australia, 86

Note: *Kangeroo* was adapted from Lawrence's autobiographical novel of the same name; Lawrence's German-born wife Frieda (six years his elder and the mother of three children) was played by Janet Suzman in *Priest Of Love* and Judy Davis in *Kangeroo.*

Lawrence, Gertrude

R

(1898 or 1902–52) Vivacious British revue star of the 20s, associated for many years with Noel Coward and famous for her singing and dancing stage roles – 'Lady In The Dark', 'The King And I', etc. Never achieved anywhere near the same success on screen, appearing in only a handful of films, but played with vigour and authority by Julie Andrews in Robert Wise's underrated biography, *Star!*

Julie Andrews — *Star!* (Wise) USA, 68

Lawrence, Marjorie

R

(1907–79) Australian-born operatic soprano whose brilliant career as a Wagnerian singer was cruelly curtailed by an attack of polio in 1941. Succeeded in making a courageous comeback but subsequently concentrated on teaching in American universities and running summer opera workshops. Eleanor Parker won an Oscar nomination for her portrayal of Miss Lawrence in 1955.

Eleanor Parker — *Interrupted Melody* (Bernhardt) USA, 55

Lawrence, T.E.

(1888–1935) Enigmatic British soldier and scholar who during his two years in Arabia in the First World War succeeded in uniting the Arab tribes against the Turks and became known as the legendary 'El Aurens'. Once described by Winston Churchill as 'the greatest living Englishman', he died in obscurity in a motor cycle accident in Dorset after serving in the RAF under the name of Shaw. Peter O'Toole's performance as Lawrence in David Lean's film turned him into a major star; Albert Finney, first choice for the role, turned the part down.

Peter O'Toole — *Lawrence Of Arabia* (Lean) GB, 62

King Lear

Legendary British king who seeks nothing but peace in his old age but declines into madness after enduring long and bitter conflicts with his three daughters. The central figure in what is generally considered to be Shakespeare's greatest work, he was portrayed twice on screen in the 70s, Peter Brook's film in particular reflecting the sadness of a man growing old before his time. More recently he has been played by Tatsuya Nakadai in Kurosawa's epic *Ran,* set in sixteenth century Japan, and Burgess Meredith (as a Mafia chieftain!) in Godard's bizarre updating set in a post-Chernobyl world.

Paul Scofield — *King Lear* (Brook) GB/Den, 71

Yuri Jarvet — *King Lear* (Kozintsev) USSR, 71

Tatsuya Nakadai — *Ran* (Kurosawa) Fra/Japan, 85

Burgess Meredith — *King Lear* (Godard) USA/Swi, 87

Note: *House Of Strangers* (49), a story of New York big business starring Edward G. Robinson, was a reworking of the Lear theme as was its western remake *Broken Lance* (54) with Spencer Tracy as a cattle baron. William V. Ranous (USA, 09), Maurice

D.H. Lawrence on screen! (Above) Colin Friels and Judy Davis in *Kangaroo;* (right) Ian McKellen as the controversial author in Christopher Miles' production *Priest Of Love,* an account of Lawrence's final years and the problems surrounding the publication of *Lady Chatterley's Lover*

'The first intelligent epic' was how one British critic described David Lean's *Lawrence of Arabia*. Not the least of the film's attributes were the performances of the all-star cast including Peter O'Toole in the title role. O'Toole was cast in the film after Albert Finney had refused the part

Costello (USA, 09), Guiseppe De Liguoro (It, 10), Ermete Novelli (It, 10) and Frederick Warde (USA, 16) all appeared as Lear on the silent screen.

On TV, Orson Welles (53), Michael Hordern (twice, in 75 and 82) and Laurence Olivier (84) have all appeared as the aged king.

Ledbetter, Huddie [R]

(1885–1949) Black blues singer/songwriter who learned the blues the hard way – breaking rocks in a chain gang in the Deep South. One of America's most widely acknowledged folksingers, his influence remains a significant force in music even 40 years after his death. Among his compositions: 'Good Night, Irene', 'Midnight Special', 'Rock Island Line', 'Cotton Fields', 'Bring Me L'il Water Silvey'. The songs in the 1976 biography *Leadbelly* were sung by HiTide Harris.

Roger E. Mosley *Leadbelly* (Parks) USA, 76

Lee, Gypsy Rose [R]

(1913–70) The best known stripper in show business, she appeared on stage with her sister (June Havoc) from the age of six. An undistinguished career in films but a sensation on stage. The Broadway musical 'Gypsy' (59) celebrated her early career and baptism into burlesque, notably with the song 'Let Me Entertain You'. Real name: Louise Hovick.

Natalie Wood *Gypsy* (LeRoy) USA, 62

Ran, Akira Kurosawa's epic version of Shakespeare's tragedy, King Lear'. Tatsuya Nakadai, (bearded in white) starred as an ageing 16th century Japanese warlord who, after a lifetime of ruthless Martial exploits, turns over his domain to his three sons, thus causing jealousy and bloodshed among his kin.

'Let Me Entertain You!' Natalie Wood as the famous stripper Gypsy Rose Lee in Warners' film version of the Broadway musical *Gypsy*

Lee, Lorelei [F]

Celebrated gold-digger who, although none too bright intellectually, uses her physical charms to land one of America's richest bachelors during an ocean trip to Europe. First created by Anita Loos in her 1925 novel 'Gentlemen Prefer Blondes', she was perfectly characterized by Marilyn Monroe (just on the verge of superstardom) in Howard Hawks' comedy of 1953. Loos' book, which was subtitled 'The Illuminating Diary of a Professional Lady', became a runaway best-seller, partly because of its satirical qualities but mainly because it was used as a handbook by young women wanting to get rich quick!

Marilyn Monroe	*Gentlemen Prefer Blondes* (Hawks) USA, 53

Note: Ruth Taylor played Lorelei in a 1928 Paramount silent; 25 years after the book's initial success Anita Loos and Joseph Fields adapted it into a Broadway musical (the basis for the Monroe film) with music by Jule Styne and lyrics by Leo Robin. The show starred Carol Channing and introduced such hit numbers as 'Bye Bye Baby' and 'Diamonds Are A Girl's Best Friend'.

Lemon Drop Kid, The

Renowned Damon Runyon character, a race track tipster who has to raise 10 000 dollars by Christmas Day in order to pay off his debt to a gang of mobsters. The 1951 production, partly rewritten and directed (uncredited) by Frank Tashlin, provided Bob Hope with one of his most amusing roles.

Lee Tracy	*The Lemon Drop Kid* (Neilman) USA, 34
Bob Hope	*The Lemon Drop Kid* (Lanfield) USA, 51

Lenin, Nikolai [R]

(1870–1924) Russian revolutionary and profound student of Marxism who first took part in revolutionary activity in the 1890s and then led the Bolsheviks to supreme power in October 1917. Many notable portrayals on the Soviet screen, e.g. Boris Shchukin in *Lenin In October* and *Lenin In 1918,* and Maxim Shtraukh in *Lenin In Poland.*

Tenen Holtz	*British Agent* (Curtiz) USA, 34
Boris Shchukin	*Lenin In October* (Romm) USSR, 37
Maxim Shtraukh	*The Man With A Gun* (Yutkevich) USSR, 38
K. Miuffko	*Great Dawn* (Chiaureli) USSR, 38
Boris Shchukin	*Lenin In 1918* (Romm) USSR, 39
Maxim Shtraukh	*The Vyborg Side* (Kozintsev/Trauberg) USSR, 39
Maxim Shtraukh	*His Name Is Sukhe-Bator* (Zarkhi/Heifits) USSR, 42
Nikolai Kolesnikov	*Light Over Russia* (Yutkevich)
I. Molchanov	*The Unforgettable Year, 1919* (Chiaureli) USSR, 52
Nikolai Plotnikov	*Prologue* (Dzigan) USSR, 56
Maxim Shtraukh	*Stories About Lenin* (Yutkevich) USSR, 58
V. Chestnokov	*In The October Days* (Vasiliev) USSR, 58
Maxim Shtraukh	*Lenin In Poland* (Yutkevich) USSR, 66
Yuri Kayurov	*The Sixth Of July* (Karasik) USSR, 68

John Gabriel	*Oh! What A Lovely War* (Attenborough)	GB, 69
Michael Bryant	*Nicholas And Alexandra* (Schaffner)	USA, 71
Roger Sloman	*Reds* (Beatty)	USA, 81

Note: In Eisenstein's 1928 film about the Revolution, *October,* the role of Lenin was played by Nikandrov. On TV Ben Kingsley starred as Lenin in Damiani's four hour TV film *The Train* (88) which documented Lenin's rail journey from Zurich to the Finland station in St Petersburg, where he eventually seized control of the Revolution. Leslie Caron co-starred as Lenin's wife, Nadezhda Krupskaya.

Leonowens, Anna [R]

English governess who travelled to Bangkok in Siam in 1862 and spent five years as secretary-tutor-confidante to King Mongut, teaching the semi barbaric king a more civilized way of life and his 67 children the rudiments of the English language. Played with moving simplicity by Irene Dunne in John Cromwell's straight version in 1946 and with a rather cloying sweetness by Deborah Kerr (dubbed by Marni Nixon in the musical numbers) in the CinemaScope version of Rodgers And Hammerstein's *The King And I.*

Irene Dunne	*Anna And The King Of Siam* (Cromwell)	USA, 46
Deborah Kerr	*The King And I* (Lang)	USA, 56

Note: Margaret Landon's novel (1944) on which the film and show were based, was first conceived as musical material by Gertrude Lawrence. The show premiered in 1951 with Lawrence as Anna and Yul Brynner as The King. Brynner went on to win an Oscar for repeating his role on screen and played the part yet again on TV in 1972 when he co-starred with Samantha Eggar (as Anna) in 13 half-hour episodes of *Anna And The King.* In the 1946 film Rex Harrison (third choice after James Mason and Robert Montgomery) featured as the King.

Leopold, Nathan & Loeb, Richard [R]

Two rich Chicago youths who, in 1924, murdered a 14-year-old schoolboy in order to prove their Nietzschean theory that their intellectual superiority exempted them from moral law. Leopold, who engaged in perverse sexuality, and Loeb, an overt homosexual, were defended by Clarence Darrow, a lifelong campaigner against capital punishment. Each received 99 years for murder and kidnapping. Neither of the two films based on their gruesome activities have identified Leopold and Loeb by name.

Farley Granger and John Dall	*Rope* (Hitchcock)	USA, 48
Dean Stockwell and Bradford Dillman	*Compulsion* (Fleischer)	USA, 59

Note: In 1936 Loeb was stabbed to death for sexually molesting another inmate. Leopold died, aged 71, while on parole in Puerto Rico.

Lepke, Louis [R]

(–1943) A killer and top executive in Murder, Inc., an organization set up by Al Capone and the Mafia in the late 20s to handle contracts on Syndicate opponents. A powerful colleague of Lucky Luciano and Albert Anastasia, he died in the electric chair in 1943 after surrendering himself to J. Edgar Hoover. Until Tony Curtis' detailed performance in Menahem Golan's film, an unknown character in the *genre* of true life American gangster films. Real name: Louis 'Lepke' Buchalter.

David J. Stewart	*Murder, Inc.* (Balaban/Rosenberg)	USA, 60
Tony Curtis	*Lepke* (Golan)	USA, 75
Gordon Zimmerman	*The Private Files Of J. Edgar Hoover* (Cohen)	USA, 78

Lestrade, Inspector 

Inept Scotland Yard inspector whose incompetence is forever throwing the deductory powers of Sherlock Holmes into even sharper light in Conan Doyle's famous series of detective stories. Described by Dr Watson as 'little, sallow, rat-faced and dark-eyed', he is generally a subsidiary figure on screen, although Frank Finlay has made something of him in two Holmes adventures, *A Study In Terror* and *Murder By Decree.*

Philip Hewland	*The Sleeping Cardinal* (Hiscott)	GB, 31
Philip Hewland	*The Missing Rembrandt* (Hiscott)	GB, 32
Alan Mowbray	*A Study In Scarlet* (Marin)	USA, 33
Charles Mortimer	*The Triumph Of Sherlock Holmes* (Hiscott)	GB, 35

A lethal line up! The Brooklyn Group (better known as 'Murder Inc') as they looked in 1935 and as they were portrayed in the 1975 crime thriller *Lepke*. Tony Curtis (front row, fourth from left) starred as Louis 'Lepke' Buchalter who headed the group and, together with Lucky Luciano and Albert Anastasia, handled contracts on Syndicate opponents

John Turnbull	*Silver Blaze* (Bentley) GB, 37
Dennis Hoey	*Sherlock Holmes And The Secret Weapon* (Neill) USA, 42
Dennis Hoey	*Sherlock Holmes Faces Death* (Neill) USA, 43
Dennis Hoey	*Spider Woman* (Neill) USA, 44
Dennis Hoey	*The Pearl Of Death* (Neill) USA, 44
Dennis Hoey	*The House Of Fear* (Neill) USA, 45
Dennis Hoey	*Terror By Night* (Neill) USA, 46
Frank Finlay	*A Study In Terror* (Hill) GB, 65
Frank Finlay	*Murder By Decree* (Clark) GB, 79
Ronald Lacey	*The Hound Of The Baskervilles* (Hickox) GB, 83
Roger Ashton-Griffiths	*Young Sherlock Holmes* (Levinson) USA, 85

Note: Arthur Bell appeared as Lestrade in the first few films in the Stoll series made by Maurice Elvey in Britain in the early 20s; on TV the most recent interpretation has been by Colin Jeavons in the Granada series (84–8) starring Jeremy Brett. Earlier small screen portrayals include those of Bill Owen (51), Peter Madden (65), William Lucas (68) and Alan Caillou in the 1972 TV version of *The Hound Of The Baskervilles* starring Stewart Granger as Holmes.

Levi, Dolly F

Thornton Wilder's formidable matchmaking heroine of turn-of-the-century New York. A scheming, affable widow, she is the central figure in both Wilder's New York play 'The Matchmaker' and the subsequent Broadway musical 'Hello, Dolly!' (1964). Louis Armstrong's hit title number is a valentine to her matchmaking abilities; the song 'Put On Your Sunday Clothes' celebrates her own vigorous intentions.

Shirley Booth *The Matchmaker* (Anthony) USA, 58
Barbra Streisand *Hello, Dolly!* (Kelly) USA, 69

Lewis, Joe E. 

(1902–71) A young prohibition singer who made a courageous comeback as a stand-up comic after mobsters brought his musical career to an abrupt end by slashing his vocal cords. Frank Sinatra who had earlier worked with Lewis and become friendly with him on the nightclub circuit, portrayed him in the 1957 film *The Joker Is Wild* which included such vintage numbers as 'I Cried For You' and 'Chicago' and also the Oscar-winning Sammy Cahn/James Van Heusen song 'All The Way'.

Frank Sinatra *The Joker Is Wild* (Charles Vidor) USA, 57

Note: Sophie Tucker, who in real life helped Lewis back to the big time via the burlesque route, played herself in the film.

Liar, Billy 

Young undertaker's clerk (real name, Billy Fisher) who escapes from his humdrum life in a Northern industrial town through a series of elaborate fantasies in which he imagines himself as the ruler of the mythical kingdom of Ambrosia. A likeable, yet finally tragic character, when he does at last get the chance to start a new life in London he loses his nerve and returns to the world of his dreams. Created by Keith Waterhouse and Willis Hall in the stage play of 1960.

Tom Courtenay *Billy Liar* (Schlesinger) GB, 63

Note: Waterhouse and Hall later turned *Billy Liar* into a short-lived TV comedy series (73–4) starring Jeffe Rawle. *Billy* (79) the American equivalent starring Steve Guttenberg was unsuccessful.

Liddell, Eric R

Devout Scottish athelete (known as 'The Flying Scotsman') who in the 1920s was acclaimed as one of the fastest men in the world when he won the 400 metres at the 1924 Paris Olympics—but not before creating something of a sensation by refusing to run on a Sunday because of his religious beliefs. He subsequently became a missionary in China and died in a Japanese internment camp in 1945. Ian Charleson portrayed Liddell in the Oscar-winning 1981 film *Chariots Of Fire*.

Ian Charleson *Chariots Of Fire* (Hudson) GB, 81

Note: Harold Abrahams, the British athlete who challenged Liddell and who ran at Cambridge to overcome the anti-semitic prejudice of the teaching fraternity was portrayed by Ben Cross.

L'il Abner 

The beefcake hillbilly hero of Al Capp's cartoon village of Dogpatch, a Kentucky hamlet deemed to be the most expendable part of the United States! To date, there have been two portrayals on screen – by Granville Owen in the small-budget RKO production of 1940 and by Peter Palmer in Paramount's film version of the Broadway musical which centred on the US government's decision to use Dogpatch as a site for atomic testing. Capp often injected social and political satire into his cartoon strip which was first published in 1934.

Granville Owen *L'il Abner* (Rogell) USA, 40
Peter Palmer *L'il Abner* (Frank) USA, 59

Note: Other characters made famous by the strip have included Abner's dumb-blonde girlfriend Daisy Mae (played by Martha O'Driscoll in 1940 and Leslie Parrish in 1959) and the marriage vendor Marryin' Sam essayed by Dick Elliot (40) and Stubby Kaye (59).

Liliom 

The disreputable hero of a 1909 Ferenc Molnar play, a Budapest merry-go-round barker who tries to rob a bank to provide for his wife, kills himself to avoid capture but reforms on his way to heaven and is allowed to redeem himself during another ten years on Earth. The various film versions have mostly concentrated on the American updating of the

A victorious Eric Liddell (Ian Charleson) being held aloft by his fellow athletes after winning a Gold Medal for the 400 metres at the 1924 Paris Olympics. A scene from Hugh Hudson's award winning 1981 film *Chariots of Fire*

story which has transposed Liliom's activities to such places as Coney Island and renamed him variously as Curly Flynn and Billy Bigelow. Fritz Lang's 1934 French film with Charles Boyer was an exception and remained close to Molnar's original play. The story also served as the basis for the musical *Carousel* which was filmed by Fox in CinemaScope in 1956.

Charles Farrell	*Liliom* (Borzage)	USA, 30
Charles Boyer	*Liliom* (Lang)	Fra, 34
Gordon MacRae	*Carousel* (Walter Lang)	USA, 56

Note: Bert Lytell starred in a silent 1921 version titled *A Trip To Paradise* and directed by Maxwell Karger.

Lime, Harry

F

A trafficker in diluted penicillin in the ruins of post-war Vienna. One of the screen's most famous villains, remembered with affection despite the fact that his smuggling activities bring agonizing deaths to scores of young children. Ends up, appropriately enough, as a corpse among the sewer rats of the city.

Orson Welles	*The Third Man* (Reed)	GB, 49

Note: Although created by Graham Greene in 1949, Lime was conceived some 20 years earlier when Greene scribbled a note on the back of an envelope, 'I had paid my last farewell to Harry a week ago when his coffin was lowered into the frozen

Orson Welles as penicillin racketeer Harry Lime in Carol Reed's classic thriller of post-war Vienna, *The Third Man* (1949)

February ground so that it was with incredulity that I saw him pass by, without a sign of recognition among the host of strangers in the Strand!' Michael Rennie (far removed from the screen original) played Lime as a smooth international do-gooder in the 1959–61 TV series.

Lincoln, Abraham [R]

(1809–65) The most distinguished of all American Presidents; a former storekeeper, postmaster, surveyor and lawyer who was twice elected to the Presidency (in 1861 and 1865) and served during the dark and turbulent years of his country's Civil War. His days as a lawyer in Springfield were conveyed with affection by John Ford in *Young Mr Lincoln,* his political career recounted in *Abraham Lincoln* and *Abe Lincoln in Illinois,* and the events leading to his assassination examined in *The Lincoln Conspiracy.* During the 30s, Frank McGlynn starred regularly as Lincoln in minor screen portrayals.

Actor	Film
Walter Huston	*Abraham Lincoln* (Griffith) USA, 30
Frank McGlynn	*Roaring West*/serial (Taylor) USA, 35
Frank McGlynn	*The Littlest Rebel* (Butler) USA, 35
Bud Buster	*Cavalry* (Bradbury) USA, 36
Frank McGlynn	*Hearts In Bondage* (Ayres) USA, 36
Frank McGlynn	*The Prisoner Of Shark Island* (Ford) USA, 36
Frank McGlynn	*The Plainsman* (De Mille) USA, 37
Frank McGlynn	*Wells Fargo* (Lloyd) USA, 37
Frank McGlynn	*Western Gold* (Bretherton) USA, 37
Albert Russell	*Courage Of The West* (Lewis) USA, 37
Percy Parsons	*Victoria The Great* (Wilcox) GB, 37
John Carradine	*Of Human Hearts* (Brown) USA, 38
Henry Fonda	*Young Mr Lincoln* (Ford) USA, 39
Frank McGlynn	*The Mad Empress* (Torres) Mex, 39
Raymond Massey	*Abe Lincoln In Illinois* (Cromwell) USA, 40
Victor Kilian	*Virginia City* (Curtiz) USA, 40
Charles Middleton	*Santa Fe Trail* (Curtiz) USA, 40
Charles Middleton	*They Died With Their Boots On* (Walsh) USA, 41
Joel Day	*The Days Of Buffalo Bill* (Carr) USA, 46
Jeff Corey	*Rock Island Trail* (Kane) USA, 50
Jeff Corey	*Transcontinent Express* (Kane) USA, 50
Leslie Kimmell	*The Tall Target* (Anthony Mann) USA, 51
Hans Conreid	*New Mexico* (Reis) USA, 51
Stanley Hall	*Prince Of Players* (Dunne) USA, 55
Austin Green	*The Story Of Mankind* (Allen) USA, 57
Raymond Massey	*How The West Was Won* (Hathaway/Marshall/Ford) USA, 62
Jeff Corey	*Der Schatz der Azteken* (Siodmak) W.Ger/Fra/It/Yug, 65
John Anderson	*The Lincoln Conspiracy* (Conway) USA, 77

Note: Lincoln was also a popular figure on the silent screen. D. W. Griffith selected Joseph Henabery for the role in his *Birth Of A Nation* (15); Judge Charles

Edward Bull appeared for John Ford in *The Iron Horse* (24) and George Billings featured in the 1924 biography, *Abraham Lincoln*. Like McGlynn Billings made a small career out of playing Lincoln, appearing several times as the President in the 20s, eg. *Barbara Frietchie* (24), *The Man Without A Country* (25) and *Hands Up* (26). All told there were more than 40 silent portrayals of Lincoln.

On TV, Dennis Weaver in *The Great Man's Whiskers* (73) and Gregory Peck in *The Blue And The Grey* (83) both featured as the President.

Lindbergh, Charles A. [R]

(1902–74) American aviator who made the first non-stop transatlantic flight (from New York to Paris) in May, 1927. The name of the plane, 'The Spirit Of St Louis', was also that of Lindbergh's Pulitzer Prize-winning book of 1953. James Stewart played Lindbergh in Billy Wilder's uncharacteristic but absorbing 1957 film which concentrated on the background to the flight and also the flight itself.

James Stewart	*The Spirit Of St Louis* (Wilder)	USA, 57

Note: The later, more tragic incident in Lindbergh's life i.e. the kidnapping and murder of his baby son, was explored in Buzz Kulik's 1976 TV movie *The Lindbergh Kidnapping Case* with Cliff De Young featuring as Lindbergh and Anthony Hopkins as Bruno Hauptmann, the man eventually executed for the crime. A TV documentary by Ludovic Kennedy, *Who Killed The Lindbergh Baby?*, was shown in 1982; Agatha Christie's *Murder On The Orient Express* (filmed in 1974), which centred on the kidnapping and murder of a child, also derived from the Lindbergh affair.

Liszt, Franz [R]

(1811–86) Hungarian composer and virtuoso pianist, a child prodigy who first performed in public at the age of nine. A favourite subject for film-makers, especially as he found time to appreciate the physical attractions of Lola Montes between composing his twenty Hungarian rhapsodies. Ken Russell's fantasy biography with Roger Daltrey was a rock conception of Liszt's life and innovatory music and looked at the composer as an early superstar.

Hans Schlenk	*Abschiedswalzer* (Bolvary)	Ger, 34
Ferenc Taray	*Szerelmi Almok* (Hille)	Hung, 35
Brandon Hurst	*Suez* (Dwan)	USA, 38
Fritz Leiber	*The Phantom Of The Opera* (Lubin)	USA, 43
Stephen Bekassy	*A Song To Remember* (Charles Vidor)	USA, 45
Henry Daniell	*Song Of Love* (Brown)	USA, 47
Svyatoslav Richter	*Glinka* (Alexandrov)	USSR, 52
Jacques Francois	*At The Order Of The Tsar* (Haguet)	Fra, 54
Will Quadflieg	*Lola Montes* (Ophuls)	Fra/Ger, 55
Carlos Thompson	*Magic Fire* (Dieterle)	USA, 56
Dirk Bogarde	*Song Without End* (Charles Vidor)	USA, 60
Henry Gilbert	*Song Of Norway* (Stone)	USA, 70
Imre Sinkovits	*The Loves Of Liszt* (Keleti)	Hung/USSR, 70
Roger Daltrey	*Lisztomania* (Russell)	GB, 75

Only Hollywood could have come up with a still such as this. A romantic Dirk Bogarde embracing an eager Capucine in Columbia's biography of Franz Liszt, *Song Without End*

Little Caesar

F

Small-time hoodlum who rises to become the head of a Chicago gangster outfit before slipping back into obscurity and being gunned down by the police. Dubbed 'Little Caesar' because of his size, name (Rico Bandello) and pugnacious character, he was not, as is sometimes thought, based on Al Capone but on one Salvatore Cardinella who operated in Chicago's Little Italy in the 20s. Adapted from W.R. Burnett's 1929 novel the film made Edward G. Robinson a star and also offered him the chance to gasp one of the most famous last lines in movies: 'Mother of mercy, is this the end of Rico?'

Edward G. Robinson	*Little Caesar* (LeRoy) USA, 31

Little John

F

Along with Friar Tuck, the most easily identifiable member of Robin Hood's outlaw band and a character who appears not only in several ballads, but in Walter Scott's 1825 novel 'The Talisman'. His battle with Robin with quarter-staves on a log spanning a stream was first depicted on film in the famous Warner swashbuckler of 1938. Burley Hollywood character actor Alan Hale played him three times; Nicol Williamson portrayed him as an old man in Richard Lester's *Robin And Marian*.

Edward G. Robinson as small-time hood turned underworld bigshot Rico Bandello, the role that made him a star in Mervyn Le Roy's *Little Caesar*

Alan Hale	*The Adventures Of Robin Hood* (Curtiz/Keighley) USA, 38
Ray Teal	*The Bandit Of Sherwood Forest* (Sherman/Levin) USA, 46
Walter Sande	*Prince Of Thieves* (Bretherton) USA, 48
Alan Hale	*Rogues Of Sherwood Forest* (Douglas) USA, 50
Wade Crosby	*Tales Of Robin Hood* (Tinling) USA, 51
James Robertson Justice	*The Story Of Robin Hood And His Merrie Men* (Annakin) GB, 52
Leslie Linder	*Men Of Sherwood Forest* (Guest) GB, 54
George Woodbridge	*Son Of Robin Hood* (Sherman) GB, 58
Nigel Green	*Sword Of Sherwood Forest* (Fisher) GB, 60
Leon Greene	*A Challenge For Robin Hood* (Pennington Richards) GB, 67
John Baldry	*Up The Chastity Belt* (Kellett) GB, 71
Dan Meaden	*Wolfshead: The Legend Of Robin Hood* (Hough) GB, 73
Nicol Williamson	*Robin And Marian* (Lester) USA, 76
Pat Roach	*The Zany Adventures Of Robin Hood* (Austin) TVM/USA, 84

Note: Little John was voiced by Phil Harris in Disney's 1973 cartoon, *Robin Hood;* Dean Martin played the equivalent role to that of Little John in *Robin And The Seven Hoods* (64), a modern gangster version of the story.

On TV Clive Mantle featured as the outlaw in *Robin Of Sherwood* (1984–6).

Little Women

F

Four teenage sisters who find maturity and romance as they grow up in a Massachusetts household during the turbulent days of the Civil War. Louisa May Alcott's novel, a timeless, gentle tale of lavender and lace, was published in 1868–9; the definitive screen portrayal of the tomboyish Jo, the headstrong, literary member of the family, belongs safely in the hands of Katharine Hepburn.

The sisters have been played as follows in the four silent and sound versions of the story:

Jo March

Ruby Miller	*Little Women* (Samuelson/Butler)	GB, 17
Dorothy Bernard	*Little Women* (Knowles)	USA, 19
Katharine Hepburn	*Little Women* (Cukor)	USA, 33
June Allyson	*Little Women* (LeRoy)	USA, 49

Amy March

Daisy Burrell	*Little Women* (Samuelson/Butler)	GB, 17
Florence Finn	*Little Women* (Knowles)	USA, 19
Joan Bennett	*Little Women* (Cukor)	USA, 33
Elizabeth Taylor	*Little Women* (LeRoy)	USA, 49

Beth March

Muriel Myers	*Little Women* (Samuelson/Butler)	GB, 17
Lilian Hall	*Little Women* (Knowles)	USA, 19
Jean Parker	*Little Women* (Cukor)	USA, 33
Margaret O'Brien	*Little Women* (LeRoy)	USA, 49

Meg March

Mary Lincoln	*Little Women* (Samuelson/Butler)	GB, 17
Isabel Lamon	*Little Women* (Knowles)	USA, 19
Frances Dee	*Little Women* (Cukor)	USA, 33
Janet Leigh	*Little Women* (LeRoy)	USA, 49

Note: A 200 minute TV movie, directed by David Lowell Rich, was filmed in 1978. Susan Dey featured as Jo, Ann Dusenberry as Amy, Eve Plumb as Beth and Meredith Baxter Birney as Meg.

Livingstone, David [R]

(1813–73) Scottish explorer and medical missionary who was 'found' in Africa in 1871 by Henry Stanley, but who holds somewhat higher claims to fame in the world's history books, i.e. exposing the slave trade and discovering the Victoria Falls and Lake Nyasa. There have been two biographies of his life, one silent, one sound, and also a version of the Stanley incident. Nothing since.

Percy Marmont	*David Livingstone* (Fitzpatrick)	GB, 36
Cedric Hardwicke	*Stanley And Livingstone* (Henry King)	USA, 39
Neal Arden	*The Best House In London* (Saville)	GB, 69

Note: M. A. Wetherell starred as *Livingstone* in a British production of 1925.

Lola-Lola [F]

A seductive night club entertainer, made legendary by Marlene Dietrich who, with the help of magnificent stockinged legs, a silk hat perched nonchalantly on her head and the song 'Falling In Love Again' traps and destroys the elderly schoolteacher who becomes infatuated with her. The 1959 remake starring May Britt was several notches below its predecessor; Fassbinder's 1981 film *Lola* was a vague modernist revamping of the tale with Lola cast as the star of a nightclub/bordello in a small city in provincial Germany in the 50s. No credit was given to Heinrich Mann's original novel in the Fassbinder film.

Marlene Dietrich	*The Blue Angel* (Von Sternberg)	Ger, 30
May Britt	*The Blue Angel* (Dmytryk)	USA, 59
Barbara Sukowa	*Lola* (Fassbinder)	Ger, 81

Note: In Mann's 1905 novel 'Professor Unrat' Lola was named Rosa Frohlich, a singer with a child from a previous marriage. Her affair with a middle-aged teacher leads to their marriage, the loss of his professorship and a future in corrupt politics as the teacher revenges himself on society.

Lolita [F]

The most famous nymphet in literature, an unconsciously seductive 12-year-old who enslaves a middle-aged American lecturer – with hilarious, pathetic, and ultimately tragic results. The central figure in Vladimir Nabokov's 1955 novel of murder and lust; turned into a teenager in Kubrick's film version in order to appease the censor.

Sue Lyon — *Lolita* (Kubrick) — USA/GB, 62

Loman, Willy [F]

Arthur Miller's ageing travelling salesman who, after a lifetime of failure and self delusion, comes home to die with his family. One of the most important figures in post-war literature in that his final disenchantment symbolizes the fact that American get-rich-quick philosophy and worship of success is little more than a phoney dream. Memorably played on stage by Lee J. Cobb, equally so on screen by Fredric March and Dustin Hoffman.

Fredric March — *Death Of A Salesman* (Benedek) — USA, 51
Nikolai Volkov — *Most Pereyti Nelzya* (Vulfovitch/Kurihin) — USSR, 60
Dustin Hoffman — *Death Of A Salesman* (Schlondorff) — TVM,USA, 85

Note: Dustin Hoffman's portrayal was in a TV movie based on his performance in the 1984 Broadway revival of Miller's play. The performance won Hoffman a best acting Emmy award.

A young lady difficult to resist! Sue Lyon as the nymphet *Lolita* in Stanley Kubrick's 1962 film version of Nabokov's controversial novel

Lombard, Carole [R]

(1908–42) High-spirited, inimitable Hollywood comedienne who featured in several of America's brightest film comedies of the 30s (*Twentieth Century, My Man Godfrey, Nothing Sacred*) before meeting an untimely death in a plane crash in 1942. Her tempestuous ten year love affair with Hollywood 'king' Clark Gable (they were married in 1939), was related in Sidney Furie's 1976 bio-pic *Gable And Lombard*.

Jill Clayburgh — *Gable And Lombard* (Furie) — USA, 76

London, Jack [R]

(1876–1916) San Francisco-born author who served as a hobo, sailor and Klondike goldminer before becoming the highest-paid American writer of the early 1900s. His violent, socialistic stories – 'Martin Eden', 'Call Of The Wild', 'Sea Wolf' – all reflect his experiences during his poverty-stricken youth; Alfred Santell's unpretentious film biography effectively transferred London's adventurous life to the screen.

Michael O'Shea — *Jack London* (Santell) — USA, 43
Jeff East — *Klondike Fever* (Carter) — USA, 79

Lone Wolf, The 

Louis Joseph Vance's society detective, an ex-jewel thief turned gentleman benefactor who re-embraces his old profession in order to bring down the American crime rate. Bert Lytell set to work as The Lone Wolf (Michael Lanyard) in the silent days; Warren William played the reformed cracksman during the 40s. The Lone Wolf first appeared in print in 1914.

Bert Lytell — *The Lone Wolf's Daughter* (Rogell) — USA, 29
Bert Lytell — *Last Of The Lone Wolf* (Boleslavsky) — USA, 30
Thomas Meighan — *Cheaters At Play* (MacFadden) — USA, 32
Melvyn Douglas — *The Lone Wolf Returns* (Neill) — USA, 36
Francis Lederer — *The Lone Wolf In Paris* (Rogell) — USA, 38

Warren William	*The Lone Wolf Spy Hunt* (Godfrey) USA, 39
Warren William	*The Lone Wolf Strikes* (Salkow) USA, 40
Warren William	*The Lone Wolf Meets A Lady* (Salkow) USA, 40
Warren William	*The Lone Wolf Takes A Chance* (Salkow) USA, 41
Warren William	*The Lone Wolf Keeps A Date* (Salkow) USA, 41
Warren William	*Secrets Of The Lone Wolf* (Dmytryk) USA, 41
Warren William	*Counter-Espionage* (Dmytryk) USA, 42
Warren William	*One Dangerous Night* (Gordon) USA, 43
Warren William	*Passport To Suez* (DeToth) USA, 43
Gerald Mohr	*The Notorious Lone Wolf* (Lederman) USA, 46
Gerald Mohr	*The Lone Wolf In Mexico* (Lederman) USA, 47
Gerald Mohr	*The Lone Wolf In London* (Goodwins) USA, 47
Ron Randell	*The Lone Wolf And His Lady* (Hoffman) USA, 49

Note: Bert Lytell featured as the Lone Wolf in the silent films *The Lone Wolf* (17), *The Lone Wolf Returns* (26), *Alias The Lone Wolf* (27). Henry B. Walthall in *The False Faces* (19) and Jack Holt in *The Lone Wolf* (24) also appeared in the role.

Long, Huey [R]

(1893–1935) Controversial Louisiana lawyer/state governor/demagogue who was turning his eyes in the direction of the White House when he was assassinated in 1935. The model for several books including Robert Penn Warren's Pulitzer Prize-winning *All The King's Men* (filmed in 1949), he has to date received only one straight screen portrayal – that of Edward Asner in the TV film *The Life And Assassination Of A Kingfish.*

Edward Asner	*The Life And Assassination Of A Kingfish* (Collins) TVM/USA, 77

Note: Broderick Crawford earned an Oscar for his portrait of the Long-type figure (renamed Willie Stark) in *All The King's Men;* in *A Lion Is In The Streets* (53), James Cagney's Hank Martin, a crusader for small sharecroppers hustling his way up from a small law practice, also derived from Long and his activities. The 1985 TV documentary *Huey Long,* directed by Ken Burns and containing much rare newsreel footage, was devoted to the life and career of the Louisiana 'Kingfish'.

The end for Willie Stark! Broderick Crawford gunned down by an assassin in the final sequence of *All The King's Men*

Lonsdale, Gordon [R]

The major figure in the true life Portland Spy case of 1961, a Russian agent who posed as a Canadian and blackmailed an ex-Navy man into stealing secret documents from the Underwater Weapon Establishment at Portland. He was eventually apprehended, along with a London bookseller and his wife, who transmitted the information by radio to Moscow.

William Sylvester	*Ring Of Spies* (Tronson) GB, 64

Note: The naval 'leak', Henry Houghton, was played by Bernard Lee; the bookseller and his wife, the Krogers, by David Kossoff and Nancy Nevinson.

Lord Jim [F]

In many ways, the most representative of Joseph Conrad's characters, a young British naval officer who makes lifelong efforts to atone for an act of instinctive cowardice (abandoning his ship when it appears to be sinking) and succeeds only when he achieves an honourable death among a tribe of Far East natives. The complex theme of honour and its redemption have so far eluded both sound and silent film-makers. The Conrad novel was published in 1900.

Peter O'Toole	*Lord Jim* (Brooks)	USA/GB, 65

Note: The only other version of the novel was produced in 1925. Percy Marmont starred as Lord Jim under Victor Fleming's direction.

Louis, Joe

(1914–81) Real name, Joseph Louis Barrow. Prior to the rise of Muhammad Ali, the most famous of the modern American heavyweights. Known as 'The Brown Bomber', he reigned as world champion from 1936 to 1948 and defended his title 25 times. He won 68 of his 71 fights. A minor screen biography was produced in 1953, two years after Louis had retired from the ring.

Coley Wallace	*The Joe Louis Story* (Gordon)	USA, 53

Note: Bernie Casey played Louis in the 1978 TV film *Ring Of Passion* which centred on the two prewar Louis/Max Schmeling fights and the way both boxers became symbols of political ideologies Stephen Macht featured as the German Schmeling.

Luciano, Charles 'Lucky'

Together with Al Capone, one of the most powerful criminals America has ever known, a gangster who began in the 20s selling protection to madams and their girls and then quickly rose to become a millionaire and Mafia overlord. Although involved in numerous gangland killings, he did not, for a change, finish up with a bullet in his brain, but died of a heart attack in 1962 after serving a jail sentence and being deported to Italy. Franco Rosi told his story in the 1973 film *Lucky Luciano*.

Cesar Romero	*A House Is Not A Home* (Rouse)	USA, 64
Angelo Infanti	*The Valachi Papers* (Young)	Fra/It, 73
Gian Maria Volonte	*Lucky Luciano* (Rosi)	It/Fra, 73
Vic Tayback	*Lepke* (Golan)	USA, 75
Lee Montague	*The Brass Target* (Hough)	USA, 78
Joe Dallesandro	*The Cotton Club* (Coppola)	USA, 84

Ludwig II

(1845–86) Mad king of Bavaria, the subject of two recent film biographies and also a German film of the 50s, which traced his bizarre life from his youth as patron of Richard Wagner, through his struggles with Bismarck and ultimate death in an asylum. Helmut Kautner's film was shot in many of the extravagant castles built by Ludwig during his lifetime.

O. W. Fischer	*Ludwig II* (Käutner)	W.Ger, 55
Gerhard Riedmann	*Magic Fire* (Dieterle)	USA, 56
Harry Baer	*Ludwig – Requiem For A Virgin King* (Syberberg)	W.Ger, 72
Helmut Berger	*Ludwig* (Visconti)	It/Fra/W.Ger, 73

Note: Olaf Fjord (Aus, 22) and Wilhelm Dieterle (Ger, 29) both appeared as Ludwig on the silent screen.

Luther, Martin

(1483–1546) German religious cleric who changed the course of history when he led the Protestant Reformation in Europe in the sixteenth century. The subject of a 1961 stage play by John Osborne, transferred to the screen in 1973 by Guy Green.

Niall MacGinnis	*Martin Luther* (Pichel)	USA/W.Ger, 53
Stacy Keach	*Luther* (Green)	USA/GB/Can, 73

Note: Eugen Klopfer appeared as Luther in a German silent film of 1927.

Luxemburg, Rosa

(1871–1919) German revolutionary born at Zamosc in Poland, who together with socialist leader Karl Liebknecht formed The Spartacus Group, a communist party which sympathized with the Bolsheviks in Russia but failed to organize a similar uprising in Germany. Assassinated in 1919, she was the subject of the 1986 feminist film of Margarethe Von Trotta which fictionalized many of the events of her private life and also idealized her politically but emphasized her enormous courage and resilience. Barbara Sukowa shared the best actress prize at Cannes in 1986; Otto Sander featured as Karl Liebknecht.

Barbara Sukowa *Rosa Luxembourg* (Von Trotta) W.Ger, 86

Lydecker, Waldo [F]

Arguably the most literate screen villain of the 40s, an urbane New York columnist whose delight in dropping epigrams at every opportunity ('I don't use a pen. I write with a goosequill dipped in venom') was equalled only by his obsession with the beautiful Laura Hunt whom he murders when he knows he can never possess her. A great scene-stealing role, much appreciated by Clifton Webb who made a comback to the screen in Otto Preminger's version of Vera Caspary's novel. Webb was nominated for a supporting Academy Award. Caspary's novel was published in 1942.

Clifton Webb *Laura* (Preminger) USA, 44

Lynn, Loretta [R]

A poor-born Tennessee girl who was married at 13, bore seven children during her stormy marriage and still found time to become America's number one female country and western star. Sissy Spacek, using her own singing voice, won an Oscar for playing Lynn in Michael Apted's 1980 film which covered the singer's life from her marriage to her initial success, then through her breakdown due to overwork and her triumphant comeback. 'I'm A Honky Tonk Girl', 'Coal Miner's Daughter' and 'You're Looking At Country' were among the Lynn songs included in the film.

A star is born! Sissy Spacek as the *Coal Miner's Daughter,* Loretta Lynn, who was married when she was just 13, gave birth to several children and eventually became a country and western star with her hit record 'Honky Tonk Girl'

Sissy Spacek *Coal Miner's Daughter* (Apted) USA, 80

MacArthur, General Douglas [R]

(1880–1964) 'I shall return' was the rallying cry of this flamboyant American general when early Japanese victories forced him to leave the Philippines in 1942. He was as good as his word and in 1945 received the surrender of the Japanese on the battleship 'Missouri'. One of America's controversial heroes of World War II, he was later relieved of command in Korea after refusing to obey orders from President Truman. Usually a subsidiary figure in movies, he has also been the subject of a full-length screen biography, Joseph Sargent's *MacArthur.*

Robert Barrat	*They Were Expendable* (Ford)	USA, 45
Robert Barrat	*American Guerilla In The Philippines* (Fritz Lang)	USA, 50
Dayton Lummis	*The Court Martial Of Billy Mitchell* (Preminger)	USA, 55
Gregory Peck	*MacArthur* (Sargent)	USA, 77
Laurence Olivier	*Inchon* (Young)	USA, 80
Jon Sidney	*Death Of A Soldier* (Mora)	Austral, 86

Note: Henry Fonda starred as MacArthur in the 1976 TV film *Collision Course* which centred on his famous clash with President Truman; the 1985 ten-part TV series *American Caesar,* based on William Manchester's biography, was narrated by John Colicos with John Huston speaking MacArthur's words.

Macbeth [F]

Shakespeare's Scots nobleman, driven to commit murder for the throne by the supernatural prophecies of three witches and the ambitions of his power-crazed wife. Orson Welles' cheaply budgeted *Macbeth* resembled, at times, 'Dante's Inferno', Roman Polanski's 1971 adaptation came closest to the description of the play as being 'a nightmare study in fear'. 'Macbeth' was first performed on stage in 1606.

Ratnaprabha	*Macbeth*	(Vinayak)	Ind, 38
David Bradley	*Macbeth*	(Blair)	USA, 46
Orson Welles	*Macbeth*	(Welles)	USA, 48
Maurice Evans	*Macbeth*	(Schaefer)	GB, 61
Jon Finch	*Macbeth*	(Polanski)	GB, 71

Note: Toshiro Mifune starred as a Japanese Macbeth in Kurosawa's *Throne Of Blood* (57), Paul Douglas as the modern gangster equivalent, *Joe Macbeth* in 1955 (GB); William V. Ranous (USA, 08), Dante Capelli (It, 09), Paul Mounet (Fra, 10), Frank R. Benson (GB, 11), Arthur Bourchier (Ger, 13), Herbert Beerbohm Tree (USA, 16) and Amleto Novelli (It, 17) appeared in the role in silent versions.

The following actresses have starred as Lady Macbeth: Miss Carver (08), Maria Gasperini (09), Joanne Delvair (10), Mrs Benson (11), Violet Vanbrugh (13), Constance Collier (16), Jain Wilimovsky (46), Jeanette Nolan (48), Judith Anderson (61) and Francesca Annis (71).

Ruth Roman appeared in *Joe Macbeth;* Isuzu Yamada in *Throne Of Blood.*

Ian McKellen and Judi Dench (79) and Nicol Williamson and Jane Lapotaire (83) have appeared in British TV versions of *Macbeth.*

Macheath 

Highwayman-adventurer of John Gay's 'The Beggar's Opera' (1728) and subsequently Bertolt Brecht's updated 'Die Dreigroschenoper'. Renamed in the latter as Mackie Messer (Mac The Knife), he operates in a seamy Victorian London where he marries the daughter of Soho's underworld boss and is eventually betrayed by his former mistress. The satirical Brecht musical (with lyrics by Kurt Weill) was premiered exactly 200 years after the first performance of Gay's ballad opera. One screen version of the original, two of 'Die Dreigroschenoper' ('The Threepenny Opera').

Rudolf Forster	*Die Dreigroschenoper* (Pabst)	Ger, 31
Laurence Olivier	*The Beggar's Opera* (Brook)	GB, 53
Curt Jurgens	*Die Dreigroschenoper* (Staudte)	Fra/W.Ger, 63

Note: Polly Peachum, Macheath's wife, was played by Caroline Neher in 1931, Dorothy Tutin in 1953

(Right) Gregory Peck as *MacArthur* in a scene from Joseph Sargent's 1977 biography that looked at the controversial American general's role in both World War II and the Korean War; (above) portraits of two presidents—Dan O'Herlihy as Franklin Roosevelt and Ed Flanders as Harry Truman in the same film

and June Ritchie in 1963; Pirate Jenny, his former mistress, by Lotte Lenya (31) and Hildegard Neff (63); *Malandro* (86), a Brazilian/French film of Ray Guerra derived loosely from *The Threepenny Opera* and updated events to the 1940s. Macheath (renamed Max and played by Edson Celulari) was recast as a pimp and smalltime smuggler; Elba Ramalho starred as his mistress Margot.

Madame X

F

Long-suffering martyr of Alexandre Bisson's 1910 play, a tragic woman, forced to abandon her husband and child, who sinks to the depths and then years later finishes up accused of murder, defended by a son who doesn't recognize her. One of the most artificial of all tearjerking roles, yet one that is still brought out and dusted down with surprising regularity. Lana Turner's fall from gloss to gloom is the best-known of the talkie interpretations.

Ruth Chatterton	*Madame X*	(Barrymore)	USA, 29
Gladys George	*Madame X*	(Wood)	USA, 37
Mme Kyveli	*Madame X*	(Laskos)	Gre, 60
Lana Turner	*Madame X*	(Rich)	USA, 66

Note: Dorothy Donnelly (15) and Pauline Frederick (20) both appeared in silent screen versions of the story; Tuesday Weld appeared in an updated TV movie (81) scripted by Edward Anhalt and directed by Robert Ellis Miller.

Madden, Owney

R

British-born mobster who became one of the toughest racketeers in America and earned himself the nickname 'Owney The Killer' when he was just 17. The only screen portrayal has been in Francis Ford Coppola's colourful homage to Harlem's 'Cotton Club' in which black entertainers performed during the 20s and 30s. Madden was played by British actor Bob Hoskins some four years after his performance as the gangster overlord in *The Long Good Friday;* Madden boasted that he had never done a day's work in his life and never intended to. Unlike many of his kind he survived, lived in luxury and died peacefully in his sleep.

Bob Hoskins	*The Cotton Club*	(Coppola)	USA, 84

Note: The black artists who entertained at The Cotton Club included many of the all-time greats. Among those portrayed briefly in Coppola's film were Cab Calloway (Larry Marshall) and Duke Ellington (Zane Mark).

Mad Max

Violent Australian super-hero who operates in a desolate future after civilization has been destroyed by a nuclear holocaust. Began his screen adventures in 1979 when he set out to revenge himself on the motor cycle barbarians who had murdered his wife and child. Has since carried on his activities in two sequels – defending first a tiny community producing oil and then coming up against the outrageous Aunt Entity (in the person of Tina Turner) and embarking in a fight to the death in the Roman-styled arena of Thunderdome. Mel Gibson emerged from all the mayhem, car stunts and general confusion as a major star.

Mel Gibson	*Max Max*	(Miller)	Austral, 79
Mel Gibson	*Mad Max 2*	(Miller)	Austral, 81
Mel Gibson	*Mad Max Beyond Thunderdome*	(Miller)	Austral, 85

Mel Gibson as the vengeful high-speed ex-cop Mad Max operating in a violent future in the three Australian films of George Miller

Magnificent Seven, The

F

The most famous outlaw band in movie history – seven men down on their luck who are hired by Mexican peasants to defend a village against marauding bandits. Derived from Kurosawa's *Seven Samurai,* the initial seven comprised of a cynical gunman (Yul Brynner), a young drifter (Steve McQueen), a black-gloved killer who has lost his nerve (Robert Vaughn), a knife man (James Coburn), a wood cutter (Charles Bronson), a gambler on the lookout for gold (Brad Dexter) and a young Mexican boy (Horst Buchholtz) eager to join the band. In the three sequels made between 1966 and 1972 only Yul Brynner reprised his role when he again played Chris in *Return Of The Seven* (66).

Yul Brynner	Chris	
Steve McQueen	Vin	
Horst Buchholtz	Chico	
James Coburn	Britt	
Charles Bronson	Bernardo	
Robert Vaughn	Lee	
Brad Dexter	Harry Luck	
The Magnificent Seven	(Sturges)	USA, 60

Note: In *Battle Beyond The Stars* (80), Roger Corman's science fiction reworking of the original, Robert Vaughn repeated his role as a world weary space samurai named Gelt.

Mahler, Gustave

R

(1860–1911) Austrian composer whose symphonies have become increasingly popular in recent decades. The only screen biography to date, starring Robert Powell, was directed by Ken Russell who recalled, in flashback, the events and people who influenced the composer's life. Some inspired visual passages were offset by scenes of Powell composing three symphonies at once and uttering the line, 'I don't care a shit for military band music'.

Robert Powell	*Mahler* (Russell)	GB, 74

Note: The character of Gustave von Aschenbach, the dying composer in Luchino Visconti's *Death In Venice* (71) was based on Mahler. Dirk Bogarde starred as Aschenbach.

Maid Marian

F

'Welcome to Sherwood, my lady!' Few screen heroines can have received such an engaging welcome as Olivia de Havilland in *The Adventures Of Robin Hood.* The handsome Errol Flynn made the greeting and a suitably wet-eyed Miss de Havilland made the most of it. Unfortunately, subsequent Maid Marians have been decidedly wishy-washy, all, that is, except the lovely ageing Marian of Audrey Hepburn in Richard Lester's *Robin And Marian.*

Olivia de Havilland	*The Adventures Of Robin Hood* (Curtiz/Keighley)	USA, 38
Patricia Morison	*Prince Of Thieves* (Bretherton)	USA, 48
Diana Lynn	*Rogues Of Sherwood Forest* (Douglas)	USA, 50
Mary Hatcher	*Tales Of Robin Hood* (Tinling)	USA, 51
Joan Rice	*The Story Of Robin Hood And His Merrie Men* (Annakin)	GB, 52
Sarah Branch	*Sword Of Sherwood Forest* (Fisher)	GB, 60
Gay Hamilton	*A Challenge For Robin Hood* (Pennington Richards)	GB, 67

Richard Todd as a young Robin of Sherwood and Joan Rice as Maid Marian in Walt Disney's version of *The Story of Robin Hood*

Rita Webb	*Up The Chastity Belt* (Kellett) GB, 71
Ciaran Madden	*Wolfshead: The Legend Of Robin Hood* (Hough) GB, 73
Audrey Hepburn	*Robin And Marian* (Lester) USA, 76
Morgan Fairchild	*The Zany Adventures Of Robin Hood* (Austin) TVM/USA, 84

Note: Monica Evans voiced Maid Marian in Disney's cartoon feature of 1973; Barbara Rush played the modern equivalent in the 1964 gangster film *Robin And The Seven Hoods*; Barbara Tennant (USA, 12), Gerda Holmes (USA, 13), Enid Bennett (USA, 22) all played the role on the silent screen. On TV Judi Trott featured as Marian in the 1984–86 series *Robin Of Sherwood.*

Maigret, Jules F

Pipe-smoking police inspector of Georges Simenon, in many ways the French equivalent of Sherlock Holmes, but relying less on intellectual deduction and more on an uncanny intuition to solve his cases. Played only once on the English-speaking screen – by Charles Laughton in *The Man On The Eiffel Tower* – although Rupert Davies, who scored such a triumph as Maigret on British TV, also featured in a German production of 1966. Jean Gabin and Albert Prejean both appeared three times as the Inspector; author Simenon first created Maigret in 'Death Of Monsieur Gallet' in 1931.

Pierre Renoir	*La Nuit du Carrefour* (Renoir) Fra, 32
Abel Tarride	*La Chien Jaune* (Tarride) Fra, 32
Harry Baur	*La Téte d'un Homme* (Duvivier) Fra, 33
Albert Prejean	*Picpus* (Pottier) Fra, 43
Albert Prejean	*Cecile est Morte* (Tourneur) Fra, 44
Albert Prejean	*Les Caves du Majestic* (Pottier) Fra, 45
Charles Laughton	*The Man On The Eiffel Tower* (Meredith) USA, 50
Michel Simon	*Brelan D'As* (Verneuil) Fra, 52
Maurice Manson	*Maigret Mene L'Enquete* (Cordier) Fra, 56
Jean Gabin	*Maigret Sets A Trap* (Delannoy) Fra, 58
Jean Gabin	*Maigret et L'Affaire St. Fiacre* (Delannoy) Fra, 59
Jean Gabin	*Maigret Voit Rouge* (Grangier) Fra, 63
Gino Cervi	*Maigret a'Pigalle* (Landi) Fra/It, 66
Rupert Davies	*Maigret Spielt Falsch* (Weidenmann) W.Ger, 66
Heinz Ruhmann	*Maigret und Sein Grosster Fall* (Weidenmann) Aus/Fra/It, 66

Note: In recent years Maigret has been portrayed regularly on French television by Jean Richard. Since the mid 70s and through the 80s he has appeared in a series of TV films that have included *Maigret Hesite* (75), *Maigret En Meubte* (72), *Maigret et Les Gangsters* (77), *Liberty Bar* (79), *Maigret A Vichy* (84) and *Maigret et le Marchand* (86). The British TV series starring Rupert Davies was transmitted by the BBC in the late 50s; author Georges Simenon was profiled in the 1971 documentary *Mirror Of Maigret* (71). The most recent TV portrayal of Maigret has been by Richard Harris in the 1988 TV film *Maigret* directed by Paul Lynch.

Maine, Norman F

A once great movie star who sinks into oblivion because of alcoholism but manages to help a young actress to the top while he is on the downward slide. One of the most famous 'fictional' creations of Hollywood writers although he was in fact based closely on John Barrymore who suffered a similar fate and hit the bottle after failing to make a career in talkies. To-date, Maine has been a film star twice (in 37 and 54) and a rock star once (76) in the three versions of the story. An earlier picture called *What Price Hollywood?* (32) cast him as an alcoholic director (named Maximilian Carey) whose career nosedives when he helps a waitress become a movie star.

Fredric March	*A Star Is Born* (Wellman) USA, 37
James Mason	*A Star Is Born* (Cukor) USA, 54
Kris Kristofferson	*A Star Is Born* (Pierson) USA, 76

Note: The actresses who enjoyed their rise to fame whilst Maine descended into alcoholic ruin have been played by Janet Gaynor (37), Judy Garland (54) and Barbra Streisand (76). In *What Price Hollywood?* Lowell Sherman starred as the director and Constance Bennett as the waitress.

Mame, Auntie [F]

Patrick Dennis' one and only eccentric aunt, a volatile, high-living but warm-hearted extrovert whose sophisticated way of life is suddenly disrupted when she finds herself responsible for her young nephew's upbringing. Vividly described by Dennis in his best-selling book which was later adapted for the stage by Jerome Lawrence and Robert E. Lee and then into a hit musical.

Rosalind Russell	*Auntie Mame* (DaCosta)	USA, 58
Lucille Ball	*Mame* (Saks)	USA, 75

Manon Lescaut [F]

Luxury-craving whore who enslaves her weak-willed student lover and drives him to petty crime and murder before meeting her own violent end in the desert. A sordid, unregenerate character, first created by Abbe Prevost in 1731, many times interpreted on the screen, notably by Cecile Aubry in Clouzot's 1949 updating which set her story in the brothels of post-war Paris and the deserts of Palestine.

Alida Valli	*Manon Lescaut* (Gallone)	It, 39
Cecile Aubry	*Manon* (Clouzot)	Fra, 49
Myriam Bru	*The Loves Of Manon Lescaut* (Costa)	It/Fra, 54
Catherine Deneuve	*Manon 70* (Aurel)	Fra/W.Ger/It, 68
Setsuko Karasuma	*Manon* (Higashi)	Jap, 82
Mayra Alejandra	*Manon* (Chalbaud)	Venez, 86

Note: Silent portrayals include those by Stacia Napierkowski (Fra, 11), Lina Cavalieri (USA, 14), Lya Mara (Ger, 19), Lya de Putti (Ger, 26) and Dolores Costello in Alan Crosland's 1927 film *When A Man Loves*.

Manson, Charles [R]

Described by the prosecution as 'one of the most evil, satanic men who ever walked the face of the earth', this demented psychopath and his followers were responsible for the murder of Roman Polanski's wife, Sharon Tate, and five other victims in Hollywood in August, 1969. Manson, regarded by his followers as a 'Christ-like figure', was sentenced to life imprisonment in 1970 and was the subject of a 1976 film *Helter Skelter*. A 1972 documentary was also made of his life and trial.

Steve Railsback	*Helter Skelter* (Gries)	USA, 76

Marie Antoinette [R]

(1755–93) The Austrian queen consort of Louis XVI, an unpopular lady who surrounded herself with a dissipated clique, was found guilty of treason by French Revolutionary forces and eventually met her death on the guillotine. Seen mostly as a minor character in historical films but afforded a major biography by MGM in 1938 who spent 1.8 million dollars on the lavish 160-minute epic, advertising it with the slogan: 'The scandals of a glamorous queen! With escapades that rocked a nation as an adulterous beauty seeks romance!' The adulterous beauty was played by Irving Thalberg's widow Norma Shearer who in one scene was clad by the studio's costumiers in a dress of 500 yards of white satin. Tyrone Power provided the romance.

Evelyn Hall	*Captain Of The Guard* (Robertson)	USA, 30
Anita Louise	*Madame DuBarry* (Dieterle)	USA, 34
Lise Delamare	*La Marseillaise* (Renoir)	Fra, 37
Norma Shearer	*Marie Antoinette* (Van Dyke)	USA, 38
Marion Dorian	*The Queen's Necklace* (L'Herbier)	Fra, 47
Nancy Guild	*Black Magic* (Ratoff)	USA, 49
Lana Marconi	*Versailles* (Guitry)	Fra, 53
Isabelle Pia	*Madame DuBarry* (Christian-Jaque)	Fra/It, 54
Lana Marconi	*Si Paris Nous Était Conté* (Guitry)	Fra, 55
Michele Morgan	*Shadow Of The Guillotine* (Delannoy)	Fra/It, 56
Marie Wilson	*The Story Of Mankind* (Allen)	USA, 57
Susana Canales	*John Paul Jones* (Farrow)	USA, 59
Liselotte	*La Fayette* (Dréville)	Fra/It, 65
Billie Whitelaw	*Start The Revolution Without Me* (Yorkin)	USA, 70
Ursula Andress	*Liberty, Equality, Sauerkraut* (Yanne)	Fra/It, 85

Note: Clotilde Delano in *Scaramouche* (USA, 23) and Princess De Bourbon in *Janice Meredith* (USA, 24) were among the silent actresses who played Marie Antoinette on screen.

Marlowe, Philip

F

The one American private-eye who continues to hold the fascination of movie audiences the world over. Tough, honest and laconic, he has operated in a nightmare world of drugs, murder and double-cross since the 1940s. The creation of Raymond Chandler and always worth listening to ('It was a nice little front yard. OK for the average family only you'd need a compass to go to the mail box'), he first appeared in print in 1939 in 'The Big Sleep'. Bogart's performance in Hawks' 1946 film remains the most famous screen interpretation. Chandler himself wanted Cary Grant to play the part.

Dick Powell	*Farewell My Lovely* (Dmytryk) USA, 44
Humphrey Bogart	*The Big Sleep* (Hawks) USA, 46
Robert Montgomery	*Lady In The Lake* (Montgomery) USA, 46
George Montgomery	*The Brasher Doubloon* (Brahm) USA, 47
James Garner	*Marlowe* (Bogart) USA, 69
Elliott Gould	*The Long Goodbye* (Altman) USA, 73
Robert Mitchum	*Farewell My Lovely* (Richards) USA, 75
Robert Mitchum	*The Big Sleep* (Winner) GB, 78

Note: *The Brasher Doubloon* was a version of Chandler's 'The High Window', *Marlowe* an adaptation of 'The Little Sister'. On TV Marlowe has been played by Philip Carey in a 1959 series that bore little resemblance to the original novels and, more recently, by Powers Boothe in *Marlowe – Private Eye* (84), an ambitious series based on Chandler short stories, among them 'Smart Aleck Kill', 'Fingerman' and 'Nevada Gas'.

Miss Marple

F

Spinster sleuth of crime writer Agatha Christie, the very antithesis of her other detective Hercule Poirot. Tall and thin in the 16 novels but short and chubby in the four films of Margaret Rutherford. Fussy and gossipy in both! First case: 'Murder At The Vicarage' (1930). Vaguely based on the character of Christie's own grandmother, she has been most accurately portrayed by Joan Hickson in a long series of BBC TV adaptations (1984–7).

Margaret Rutherford	*Murder She Said* (Pollock) GB, 61
Margaret Rutherford	*Murder At The Gallop* (Pollock) GB, 63
Margaret Rutherford	*Murder Most Foul* (Pollock) GB, 64
Margaret Rutherford	*Murder Ahoy* (Pollock) GB, 64
Angela Lansbury	*The Mirror Crack'd* (Hamilton) GB, 80

Note: Miss Marple (again played by Margaret Rutherford) also made a fleeting guest appearance in Frank Tashlin's 1966 Poirot melodrama *The Alphabet Murders*. On TV Joan Hickson's cases have included *The Body In The Library, A Murder Is Announced, The Moving Finger, A Pocket Full Of Rye, The Murder At The Vicarage, Sleeping Murder, Bertram's Hotel, Nemesis* and *The 4.50 from Paddington*. Helen Hayes has played Miss Marple in the American TV films *A Caribbean Mystery* (83) and *Murder With Mirrors* (85).

Mary, Queen Of Scots

R

(1542–87) Sixteenth century Queen of Scotland, from the Catholic viewpoint the rightful claimant to the throne of England, but eventually brought to trial and executed for conspiring against Elizabeth. Two compelling, if historically inaccurate screen performances – by Katharine Hepburn in John Ford's *Mary Of Scotland* and Vanessa Redgrave, an Oscar nominee for *Mary, Queen Of Scots*.

Katharine Hepburn	*Mary Of Scotland* (Ford) USA, 36
Jacqueline Delubac	*The Pearls Of The Crown* (Guitry/Jaque) Fra, 37
Zarah Leander	*Heart Of A Queen* (Froelich) Ger, 40
Esmeralda Ruspoli	*Seven Seas To Calais* (Mate) It, 62
Vanessa Redgrave	*Mary, Queen Of Scots* (Jarrott) GB, 71

Note: On the silent screen Mary was played by Mary Fuller in *Mary Stuart* (USA, 13), Fay Compton in *Loves Of Mary, Queen Of Scots* (GB, 23) and Maisie Fisher in *The Virgin Queen* (GB, 23).

Mata Hari

R

(1876–1917) The stage name of the most notorious female spy in history. Under her real name of

Mame—Patrick Dennis' eccentric aunt whose philosophy is that 'life is a banquet and most poor suckers are starving to death!' (above) Lucille Ball featured in the musical version of 1974; (left) Rosalind Russell played the colourful lady in the straight comedy adaptation in 1958

Margarete Gertrude Zelle, she might not have fared so well, but as dancer Mata Hari she was as alluring an espionage agent as the Germans could have wished for, achieving notable success before finishing up in front of a French firing squad in 1917. The highspot of George Fitzmaurice's 1932 film was Greta Garbo's exotic temple dance.

Greta Garbo	*Mata Hari* (Fitzmaurice)	USA, 32
Judith Voselli	*Stamboul Quest* (Wood)	USA, 34
Delia Col	*Marthe Richard au Service de la France* (Bernard)	Fra, 37
Jeanne Moreau	*Mata Hari, Agent H-21* (Richard)	Fra/It, 65
Zsa Zsa Gabor	*Up The Front* (Kellet)	GB, 72
Sylvia Kristel	*Mata Hari* (Harrington)	GB, 85

Note: Magda Sonja was a silent Mata Hari in *Mata Hari: The Red Dancer* (28); Ludmilla Tcherina featured as *The Daughter of Mata Hari* in the 1954 French/Italian co-production directed by Carmine Gallone and Renzo Merusi.

Maugham, W. Somerset R

(1874–1965) Distinguished English novelist and short story writer, twice played on screen by Herbert Marshall in the 40s, i.e. in *The Moon And Sixpence* (as Geoffrey Wolfe) and *The Razor's Edge*. In the post-war years he appeared as himself when he introduced three omnibus films of his short stories: *Quartet* (48), made up from 'The Facts Of Life', 'The Alien Corn', 'The Kite' and 'The Colonel's Lady'; *Trio* (50) from 'The Verger', 'Mr Know-All' and 'Sanatorium'; and *Encore* (51) from 'The Ant And The Grasshopper', 'Winter Cruise' and 'Gigolo and Gigolette'.

Herbert Marshall	*The Moon And Sixpence* (Lewin)	USA, 42
Herbert Marshall	*The Razor's Edge* (Goulding)	USA, 46

Note: Maugham's days as a medical student before he turned to a writing career were reflected in his 1915 novel 'Of Human Bondage'. The character of the young Philip Carey who becomes infatuated with a worthless tart was a semi-autobiographical portrait. Carey has been played three times on film – by Leslie Howard in 1934, Paul Henreid in 1946 and Laurence Harvey in 1964. Bette Davis, Eleanor Parker and Kim Novak bitched their way through the respective adaptations. On TV Duncan Ross briefly portrayed Maugham in *The Winds Of War* (83).

Maupassant, Guy de R

(1850–93) French short story writer and novelist whose realistic and ironic style encompassed tales of Norman peasant life, the behaviour of the bourgeoisie and those living in the fashionable areas of nineteenth century Paris. Michael Drach's 1982 biography looked at the writer in his final tragic months when he was dying from syphilis (contracted 16 years earlier) and concentrated on his physical and mental deterioration as he sought the aid of doctors to forestall madness and death. His earlier life was related in flashback.

Claude Brasseur	*Guy de Maupassant* (Drach)	Fra, 82

McCarthy, Joe

(1908–57) American senator who rose to notoriety after World War II by claiming that Communist infiltration was rife in the State Department and other areas of public life. His much publicized 'Un-American Activities investigative committees' made him at one time seem even more powerful than the president but he was eventually destroyed by lawyer Joseph Welch during the televised investigations of the Army and Department of Defence in 1954. None of McCarthy's allegations were actually proved but his ruthless tactics were enough to ensure that many lives were ruined and jobs lost during the 50s. No large screen biography as yet although the TV movie *Tail Gunner Joe* efficiently charted his rise and fall.

Peter Boyle	*Tail Gunner Joe* (Taylor)	TVM,USA, 77

Note: The senator (unnamed) played by Tony Curtis in Nicolas Roeg's *Insignificance* (85) was clearly patterned on McCarthy; on TV he has been played by, among others, Charles Hallahan in *J. Edgar Hoover* (87).

Melba, Dame Nellie

(1861–1931) Australian soprano who became the prima donna of the Royal Opera at Covent Garden. The wonderful purity of her voice won her world fame, as did her stage surname which inspired not only two operas but the delicacies peach melba and melba toast. One of the few opera stars to be given a screen biography, she was played by Patrice Munsel in Lewis Milestone's bio-pic of 1953. Real name: Helen Porter Armstrong.

Patrice Munsel — *Melba* (Milestone) GB, 53

Mengele, Dr Josef [R]

For years the world's most wanted criminal, a sadistic ex-Nazi doctor, known as 'The Angel Of Death', who was directly responsible for the destruction of 300 000 Jews in Auschwitz. Lived under presidential protection in Paraguay until his death from drowning in 1978 and was the number one target of famed Nazi hunter Simon Wiesenthal. Portrayed on screen by Gregory Peck in Ira Levin's bizarre thriller *The Boys From Brazil.*

Gregory Peck — *The Boys From Brazil* (Schaffner) USA, 78

Note: Wiesenthal has been played by Shmuel Rodensky in Ronad Neame's *The Odessa File* (74) and by Laurence Olivier (as Ezra Lieberman) in *The Boys From Brazil.*

Mercader, Ramon 

(1914–78) A man of many aliases but whose real name is firmly etched in the history books as the assassin of the exiled Leon Trotsky. As Frank Jacson he infiltrated the Trotsky household in Mexico and on 21 August 1940, drove an ice pick into the skull of the Communist idealist who died the following day. Jacson served 20 years in prison but never once revealed the names of his paymasters. The weeks leading up to the assassination were reconstructed in Joseph Losey's 1972 film, with Alain Delon as Jacson and Richard Burton as Trotsky.

Alain Delon — *The Assassination Of Trotsky* (Losey) Fra/It/GB, 72

Merlin 

Legendary magician, generally hovering in the background in movies about the Round Table, but whose magical powers helped Arthur remain invincible during his reign on the throne. Legend has it that he was destroyed by The Lady in the Lake, a sorceress who tired of him and imprisoned him

A nasty but deserved end for Dr Josef Mengele! Gregory Peck's Nazi doctor is savaged by Dobermans at the grisly climax of *The Boys from Brazil,* an adaptation of Ira Levin's bestseller about a monstrous plot to breed a new race of Hitlers

forever in an enchanted tower. Nicol Williamson's weird and jokey playing of the old wizard in *Excalibur* remains the most unusual and controversial portrayal of the character to date.

Actor	Film	Director	Country, Year
Brandon Hurst	*A Connecticut Yankee*	(Butler)	USA, 31
Murvyn Vye	*A Connecticut Yankee In King Arthur's Court*	(Garnett)	USA, 49
Felix Aylmer	*Knights Of The Round Table*	(Thorpe)	GB, 54
John Laurie	*Siege Of The Saxons*	(Juran)	GB, 63
Mark Dignam	*Lancelot And Guinevere*	(Wilde)	GB, 63
Laurence Naismith	*Camelot*	(Logan)	USA, 67
Ron Moody	*The Spaceman And King Arthur*	(Mayberry)	GB, 79
Nicol Williamson	*Excalibur*	(Boorman)	USA, 81

Note: Karl Swenson voiced Merlin in Disney's cartoon *The Sword And the Stone* (63) and Chinese

Master Magician! Nicol Williamson as King Arthur's counsellor, the wizard Merlin in John Boorman's recreation of the world of Camelot in *Excalibur*. The legendary magician has been played on many occasions on screen—by Felix Aylmer in *Knights of the Round Table*, Ron Moody in *The Spaceman and King Arthur* and Karl Swenson (voice only) in Walt Disney's animated feature *The Sword And The Stone*

showman Tony Randall donned the disguise of the magician in *The Seven Faces Of Dr Lao* (64); on the silent screen William V. Mong featured as the character in the 1921 version of *A Connecticut Yankee In King Arthur's Court.* The most recent portrayal has been by Edward Woodward in Clive Donner's 1983 TV movie *Arthur The King.*

Messalina, Valeria R

(*d.* AD 48) Temptress and lascivious third wife of the emperor Claudius who was eventually executed by orders of her husband but not before she'd 'gone through' some of the most virile men in ancient Rome. Actresses, both European and American, have revelled in her wickedness; Susan Hayward purred venom in CinemaScope in *Demetrius And The Gladiators* and in more recent years, Anneka Di Lorenzo, Betty Roland and others have wallowed in debauchery thanks to the relaxation of censorship.

Maria Felix	*Messalina* (Gallone)	Fra/It, 51
Susan Hayward	*Demetrius And The Gladiators* (Daves)	USA, 54
Belinda Lee	*Messalina, Venere Imperatrice* (Cottafavi)	It, 60
Anneka Di Lorenzo	*Messalina, Messalina* (Corbucci)	It, 77
Anneka Di Lorenzo	*Caligula* (Brass)	USA/It, 80
Betty Roland	*Caligula And Messalina* (Pass)	Fra, 82

Note: On the silent screen Rina De Liguoro starred in *Messalina,* directed by Enrico Guazzoni in Italy in 1923; Sheila White, in *I Claudius* (76) and Jennifer O'Neill in *AD–Anno Domini* (85) are among the actresses who have featured in the role on television.

Mesta, Pearl R

(1889–1975) According to the Irving Berlin musical *Call Me Madam* 'The Hostess With The Mostess'; in real life the most celebrated unofficial hostess in Washington during the 40s and a lady who became the official US envoy to Luxemburg between 1949 and 1953. Berlin's political satire which renamed her Sally Adams centred on her capacity in the latter years when she operated in 'two mythical countries, one Lichtenburg, the other the United States Of America' Ethel Merman recreated her Broadway role in one of the last Fox musicals to be made before the advent of CinemaScope. Among her songs: 'Can You Use Any Money Today?'; 'You're Just In Love' and 'International Rag'.

Ethel Merman	*Call Me Madam* (Lang)	USA, 53

Micawber, Wilkins F

The eternal optimist of 'David Copperfield' (1850), always on the bread line but forever confident that something will 'turn up'. For most of his life it usually does, in the form of his creditors. In the end, though, his joviality and kindness to Dickens' boy hero serve him well and he emigrates to Australia to become a magistrate. Ralph Richardson's screen Micawber comes closest to Dickens' original conception; W C Fields' unique vaudeville turn defies criticism.

W. C. Fields	*David Copperfield* (Cukor)	USA, 35
Ralph Richardson	*David Copperfield* (Delbert Mann)	GB, 70

Note: Micawber was played by H. Collins in Thomas Bentley's British silent version of 1913 and by Frederik Jensen in A. W. Sandburg's Danish film of 1923.

The other characters in Dickens' partly autobiographical novel include the boy David, his cruel stepfather Mr Murdstone, Aunt Betsy Trotwood, the kindly Yarmouth fisherman Dan Peggotty and the devious, 'ever so 'umble' solicitor's clerk Uriah Heep. They have been played on screen as follows:

David (as a boy)

Freddie Bartholomew	*David Copperfield* (Cukor)	USA, 35
Alistair Mackenzie	*David Copperfield* (Delbert Mann)	GB, 70

David (as a man)

Frank Lawton	*David Copperfield* (Cukor)	USA, 35
Robin Phillips	*David Copperfield* (Delbert Mann)	GB, 70

Note: Eric Desmond and Kenneth Ware (GB, 13) and Martin Herzberg and Gorm Schmidt (Den, 23) played the child and adult Copperfield in silent productions.

Two screen portrayals of Charles Dickens' eternal optimist—Wilkins Micawber—(above) W.C. Fields with Freddie Bartholomew in George Cukor's 1935 version of *David Copperfield*; (left) Ralph Richardson as Micawber in Delbert Mann's 1970 remake

Mr Murdstone

Basil Rathbone — *David Copperfield* (Cukor) USA, 35

James Donald — *David Copperfield* (Delbert Mann) GB, 70

Silent: Johnny Butt (GB, 13) and Robert Schmidt (Den, 23).

Betsy Trotwood

Edna May Oliver — *David Copperfield* (Cukor) USA, 35

Edith Evans — *David Copperfield* (Delbert Mann) GB, 70

Silent: Miss Harcourt (GB, 13) and Marie Dinesen (Den, 23).

Dan Peggotty

Lionel Barrymore — *David Copperfield* (Cukor) USA, 35

Michael Redgrave — *David Copperfield* (Delbert Mann) GB, 70

Silent: James Darling (GB, 13) and K. Caspersen (Den, 23).

Uriah Heep

Roland Young — *David Copperfield* (Cukor) USA, 35

Ron Moody — *David Copperfield* (Delbert Mann) GB, 70

Silent: Jack Hulcup (GB, 13) and Rasmus Christiansen (Den, 23).

Michelangelo [R]

(1475–1564) Renaissance painter, sculptor and poet whose conflict with Pope Julius II during his four-year painting of the ceilings of the Sistine Chapel provided the basis for Irving Stone's novel, and later Carol Reed's film. *The Agony And The Ecstasy.* Charlton Heston suffered producing a masterpiece of decorative design, Rex Harrison fretted as the impatient Julius.

Wilfred Fletcher — *The Cardinal* (Hill) GB, 36

Andrea Bosic — *The Magnificent Adventurer* (Freda) It/Fra/Spa, 63

Charlton Heston — *The Agony And The Ecstasy* (Reed) USA, 65

Milady de Winter [F]

Beautiful *femme fatale* in many of the screen versions of Dumas' 'The Three Musketeers', a spy for Cardinal Richelieu and former wife of Athos, she murders without compunction and is eventually executed by the musketeers. A bejewelled Faye Dunaway sparkled with venom in Richard Lester's two films of the 70s; Lana Turner was even more effective in George Sidney's 1948 version for MGM.

Dorothy Revier — *The Iron Mask* (Dwan) USA, 29

Edith Mera — *The Three Musketeers* (Diamant-Berger) Fra, 32

Margot Grahame — *The Three Musketeers* (Lee) USA, 35

Binnie Barnes — *The Three Musketeers* (Dwan) USA, 39

Lana Turner — *The Three Musketeers* (Sidney) USA, 48

Yvette Lebon — *Milady And The Musketeers* (Cottafavi) It, 51

Yvonne Sanson — *The Three Musketeers* (Hunebelle) Fra, 53

Dawn Addams — *Le Vicomte de Bragelonne* (Cerchio) Fra/It, 55

Mylene Demengeot — *The Three Musketeers* (Borderie) Fra, 61

Faye Dunaway — *The Three Musketeers* (Lester) Panama/Spa, 74

Charlton Heston as the Renaissance painter and sculptor Michelangelo in Carol Reed's 1965 version of Irving Stone's novel *The Agony and the Ecstasy*

Faye Dunaway — *The Four Musketeers* (Lester) Panama/Spa, 75

Note: Carey Lee starred as Milady in an American silent of 1911, Barbara LaMarr appeared in Fred Niblo's 1921 *The Three Musketeers* and Mademoiselle Claude Merelle in Berger's 18-part serial of 1922.

Miller, Glenn [R]

(1904–44) American bandleader who brought a new sound to popular dance music in the 30s and 40s and whose music enjoyed a rebirth a decade after his death with the release of Universal's *The Glenn Miller Story*. Lost in a World War II plane crash, Miller earned his enormous popularity with such hit numbers as 'Moonlight Serenade', 'In The Mood' and 'String Of Pearls'. He featured with his band in the Fox musicals, *Orchestra Wives* and *Sun Valley Serenade*.

James Stewart — *The Glenn Miller Story* (Anthony Mann) USA, 54
Ray Daley — *The Five Pennies* (Shavelson) USA, 59

Miller, Marilyn [R]

(1898–1938) Tiny blonde musical comedy star of the 20s who appeared in several revues for Ziegfeld, as well as the hit Broadways shows 'Sally', 'Sunny' and 'As Thousands Cheer'. Helped make popular such songs as 'Who?', 'Wild Rose' and 'Easter Parade'. Her career, including her early vaudeville days with her mother and stepfather, was recounted in the Warner biography *Look For The Silver Lining*. Judy Garland featured as Miller in *Till The Clouds Roll By*.

Rosina Lawrence — *The Great Ziegfeld* (Leonard) USA, 36
Judy Garland — *Till The Clouds Roll By* (Whorf) USA, 46
June Haver — *Look For The Silver Lining* (Butler) USA, 49

Note: Pamela Peadon appeared as Miller in Buzz Kulik's 1978 TV film, *Ziegfeld: The Man And His Women*.

Miner, Bill [R]

(1847–1913) A Californian outlaw forever robbing stagecoaches and trains in the later years of the nineteenth century. Credited for being the first man to use the expression 'Hands-Up!' he operated from the Civil War days to as late as 1911 and was in and out of jail many times before being finally apprehended by a Pinkerton detective. He lived out his last years tending his flower garden and died peacefully in his sleep. Some of his more colourful escapades, plus a scene in which he learns a thing or two from watching *The Great Train Robbery*, were portrayed in the Canadian film *The Grey Fox*. Miner was played by the veteran Richard Farnsworth who began in films in the 30s and worked as a stunt man for Roy Rogers.

Richard Farnsworth — *The Grey Fox* (Borsos) Can, 82

Miniver, Mrs

Middle-class British housewife who takes all the Nazis can throw at her home and country in World War II. In William Wyler's famous film of 1942 she reads to her children in an air raid shelter, waits for her husband to return from Dunkirk and even captures a German airman in her back garden. Whether or not many Mrs Minivers actually existed in Britain during the war is difficult now to ascertain. If they didn't, they should have! Played to perfection in two movies by Greer Garson.

Greer Garson — *Mrs Miniver* (Wyler) USA, 42
Greer Garson — *The Miniver Story* (Potter) GB, 50

Mishima, Yukio

(1925–70) Japan's most controversial post-World War II author and playwright, a fanatical patriot and political agitator who led his own private army (The Shield Society) and in 1970 shook the world by committing ritual suicide when he failed to overthrow the constitution and restore unrestricted powers to the emperor. Paul Schrader's 1985 film (produced by Coppola and Lucas) told Mishima's remarkable story in flashback, combining scenes of his personal life (photographed in black and white) with colour dramatizations of his most emotional works of fiction.

Ken Ogata — *Mishima: A Life In Four Chapters* (Schrader) USA/Jap, 85

Note: Go Riju (Mishima, age 18–19), Masato Aizawa (age 9–14) and Yuki Nagahara (age 5) featured as the writer in the earlier stages of his life.

Miss Julie

F

The repressed daughter of a Swedish nobleman who tempts her father's valet into seducing her then commits suicide rather than face the consequences of her act. The central figure of Strindberg's 1888 play in which the author explores the social conflict between the working classes and decadent aristocracy of nineteenth century Sweden. Faultlessly played by Anita Björk in Sjöberg's 1950 screen version.

Amelia Bence	*Miss Julie*	(Soffici)	Arg, 47
Anita Björk	*Miss Julie*	(Sjöberg)	Swe, 50
Helen Mirran	*Miss Julie*	(Phillips)	GB, 72

Note: Four silent films were made of Strindberg's play. Manda Björling starred in a 1912 production Olga Preobrajenskaia in a 1915 Russian adaptation, Gizi Bajor in a 1919 Hungarian film and Asta Nielsen in a German version released in 1921.

Mitchell, Billy

(1879–1936) Controversial American brigadier-general who tried to convince the officials of the Army and Navy of the importance of Air Power, even predicting that the American naval base in Hawaii might eventually be the target of attack by Japanese bombers. Otto Preminger's 1955 film concentrated on the most important episode in Mitchell's life when he publicly charged the War and Navy Departments with 'incompetence and criminal negligence' and was arrested and court-martialled.

Gary Cooper — *The Court-Martial Of Billy Mitchell* (Preminger) USA, 55

Mitchell, Reginald

(1895–1937) English aircraft designer of the famous Spitfire fighter plane used with such devastating effect by the RAF in World War II. The development and testing of the plane are covered in detail in Leslie Howard's bio-pic *The First Of The Few.*

Leslie Howard — *The First Of The Few* (Howard) GB, 42

Mitty, Walter

Frustrated, middle-aged husband who daydreams away his mundane existence by imagining himself

Dreamland! Danny Kaye enjoying one of his many fantasies in Sam Goldwyn's production of *The Secret Life of Walter Mitty.* Helping things along—Virginia Mayo!

in all kinds of heroic situations. First created by James Thurber in his 1939 'New Yorker' story 'The Secret Life Of Walter Mitty' he was later given the Hollywood treatment by producer Sam Goldwyn who spent three million dollars turning his imaginings into a lavish Technicolor vehicle for Danny Kaye. Thurber, who had stated that he would prefer to pay Goldwyn $10,000 for him *not* to touch his story, was, perhaps not surprisingly, unhappy with the final result.

Danny Kaye — *The Secret Life Of Walter Mitty* (McLeod) USA, 47

Note: Kaye romped through several characterizations in the film, playing a daring sea captain guiding his ship through a raging typhoon, a French fashion designer, a western gunfighter, a Mississippi riverboat gambler, a noted surgeon performing an impossible operation, and a dashing RAF pilot. In 1969 William Windom (although not named Walter Mitty) got rather closer to the Thurber daydreamer in the TV series *My World And Welcome To It,* the story of a cartoonist who sees his home life in terms of his drawings.

Molière

R

(1622–73) Satirical French playwright, a master of prose and comic verse, and sometimes referred to as the father of modern French comedy. In 1978 afforded the luxury of a four and a quarter hour screen biography by director Ariane Mnouchkine.

Otto Gebuhr	*Nanon* (Maisch)	Ger, 38
Fernand Gravey	*Versailles* (Guitry)	Fra, 54
Philippe Caubere	*Molière* (Mnouchkine)	Fra, 78

Note: Frederic Ladonne played Molière as a child in the Mnouchkine biography.

Monroe, Marilyn

R

(1926–62) Real name, Norma Jean Baker. In many ways the last of the great Hollywood sex symbols, blonde, wide-eyed and innocently appealing. Regarded with more affection than any other star of her period (the 50s), she desired only one thing in life, i.e. to become a movie star, but she was subsequently destroyed by the very system in which she functioned so effectively. *Goodbye, Norma Jean* recounted her sordid early life up until the time she broke into films; *Marilyn: The Untold Story* told her life à la Norman Mailer's biography; and *This Year's Blonde,* a segment of the three-part *Moviola* series, told of her early relationship with her agent Johnny Hyde.

Misty Rowe	*Goodbye, Norma Jean* (Buchanan) Austral/USA, 76
Constance Forslund	*Moviola: This Year's Blonde* (Erman) TVM/USA, 80
Catherine Hicks	*Marilyn: The Untold Story* (Flynn, Arnold, Schiller) TVM/USA, 80

Note: *Marilyn* (63), released a year after her death and narrated by Rock Hudson, was a film documentary built around clips from Monroe movies; two TV documentaries have also been devoted to her life – *Marilyn Monroe: Say Goodbye To The President* (85) about her relationship with John and Bobby Kennedy, and *The Last Days Of Marilyn Monroe* (85).

The blonde actress (played by Theresa Russell) who meets up with Albert Einstein in a New York hotel room in *Insignificance* (85) was derived from Monroe.

Montes, Lola

R

(1818–61) Nineteenth century adventuress and dancer who crammed into her 43 years more 'living' than perhaps any other woman of her century. On screen, she emerges frequently in films about Liszt and King Ludwig of Bavaria, just two of her many illustrious lovers. She was given star treatment in the last film of Max Ophuls, who traced her career in flashback from the time of her love affairs with Liszt and Ludwig, to her final degradation as a circus sideshow attraction.

Rebecca Wassem	*Wells Fargo* (Lloyd) USA, 37
Yvonne DeCarlo	*Black Bart* (Sherman) USA, 48
Martine Carol	*Lola Montes* (Ophuls) Fra/Ger, 55
Larissa Trembovelskaya	*The Loves Of Liszt* (Keleti) Hung/USSR, 70
Ingrid Caven	*Ludwig – Requiem For A Virgin King* (Syberberg) W.Ger, 72
Anulka Dziubinska	*Lisztomania* (Russell) GB, 75
Florinda Bolkan	*Royal Flash* (Lester) GB, 75

Note: Leopoldine Konstantin (Ger, 18), Maria Leiko (Ger, 19) and Ellen Richter (Ger, 22) all played Lola Montes on the silent screen.

Montgomery, Field Marshal Bernard

R

(1887–1976) Britain's most celebrated commander of World War II (a hero of El Alamein and Commander-in-Chief of the British armies in France and Germany) but not yet awarded a major screen biography to set alongside those of Patton and MacArthur. Michael Bates, in Schaffner's *Patton,* showed Monty to be a somewhat petulant figure, in constant rivalry with his American colleagues.

Trevor Reid	*The Longest Day* (Wicki/Marton/Annakin)	USA, 62
Michael Rennie	*Desert Tanks* (Padget)	It/Fra, 68
Michael Bates	*Patton* (Schaffner)	USA, 70

Note: Ironically, Montgomery's 'stand-in', Clifton James, has been given wider exposure on screen. The film, *I Was Monty's Double,* showed how the British fooled the Germans on the eve of D-Day by

Imitation Monroe. Misty Rowe (right) as the legendary blonde in the 1976 biography *Goodbye, Norma Jean* and (below) Theresa Russell as the mysterious Monroe – like blonde in Nicolas Roeg's 1985 film *Insignificance*

sending his look-alike to review the troops in the Middle East while the real Monty was putting the final touches to the plans for the invasion of Europe. Clifton James played himself in the film which was released in 1958.

Moore, Grace R

(1901–47) Operatic singer who enjoyed a brief movie career at Columbia during the 30s. An Oscar nominee for *One Night Of Love* (34), she retired from the screen in 1939 and met a premature death in a Copenhagen aircrash just eight years later. Warners' screen biography focused on her life up until her debut at the Metropolitan Opera in 1928.

Kathryn Grayson — *So This Is Love* (Douglas) USA, 53

Moran, Bugs 

American gangster who took over Chicago's North Side Mob after the murder of Dion O'Bannion in the bootlegging wars of the 20s. By a lucky chance escaped death in the St Valentine's Day Massacre of 1929 when six of his gang were shot down in a garage by Al Capone's men. Never again a force to be reckoned with, he turned to petty crime and died in prison in 1957. A substantial performance was given by Ralph Meeker in Roger Corman's film of 1967.

Ben Hendricks Jr — *The Public Enemy* (Wellman) USA, 31
Murvyn Vye — *Al Capone* (Wilson) USA, 58
Ralph Meeker — *The St Valentine's Day Massacre* (Corman) USA, 67
Robert Phillips — *Capone* (Carver) USA, 75

More, Sir Thomas 

(1478–1535) Sixteenth century statesman who refused, as a matter of conscience, to sign the Act of Succession which condoned Henry VIII's divorce from Catherine of Aragon and marriage to Anne Boleyn. After resigning the post of Lord Chancellor, he was imprisoned, tried for high treason and executed. Fred Zinnemann's film of Robert Bolt's stage play, 'A Man For All Seasons' (1961) examined the man and his principles; Paul Scofield's performance won him a best actor Academy Award.

Paul Scofield — *A Man For All Seasons* (Zinnemann) GB, 66

Paul Scofield repeating his stage role as Sir Thomas More in Fred Zinnemann's screen version of the Robert Bolt play, *A Man For All Seasons*

William Squire — *Anne Of The Thousand Days* (Jarrott) GB, 70
Michael Goodliffe — *Henry VIII And His Six Wives* (Hussein) GB, 72

Morgan, Harry 

Tough, disillusioned Hemingway hero of 'To Have And Have Not' (1937), a man who wearies of hiring out his motor boat for unprofitable fishing trips and becomes involved with smugglers and racketeers. Portrayed by Bogart in the famous 1944 film of Howard Hawks, but more effectively by John Garfield in Michael Curtiz's adaptation, *The Breaking Point*.

Humphrey Bogart — *To Have And Have Not* (Hawks) USA, 44
John Garfield — *The Breaking Point* (Curtiz) USA, 50
Audie Murphy — *The Gun Runners* (Siegel) USA, 58

Morgan, Helen 

(1900–41) Famed torch singer, at her peak during the 20s and early 30s. She enjoyed success and accl-

'If you want anything just whistle'. Bogart (as Hemingway's Harry Morgan) and Bacall (debut), together for the first time in Howard Hawks' version of *To Have and Have Not.* The film reworked the Hemingway original and cast Bogart as a skipper-for-hire operating in Martinique in World War II

in vaudeville and on Broadway, but failure and alcoholism in her private life. She introduced 'Bill' and 'Can't Help Lovin' Dat Man' in 'Show Boat', appeared in the movies *Applause* (29), *Show Boat* (30, *Marie Galante* (34), etc. Gogi Grant dubbed the musical numbers for Ann Blyth in Michael Curtiz' 1957 bio-pic.

Ann Blyth	*The Helen Morgan Story* (Curtiz) USA, 57

Morgan, Sir Henry [R]

(*c.* 1635–88) Notorious Welsh buccaneer who reformed to become the Lieutenant Governor of Jamaica and who died, not as the result of a rope around the neck or a sword through the chest, but of simple dissipation. Portrayed as a swashbuckler by Steve Reeves in *Morgan The Pirate,* and as the overlarge, ageing governor by Laird Cregar in *The Black Swan.*

Laird Cregar	*The Black Swan* (Henry King) USA, 42
Robert Barrat	*Double Crossbones* (Barton) USA, 50
Torin Thatcher	*Blackbeard The Pirate* (Walsh) USA, 52
Steve Reeves	*Morgan The Pirate* (De Toth/Zeglio) It, 60
Timothy Carey	*The Boy And The Pirates* (Gordon) USA, 60
Robert Stephens	*Pirates Of Tortuga* (Webb) USA, 61

Moriarty [F]

In the words of Sherlock Holmes, 'the Napoleon of crime', a master criminal with a far-flung organization, who is forever lurking in the background in the Holmes stories and finally meets his death amid the roaring waters of the Reichenbach Falls. More in the thick of things in the movies, especially in *The Adventures Of Sherlock Holmes* in which he attempts to steal the Crown Jewels. No definitive screen portrait as yet but several enjoyable ones from Zucco, Atwill, Daniell and co.

Harry T. Morey	*The Return Of Sherlock Holmes* (Dean/Brook) USA, 29
Ernest Torrence	*Sherlock Holmes* (Howard) USA, 32
Lyn Harding	*The Triumph Of Sherlock Holmes* (Hiscott) GB, 35
Lyn Harding	*Silver Blaze* (Bentley) GB, 37
George Zucco	*The Adventures Of Sherlock Holmes* (Werker) USA, 39
Lionel Atwill	*Sherlock Holmes And The Voice Of Terror* (Rawlins) USA, 42
Henry Daniell	*The Woman In Green* (Neill) USA, 45
Hans Sohnker	*Sherlock Holmes And The Secret Necklace* (Fisher) Ger, 62
Leo McKern	*The Adventures Of Sherlock Holmes' Smarter Brother* (Gene Wilder) USA, 75
Laurence Olivier	*The Seven-Per-Cent Solution* (Ross) GB, 76
Anthony Higgins	*Young Sherlock Holmes* (Levinson) USA, 85

Note: Booth Conway in *The Valley Of Fear* (GB, 16) and Gustav von Seyffertitz in *Sherlock Holmes* (USA, 22) both featured as Moriarty on the silent screen.

On TV John Huston featured in *Sherlock Holmes In New York* (76), George Morfogen in *Sherlock Holmes* (81) and Eric Porter in *The Final Problem* (85) episode of the Granada series with Jeremy Brett. The animated rat-villain Professor Ratigan, voiced by Vincent Price in Disney's feature cartoon *The Great Mouse Detective* (USA, 86), derived from the Moriarty figure.

Moses [R]

The Hebrew lawgiver who led the Israelites out of Egypt, through the wilderness and to the promised land. According to the Bible, the meekest of men; according to Hollywood, somewhat more dominant in the form of Charlton Heston, who parted the Red Sea without any difficulty and took the tablets on top of Mount Sinai. Comedian Mel Brooks presented him as a man prone to clumsiness, descending the mountain with 15 commandments then dropping a tablet and reducing them to ten!

Charlton Heston	*The Ten Commandments* (DeMille) USA, 56
Francis X. Bushman	*The Story Of Mankind* (Allen) USA, 57
Burt Lancaster	*Moses* (De Bosio) It/GB, 75
Mel Brooks	*History Of The World Part I* (Brooks) USA, 81

Note: William Lancaster played the young Moses in the 1975 film; Theodore Roberts appeared for DeMille as the lawgiver in the silent version of *The Ten Commandments* (USA, 23), Hans Marr for Michael Curtiz in the Austrian production, *Moon Of Israel* (24).

Rameses II, the Pharaoh who oppressed the Jews at the time of the Exodus from Israel, has been played by Charles de Roche (23), Yul Brynner (56) and Mario Ferrari (75).

Mowgli [F]

The 'Boy Cub' of Rudyard Kipling's two-volume fable 'The Jungle Book' (1894–5), a foundling who is raised by a family of wolves and instructed in the lore of the jungle. On screen, best known as the animated character in Walt Disney's full-length cartoon, but portrayed earlier by Sabu in a 1942 Korda film in which he ventures out against wild animals, wicked natives and discovers the treasures of a lost city.

Sabu	*The Jungle Book* (Zoltan Korda) USA, 42
Bruce Reitherman (voice only	*The Jungle Book* (Disney) USA, 67

Mozart, Wolfgang Amadeus [R]

(1756–91) Austrian composer and child prodigy, a supreme musical genius who produced more than 600 works in his 35 years, including concertos, symphonies and the operas 'The Marriage Of Figaro', 'Don Giovanni' and 'The Magic Flute'.

The two faces of Moses. (above) Charlton Heston – third from the left – as the young adopted son of the Pharoah Sethi and (left) as the aged Moses, descending with the Commandments from Mount Sinai. Two scenes from DeMille's 1956 epic *The Ten Commandments*

Unlike Liszt, Chopin and others he has received distinguished treatment from film-makers, Karl Hartl telling his life story in two films in the 40s and 50s and Kirschner concentrating on Mozart's boyhood and youth in his 1976 film *Mozart: A Childhood Chronicle*. The Oscar-winning *Amadeus* was an adaptation of Peter Shaffer's celebrated stage play and focused on the conflict between Mozart and court composer Salieri who, the film suggests, was responsible for Mozart's early death. The death of the composer was also the central theme of the subsequent *Forget Mozart*, filmed in West Germany in 1985.

Stephen Haggard	*Whom The Gods Love* (Dean) GB, 36
Gino Cervi	*Eternal Melodies* (Gallone) It, 39
Hannes Stelzer	*Die Kleine Nachtmusik* (Hainisch) Ger, 39
Hans Holt	*Whom The Gods Love* (Hartl) Aus, 42
Oscar Werner	*Mozart – Put Your Hand In Mine Dear* (Hartl) Aus, 55
Diego Crovetti Santiago Ziesmer	*Mozart: A Childhood Chronicle* (Kirschner) W.Ger, 76
Tom Hulce	*Amadeus* Ⓞ (Forman) USA, 84
Tidof	*Forget Mozart* (Luther) W.Ger, 85
Philip Zander	*The Mozart Brothers* (Osten) Swe, 86

The most famous of all the screen Mozarts—Tom Hulce as the Austrian composer in Milos Forman's Academy Award winning *Amadeus* (1984)

Note: In Kirschner's film Crovetti played Mozart when he was 12, Ziesmer when he was 20; F Murray Abraham played Salieri in *Amadeus* and Winfried Glatzeder in *Forget Mozart*.

In the Swedish comedy *The Mozart Brothers* Philip Zander featured as Mozart's ghost who looks on in amusement as a director decides to stage 'Don Giovanni' without its libretto and with the cast clad only in rags!

Moto, Mr

Oriental super sleuth of Pulitzer Prize-winning novelist John P. Marquand. Shrewd, courteous and more active than his elderly competitors, Charlie Chan and Mr Wong, he frequently worked under cover and employed many disguises during his cases. First appeared in print in 'Saturday Evening Post' serials then graduated to the screen in the person of Peter Lorre, whose well-known features were partly obscured by steel-rimmed glasses, plastered down hair and false buck teeth.

Peter Lorre	*Think Fast, Mr Moto* (Foster) USA, 37
Peter Lorre	*Thank You, Mr Moto* (Foster) USA, 37
Peter Lorre	*Mr Moto's Gamble* (Tinling) USA, 38
Peter Lorre	*Mr Moto Takes A Chance* (Foster) USA, 38
Peter Lorre	*Mysterious Mr Moto* (Foster) USA, 38
Peter Lorre	*Mr Moto's Last Warning* (Foster) USA, 39
Peter Lorre	*Mr Moto In Danger Island* (Leeds) USA, 39
Peter Lorre	*Mr Moto Takes A Vacation* (Foster) USA, 39
Henry Silva	*The Return Of Mr Moto* (Morris) USA, 65

Montague, Ewan

(1901–85) World War II Intelligence Officer and lawyer who masterminded 'Operation Mincemeat', an ingenious Allied plot to foil the Nazis in which a body (complete with official documents) was deliberately placed in the sea near Spain in order to persuade the enemy that an Allied offensive would occur in Greece or Turkey and not Sicily. Montague's subsequent book of the affair — 'The Man Who Never Was' — was written over a single weekend (Friday night to Sunday night) and sold two million copies; the film of the book followed two years later.

Clifton Webb — *The Man Who Never Was* (Neame) GB, 56

Muhammad Ali R

(1942–) The only man ever to win the heavyweight championship of the world three times and, without doubt, the supreme boxer of the post-war generation. His life, from his early years when he won the light heavyweight gold medal at the Rome Olympics, to his regaining the title from George Foreman in Zaire, was recounted in Tom Gries' *The Greatest.* To no-one's surprise, Ali played himself.

Muhammad Ali — *The Greatest* (Gries) USA, 77

Note: The 18-year-old Cassius Clay was played in the film by Phillip 'Chip' McAllister; Ernest Borgnine appeared as Angelo Dundee, Roger E. Mosley as Sonny Liston. Clay appeared as himself in the 1962 film *Requiem For a Heavyweight;* William Clayton directed *AKA Cassius Clay,* a 1970 documentary that looked at Ali's career in and out of the ring.

Mummy, The 

Since 1932, one of the great figures of screen horror, a 3700-year-old mummified Egyptian priest who guards the tomb of a princess and is accidentally brought back to life by an English archaeologist. Known as Imhotep in Karl Freund's film and, more usually, Kharis in the sequels. Changed sex in the movies *Blood From The Mummy's Tomb* and *The Awakening.* There have been just two versions of the original story, the first with Karloff, the second with Christopher Lee.

Boris Karloff — *The Mummy* (Freund) USA, 32

Tom Tyler — *The Mummy's Hand* (Cabanne) USA, 40

Lon Chaney, Jr — *The Mummy's Tomb* (Young) USA, 42

Lon Chaney, Jr — *The Mummy's Ghost* (Le Borg) USA, 44

Lon Chaney, Jr — *The Mummy's Curse* (Goodwins) USA, 45

Eddie Parker — *Abbott And Costello Meet The Mummy* (Lamont) USA, 55

Christopher Lee — *The Mummy* (Fisher) GB, 59

Dickie Owen — *The Curse Of The Mummy's Tomb* (Carreras) GB, 64

Toolsie Persaud — *The Mummy's Shroud* (Gilling) GB, 67

Valerie Leon — *Blood From The Mummy's Tomb* (Holt) GB, 71

Stephanie Zimbalist — *The Awakening* (Newell) GB, 80

Note: Both *Blood From The Mummy's Tomb* and *The Awakening* derived from the Bram Stoker novel 'The Jewel Of Seven Stars' (1903).

Munch, Edvard 

(1863–1944) Melancholic Norwegian artist of portraits and landscapes, a pioneer of modern art who became one of the most influential figures in European Expressionism. Peter Watkins' 215-minute film chronicled his turbulent years in Norway and photographed all Munch's major canvases.

Geir Westby — *Edvard Munch* (Watkins) Swe/Nor, 76

Note: Erik Allum appeared as Munch, aged five, and Amund Berge as the artist, aged 14.

Münchhausen, Baron 

Legendary adventurer and teller of tall tales, forever involved in remarkable escapades and always escaping from impossible situations by the skin of his teeth. Most film-makers have offered their own interpretation of the Baron's adventures, drawing inspiration from early nineteenth century novels by Gottfried Burger and Karl Immermann, and also the work of Carl Haensel who reworked the exploits in the 1920s. The most spectacular version has been the 1943 German production which sent the Baron on far-fetched adventures to Russia, Constantinople (on a cannon ball) and Venice; the most recent portrayal has been by John Neville in the surrealist adaptation of Terry Gilliam.

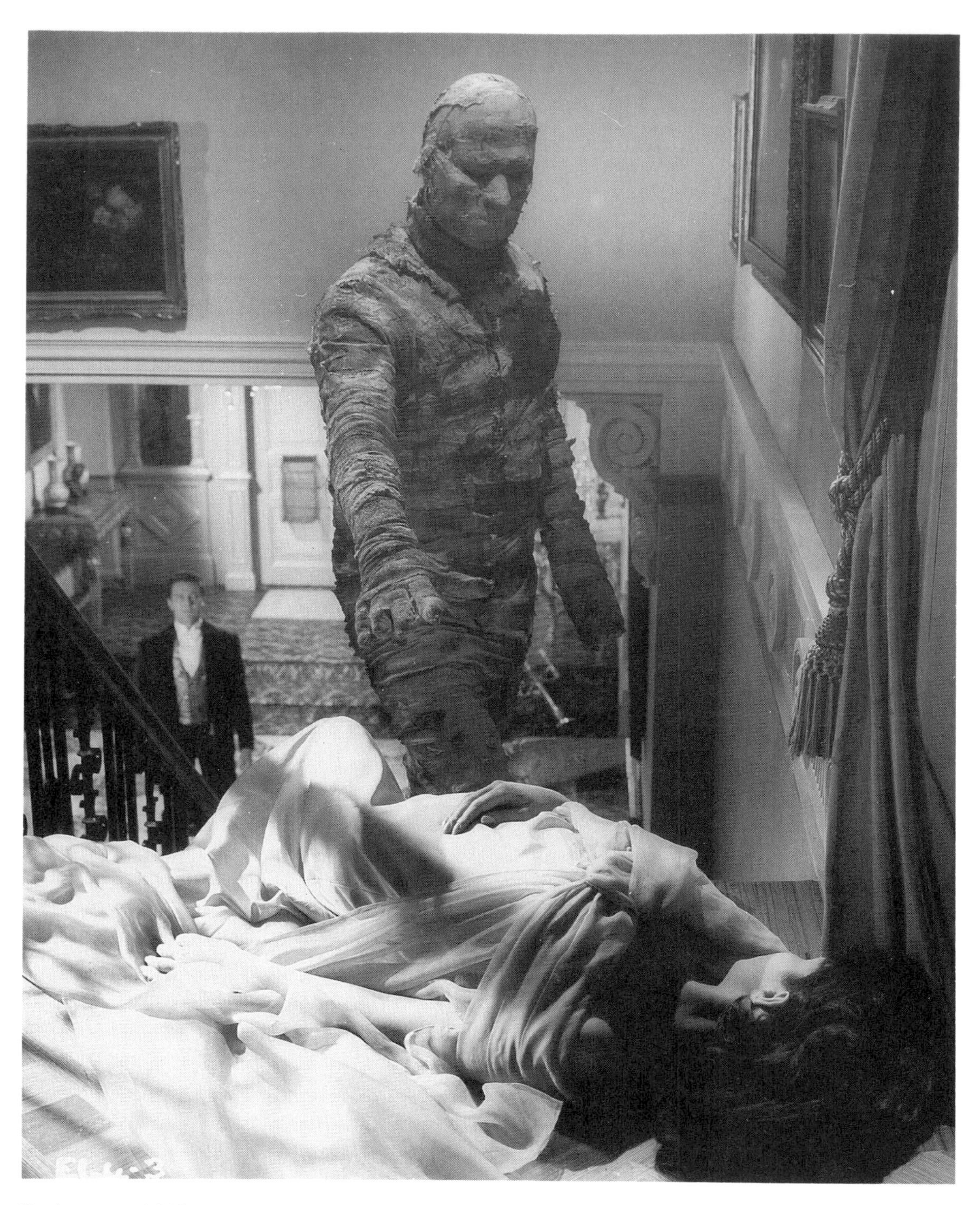

On the rampage! Dickie Owen as the mummy of Pharoah Ra-Antef — brought back to life by 20th century archaeologists and an American showman in a scene from *The Curse Of The Mummy's Tomb*

Hans Albers	*Münchhausen* (Von Baky) Ger, 43
Milos Kopecky	*Baron Münchhausen* (Zeman) Cze, 62
John Neville	*The Adventures Of Baron Münchhausen* (Gilliam) GB, 88

Note: Münchhausen was supposedly a real person, an eighteenth century German baron who travelled the world and fought for Catherine The Great and later entertained his drinking companions with accounts of his exploits. The 1979 film *The Fabulous Adventures Of The Legendary Baron Münchhausen* (Fra, 79) was an animated feature directed by Jean Image. *Münchhausen* (Ger, 20) was a silhouette film conceived and executed by Richard Felgenauer.

Murphy, Audie [R]

(1924–71) America's most decorated hero of World War II; later a movie star in over 30 double-feature westerns. Appeared as himself in Universal's version of his war experiences, *To Hell And Back.* Died in a plane crash in 1971.

Audie Murphy	*To Hell And Back* (Hibbs) USA, 56

Mussolini, Benito 

(1883–1945) 'Il Duce', the Italian dictator who marched on Rome with his black shirts in October, 1922 and ruled Italy with force – and efficiency – until the Second World War brought about his collapse. Chaplin satirized him through Jack Oakie's Benzini Napaloni in *The Great Dictator;* Rod Steiger portrayed him in the last days of his life when he was hounded across Italy by partisans and finally executed by firing squad.

Jack Oakie	*The Great Dictator* (Chaplin) USA, 40
Joe Devlin	*The Devil With Hitler* (Douglas) USA, 42
Joe Devlin	*That Nazty Nuisance* (Tryon) USA, 43
Ivo Garrani	*The Great Battle* (Ozerov) USSR/Pol/Yug/E.Ger/It, 69
Mario Adorf	*The Assassination of Matteotti* (Vancini) It, 73
Vladimir Stach	*Day Of Betrayal* (Vavra) Czech, 74
Rod Steiger	*The Last Days Of Mussolini* (Lizzani) It, 74
Rod Steiger	*Lion Of The Desert* (Akkad) USA, 80

Note: In 1985 two actors appeared as Mussolini on TV – Bob Hoskins featured as the dictator in Alberto Negrin's Italian/USA co-production *Mussolini: The Decline And Fall Of Il Duce,* and George C. Scott starred in the six hour *Mussolini – The Untold Story,* directed by William A. Graham. The former viewed events through the eyes of Mussolini's daughter Edda (Susan Sarandon), the latter told Mussolini's story from when he seized power to his death at the end of World War II.

Nana

[F]

The prostitute daughter of Gervaise in Zola's 'Nana' (1880). Yet another victim of her slum environment, she goes from man to man in the Paris of the 1880s, ruining both her lovers and herself until she dies a lingering death from smallpox. Her hard, unrepentant nature has appealed to many actresses, although none has yet managed to capture her true character on screen. For the Sam Goldwyn version starring Anna Sten, Rodgers and Hart were commissioned to write a torch song called 'That's Love'.

Actor	Film	Country, Year
Anna Sten	*Nana* (Arzner)	USA, 34
Lupe Velez	*Nana* (Gorostiza)	Mex, 44
Martine Carol	*Nana* (Christian-Jaque)	Fra/It, 55
Anna Gael	*Take Me, Love Me* (Ahlberg)	Swe/Fra, 70
Katya Berger	*Nana* (Wolman)	It, 83
Irma Serrano	*Nana* (Baledon/Bolanos)	Mex, 85

Note: Silent portrayals include those of Ellen Lumbye (Den, 12), Lilla Pescatori (It, 14), Tilda Kassay (It, 19) and Catherine Hessling who featured in Jean Renoir's French version of 1926; Katharine Schofield in a four-part 1968 BBC adaptation and Veronique Genest in a six episode French version (83) have both appeared as Nana on TV.

Nelson, George 'Baby Face'

[R]

(–1935) Real name: Lester Gillis. One of the nastiest hoodlums to flourish in Depression America. Just five feet five inches tall and with the face of a choir boy, he was a cold-blooded killer of the most ruthless kind and, after the death of Dillinger, with whom he teamed for a while, featured prominently on the FBI's wanted list. He was eventually killed in Illinois in a shootout with two FBI agents. Nelson's ruthlessness was most accurately conveyed in Don Siegel's 1957 biography with Mickey Rooney.

Actor	Film	Country, Year
Mickey Rooney	*Baby Face Nelson* (Siegel)	USA, 57
William Phipps	*The FBI Story* (LeRoy)	USA, 59
John Ashley	*Young Dillinger* (Morse)	USA, 64
Richard Dreyfuss	*Dillinger* (Milius)	USA, 73

Note: Elliott Street played Nelson in the TV movie *The Kansas City Massacre,* directed by Dan Curtis in 1975.

Nelson, Horatio

[R]

(1758–1805) British naval hero of the battles of the Nile and Trafalgar, but of more interest to film-makers for his victories below decks i.e. with Lady Hamilton, than those against Napoleon. Nonetheless, a major figure in several screen biographies, both silent and sound. The romanticized *Lady Hamilton* was said to be one of the favourite films of Winston Churchill who reputedly saw it many times.

Actor	Film	Country, Year
Victor Varconi	*The Divine Lady* (Lloyd)	USA, 29
John Burton	*Lloyds Of London* (Henry King)	USA, 36
Laurence Olivier	*Lady Hamilton* (Korda)	GB, 41
Stephen Haggard	*The Young Mr. Pitt* (Reed)	GB, 42
Roland Bartrop	*Austerlitz* (Gance)	Fra/It/Yug, 60
Richard Johnson	*Lady Hamilton* (Christian-Jaque)	W.Ger/It/Fra/USA, 69
Peter Finch	*Bequest To The Nation* (Jones)	GB, 73

Note: Jimmy Thompson spoofed Nelson in *Carry On Jack* (64); Donald Calthrop in *Nelson* (GB, 18), Humberstone Wright in *The Romance Of Lady Hamilton* (GB, 19), Conrad Veidt in Richard Oswald's *The Affairs Of Lady Hamilton* (Ger, 21) and Cedric Hardwicke in *Nelson* (GB, 26) all played him on the silent screen.

Nemo, Captain

The megalomaniac genius of Jules Verne's novels, '20 000 Leagues Under The Sea' and 'The Mysterious Island' (both 1870); an embittered inventor who finds a new world for himself beneath the ocean as he patrols the lower depths in his revolutionary nineteenth century submarine *Nautilus.* Numerous portrayals in spin-offs from the original story but played with most conviction by James Mason in Disney's relatively straight adaptation of 1954.

Lionel Barrymore	*The Mysterious Island* (Hubbard) USA, 29
James Mason	*20,000 Leagues Under The Sea* (Fleischer) USA, 54
Herbert Lom	*Mysterious Island* (Endfield) GB, 62
Robert Ryan	*Captain Nemo And The Underwater City* (Hill) GB,69
Omar Sharif	*The Mysterious Island* (Bardem) Fra/It/Spa, 73
Jose Ferrer	*The Amazing Captain Nemo* (March) USA, 78

Note. Nemo was renamed Dakkar in the 1929 version with Lionel Barrymore; Allan Holubar played the role in a 1916 production released by Universal.

Nero

R

(AD 37–68) Mad Roman emperor who supposedly fiddled while Rome burned, kicked his mistress Poppaea and her unborn child to death and fed hundreds of Christians to the lions. A natural for any actor with a tendency towards ham, as was proved by Charles Laughton's Nero which was laced with effeminacy, and that of Peter Ustinov who combined humour with the sadism and insanity and won himself an Academy Award nomination. The most recent portrayal has been that of Klaus Maria Brandauer in the six-hour TV version of *Quo Vadis* in 1985.

Charles Laughton	*The Sign Of The Cross* (DeMille) USA, 32
Francis L. Sullivan	*Fiddlers Three* (Watt) GB, 44
Peter Ustinov	*Quo Vadis* (LeRoy) USA, 51
Gino Cervi	*O K Nero!* (Soldati) It, 51
Jacques Aubuchon	*The Silver Chalice* (Saville) USA, 54
Alberto Sordi	*Nero's Big Weekend* (Steno) It/Fra, 56
Peter Lorre	*The Story Of Mankind* (Allen) USA, 57
Gianni Rizzo	*The Ten Desperate Men* (Parolini) It, 63
Vladimir Medar	*Revenge Of The Gladiators* (Malatesta) It, 63
Dom De Luise	*History Of The World Part I* (Brooks) USA, 81
Klaus Maria Brandauer	*Quo Vadis* (De Concini, Scardamaglia, Rossi) TVM/It, 85

Note: Jacques Gretillat in *Nero* (It/USA, 22) and Emil Jannings in *Quo Vadis* (It, 24) both featured as Nero on the silent screen.

Poppaea has not appeared in all the films about the emperor but has been played by the following actresses: Paulette Duval in *Nero,* Elena Sangro in *Quo Vadis* (24), Claudette Colbert in *The Sign Of The Cross,* Patricia Laffan in *Quo Vadis* (51), Silvana Pampanini in *O K Nero!,* Brigitte Bardot in *Nero's Big Weekend,* Margaret Taylor in *The Ten Desperate Men,* Moira Orfei in *Revenge Of The Gladiators,* and Cristina Raines in *Quo Vadis* (TV, 85).

On TV Nero has also been played by Julian Fellowes in *Peter And Paul* (81) and Anthony Andrews in *AD Anno Domini* (85).

Ness, Eliot

R

(1902–57) One of the most romanticized folk heroes of contemporary America, a Chicago lawman who was put in charge of a special Prohibition detail to try and nail Al Capone. His squad of nine agents (known as 'The Untouchables' because they could not be bribed) helped fight bootlegging in the 30s but although they did make inroads into Capone's operation they were not responsible for his eventual imprisonment – which was due to tax evasion. Robert Stack led his team through many TV adventures in the late 50s/early 60s; Kevin Costner did the same with his squad in Brian DePalma's 1987 film *The Untouchables.*

Phillip R. Allen	*The Lady In Red* (Teaque) USA, 79
Kevin Costner	*The Untouchables* (De Palma) USA, 87

Note: The TV series starring Robert Stack (1959–62) ran for four consecutive seasons and comprised of 117 50-minute episodes, all of them shot in black and white.

Nevsky, Alexander

R

(1218–63) Legendary Russian prince who led his country's peasants to great victories against the

The best-known American gangbuster of the 30s—Eliot Ness as played by Kevin Costner in Brian De Palma's *The Untouchables*

The same character portrayed 25 years earlier by Robert Stack in *The Scarface Mob,* adapted from two episodes of *The Untouchables* TV series

invading Teutonic Knights during the war between Russia and Germany in the thirteenth century. Presented as a hero of epic proportions by Sergei Eisenstein in his 1938 film, which included the famous battle on the ice of Lake Peipus.

Nikolai Cherkasov	*Alexander Nevsky* (Eisenstein) USSR, 38

Nicholas II [R]

(1868–1918) The last emperor of Russia, a Tsar whose ill-fated reign was filled with political blunders, social upheaval, and ended violently in the Bolshevik revolution of 1917. Often a shadowy figure in films made about his turbulent times, he was put into historical perspective in *Nicholas And Alexandra* which focused on the final decay of the Romanovs during the years 1904 to 1918.

Paul Otto	*Rasputin* (Trotz) Ger, 32
Ralph Morgan	*Rasputin And The Empress* (Boleslawsky) USA, 32
Reinhold Schuenzrel	*1914: The Last Days Before The War* (Oswald) Ger, 32
Jean Worme	*Rasputin* (L'Herbier) Fra, 39
Robert Bernier	*Rasputin* (Bernier) It/Fra, 54
Ugo Sasso	*The Nights Of Rasputin* (Chenal) Fra/It, 60
Paul Daneman	*Oh! What A Lovely War* (Attenborough) GB, 69
Michael Jayston	*Nicholas And Alexandra* (Schaffner) USA, 71
Anatoly Romashin	*Agony* (Klimov) USSR, 75

Note: Alfred Hickman in *The Fall Of The Romanoffs* (USA, 17) H. C. Simmons in *Into Her Kingdom* (USA, 26) and Erwin Kalser in *Rasputin, The Holy Devil* (Ger, 28) were among the actors who appeared as Nicholas on the silent screen.

Nichols, Red [R]

(1905–65) Jazz trumpeter of the 20s and 30s who led several large and small bands, notably 'The Five Pennies', on his rise to the top. Mel Shavelson's sentimental biography included a guest appearance by Louis Armstrong and several soundtrack solos by Nichols. Top numbers: 'Indiana' 'Runnin' Wild' and 'My Blue Heaven'.

Louis 'Satchmo' Armstrong and Danny Kaye swinging together in Mel Shavelson's musical biography *The Five Pennies*, the story of jazz trumpeter Red Nichols. Kaye played Nichols; other jazz greats portrayed in the film included Glenn Miller (Ray Daley) and Jimmy Dorsey (Ray Anthony)

Danny Kaye	*The Five Pennies* (Shavelson)	USA, 59

Note: Nichols appeared as himself in the movies *Wabash Avenue* (50) in which he backed Betty Grable on 'I Wish I Could Shimmy Like My Sister Kate', *Disc Jockey* (51), the Mickey Rooney melodrama *Quicksand* (51) and *The Gene Krupa Story* (59).

Nightingale, Florence [R]

(1820–1910) English nurse and hospital reformer, known as 'The Lady With The Lamp', who founded the modern nursing profession when she set up a hospital with other nurses to tend the wounded in the Crimean War. A miscast Kay Francis featured in the first sound biography at Warners in 1936; 15 years later Anna Neagle, in the last of her long line of real life British heroines, made the role her own in a refined bio-pic of Herbert Wilcox.

Kay Francis	*The White Sister* (Dieterle)	USA, 36
Joyce Bland	*Sixty Glorious Years* (Wilcox)	GB, 38
Anna Neagle	*The Lady With The Lamp* (Wilcox)	GB, 51

Note: Elizabeth Risdon starred in a British silent biography directed by Maurice Elvey in 1915; on TV Jaclyn Smith starred as the famous nurse in Daryl Duke's TV Movie *Florence Nightingale* (85).

Nijinsky, Vaslav [R]

(1890–1950) Legendary Russian dancer, an outstanding member of the Diaghilev company and the first

(Top and opposite page) George De La Pena as the legendary Russian dancer Nijinsky in scenes from Herbert Ross' 1980 biography; (above right) Alan Bates as the Ballet Russe impresario Sergei Diaghilev with whom Nijinsky enjoyed a long standing sexual relationship

man to appear as Petrouchka in Stravinsky's ballet of 1911. Herbert Ross' film hinged on Nijinsky's sexual relationships with impresario Diaghilev and the young Russian girl Romola de Pulsky, a relationship that culminated in Nijinsky's decline and ultimate descent into madness.

George De La Pena	*Nijinsky* (Ross)	USA, 80
Michael Kradunin	*Pavlova – A Woman For All Time* (Lotianou)	GB/USSR, 83

Note: Alan Bates played Diaghilev in the 1980 biography, Vsevolod Larionov in *Pavlova* (83).

Nimitz, Admiral Chester W. [R]

(1885–1966) Commander-in-Chief of all US naval forces in the Pacific from 17 December 1941 (when Kimmel was relieved of command) to the end of World War II. An outstanding strategist, he was responsible for re-establishing the power of the American Fleet after the disaster of Pearl Harbour, i.e. at the famous Battle of Midway in 1942.

Selmer Jackson	*Hellcats Of The Navy* (Juran)	USA, 57
Selmer Jackson	*The Gallant Hours* (Montgomery)	USA, 60
Henry Fonda	*Midway* (Smight)	USA, 76
Addison Powell	*MacArthur* (Sargent)	USA, 77

Ninotchka [F]

Garbo's favourite of all her roles, a humourless Soviet commissar who learns the meaning of laughter and love from a debonair American in 30s Paris. The film was advertised by MGM with the slogan, 'Garbo Laughs' and proved to be the actresses penultimate film. Just two years later, aged 36, she retired after making *Two-faced Woman*. In 1957 the solemn commissar (played by Cyd Charisse) was warmed up all over again, this time by Fred Astaire who, although not quite as suave as Melvyn Douglas in the original, had such Cole Porter songs as 'Fated To Be Mated' and 'All Of You' to help him with the defrosting!

Greta Garbo	*Ninotchka* (Lubitsch)	USA, 39
Cyd Charisse	*Silk Stockings* (Mamoulian)	USA, 57

Nitribitt, Rosemarie [R]

Frankfurt call girl, no more important than countless others in her sordid trade, but whose murder caused sensational headlines when it was discovered that she included among her clients several leading West German industrialists. Her murder was never solved and started a political scandal that was reflected in two films of the late 50s.

Nadja Tiller	*The Girl Rosemarie* (Thiele)	W.Ger, 58
Belinda Lee	*Love Now, Pay Later* (Jugert)	W.Ger, 59

Nixon, Richard Milhous [R]

(1913–) Compared to John Kennedy, the screen portrayals of 'Tricky Dicky' have been relatively mundane despite the sterling efforts of look-alike Richard Dixon who made something of a career portraying the American president in the 70s and 80s. The two notable exceptions have been the performances of Jason Robards (renamed Richard Monckton) in the 1977 TV series *Washington Behind Closed Doors* which dealt with the ruthless rise of a power mad politician, and Philip Baker Hall in *Secret Honour* (84) set late one night in the Oval Office where a paranoid Nixon recollects his early history and begins to tape his justification of the Watergate Affair that forced his resignation.

Jean-Pierre Biesse	*Made In USA*	Fra, 67
Jim Dixon	*Is There Sex After Death?* (Jeanne and Alan Abel)	USA, 71
Richard M. Dixon	*The Faking Of The President 1974* (Jeanne and Alan Abel)	USA, 76
Richard M. Dixon	*The Private Files Of J. Edgar Hoover* (Cohen)	USA, 77
Anderson Humphreys	*The Cayman Triangle* (Humphreys)	Cay, 77
Harry Spillman	*Born Again* (Rapper)	USA, 78
Richard M. Dixon	*Hopskotch* (Neame)	USA, 80
Richard M. Dixon	*Where The Buffalo Roam* (Linson)	USA, 80
Philip Baker Hall	*Secret Honour* (Altman)	USA, 84

Note: *Secret Honour* was based on the stage play by Donald Freed and Arnold M. Stone. On TV Jason Robards in *Washington Behind Closed Doors* (77) and Anthony Palmer in *J. Edgar Hoover* (87) have both featured as Nixon.

The perfect team! Cyd Charisse and Fred Astaire, together in one of the last of MGM's great musicals, *Silk Stockings,* a remake of the 1939 classic of Ernst Lubitsch's, *Ninotchka,* about a Russian commissar (Charisse) who is defrosted by a debonair film producer (Astaire) in Paris. Garbo and Melvyn Douglas played the roles in the 1939 original

Nobile, General Umberto [R]

(1885–1978) Italian airship designer whose attempt to reach the North Pole by dirigible in 1928 ended in disaster when the airship crashed in a blizzard and many lives were lost. Amundsen, flying to the rescue, perished in the attempt; Nobile and a handful of survivors were rescued.

Peter Finch — *The Red Tent* (Kalatozov) — It/USSR, 71

Nolan, Gypo 

Liam O'Flaherty's tragic, doom-laden police informer who sells his best friend for a £20 reward during the Sinn Fein rebellion of the 20s. The central figure in O'Flaherty's 1925 novel 'The Informer'. Victor McLaglen won an Oscar for his portrait of Nolan in 1935; the third version of the story, *Uptight*, was updated to an all-black Cleveland setting.

Lars Hanson — *The Informer* (Robinson) — GB, 29
Victor McLaglen — *The Informer* (Ford) — USA, 35
Julian Mayfield — *Uptight* (Dassin) — USA, 68

Awaiting Arctic rescue! Peter Finch as the ill-fated explorer General Umberto Nobile in the 1971 film *The Red Tent*

Nostradamus [R]

(1503-66) French astrologer and physician (real name Michel de Nostre-Dame) who in the sixteenth century foresaw the future and in his book *Centuries* (55) published a collection of prophecies that many have seen as coming true in the form of The French Revolution, Napoleon's dynasty and World Wars I and II. Many scorn his predictions, others point to the fact that he mentioned, by name, Montgolfier, Pasteur, Franco and a Teutonic despot whom he called 'Hister'. Also among his predictions was Armageddon before the end of this century. Richard Butler portrayed Nostradamus in a dramatized 1981 documentary narrated by Orson Welles.

Richard Butler — *The Man Who Saw Tomorrow* (Guenette) — USA, 81

Note: Philip L. Clarke voiced Nostradamus in Robert Guenette's film; Howard Ackerman appeared as the astrologer as a youth, Jason Nesmith as a child.

Nozière, Violette 

(1915–63) Young French girl (at night a petty thief and amateur whore in the Latin Quarter of Paris) who in 1934 was accused and convicted of poisoning her father and attempting to kill her mother. Sentenced to be beheaded in a public place she eventually had her death sentence commuted to life imprisonment, serving just 12 years and finally marrying the prison clerk's son. In 1978, Claude Chabrol reconstructed Nozière's story, examining her anti-social attitudes and also investigating her claim that she had been raped by her father at 13 and that there may have been an accomplice to the murder.

Isabelle Huppert — *Violet Nozière* (Chabrol) — Fra/Can, 78

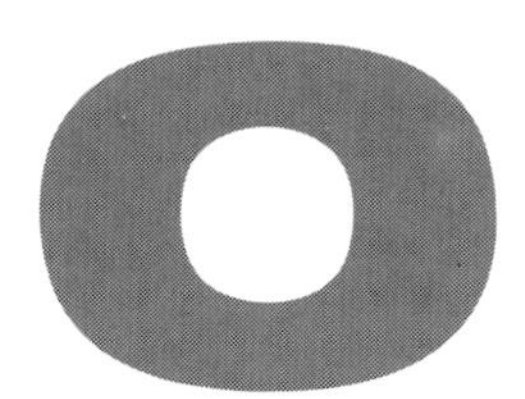

Oakes, Sir Harry

R

(1874–1943) A self-made millionaire who struck it rich in the Klondike in his early 20s but was later murdered at his Bahamas home where he was battered and burned and his body mysteriously covered with feathers. Nicolas Roeg's *Eureka* was inspired by the Oakes case and presented the millionaire (renamed Jack McGann) as a mystical figure not dissimilar to Orson Welles' Kane whose wealth cuts him off from mankind and leaves him in a kind of spiritual isolation. Roeg's film offered no explanation for the murder although it hinted at times that the Mafia may have been involved in the killing.

Gene Hackman — *Eureka* (Roeg) USA/GB, 83

Oakley, Annie

R

(1859–1926) Famed western sharpshooter – a crack-shot from the age of nine – who reigned as a top attraction in Buffalo Bill's Wild West Show for some 17 years. Her feud with variety performer Frank Butler, whom she later married, has been the subject of several movies, i.e. George Stevens' *Annie Oakley* and the MGM musical *Annie Get Your Gun.* Her full name was Phoebe Anne Oakley Mozee. She was partially paralysed by injury in a train wreck in 1902, but continued her sharpshooting after the accident.

Barbara Stanwyck — *Annie Oakley* (Stevens) USA, 35

Betty Hutton — *Annie Get Your Gun* (Sidney) USA, 50

Gail Davis — *Alias Jesse James* (McLeod) USA, 59

Nancy Kovack — *The Outlaws Is Coming* (Maurer) USA, 65

Angela Douglas — *Carry On Cowboy* (Thomas) GB, 66

Geraldine Chaplin — *Buffalo Bill And The Indians, or Sitting Bull's History Lesson* (Altman) USA, 76

Note: Gail Davis appeared as Oakley in eighty episodes of a 1953–7 TV series.

Odd Couple, The (Felix Ungar and Oscar Madison)

F

Arguably the most famous male double act in the movies; one a distraught, about-to-be-divorced family man (Jack Lemmon), the other his sloppy buddy (Walter Matthau) who works as a sports commentator and who offers to share his apartment while his friend is in emotional crisis. The resulting conflict between Lemmon's fussiness and hypochondria and Matthau's sullen inefficiency made for one of the most amusing movies of the 60s even though it was not, as had originally been hoped, directed by Billy Wilder. Among the best of Neil Simon's sharp one-liners was the opening question asked

Neil Simon's *The Odd Couple:* sloppy (Walter Matthau) and fussy (Jack Lemmon) in Gene Saks' 1968 version of Simon's Broadway success

by a suicidal Lemmon of a hotel clerk: 'Haven't you got anything higher?'

Jack Lemmon and Walter Matthau	*The Odd Couple* (Saks) USA, 68

Note: *The Odd Couple* was later adapted into a TV series which ran for 90 episodes between 1970 and 1974. Tony Randall featured as Felix and Jack Klugman as Oscar. In the very last episode Felix moved out to remarry his wife. In 1983 the series was revived under the title *The New Odd Couple* (1982–3) with black actors Ron Glass and Desmond Wilson as Felix and Oscar.

Oedipus Rex F

One of the most tragic figures of Greek mythology, a young man who unknowingly kills his father and marries his mother and then blinds himself with his mother's brooch when he learns the awful truth. His claim to the throne of Thebes and subsequent wanderings as a banished outcast have been filmed several times, the most unusual version being that of Pasolini who presented the tale in both contemporary and historical settings. The 1956 Canadian film was a record of the Stratford Ontario stage production directed by Tyrone Guthrie.

Douglas Campbell	*Oedipus Rex* (Guthrie) Can, 56
Christopher Plummer	*Oedipus The King* (Saville) GB, 68
Franco Citti	*Oedipus Rex* (Pasolini) It, 67

Note: Michael Pennington featured as Oedipus in the 1986 TV production of Sophocles' *Oedipus The King*, directed by Don Taylor.

O'Hara, Scarlett

The most famous Southern belle in literature; a scheming Georgia vixen who works her way through three marriages (and the American Civil War) in pursuit of the man she loves only to find, after three hours and forty minutes of screen time, that she isn't so keen after all. Eventually pulls herself together with the optimistic hope that 'tomorrow is another day!' Created by Margaret Mitchell in her Pulitzer-Prize winning novel of 1936 and played by Vivien Leigh after many top actresses had been considered for the role, among them Paulette Goddard, Susan Hayward, Joan Bennett, Lana Turner, Jean Arthur and Bette Davis.

Vivien Leigh	*Gone With The Wind* (Fleming) (USA, 39

Note: Leslie Howard featured as Ashley Wilkes, the long-suffering object of Scarlett's affections, and Clark Gable appeared as the dashing blockade runner Rhett Butler. The story of the search for the actress to play Scarlett O'Hara was filmed by John Erman in the 1980 TV movie, *The Scarlett O'Hara War*.

Oppenheimer, J. Robert

(1904-67) 'Now I am become death, the destroyer of worlds', said this father of the atom bomb when he witnessed the horrific results of his experiments at Los Alamos in 1945. Few would disagree with him although the dramatic potential of Oppenheimer's story seems to have been lost on film-makers, the only major screen portrayal of the physicist being by Hume Cronyn in a 1947 film about the development of the A-bomb. The most notable portrayal has been by Sam Waterston in the 1981 BBC TV production which covered Oppenheimer's life from when he was an eager young physicist in the 1920s to when he became a victim of the McCarthy witch-hunts and was accused of disloyalty and communist sympathies.

Hume Cronyn	*The Beginning Or The End?* (Taurog) USA, 47
Sam Waterston	*Oppenheimer* (Goodchild) TV/GB, 81

Note: Robert Walden had a featured role as Oppenheimer in the 1980 TV movie *Enola Gay*; Jon Else's TV documentary *The Day After Trinity* (80) looked at Oppenheimer's role in producing the bomb and used newly declassified government footage together with the recollections of Oppenheimer's friends and associates at Los Alamos.

Orlac, Stephen

Celebrated concert pianist who has the hands of a murderous psychopath grafted onto his wrists when he is badly mutilated in an accident. A favourite horror character who has grown steadily in popularity since he was first adapted to the screen in

It took months to find her but when they did they got it right! Vivien Leigh, perfection as the Southern belle, Scarlett O'Hara in David O. Selznick's *Gone With The Wind.* Paulette Goddard, Jean Arthur, Joan Crawford, Susan Hayward, Joan Bennett and Bette Davis were among the actresses considered for the role before Selznick eventually signed Leigh, reputedly on the day he began shooting the film with the burning of Atlanta sequence

Gary Oldman as controversial playwright Joe Orton in the Stephen Frears film *Prick Up Your Ears* the story of Orton's life as a writer and of his homosexual affair with his jealous lover Kenneth Halliwell, an affair that ended in tragedy and murder

1925. First appeared in Maurice Renard's 1920 novel 'Les Mains d'Orlac'.

Colin Clive	*Mad Love*	(Freund)	USA, 35
Mel Ferrer	*The Hands Of Orlac*	(Greville)	GB/Fra, 60
James Stapleton	*Hands Of A Stranger*	(Newt Arnold)	USA, 62

Note: Conrad Veidt was the first actor to appear in the role in Robert Wiene's German silent of 1925. Howard Vernon appeared as the demented son of Dr Orloff in Jesus Franco's 1982 Spanish production *The Sinister Dr Orloff.*

Orton, Joe

R

(1933–67) Controversial British playwright who stemmed from the provinces (Leicester) and who shocked the British public in the 60s with a series of plays that challenged the accepted notions of natural behaviour and openly commented on the homosexual milieu. His short, turbulent period as a writer and his life – plus his death at the hands of his lover Kenneth Halliwell – was recounted in the Stephen Frears film *Prick Up Your Ears.* Gary Oldman featured as Orton and Alfred Molina as Halliwell; Vanessa Redgrave cameoed as Peggy Ramsey, the agent who helped launch Orton on his career.

Gary Oldman	*Prick Up Your Ears*	(Frears)	GB, 87

Note: Orton's plays *Entertaining Mr Sloane* and *Loot* have both been filmed, the former in 1969, the latter in 1972.

Othello

The man who 'loved not wisely but too well', a noble Moor who murders his wife Desdemona in a jealous rage after the scheming Iago has cast doubts in his mind about her infidelity. The central figure in Shakespeare's tragedy of 1604. Three distinguished screen performances to date: by Orson Welles (52) who filmed the story among the old Arab citadels of North Africa, Sergei Bondarchuk (55) and Laurence Olivier (65) who repeated for the cameras, his performance at Britain's National Theatre.

John Slater	*Othello*	(Mackane)	GB, 46
Orson Welles	*Othello*	(Welles)	Morocco, 52
Sergei Bondarchuk	*Othello*	(Yutkevich)	USSR, 55
Laurence Olivier	*Othello*	(Burge)	GB, 65

Note: On the silent screen Franz Porten (Ger, 07), Mario Caserini (It, 07), William V. Ranous (USA, 08), Ferrucio Garavaglia (It, 09), Paslo Colaci (It, 14), Beni Montano (Ger, 18) and Emil Jannings (Ger, 22) all appeared as the Moor. In 1981 Anthony Hopkins played Othello in Jonathan Miller's TV adaptation.

Ernest Borgnine (as a rancher) starred in *Jubal* (56), a western variation of the Othello theme, Paul Harris (as a black jazz pianist) featured as the Othello character in a modern updating of the story, *All Night Long* (62) and Richie Havens appeared in a loose rock musical adaptation *Catch My Soul* (73).

The innocent Desdemona has been played by Henny Porten (07), Maria Gasperini (07), Julia Swayne-Gordon (08), Vittoria Lepanto (09), Lena Lenard (14), Ellen Korth (18), Ica de Lenkoffi (22), Luanna Shaw (46), Suzanne Cloutier (52), Irina Skobtseva (55) and Maggie Smith (65); Valerie French featured in *Jubal,* Marti Stevens in *All Night Long* and Season Hubley in *Catch My Soul.*

Paganini, Nicolo R

(1782–1840) Italian violinist and composer, a virtuoso both as a performer and a personality, who built up an almost legendary reputation and was said by some to be in league with the Devil. A man who revolutionized violin technique, he played his first concert at the age of eleven, a fact that proved of little interest to the makers of the inept 1946 biography *The Magic Bow* in which Stewart Granger found time to duel, gamble and make love to aristocrat Phyllis Calvert. A more recent biography starred Klaus Kinski.

Roxy Roth	*A Song To Remember* (Charles Vidor)	USA, 45
Karel Dostal	*Bohemian Rapture* (Krska)	Cze, 48
Stewart Granger	*The Magic Bow* (Knowles)	GB, 46
Klaus Kinski	*Paganini* (Kinski)	It, 88

Note: Conrad Veidt appeared in a silent biography, *Paganini* which he also produced in 1923.

Pal Joey 

One of the first anti-heroes of the modern musical theatre, an unscrupulous, self-seeking entertainer who relies on the sexual favours and patronage of a wealthy matron to see him through life. Gene Kelly became a star playing him on Broadway in 1940; Frank Sinatra portrayed him on screen during the 50s when his image was softened somewhat to accommodate the censor. Songs in the original Rodgers and Hart score included 'Zip', 'Bewitched' and 'I Could Write A Book'.

Frank Sinatra	*Pal Joey* (Sidney)	USA, 57

Note: The character of Pal Joey (Joey Evans) first appeared in a series of short stories published in the New Yorker. The stories were written as a series of letters from 'Our Pal Joey' to a bandleader friend and were later adapted by John O'Hara into the 1940 musical play. Billy Wilder's plans to direct a film version starring Marlon Brando and Mae West unfortunately came to nothing.

Palmer, Harry 

A poor man's 007 but far, far removed from Fleming's super-hero in that he is working-class, unenthusiastic and basically a loser. A liking for good food is just about the only thing he has in common with Bond. Featured in three movies during the 60s, but, like most of 007's competitors, quickly faded from the scene. The first of Len Deighton's novels 'The Ipcress File' was published in 1962. Palmer remains unnamed in all of Deighton's books.

Michael Caine	*The Ipcress File* (Furie)	GB, 65
Michael Caine	*Funeral In Berlin* (Hamilton)	GB, 66
Michael Caine	*Billion Dollar Brain* (Russell)	GB, 67

Papillon 

The nickname (meaning 'Butterfly') of Frenchman Henri Charriere, falsely accused of murder in the 1930s and who survived the horrors of the infamous penal colony on Devil's Island. An indestructible hero-victim, he survived all the system could throw at him and escaped to tell his tale in a novel that became a best-seller the world over.

Steve McQueen	*Papillon* (Schaffner)	USA, 73

Parker, Charlie 

(1920–55) Legendary jazz pioneer whose brilliant saxophone playing and musical genius influenced succeeding generations of jazz musicians. Several guest appearances in jazz shorts of the late 40s and early 50s but no screen biography until 1988 when Clint Eastwood filmed his tragic story, cut short by the usual jazzman's afflictions – drug addiction and alcoholic excess. Forest Whitaker who appeared as a young pool hustler in Scorsese's *The Colour Of Money*, featured in the lead role.

Forest Whitaker	*Bird* (Eastwood)	USA, 88

Note: Parker can be glimpsed in the shorts *J.A.T.P.* (50) and *Stage Entrance* (51) and in the 60-minute B feature *Jivin In Be-Bop* (47), made up of a continuous series of musical numbers and dance

More at home—and certainly more competent—in the kitchen than in the world of spies and spymasters. Michael Caine (as the Cockney gourmet Harry Palmer, the poor man's 007) in *The Ipcress File,* the first and best of the three thrillers he made from the novels of Len Deighton

routines; Richard Pryor was originally set to star in a 1979 biography *The Charlie Parker Story* but the project never got beyond the planning stage.

Pasteur, Louis [R]

(1822–95) Dedicated French chemist who succeeded in pasteurizing milk in order to free it from harmful bacteria and also discovered vaccines for anthrax and rabies. A man constantly at odds with his own profession and the subject of the first of Warners' famous screen biographies of the 30s. For his performance as Pasteur, Paul Muni won the best actor Academy Award of 1936.

Sacha Guitry	*Pasteur* (Guitry)	Fra, 35
Paul Muni	*The Story Of Louis Pasteur* (Dieterle)	USA, 36
Theodor Vogeler	*Semmelweis, der Hetter der Mutter* (Klaren)	E.Ger, 50

Patton, General George S. [R]

(1885–1945) Old 'Blood And Guts' to his men, this controversial American General was one of the leaders of the Allied march across France and Germany during the latter stages of World War II. At one time relieved of his command for slapping the face of a soldier suffering from combat fatigue, he later made a decisive intervention in the Battle of the Bulge. Franklin Schaffner's three-hour account of his final years remains one of the most distinguished biographies of a military leader ever to reach the screen.

John Larch	*Miracle Of The Wild Stallions* (Hiller)	USA, 63
Kirk Douglas	*Is Paris Burning?* (Clement)	Fra/USA, 66
George C. Scott	*Patton* (Schaffner)	USA, 70
George Kennedy	*Brass Target* (Hough)	USA, 78

Note: George C Scott reprised his role in Delbert Mann's 1986 TV Movie, *The Last Days Of Patton.*

Pavlova, Anna [R]

(1885–1931) Legendary Russian ballerina, considered one of the greatest dancers of the twentieth century, whose life was recalled in an expensive but fragmentary co-production that concentrated on her career after she had left Russia and toured the world with her own company. Appropriately, the film's highlights were the performances of 'Swan Lake' and 'Giselle' for which Pavlova was renowned and which were danced by Galina Beliaeva who both danced and acted the role of the great ballerina. Michael Powell was supervisor of the western version of the film which made little attempt to elaborate on Pavlova's personal life or artistic motives.

Galina Beliaeva	*Pavlova – A Woman For All Time* (Emil Lotianou)	GB/USSR, 83

Payne, Cynthia 

Redoubtable suburban madam (known affectionately as Madam Cyn) whose activities running a Streatham brothel hit the headlines when her house was raided and it was discovered that inland revenue clerks, barristers, policemen and politicians figured high among her clients. Terry Jones' 1987 film *Personal Services* charted the career of the adult Cynthia; David Leland's *Wish You Were Here* looked at her early teenage life in Worthing in the early 50s. Payne was renamed Christine Painter in Jones' film and known simply as Lynda in the Leland picture.

Julie Walters	*Personal Services* (Jones)	GB, 87
Emily Lloyd	*Wish You Were Here* (Leland)	GB, 87

Note: Cynthia Payne acted as 'consultant' on *Personal Services.*

Peace, Charles Frederick 

(1832–79) A man frequently referred to as Britain's most notorious criminal, yet one who has been portrayed only once in sound cinema – by Michael Martin Harvey in 1949. His criminal career lasted for nearly 20 years and included countless burglaries and two murders. In between times he became an accomplished violinist, reciter of monologues, woodweaver, picture framer and pacifist. He ate his pre-execution breakfast with great calm but quickly complained, 'This is bloody rotten bacon!'

Michael Martin Harvey	*The Case Of Charles Peace*	GB, 49

Note: Walter Haggar in the 1905 British film *Charles Peace,* and Jeff Barlow in *Charles Peace, King Of Criminals* (1914), both played the role in the silent days.

(Above) George C. Scott as the brilliant but controversial American World War II General, *Patton,* in Franklin Schaffner's Academy Award winning biography of 1970; (right) George Kennedy as Patton in the 1978 assassination thriller, *Brass Target*

The two lives of Cynthia Payne—(above) as a promiscuous teenager (Emily Lloyd) in '50s Worthing in *Wish You Were Here* and (right) as a brothel madam (Julie Walters, far right) indulging in kinky sex in *Personal Services*

Pepe-Le-Moko

F

Parisian jewel thief who finds temporary safety from the police in the Algerian Casbah only to be tempted into the outside world and certain death because of his love for a beautiful woman. As portrayed in the original French film by Duvivier, a doomed tragic figure fighting against authority; as played by Charles Boyer and Tony Martin in the remakes little more than a crook on the run.

Jean Gabin	*Pepe-Le-Moko* (Duvivier)	Fra, 37
Charles Boyer	*Algiers* (Cromwell)	USA, 38
Tony Martin	*Casbah* (Berry)	USA, 48

Peter, St

R

Disciple who, after Christ's death on the cross, travelled as a missionary preaching God's word. History has it that in 66 AD he was crucified upside down because he believed himself unworthy to suffer the same fate as Jesus. Screen portraits have covered most periods of his life, Finlay Currie featuring as the aged Peter in MGM's *Quo Vadis*.

Finlay Currie	*Quo Vadis* (Leroy)	USA, 51
Michael Rennie	*The Robe* (Koster)	USA, 53
Michael Rennie	*Demetrius And The Gladiators* (Daves)	USA, 54
Lorne Greene	*The Silver Chalice* (Saville)	USA, 54
Tyler McVey	*The Day Of Triumph* (Pichel/Coyle)	USA, 54
Howard Keel	*The Big Fisherman* (Borzage)	USA, 59
Harry Andrews	*Barabbas* (Fleischer)	It, 62
Settimio Di Porto	*The Gospel According To St Matthew* (Pasolini)	It/Fra, 64
Gary Raymond	*The Greatest Story Ever Told* (Stevens)	USA, 65
Antonio Vilar	*The Redeemer* (Breen)	Spa/USA, 65
Jean Clarieux	*The Milky Way* (Bunuel)	Fra/It, 69
Paul Smith	*The Gospel Road* (Elfstrom)	USA, 73
James Farentino	*Jesus Of Nazareth* (Zeffirelli)	GB, 77
Niko Nitai	*Jesus* (Sykes/Krish)	USA, 79
Jay O. Sander	*The Day Christ Died* (Manulis)	TVM/USA, 80
Robert Foxworth	*Peter And Paul* (Day)	TVM/USA, 81

Note: Philip Toubus featured as Peter in *Jesus Christ, Superstar* (USA, 73); Bruno Ziener (Ger, 23) and Ernest Torrence in DeMille's *King Of Kings* (USA, 27) played the disciple on the silent screen.

Petrovich, Porfiri

Wily Russian police inspector who patiently breaks down the will of the haunted murderer Raskolnikov in 'Crime And Punishment'. A master of psychological observation, he is the cat figure in Dostoievsky's famous cat and mouse crime story and simply awaits the confession he knows will come. The performance of Frank Silvera in the 1959 updating, *Crime And Punishment, USA*, is one of the most accomplished interpretations of the role. Dostoievsky's novel was published in 1866.

Harry Baur	*Crime And Punishment* (Chenal)	Fra, 35
Edward Arnold	*Crime And Punishment* (von Sternberg)	USA, 35
Sigurd Wallen	*Crime And Punishment* (Faustman)	Swe, 45
Jean Gabin	*Crime And Punishment* (Lampin)	Fra, 56
Jean Pelegri	*Pickpocket* (Bresson)	Fra, 59
Frank Silvera	*Crime And Punishment, USA* (Sanders)	USA, 59
Innokenti Smoktounovski	*Crime And Punishment* (Kulidjanov)	USSR, 70

Note: Andrei Gromov in the Russian 1910 adaptation and Pavel Pavlov in Robert Wiene's 1923 German film both appeared in silent versions of Dostoievsky's novel.

Petruchio

The wily opportunist who takes and weds the fiery man-eater Katharina in Shakespeare's 'The Taming Of The Shrew' (1594). Douglas Fairbanks portrayed him (opposite real-life wife Mary Pickford) in the first talking screen version of a Shakespearean play; Richard Burton roared his way through the part in Zeffirelli's opulent production of 1967. Elizabeth Taylor, then Mrs Burton, fought tooth and nail to get on even terms.

Douglas Fairbanks	*The Taming Of The Shrew* (Taylor)	USA, 29

Amadeo Nazzari	*La Bisbetica Domata* (Poggioli) It, 42
Miklos Hajmassy	*The Taming Of The Shrew* (Banky) Hung, 43
Alberto Closas	*The Taming Of The Shrew* (Roman) Fra/Spa, 55
Andrei Popov	*Ukroshchenie Stroptivoi* (Kolosov) USSR, 61
Richard Burton	*The Taming Of The Shrew* (Zeffirelli) USA/It, 67

Note: On the silent screen Arthur Johnson and Florence Lawrence (USA, 08), Romuald Joube and Cecile Didier (Fra, 11), Eleuterio Rodolfi and Gigotta Morano (It, 13) and Lauderdale Maitland and Mlle Dacia (GB, 23) all featured as Shakespeare's ill-matched couple; John Cleese and Sarah Badel appeared in a BBC/Time Life TV adaptation in 1980.

Katharina has been played by Mary Pickford (28), Emmy Buttykay (43), Lilia Silvi (49), Carmen Serilla (55), Ludmila Kasatkina (61), and Elizabeth Taylor (67).

In Cole Porter's musical *Kiss Me Kate* (53), Howard Keel and Kathryn Grayson featured as a married couple whose offstage lives intertwine with their performances in 'The Taming Of The Shrew'. Snatches of Shakespearean dialogue combined with such classic Porter songs as 'So In Love', 'Too Darn Hot' and 'Wunderbar'.

Real-life husband and wife team Richard Burton and Elizabeth Taylor enjoying one of their few lyrical moments together in Zeffirelli's version of Shakespeare's *The Taming of the Shrew*

Phantom Of The Opera, The [F]

Gaston Leroux's classical figure of horror, a demented musician with a disfigured face who haunts the underground caves of the Paris Opera House and secretly aids a young prima donna in her career. Known as Erik in the classic silent version of 1925, Enrique in 1943, The Phantom in 1962 and Winslow in Brian DePalma's rock updating of 1974. Gaston Leroux's novel was first published in 1911.

Lon Chaney	*The Phantom Of The Opera* (Julian) USA, 25
Claude Rains	*The Phantom Of The Opera* (Lubin) USA, 43
Herbert Lom	*The Phantom Of The Opera* (Fisher) GB, 62
William Finley	*Phantom Of The Paradise* (DePalma) USA, 74

Note: Maximilian Schell, cast as a deranged Hungarian voice coach, played the Phantom in Robert Marowitz's 1983 TV Movie, *The Phantom Of The Opera;* Jack Cassidy enjoyed himself in the 1974 *Phantom Of Hollywood* which reworked the plot to accommodate a masked monster who goes on a deadly rampage against those who have decided to sell his home – the legendary MGM backlot.

Piaf, Edith [R]

(1915–63) The French singer (real name, Edith Gassion) whose life was described by Sacha Guitry as being so sad it was almost too beautiful to be true. Raised in a brothel and blind until she was seven, she was noisy, demanding, egotistical and possessor of that magical talent which only the greatest artistes enjoy. Primarily a stage performer, she appeared in just a handful of films (including Renoir's *French Can Can*) and made famous such songs as 'La Vie en Rose' and 'Je ne Regrette Rien'. Guy Casaril's 1974 film covered her early years with Betty Mars miming the songs to Brigitte Ariel's performance; Lelouch's *Edith And Marcel* told of Piaf's love affair with middleweight boxer Marcel Cerdan who died in a plane crash in 1979.

Brigitte Ariel	*The Sparrow Of Pigalle* (Casaril) Fra, 74
Evelyne Bouix	*Edith And Marcel* (Lelouch) Fra, 83

'You *will* take notice of me', Lon Chaney seems to be saying to Mary Philbin in this scene from Rupert Julian's classic piece of horror hokum *The Phantom of the Opera*—although how she could ignore him in the first place is something of a mystery. The film was released in 1925 and was the first of several screen versions of Gaston Leroux's story

Picasso, Pablo [R]

(1881–1973) Prolific Spanish-born painter, creator of Cubism and generally considered to be the greatest of the twentieth century masters. The Swedish film, *The Adventures Of Picasso,* paid affectionate homage in a crazy, comic vein; Clouzot's 75-minute documentary, *The Mystery Of Picasso,* observed the artist at work on some 15 original pictures, especially painted for the cameras.

Himself — *The Mystery Of Picasso* (Clouzot) Fra, 56
Goesta Ekman — *The Adventures Of Picasso* (Danielsson) Swe, 78

Pickwick, Samuel [F]

The benign founder of The Pickwick Club in Charles Dickens' novel 'The Pickwick Papers', published in 1836–7. The first of the author's optimistic heroes – middle-aged, jovial and not a little naive – he sets out on a series of adventures to investigate scientific and cultural matters, accompanied always by his three close friends – the would-be sportsman Nathaniel Winkle, the romantic Augustus Snodgrass, and the plump and amorous Tracy Tupman. Pickwick has been portrayed but once on the sound screen although the novel was filmed twice in the silent days.

James Hayter — *The Pickwick Papers* (Langley) GB, 53

Note: John Bunny in the three part *The Pickwick Papers* (GB, 13) and Fred Volpe in *The Adventures Of Mr Pickwick* (GB, 21) were the actors who played

Pickwick on the silent screen. Winkle has been played by Fred Hornby (GB, 13), Arthur Cleave (GB, 21) and James Donald (GB, 53); Snodgrass by Sidney Hunt (GB, 13), John Kelt (GB, 21) and Lionel Murton (GB, 53); Tupman by James Pryor (GB, 13) and Alexander Gauge (GB, 53).

Pilate, Pontius [R]

The Roman governor of Judaea who presided over the trial of Jesus and eventually ordered his crucifixion, despite being unable to find him guilty of any crime. A challenging, if brief role in which many actors have excelled, notably Rod Steiger in Zeffirelli's *Jesus Of Nazareth*. Telly Savalas earned himself world fame by shaving his head for the part in George Stevens' *The Greatest Story Ever Told*.

Basil Gill	*The Wandering Jew* (Elvey) GB, 33
Basil Rathbone	*The Last Days Of Pompeii* (Schoedsack) USA, 35
Jean Gabin	*Golgotha* (Duvivier) Fra, 35
Richard Boone	*The Robe* (Koster) USA, 53
Basil Sydney	*Salome* (Dieterle) USA, 53
Lowell Gilmore	*The Day Of Triumph* (Pichel/Coyle) USA, 54
Frank Thring	*Ben-Hur* (Wyler) USA, 59
Hurd Hatfield	*King Of Kings* (Ray) USA, 61
Jean Marais	*Ponzio Pilato* (Callegari) It/Fra, 61
Arthur Kennedy	*Barabbas* (Fleischer) It, 62
Alessandro Tasca	*The Gospel According To St Matthew* (Pasolini) It/Fra, 64
Telly Savalas	*The Greatest Story Ever Told* (Stevens) USA, 65
Antonio Vilar	*The Redeemer* (Breen) USA/Spa, 65
Ljuba Tadic	*The Master And Margarita* (Petrovic) Yug/It, 72
Donald Pleasence	*The Passover Plot* (Campus) Israel/USA, 76
Rod Steiger	*Jesus Of Nazareth* (Zeffirelli) GB, 77
Peter Frye	*Jesus* (Sykes/Krish) USA, 79
Keith Michell	*The Day Christ Died* (Manulis) TVM/USA, 80
David Bowie	*The Passion* (Scorsese) USA, 88

James Hayter as the benevolent Samuel Pickwick in the only sound version made to date of Dickens' *The Pickwick Papers*

Note: Barry Dennen featured as the Pilate character in *Jesus Christ, Superstar* (73); Werner Krauss (Ger, 23), Victor Varconi (USA, 27) and Charles McCaffrey (USA, 28) all appeared in the role in silent productions.

Pitt, William [R]

(1759–1806) For many historians, the greatest of English Prime Ministers, a major reformer who enjoyed one of the longest ministries in English history—from 1783 to 1801 and again between 1804–5. Carol Reed's biography followed his career in the days preceding and during the first phase of the Napoleonic wars and drew strong parallels with Britain's fight against the Nazis.

Ian MacLaren	*The Last Of The Mohicans* (Seitz) USA, 36
Robert Donat	*The Young Mr Pitt* (Reed) GB, 42
Anthony Nicholls	*The Laughing Lady* (Stein) GB, 46
Paul Rogers	*Beau Brummel* (Bernhardt) GB, 54
Anthony Stuart	*Austerlitz* (Gance) Fra/It/Yug, 60

Note: Ernest Thesiger featured as Pitt in Maurice Elvey's 1918 British production, *Nelson*.

Poe, Edgar Allan

R

(1809–49) American poet and short story writer whose tortured private life was reflected in many of his macabre stories of the supernatural—'The Black Cat', 'The Fall Of The House Of Usher', 'The Tell-Tale Heart', etc. Credited with establishing the form of the modern short story, Poe has been featured many times on screen, i.e. as a struggling writer in *The Loves Of Edgar Allan Poe,* an alcoholic poet in *The Man with A Cloak,* and an explorer of the occult in *The Spectre of Edgar Allan Poe.* He died of exhaustion and alcoholism in 1849.

John Shepperd	*The Loves Of Edgar Allan Poe* (Lachman)	USA, 42
Joseph Cotten	*The Man With A Cloak* (Markle)	USA, 51
Laurence Payne	*The Tell-Tale Heart* (Morris)	GB, 60
Robert Walker	*The Spectre Of Edgar Allan Poe* (Quandour)	USA, 74

Note: John Shepperd who appeared in the 1942 film became known as Shepperd Strudwick.

Poirot, Hercule

F

Dapper Belgian detective who features in more than 40 Agatha Christie novels. Almost a comic figure – fastidious, short and sporting a waxed moustache – he solves his cases through a fine intellect and massive ego. Until Albert Finney's portrayal in *Murder On The Orient Express,* an unappealing character on screen, although Charles Laughton and Francis L. Sullivan were both admirable stage Poirots during the 30s. Peter Ustinov's recent performances on the big screen and on TV have been more Ustinov than Poirot but have at least instilled some humour into the character.

Austin Trevor	*Alibi* (Hiscott)	GB, 31
Austin Trevor	*Black Coffee* (Hiscott)	GB, 31
Austin Trevor	*Lord Edgware Dies* (Edwards)	GB, 34
Tony Randall	*The Alphabet Murders* (Tashlin)	GB, 66
Albert Finney	*Murder On The Orient Express* (Lumet)	GB, 74
Peter Ustinov	*Death On The Nile* (Guillermin)	GB, 78
Peter Ustinov	*Evil Under The Sun* (Hamilton)	GB, 82
Peter Ustinov	*13 At Dinner* (Antonio)	TVM/USA, 85
Peter Ustinov	*Dead Man's Folly* (Donner)	TVM/USA 86
Peter Ustinov	*Murder In Three Acts* (Nelson)	TVM/USA, 87
Peter Ustinov	*Appointment With Death* (Winner)	USA, 88

Note: Ian Holm featured as the little detective in the 60 minute TV film *Murder By The Book* (86) in which Poirot investigates his own murder (before it has happened) when he learns that his creator is to publish a book in which he is to be bumped off.

Pollyanna

Heroine of Eleanor Porter's 1913 novel; a young orphan girl who goes to live with her wealthy aunt in a small New England town and changes the lives of everyone she comes in contact with, primarily because of her uncanny knack of always looking on the bright side of things. The most delightful optimist in modern literature.

Hayley Mills	*Pollyanna* (Swift)	USA, 60

Note: Mary Pickford played Pollyanna on the silent screen in a version directed by Paul Powell in 1920.

Popeye

Muscle-bound, spinach-eating cartoon sailor (I'm Popeye the Sailor I am') first created by newspaper cartoonist Elzie Crisler Segar in 1929 and who made his screen debut four years later in the Max Fleischer short *Popeye The Sailor.* Portrayed in human form by Robin Williams in Robert Altman's 1980 movie which dealt with Popeye's adventures with his arch enemy, the brutish Captain Bluto. Shelley Duvall featured as Popeye's quick-tempered gawky girlfriend Olive Oyl and other Popeye favourites were played by Paul L. Smith (as Bluto), Paul Dooley (as the Hamburger-eating Wimpy) and Wesley Ivan Hurt (as Olive Oyl's nephew Swee' Pea).

Robin Williams	*Popeye* (Altman)	USA, 80

Note: The 1980 film was instigated by Robert Evans after he had failed to purchase the screen rights to *Annie.* Dustin Hoffman and Lily Tomlin were originally considered for the roles of Popeye and Olive Oyl but were replaced when three top directors – Hal Ashby, Mike Nichols and Arthur Penn – could make nothing of the idea. In the

(Top right) Albert Finney, the first postwar actor to portray Hercule Poirot on screen (in *Murder On The Orient Express)* and right Peter Ustinov, who has portrayed Christie's Belgian sleuth regularly on the cinema and TV screen during the '70s and '80s

Shelley Duvall as Olive Oyl says 'Phooey' to an obviously smitten Popeye, played by Robin Williams in Albert Altman's 1980 live-action movie based on the world-famous comic strip characters created by E.C. Segar

original Popeye cartoons (234 were produced by Fleischer including the feature-length *Popeye The Sailor Meets Sinbad The Sailor* (36) Popeye was voiced first by William Costello who did the job for a few weeks and then by Jack Mercer who went on to make it his life's work, continuing for 45 years by which time the cartoons had moved to television.

Poppins, Mary

F

The most famous fictional nanny of them all, P. L. Travers' magical child-minder who floats from the skies, complete with umbrella and carpetbag, spreading delight and wisdom all over early twentieth-century London. In her own words, 'practically perfect'. Just one screen portrayal – by Julie Andrews in the classic film of Walt Disney; who was kept waiting for 16 years (1944–60) before securing the screen rights!

Julie Andrews	*Mary Poppins* (Stevenson)	USA, 64

Porter, Cole

(1892–1964) Elegant, witty American lyricist/ composer, whose stage shows – 'Anything Goes', 'Kiss Me Kate', 'Silk Stockings' – rank with some of the best ever produced on Broadway. Seriously disabled as a result of a riding accident, he continued to write into the 50s and was played and sung ('You're The Top') by Cary Grant in Warners' 1946 biography *Night And Day*. Among his film scores: *You'll Never Get Rich, High Society, Les Girls*. Among his hit songs: 'You Do Something To Me', 'I Get A Kick Out Of You', 'Begin The Beguine'.

Cary Grant	*Night And Day* (Curtiz)	USA, 46
Ron Randell	*Kiss Me Kate* (Sidney)	USA, 53

Magical nanny Mary Poppins (Julie Andrews) blows into No. 17 Cherry Tree Lane in Walt Disney's Oscar-winning adaptation of the stories by P.L. Travers

Porter, Jimmy F

The original 'angry young man' of John Osborne's 1956 stage play 'Look Back In Anger', a working-class hero whose rebellion against the establishment emerged as a powerful comment on the mood of Britain in the mid-50s. A star part if ever there was one, although Richard Burton's screen Porter was too mature and less convincing than those of the younger stage actors who had earlier featured in the role.

Richard Burton	*Look Back In Anger* (Richardson) GB, 59

Porthos 

The most jovial of Dumas' 'Three Musketeers', good-hearted, large in stature and a frequent companion of D'Artagnan in his many screen adventures. The burly frames of Alan Hale and Alan Hale, Jr filled the role on several occasions, just as they did for the part of Little John in the Robin Hood spectators. In recent times, British actor Frank Finlay has provided an even more swaggering and ebullient Porthos in the two Musketeer films of Richard Lester.

Stanley J. Sandford	*The Iron Mask* (Dwan) USA, 29
Thomy Bourdelle	*The Three Musketeers* (Diamant-Berger) Fra, 32
Moroni Olsen	*The Three Musketeers* (Lee) USA, 35
Russell Hicks	*The Three Musketeers* (Dwan) USA, 39
Alan Hale	*The Man In The Iron Mask* (Whale) USA, 39
Gig Young	*The Three Musketeers* (Sidney) USA, 48
Mel Archer	*Sword Of D'Artagnan* (Boetticher) USA, 52
Alan Hale, Jr	*Lady In The Iron Mask* (Murphy) USA, 52
Gino Cervi	*The Three Musketeers* (Hunebelle) Fra, 53
Sebastian Cabot	*The Knights Of The Queen* (Bolognini) It, 54
Bernard Woringer	*The Three Musketeers* (Borderie) Fra, 61
Mario Petri	*The Secret Mark Of D'Artagnan* (Marcellini) It/Fra, 62
Livio Lorenzon	*Zorro And The Three Musketeers* (Capuano) It, 63
Walter Barnes	*Revenge Of The Musketeers* (Tull) It, 64
Frank Finlay	*The Three Musketeers* (Lester) Panama/Spa, 74
Frank Finlay	*The Four Musketeers* (Lester) Panama/Spa, 75
Alan Hale, Jr	*The Fifth Musketeer* (Annakin) Austria, 79

Note: Moroni Olsen repeated his role, as the aged Porthos, in *At Sword's Point* (52), a film in which Alan Hale, Jr played his son; on the silent screen Jack Chagnon (USA, 11), George Siegmann (Fra, 21) and Charles Martinelli who appeared in Henri Berger's two French serials *The Three Musketeers* (22) and *Twenty Years After* (22) all appeared as the burly musketeer.

Powell, Bud R

(1924–66) One of the most important figures in the history of jazz, a pianist whose musical genius was destroyed by drink and ill-health and whose death was mourned by 5000 people who lined the streets of Harlem on the day of his funeral. Bertrand Tavernier's film *'Round Midnight* was based on incidents in the life of Powell and the young Frenchman Francis Paudras who helped the jazzman make a comeback in the 60s. The film renamed him Dale Turner and recast him as an ageing saxophonist facing drink and drug problems. Real life saxophonist Dexter Gordon earned a best actor Oscar nomination for his performance as Turner/Powell.

Dexter Gordon — *'Round Midnight* (Tavernier) USA/Fra, 86

Note: Powell's appearances on film are brief. He featured in the 10-minute 1944 short *Cootie Williams And His Orchestra* and also in the 12-minute *Stopforbud* (63), a Danish experimental film showing Powell at leisure and at work in Copenhagen. The commentary for the latter film was spoken by Dexter Gordon.

Presley, Elvis [R]

(1935–77) The king of 'Rock n' Roll' and the man who started it all back in the 50s with a succession of hits that included 'Heartbreak Hotel', 'Hound Dog', 'It's Now Or Never' and 'All Shook Up'. His film career, which began in 1956 with *Love Me Tender,* spanned 15 years and included over 30 movies. Denis Sanders' documentary *Elvis: That's The Way It Is* (70) looked at Presley off-stage, John Carpenter's 1979 TV film at his career from youth to club entertainer and *Elvis And The Beauty Queen* (81) at his five year romance with Linda Thompson.

Kurt Russell — *Elvis – The Movie* (Carpenter) TVM/USA, 79
Don Johnson — *Elvis And The Beauty Queen* (Trikonis) TVM/USA, 81

Note: *Elvis On Tour* (72) directed by Pierre Adidge and Robert Abel also took a look at the concert Presley; in the John Carpenter biography country singer Ronnie McDowell dubbed the songs for Kurt Russell.

Purvis, Melvin [R]

Midwest FBI chief who challenged J. Edgar Hoover as a headline hero of the 30s when he shot down John Dillinger in Chicago. His career was brief, however, and after leaving the bureau he eventually committed suicide, supposedly with the very gun that killed Dillinger. He figured in several movies of the 70s which revealed his vain, glory-seeking character to be little different from those of the gangsters he tracked down.

Myron Healy — *Guns Don't Argue* (Karn/Kahn) USA, 55
Ben Johnson — *Dillinger* (Milius) USA, 73
Dale Robertson — *The Legend Of Machine Gun Kelly* (Curtis) USA, 74
Michael Sacks — *The Private Files Of J. Edgar Hoover* (Cohen) USA, 78
Alan Vint — *The Lady In Red* (Teague) USA, 79

Note: *The Legend Of Machine Gun Kelly* was originally a TV movie entitled *Melvin Purvis G-Man* (74); Robertson also appeared in a subsequent TV movie, *Kansas City Massacre* (75) which was not released theatrically. Geoffrey Binney starred as Purvis in Clyde Ware's *The Story Of Pretty Boy Floyd* (TV, 74).

Pu Yi [R]

(1906–67) China's last emperor, just three years old when he came to the throne and who 60 years later died a normal, happy man after working as a gardener in the Peking botanical gardens and travelling around the capital by bike and bus. During his remarkable life he lived in the forbidden city of Peking surrounded by dozens of retainers and 1500 eunuchs, became emperor of the puppet state of Manchukuo when the Japanese invaded Manchuria in the 30s and spent ten years in jail when the communists took over in China in 1949. The Chinese-American actor John Lone played Pu Yi in Bernardo Bertolucci's 160-minute film of 1987, the first to be shot on location in China by a western film-maker. Tony Leung also featured as the emperor in an earlier film which concentrated only on the final stages of Pu Yi's life.

Tony Leung — *The Last Emperor: Pu Yi's Latter Life* (Hsiang) Hong Kong/China, 86
John Lone — *The Last Emperor* (Bertolucci) Italy/Hong Kong, 87

Note: In the Bertolucci film Richard Vuu (Pu Yi aged 3), Tijger Tsou (aged 8) and Wu Tao (aged 15) all played the emperor in childhood; Sir Reginald

The heavy mob, although not, as this still would suggest, gangsters on the wrong side of the law, but gangbusters, led by ruthless FBI agent Melvin Purvis (Ben Johnson, centre). A scene from the John Milius 1973 biopic *Dillinger*

Johnson, Pu Yi's English tutor in his early years was played by Peter O'Toole. Bertolucci's picture was inspired by Pu Yi's autobiography 'From Emperor To Citizen'.

Pyle, Ernie

R

(1900–45) American newspaper correspondent of World War II, much admired by soldiers and civilians for the honesty and warmth of his dispatches from the front line. A Pulitzer Prize winner for his vivid eyewitness accounts, he covered many campaigns in North Africa and Europe before being killed by Japanese machine gun fire on an island near Okinawa. Portrayed on screen by Burgess Meredith in Wellman's *The Story Of G.I. Joe*.

Burgess Meredith *The Story Of G.I. Joe* (Wellman) USA, 45

The Emperor Pu Yi (Wu Tao) as an adolescent bridegroom with his new bride Wan Jung (Joan Chen) on their wedding night. A scene from Bernardo Bertolucci's award-winning *The Last Emperor* (1987), the first Western film to be shot inside China

Quartermain, Allan

F

The most famous white hunter of them all, a cynical weather-beaten hero who, in Rider Haggard's adventure classic *King Solomon's Mines* (1885) leads a search for legendary diamonds in darkest Africa. The prewar portrayal by Hardwicke and to a lesser extent Stewart Granger's 1950 interpretation bear a reasonable likeness to Rider Haggard's creation; the more recent characterizations by Richard Chamberlain are closer to Indiana Jones than the Haggard original.

Cedric Hardwicke	*King Solomon's Mines* (Stevenson)	GB, 37
Stewart Granger	*King Solomon's Mines* (Bennett/Marton)	USA, 50
Richard Chamberlain	*King Solomon's Mines* (Lee Thompson)	USA, 85
Richard Chamberlain	*Allan Quartermain And The Lost City Of Gold* (Nelson)	USA, 87

Note: George Montgomery (as Harry, son of Allan) played Quartermain in Kurt Neumann's 1959 production *Watusi*.

Quatermass, Professor Bernard

F

Fictional British rocket scientist, first created by Nigel Kneale for BBC TV and then transferred to the movie screen for three above average adventures against beings from outer space. Americanized to the point of rigidity by Brian Donlevy; more acceptably played by Andrew Keir in the best in the series, *Quatermass And The Pit,* an inventive tale about the unearthing of a spacecraft and the remains of a far from dead Martian crew in modern day London.

Brian Donlevy	*The Quatermass Experiment* (Guest)	GB, 55
Brian Donlevy	*Quatermass II* (Guest)	GB, 57
Andrew Keir	*Quatermass And the Pit* (Ward Baker)	GB, 67

Note: In 1979 Nigel Kneale resurrected his character in the four-part TV series *Quatermass,* a disturbingly bleak portrait of Britain in the near future when law and order has broken down and a predatory life force from space has taken over the human race. John Mills featured in *Quatermass* which, unlike the other three TV serials, was not adapted to the big screen.

Queeg, Captain

F

The 'I kid you not' captain of the minesweeper/destroyer *Caine,* a paranoid who has cracked after the strain of years of command and is relieved by his executive officer when he panics during a typhoon. A gem of a role for any actor, not least during his court martial when he finally breaks, constantly clicking between finger and thumb, the two steel balls he always carries with him. Humphrey Bogart (Oscar-nominated but miscast for some) played him on screen; Lloyd Nolan on TV in *The Caine Mutiny Court Martial* (56), a version of the stage play, adapted by Herman Wouk from his Pulitzer Prize winning novel of 1951.

Panic during a storm at sea! Humphrey Bogart's Captain Queeg on the way to a court-martial in *The Caine Mutiny*

Stewart Granger as Rider Haggard's intrepid white hunter Allan Quartermain in the 1950 version of *King Solomon's Mines*, a somewhat romanticized version of Haggard's novel and the film that began Granger on a long series of swashbuckling adventure movies at the MGM studio. Richard Chamberlain essayed the role twice in even looser adaptations of the '80s

(Above) Brian Donlevy as Professor Quatermass in the second of the three films adapted from Nigel Kneale's British TV series

Humphrey Bogart	*The Caine Mutiny* (Dmytryk) USA, 54
Lloyd Nolan	*The Caine Mutiny Court-Martial* (Schaffner) TVM/USA, 56
Brad Davis	*The Caine Mutiny Court-Martial* (Altman) TVM/USA, 88

Note: Lloyd Nolan also appeared in the original stage play of *The Caine Mutiny Court-Martial,* first performed on Broadway in 1954.

Quilp, Daniel F

The fiendish, deformed moneylender in Charles Dickens' 'The Old Curiosity Shop' (1840), a cunning, malicious dwarf who is permanently leching after

(Right) Charles Dickens' deformed moneylender Daniel Quilp as played by Anthony Newley in Michael Tuchner's film *Mr Quilp*

the innocent Little Nell whose gambling grandfather is forever in his clutches. One of Dickens' larger than life characters he is difficult to portray realistically on screen and has generally been overplayed, not least by Anthony Newley in the 1975 musical adaptation *Mister Quilp,* the only post-war screen version of the tale.

Hay Petrie	*The Old Curiosity Shop*	(Bentley)	GB, 35
Anthony Newley	*Mister Quilp*	(Tuchner)	GB, 75

Note: Thomas Bentley who directed the 1935 adaptation was obviously obsessed with the story, filming it three times in all, E. Felton (GB, 13) and Pino Conti (GB, 21) appearing as Quilp in his earlier versions.

Little Nell has been played by Mai Deacon (13), Mabel Poulton (21), Elaine Benson (35) and Sarah-Jane Varley (75); Grandfather Trent by Warwick Buckland (13), William Lugg (21), Ben Webster (35) and Michael Hordern (75).

Raffles [F]

Debonair British jewel thief who steals 'purely for the sport of it all' and lives by his wits and skill in absolute luxury in his expensive rooms in London's Albany. An old-style gentleman hero, personified on screen by Ronald Colman and David Niven, but nowadays somewhat out of fashion, although a TV series starring Anthony Valentine enjoyed recent success in England. Created by Ernest William Hornung in 'The Amateur Cracksman' in 1899.

Ronald Colman	*Raffles* (D'Arrast/Fitzmaurice) USA, 30
George Barraud	*The Return Of Raffles* (Markham) GB, 32
David Niven	*Raffles* (Wood) USA, 40

Note: J. Barney Sherry (USA, 05), Ubaldo Maria del Colle (It, 11), John Barrymore (USA, 17), Gerald Ames (GB, 21) and House Peters (USA, 25) all played Raffles on the silent screen.

Raleigh, Sir Walter [R]

(1552–1618) English explorer and courtier, a favourite of Elizabeth I, who fell from favour because of his seduction of one of her maids of honour. The affair formed the basis of the 1955 CinemaScope production, *The Virgin Queen.*

Vincent Price	*The Private Lives Of Elizabeth And Essex* (Curtiz) USA, 39
Richard Todd	*The Virgin Queen* (Koster) USA, 55
Edward Everett Horton	*The Story Of Mankind* (Allen) USA, 57

Raskolnikov [F]

One of the most tormented characters in all fiction, a brilliant young student who meticulously carries out the murder of an old pawnbroker only to find that the memory of the killing haunts him day and night. Dogged by the deceptively patient Inspector Petrovich, he finally confesses and is saved by the love of a young girl. Dostoievsky's original novel, 'Crime And Punishment' was set in nineteenth century St Petersburg. Locations have varied in the different screen versions.

Pierre Blanchar	*Crime and Punishment* (Chenal) Fra, 35
Peter Lorre	*Crime And Punishment* (von Sternberg) USA, 35
Hampe Faustman	*Crime And Punishment* (Faustman) Swe, 45
Roberto Canedo	*Crimen y castigo* (De Fuentes) Mex, 50
Robert Hossein	*Crime And Punishment* (Lampin) Fra, 56
Martin Lassalle	*Pickpocket* (Bresson) Fra, 59
George Hamilton	*Crime And Punishment, USA* (Sanders) USA, 59
Gueorgui Taratorkine	*Crime And Punishment* (Kulidjanov) USSR, 70

Note: V. Krivtsov (USSR, 10), Carl Gerard (USA, 17), Theodor Loos (Ger, 22) and Grigori Khmara (Ger, 23) all appeared in silent versions of the novel.

Rasputin [R]

(1871–1916) Notorious Russian peasant monk who acquired great influence over Empress Alexandra in the Russian Imperial Court when he saved her son Alexis several times from near-fatal attacks of haemophilia. The screen has concentrated more on his lecherous traits than on his supposed healing powers and also on his remarkable death, when he was given enough cyanide to kill six men but was still alive when thrown into the River Neva. Film portraits have been variable, although Conrad Veidt, Lionel Barrymore, Christopher Lee and, more recently Alexei Petrenko, have all revelled in the part.

Conrad Veidt	*Rasputin* (Trotz) Ger, 32
Lionel Barrymore	*Rasputin And The Empress* (Boleslawsky) USA, 32
Harry Baur	*Rasputin* (L'Herbier) Fra, 39
Pierre Brasseur	*Rasputin* (Combret) It/Fra, 54
Edmund Purdom	*The Nights Of Rasputin* (Chenal) Fra/It, 60
Christopher Lee	*Rasputin – The Mad Monk* (Sharp) GB, 66

Youssoupov's Palace, 1916. Rasputin (Tom Baker), poisoned with cyanide and shot in the back, makes a desperate attempt to crawl away from his murderers. A scene from the Sam Spiegel/Franklin Schaffner epic *Nicholas and Alexandra*

Gert Frobe	*I Killed Rasputin* (Hossein)	Fra/It, 67
Wes Carter	*Why Russians Are Revolting* (Sullivan)	USA, 70
Tom Baker	*Nicholas And Alexandra* (Schaffner)	USA, 71
Alexei Petrenko	*Agony* (Klimov)	USSR, 75

Note: Edward Connolly in *The Fall Of The Romanoffs* (USA, 17), Max Neufield in *Rasputin* (USA, 17), Montague Love in *Rasputin The Black Monk* (USA, 17), Grigori Khmara in *Rasputin* (Ger, 28), Nikolai Malikoff in *Rasputin, The Holy Devil* (Ger, 28) and Demetrius Alexis in *The Red Dance* (USA, 28) all appeared in the role on the silent screen.

Rassendyll, Rudolf F

Noble, self-sacrificing English hero who assumes the guise of his double, the abducted King Rudolf of Ruritania, in order to prevent a take-over of the throne. The central character in Anthony Hope's romantic adventure 'The Prisoner Of Zenda' (1896), never better realized on screen than by Ronald Colman in John Cromwell's definitive 1937 film for Selznick.

Ronald Colman	*The Prisoner Of Zenda* (Cromwell)	USA, 37
Stewart Granger	*The Prisoner Of Zenda* (Thorpe)	USA, 52
Peter Sellers	*The Prisoner Of Zenda* (Quine)	USA, 79

Note: The character was spoofed by Tony Curtis in a duelling episode with Ross Martin in *The Great Race* (65) and by Malcolm McDowell (as Flashman) in his duel with Alan Bates in *Royal Flash* (75).

Rassendyll was played by James K. Hackett (USA, 13), Henry Ainley (GB, 15) and Lewis Stone (USA, 22) in silent versions of *The Prisoner Of Zenda*; by Henry Ainley (GB, 15) and Bert Lytell (USA, 23) in *Rupert Of Hentzau.*

Rawlings, Marjorie Kinnan [R]

(1896–1953) American novelist who, in 1928, left her journalist husband and a comfortable life in New York for the primitive Florida backwoods where she carved a new life for herself and began writing novels based on the day-to-day experiences of her simple-living neighbours. Her best-known novel, *The Yearling,* the story of a boy and his pet fawn, was filmed in 1946 with Gregory Peck and Jane Wyman; much the same ground was covered in Martin Ritt's lyrical biography *Cross Creek* which looked at Rawlings' first years in her Florida home.

Mary Steenburgen — *Cross Creek* (Ritt) USA, 83

Note: In *Cross Creek* Malcolm McDowell featured in a cameo role as the famed New York editor Maxwell Perkins.

Reed, John [R]

(1887–1920) Radical American journalist and war correspondent who helped form the first Communist Party in the United States and whose eye-witness account of the Russian Revolution in November, 1917 was published as 'Ten Days That Shook The World'. The last five years of Reed's life in Russia and America (including his involvement with fellow American journalist Louise Bryant) were portrayed at length by Warren Beatty in his three and a quarter hour film, *Reds.* Diane Keaton co-starred as Bryant and the narrative of the film was linked by interviews with many who knew Reed and Bryant during their lifetime, among them Rebecca West, Henry Miller, Adela Rogers St Johns, Oleg Kerensky and George Jessel.

Warren Beatty — *Reds* (Beatty) USA, 81

Rembrandt [R]

(1609–69) Dutch painter who achieved greatness with his series of self-portraits and proved that quality could be synonymous with quantity by providing over 650 oil paintings, 2000 drawings and 300 etchings! As far as films are concerned the quality of performance has been more varied. Laughton's Rembrandt in Korda's film of 1936 was only fitfully impressive; Frans Stelling's performance in the 1978 Dutch production treated the character more as a soap opera figure than an artist of genius.

Charles Laughton — *Rembrandt* (Korda) GB, 36
Ewald Balser — *Rembrandt* (Steinhoff) Ger, 42
Frans Stelling — *Rembrandt-Feigt 1669* (Stelling) Holl, 78

Note: Carl de Vogt played Rembrandt in a German silent of 1920.

Reuter, Paul Julius [R]

(1816–99) German-born founder of the famous Reuters News Agency (set up in London in 1851), the first organization to transmit commercial news by telegraph. The subject of the final film biography made by William Dieterle at Warners.

Edward G. Robinson — *A Dispatch From Reuters* (Dieterle) USA, 40

Rhodes, Cecil 

(1853–1902) British financier and statesman who made a fortune at the Kimberley diamond diggings and succeeded in opening up that part of Africa which later became known as Rhodesia. Prime Minister of Cape Colony from 1890 to 1896, he was played by Walter Huston in a British screen biography of the mid-thirties.

Walter Huston — *Rhodes Of Africa* (Viertel) GB, 36
Wyndham Goldie — *Victoria The Great* (Wilcox) GB, 37
Ferdinand Marian — *Ohm Krüger* (Steinhoff) Ger, 41

Rice, Archie 

Almost as famous a John Osborne creation as Jimmy Porter, a third-rate music hall performer on the skids who drags down all the people around him to his own shabby level. A sordid, pathetic character, especially written for Laurence Olivier who played him with great skill both on stage (1957) and on screen. The 1975 remake switched the action from the Suez crisis days in Britain to the America of 1944.

Laurence Olivier	*The Entertainer* (Richardson)	GB, 60
Jack Lemmon	*The Entertainer* (Wrye)	USA, 75

Richard I

[R]

(1157–99) The son of Henry II and Eleanor of Aquitaine; something of a whitewashed historical figure whose feats in the Third Crusade were often over-glamorized and whose character was never quite as noble as implied in the Robin Hood films. Anthony Hopkins featured as the ambitious Prince Richard in *The Lion In Winter,* Richard Harris as a weary, ageing monarch in *Robin And Marian.*

Henry Wilcoxon	*The Crusades* (DeMille)	USA, 35
Ian Hunter	*The Adventures Of Robin Hood* (Curtiz/Keighley)	USA, 38
Norman Wooland	*Ivanhoe* (Thorpe)	GB, 52
Patrick Barr	*The Story Of Robin Hood And His Merrie Men* (Annakin)	GB, 52
George Sanders	*King Richard And The Crusaders* (Butler)	USA, 54
Patrick Holt	*Men Of Sherwood Forest* (Guest)	GB, 54
Salah Zulficar	*Saladin* (Sebal)	Egy, 63
Anthony Hopkins	*The Lion In Winter* (Harvey)	GB, 68
Frankie Howerd	*Up The Chastity Belt* (Kellett)	GB, 71
Richard Harris	*Robin And Marian* (Lester)	USA, 76
Robert Hardy	*The Zany Adventures Of Robin Hood* (Austin)	TVM/USA, 84

Note: A. Scott Craven in *Ivanhoe* (USA, 13) and Wallace Beery in both *Robin Hood* (USA, 22) and *Richard The Lion-Hearted* (USA, 23) were among the actors who played Richard on the silent screen.

Richard III

(1452–85) England's last Plantagenet king, a ruthless hunchback who allegedly schemed his way to the throne via several murders including those of the boy princes, Edward and Richard, in the Tower Of London. Powerfully represented by Shakespeare in his 1594 stage play, transferred to the sceen by Olivier who duly made his desperate cry, 'A horse! A horse! My kingdom for a horse!' when on the losing end at the Battle of Bosworth.

Basil Rathbone	*Tower Of London* (Lee)	USA, 39
Laurence Olivier	*Richard III* (Olivier)	GB, 55
Vincent Price	*Tower Of London* (Corman)	USA, 62

Note: William V. Ranous (USA, 08), Frank R. Benson (GB, 11), Frederick B. Warde (USA, 13) and Conrad Veidt (Ger, 19) all appeared in silent versions of Shakespeare's *Richard III;* Ron Cook starred as Richard in the 1983 BBC/Time Life TV production.

Richelieu, Cardinal

(1585–1642) Powerful chief minister to Louis XIII in seventeenth century France. In the history books, a man largely responsible for the downfall of Protestantism and who greatly strengthened the French monarchy; in the films about the musketeers, always the chief villain, scheming to extend his influence over the weak king and enjoying the physical pleasures of Milady de Winter. Vincent Price and an oversized Charlton Heston are among those who have plotted against D'Artagnan and company. George Arliss appeared in a screen biography of 1935.

Nigel De Brulier	*The Iron Mask* (Dwan)	USA, 29
Osgood Perkins	*Madame DuBarry* (Dieterle)	USA, 34
Nigel De Brulier	*The Three Musketeers* (Lee)	USA, 35
George Arliss	*Cardinal Richelieu* (Lee)	USA, 35
Raymond Massey	*Under The Red Robe* (Seastrom)	GB, 37
Nigel De Brulier	*The Man In The Iron Mask* (Whale)	USA, 39
Miles Mander	*The Three Musketeers* (Dwan)	USA, 39
Aime Clariond	*Monsieur Vincent* (Cloche)	Fra, 47
Vincent Price	*The Three Musketeers* (Sidney)	USA, 48
Paul Cavanaugh	*Sword Of D'Artagnan* (Boetticher)	USA, 52
Renaud-Mary	*The Three Musketeers* (Hunebelle)	Fra, 53

Denis d'Ines	*Mistress DuBarry* (Christian-Jaque)	Fra/It, 54
Daniel Sorano	*The Three Musketeers* (Borderie)	Fra, 61
Rafael Rivelles	*Cyrano And D'Artagnan* (Gance)	Fra, 62
Massimo Serato	*The Secret Mark Of D'Artagnan* (Marcellini)	Fra/It, 62
Christopher Logue	*The Devils* (Russell)	GB, 71
Charlton Heston	*The Three Musketeers* (Lester)	Panama/Spa, 74
Charlton Heston	*The Four Musketeers* (Lester)	Panama/Spa, 75

Note: Silent portrayals of Richelieu included those by Murdoch MacQuarrie in Allan Dwan's *Richelieu* (USA, 14), Nigel De Brulier in the 1921 version of *The Three Musketeers,* Robert B. Mantell in *Under The Red Robe* (USA, 23) and Edward Connelly in *Bardeleys The Magnificent* (USA, 26).

Richthoven, Baron Manfred von [R]

(1882–1918) The most famous German air ace of World War I, noted for his high number of aerial victories (80) and the scourge of the Allies in his deadly red triplane. Roger Corman's 1971 film traced Richthoven's career from 1916 to 1918, alternating his story with that of Roy Brown, the Canadian pilot who eventually shot him down in the last year of the war.

William von Brincken	*Hell's Angels* (Hughes)	USA, 30
Carl Schell	*The Blue Max* (Guillermin)	GB, 66
Ingo Mogendorf	*Darling Lili* (Edwards)	USA, 70
John Phillip Law	*The Red Baron* (Corman)	USA, 71

Note: In *The Red Baron,* Roy Brown was played by Don Stroud.

Rimsky-Korsakov, Nikolai [R]

(1844–1908) Russian composer, best known for his symphonic suites 'Scheherazade' and 'Capriccio Espagnol' and operas based on Russian legends. His native country afforded him a respectful tribute in the early 50s; Hollywood offered *Song Of Scheherazade* and an affair with dance-hall girl Yvonne de Carlo who, according to Universal's scriptwriters, inspired his greated music. Universal also threw in Eve Arden who gingered up the proceedings by referring to the composer as 'the Russian with two names'.

Jean Pierre Aumont	*Song Of Scheherazade* (Reisch)	USA, 47
David Leonard	*Song Of My Heart* (Glazer)	USA, 48
Andrei Popov	*Musorgskij* (Roshal)	USSR, 50
Grigori Belov	*Rimsky-Korsakov* (Roshal/Kazansky)	USSR, 52

Ringo Kid, The [F]

Western hero and the character that propelled John Wayne to genuine stardom in John Ford's celebrated *Stagecoach.* One of a group of passengers who are attacked by marauding Apaches when they cross dangerous New Mexico territory by stagecoach, he derives from Malpais Bill, created by Ernest Haycox in his 1937 short story 'Stage To Lordsburgh' (first published in Collier's Magazine). Wayne, first seen in the film with a rifle twirling in his right hand and a saddle on his other arm, went on to make 14 movies with Ford.

John Wayne	*Stagecoach*	(Ford)	USA, 39
Alex Cord	*Stagecoach*	(Douglas)	USA, 66

Note: Kris Kristofferson became the third actor to play The Ringo Kid in the 1986 TV movie of Ted Post. Another famous *Stagecoach* passenger, the alcoholic Doc Boone who has to sober up en route in order to deliver a baby, has been played by Thomas Mitchell (39), Bing Crosby (66) and Willie Nelson (86). In the TV movie he was renamed Doc Holliday.

Robarts, Sir Wilfrid [F]

After Miss Marple and Poirot the most famous of Agatha Christie's characters to be portrayed on screen; a barnstorming barrister who agrees to defend (and is then tricked by) a young man accused of murdering a middle-aged widow to inherit her money. Brought vividly to life by Charles Laughton ('a drowning man clutching at razor blades' he says of his client) in Billy Wilder's *Witness For The Prosecution,* less effectively by Ralph Richardson in the labouring TV version. First appeared in the 1933 short story 'Witness For The Prosecution' which predated Christie's stage play by some 20 years.

Charles Laughton	*Witness For The Prosecution* (Wilder) USA, 57
Ralph Richardson	*Witness For The Prosecution* GB/USA(TV), 82

Robespierre, Maximilien [R]

(1758–94) Arguably the most fervent of the French revolutionaries and, depending on one's viewpoint, either a champion of social change or an ambitious demagogue and dictator. Brilliantly played in Wajda's 1982 film by the Polish actor Wojciech Pszoniak who essayed the revolutionary as a chillingly inflexible authoritarian and a sick man sweating out a private nightmare that he too might finish up on the guillotine – which he did, just three months after his former comrade Danton ascended the scaffold. Apart from the Pszoniak portrayal usually only a subsidiary character on screen, often popping up with evil menace in versions of *The Scarlet Pimpernel*!

George Hackathorne	*Captain Of The Guard* (Robertson) USA, 30
Gustaf Gruendgens	*Danton* (Behrendt) Ger, 31
Ernest Milton	*The Scarlet Pimpernel* (Young) GB, 35
Henry Oscar	*The Return Of The Scarlet Pimpernel* (Schwartz) GB, 38
George Meeker	*Marie Antoinette* (Van Dyke) USA, 38
Charles Goldner	*The Laughing Lady* (Stein) GB, 46
Richard Basehart	*Reign Of Terror* (Mann) USA, 49
Jacques Berthier	*Versailles* (Guitry) Fra, 53
Peter Gilmore	*Don't Lose Your Head* (Thomas) GB, 66
Bernard Dheran	*Valmy* (Gance) Fra, 67
Wojciech Pszoniak	*Danton* (Wajda) Pol/Fra, 82
Roland Giraud	*Liberty, Equality, Sauerkraut* (Yanne) Fra/It, 85

Note: Fotheringham Lysons in *The Elusive Pimpernel* (GB, 19), Werner Krauss in *Danton* (Ger, 21), Sidney Herbert in *Orphans Of The Storm* (USA, 21), De Garcia Fuerburg in *Scaramouche* (USA, 23) and Nelson Keyes in *The Triumph Of The Scarlet Pimpernel* (GB, 28) all played Robespierre on the silent screen; Richard Morant featured as the revolutionary in the 1982 TV version of *The Scarlet Pimpernel*.

Robin Hood [F]

Legendary British outlaw who, according to ancient ballads stole from the rich to give to the poor during the tyrannical reign of Prince John in twelfth century England. As a traditional portrait, Errol Flynn's handsome pre-war swashbuckler will probably never be surpassed; more recently, however, Sean Connery shattered the legend with his ageing outlaw in *Robin And Marian* and brought realism to a character who had previously been reserved solely for escapists and the young in heart.

Errol Flynn	*The Adventures Of Robin Hood* (Curtiz/Keighley) USA, 38
Russell Hicks	*The Bandit Of Sherwood Forest* (Sherman/Levin) USA, 46
Jon Hall	*Prince Of Thieves* (Bretherton) USA, 48
Robert Clarke	*Tales Of Robin Hood* (Tinling) USA, 51
Harold Warrender	*Ivanhoe* (Thorpe) GB, 52
Richard Todd	*The Story Of Robin Hood And His Merrie Men* (Annakin) GB, 52
Don Taylor	*Men Of Sherwood Forest* (Guest) GB, 54
Richard Greene	*Sword Of Sherwood Forest* (Fisher) GB, 60
Barrie Ingham	*A Challenge For Robin Hood* (Pennington Richards) GB, 67
Hugh Paddick	*Up The Chastity Belt* (Kellett) GB, 71
David Warbeck	*Wolfshead: The Legend Of Robin Hood* (Hough) GB, 73
Brian Bedford	*Robin Hood* (Disney) USA, 73
Boris Khmielnitski	*Robin Hood* (Tarassov) USSR, 76
Sean Connery	*Robin And Marian* (Lester) USA, 76
John Cleese	*Time Bandits* (Gilliam) GB, 81
George Segal	*The Zany Adventures Of Robin Hood* (Austin) TVM/USA, 84

Note: Cornel Wilde in *The Bandit Of Sherwood Forest* (USA, 46) and John Derek in *Rogues Of*

Sherwood Forest (USA, 50) both featured as the son of Robin Hood; June Laverick as his daughter in the misleadingly titled *Son Of Robin Hood* (GB, 58).

Brian Bedford voiced the role in the Disney cartoon; in *Robin And The Seven Hoods,* the gangster updating of the tale, the equivalent role to that of Robin Hood was played by Frank Sinatra (as Robbo).

Douglas Fairbanks was the king of the silent outlaws in Allan Dwan's 1922 spectacular, *Robin Hood.* Robert Frazer (USA, 12), W. Thomas (USA, 13), William Russell (USA, 14) were others who appeared in the part.

On TV Richard Greene featured in 143 episodes of *The Adventures Of Robin Hood* (55–9); more recently Michael Praed and Jason Connery both appeared as Robin in the series *Robin Of Sherwood* (1984–86).

Robinson Crusoe

F

Seventeenth-century English squire, shipwrecked for over 20 years on an uninhabited island with only a cat, a dog and finally a young native (Man Friday) for company. A courageous figure in Daniel Defoe's novel of 1719–20, he has attracted several major film-makers, notably Luis Bunuel whose 1953 Mexican film ranks as perhaps the definitive screen version of the story. The theme was intriguingly revamped into science-fiction terms in *Robinson Crusoe On Mars;* in *Man Friday* Jack Gold told the story from Friday's viewpoint and reversed the roles of master and servant.

Douglas Fairbanks	*Mr Robinson Crusoe* (Sutherland) USA, 32
Herbert A. E. Bohme	*Robinson Crusoe* (Fanck) Ger, 40

A duel to the death in Nottingham Castle at the close of the 1938 swashbuckler *The Adventures of Robin Hood.* No-one ever defeated Errol Flynn (right) in a screen sword fight although Basil Rathbone (pictured left, as Guy of Gisbourne) was in real-life a superb swordsman and superior to all his film opponents

Pavel Kadotchnikov	*Robinson Crusoe* (Andrievski)	USSR, 47
Georges Marchal	*Robinson Crusoe* (Musso)	It, 51
Dan O'Herlihy	*The Adventures Of Robinson Crusoe* (Bunuel)	Mex, 53
Paul Mantee	*Robinson Crusoe On Mars* (Haskin)	USA, 64
Dick Van Dyke	*Lt Robinson Crusoe, USN* (Paul)	USA, 66
Hugo Stieglitz	*Robinson Crusoe* (Cardona, Jr)	Mex, 69
Leonid Kuravlev	*The Life And Surprising Adventures Of Robinson Crusoe* (Govorukin)	USSR, 72
Peter O'Toole	*Man Friday* (Gold)	GB, 76
Aidan Quinn	*Robinson Crusoe* (Deschanel)	Yug, 88

Note: Both the Douglas Fairbanks and Dick Van Dyke performances were updated variations of Defoe's story; Georges Melies (Fra, 02), Einar Zangenberg (Den, 10), Robert Z. Leonard (USA, 13), Mario Dani (Fra, 21), Harry C. Myers (USA, 22) and M. A. Wetherell (GB, 27) were among the silent actors who appeared in the role.

Rochester, Edward F

The master of Thornfield Hall in Charlotte Brontë's 'Jane Eyre' (1847). A strange, complex character, his moodiness derives from a hopeless marriage to an insane wife, a secret only revealed on the day of

Joan Fontaine as Jane Eyre and Orson Welles as the tormented Edward Rochester in Robert Stevenson's 1944 version of Charlotte Brontë's classic tale. The film was one of the first in which Welles concentrated solely on acting after his artistically triumphant but commercially disastrous productions *Citizen Kane* and *The Magnificent Ambersons*

his proposed marriage to his young governess. Eventually maimed and blinded amid the blazing walls of his huge mansion. Two notable screen portrayals: Orson Welles and George C. Scott.

Colin Clive	*Jane Eyre*	(Cabanne)	USA, 34
Orson Welles	*Jane Eyre*	(Stevenson)	USA, 44
George C. Scott	*Jane Eyre*	(Delbert Mann)	GB, 71

Note: Tom Conway appeared in the Rochester role in Val Lewton's 1943 horror updating, *I Walked With A Zombie;* Irving Cummings (14), Alan Hale (15), Richard Tucker (15), Conway Tearle (15), Norman Trevor (21) and the German actors Charles Willy Kayser (19) and Olaf Fonss (26) were among those who appeared in silent versions.

Rocky Balbao

F

Sylvester Stallone's shambling Philadelphia boxer, a 'has-been' who is given a million-to-one shot at the heavyweight title by reigning world champ Apollo Creed and surprises everyone by going the distance. Essentially little more than an old B movie hero, he has to date battered Creed into submission in *Rocky II,* lost and regained his title to a slugger in *Rocky III,* and defeated a biochemically engineered Soviet boxer in *Rocky IV.* Has yet to hang up his gloves but when he does looks likely to go out as champ. First created by Stallone in his original screenplay of 1976.

Sylvester Stallone	O	*Rocky*	(Avildsen)	USA, 76
Sylvester Stallone		*Rocky II*	(Stallone)	USA, 79
Sylvester Stallone		*Rocky III*	(Stallone)	USA, 82
Sylvester Stallone		*Rocky IV*	(Stallone)	USA, 85

Rocky Balbao the underdog, fights a savage battle with world champion Apollo Creed (Carl Weathers) in the first *Rocky* film directed by John Avildsen in 1976. Sylvester Stallone has since played his shambling Philadelphia boxing hero on four occaions even though he ran out of story ideas after film number one!

Rodgers, Richard [R]

(1902–79) The most durable of all American composers of popular stage music, a man whose melodies (with Lorenz Hart) attracted audiences of the 20s and 30s, and also (with Oscar Hammerstein) those of subsequent decades. His partnership with Hart was the subject of MGM's screen biography, *Words And Music.* Among the Rodgers and Hart shows: 'On Your Toes', 'Babes In Arms', 'The Boys From Syracuse' and 'Pal Joey'; among the Rodgers and Hammerstein musicals; 'Oklahoma', 'South Pacific', 'The King And I', 'The Sound Of Music'.

Tom Drake	*Words And Music*	(Taurog)	USA, 48

Rogers, Will [R]

(1879–1935) American actor and humorist who began as a cowboy rope-twirler in vaudeville and rose, through the Ziegfeld Follies, to become one of America's top movie stars of the early 30s. His charm, wit and cracker-barrel philosophy made him the most successful entertainer of his generation. Killed in a plane crash in 1935, he was played on screen by his look-alike son in Warners' biography of the early 50s.

A.A. Trimble	*The Great Ziegfeld*	(Leonard)	USA, 36
Will Rogers, Jr	*The Story Of Will Rogers*	(Curtiz)	USA, 52

Note: Lew Harvey featured as Rogers in the 1925 silent *Pretty Ladies* (USA, 25); Gene McLaughlin appeared in the 1978 TV Movie *Ziegfeld: The Man And His Women.*

Romberg, Sigmund 

(1887–1951) Hungarian-born composer of light operettas, popular during the 20s and 30s when several of his Broadway hits, 'The Desert Song', 'Maytime', 'The Girl Of The Golden West', 'New Moon', were filmed in Hollywood. Given MGM's lush biography treatment in the 1954 musical *Deep In My Heart.*

Jose Ferrer	*Deep In My Heart*	(Donen)	USA, 54

Rome, Tony 

Modern private-eye, the creation of novelist Marvin H. Albert. Very much in the laconic Philip Marlowe mould, but minus upturned raincoat and shabby office. Instead, a sailor's cap and a plush houseboat in sunny Miami. Portrayed twice on screen by Frank Sinatra.

Frank Sinatra	*Tony Rome*	(Douglas)	USA, 67
Frank Sinatra	*Lady In Cement*	(Douglas)	USA, 68

Romeo And Juliet 

The immortal star-crossed lovers of William Shakespeare, victims of the tragic family feud between the Montagues and the Capulets in Renaissance Italy. Screen portrayals of the doomed pair have been variable, although the pictorial values of the Castellani and Zeffirelli adaptations frequently compensated for any inadequacy of performance. 'Romeo And Juliet' was first performed on stage in 1596.

Leslie Howard and Norma Shearer	*Romeo And Juliet*	(Cukor)	USA, 36
Enrique Guitart and Marta Flores	*Julieta y Romeo*	(Castellvi)	Spa, 40
Ibrahim Hamouda and Leila Mourad	*Romeo And Juliet*	(Selim)	Egy, 42
Jaraj and Nargis	*Anjuman*	(Hussein)	Ind, 48
Laurence Harvey and Susan Shentall	*Romeo And Juliet*	(Castellani)	GB/It, 54
Meynier and Rosemarie Dexter	*Romeo And Juliet*	(Freda)	It/Spa, 64
Leonard Whiting and Olivia Hussey	*Romeo And Juliet*	(Zeffirelli)	GB/It, 68

Note: The musical *West Side Story* (61) updated the Romeo And Juliet theme to contemporary New York and set the tragedy against a feud between two rival street gangs, the Sharks and the Jets. Richard Beymer featured as the Romeo character, Natalie Wood as Juliet. André Cayatte's 1949 French film *Les Amants de Verone* starring Pierre Brasseur and Anouk Aimee was also a modernized version of Shakespeare's tale.

Silent screen portrayals of the two lovers were given by Paul Panzer and Florence Lawrence (USA, 08), Mario Caserini and Maria Gasperini (It, 08), Sir Godfrey Tearle and Mary Malone (GB, 08), George A. Lessey and Julia M. Taylor (USA, 11), Gustav Serena and Francesca Bertini (It, 11), Francis X. Bushman and Beverly Bayne (USA, 16) and Harry Hilliard and Theda Bara (USA, 16). The most recent TV performances have been by Peter McEnery and Sarah Badel (77) and Patrick Ryecart and Rebecca Saire (78).

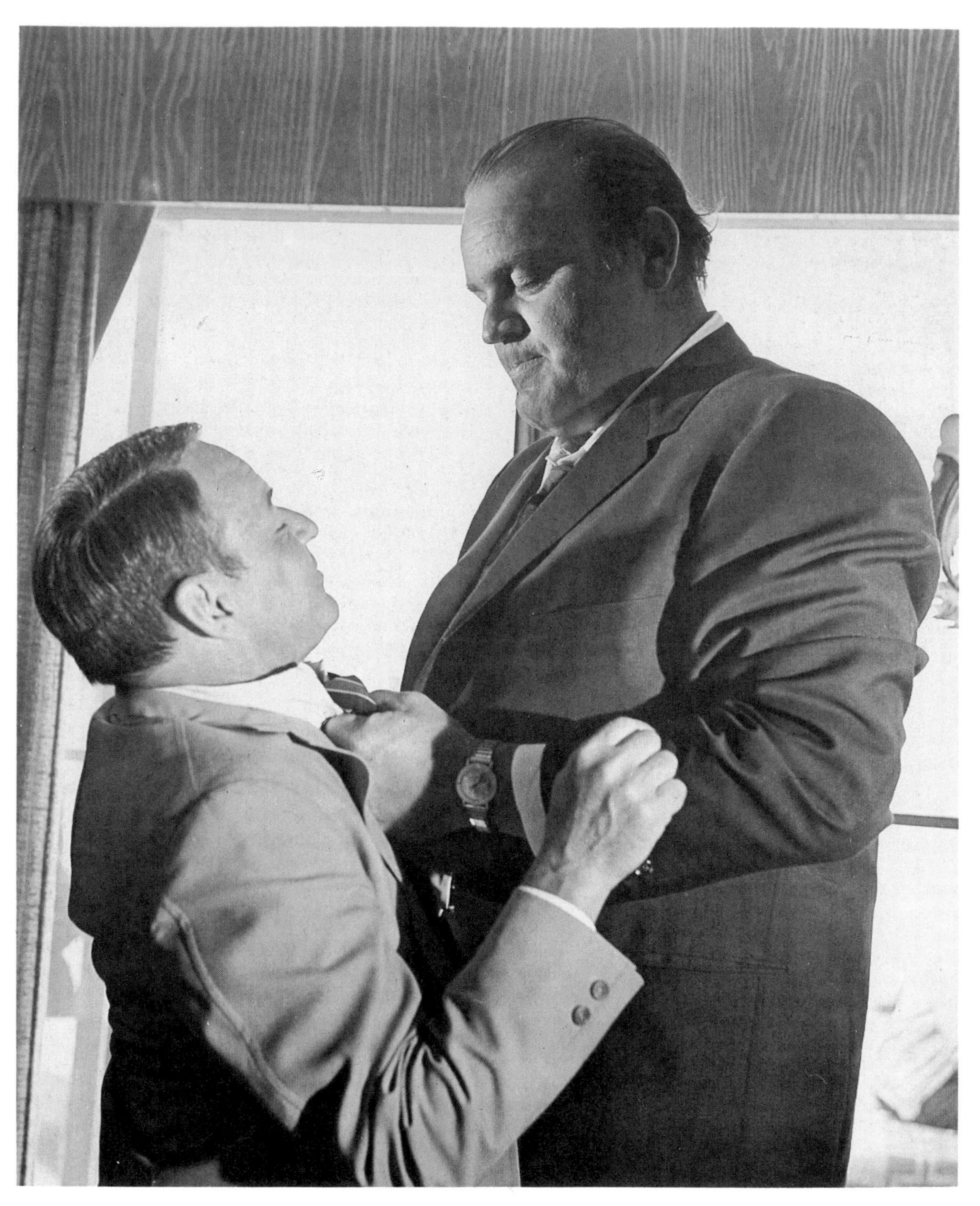

Not quite up to the job! Frank Sinatra making a bit of a hash of playing private eye Tony Rome in the Fox thriller *Lady In Cement*. The actor dwarfing Frank in this scene is the late Dan Blocker who made his screen debut in the film and became famous in the TV western series *Bonanza*. Sinatra made two Tony Rome adventures, both of them set in the sunny locale of Miami

(Right above) Leonard Whiting and Olivia Hussey as Shakespeare's tragic young lovers *Romeo And Juliet*; (top) Richard Beymer and Natalie Wood in Leonard Bernstein's musical updating *West Side Story*

Rommel, Field Marshal Erwin [R]

(1891–1944) The most famous German soldier of World War II, a man who excelled at every level of command and led the legendary Afrika Korps to decisive victories before being halted by Montgomery at El Alamein. Committed suicide in 1944 after being implicated in the bomb plot against Hitler. James Mason's performance in *The Desert Fox* remains the most distinguished screen portrayal. Erich von Stroheim's in *Five Graves To Cairo* the most melodramatic.

Erich von Stroheim	*Five Graves To Cairo* (Wilder) USA, 43
James Mason	*The Desert Fox* (Hathaway) USA, 51
James Mason	*The Desert Rats* (Wise) USA, 53
Albert Lieven	*Foxhole In Cairo* (Moxey) GB, 60
Gregory Gay	*Hitler* (Heisler) USA, 62
Werner Hinz	*The Longest Day* (Wicki/Marton/Annakin) USA, 62
Christopher Plummer	*The Night Of The Generals* (Litvak) Fra/GB, 67
Robert Hossein	*Desert Tanks* (Padget) Fra/It, 68
Karl Michael Vogler	*Patton* (Schaffner) USA, 70
Wolfgang Preiss	*Raid On Rommel* (Hathaway) USA, 71

Roosevelt, Eleanor [R]

(1884–1962) Wife of Franklin Roosevelt and mother of six children who during her term as First Lady became as famous as her husband in her promotion of liberal causes. Appointed delegate to the United Nations after her husband's death she secured the adoption of the Universal Declaration of Human Rights and during the 50s travelled extensively, becoming widely acknowledged as the world's most admired woman. Greer Garson portrayed her in *Sunrise At Campobello,* Jane Alexander in the two TV films dealing with her life with Roosevelt, and Jean Stapleton in John Erman's 1982 TV movie *Eleanor, First Lady Of The World.*

Greer Garson	*Sunrise At Campobello* (Donehue) USA, 60
Jane Alexander	*Eleanor And Franklin* (Petrie) TVM/USA, 76
Jane Alexander	*Eleanor And Franklin: The White House Years* (Petrie) TVM/USA, 77
Jean Stapleton	*Eleanor, First Lady Of The World* (Erman) TVM/USA, 82
Lois deBanzie	*Annie* (Huston) USA, 82

Note: Eileen Heckart in *F.D.R. The Last Year* (80) and Elizabeth Hoffman in *The Winds Of War* (83) have also played Eleanor Roosevelt on TV; the 90 minute documentary *The Eleanor Roosevelt Story,* directed by Richard Kaplan, covered The First Lady's life through still photographs and newsreel footage. It was named best feature documentary of 1965 at the Academy Awards ceremony in 1966.

Roosevelt, Franklin Delano [R]

(1882–1945) The only American President to be re-elected three times, a man who led his country out of the Depression and through World War II despite being crippled by polio. Famous for his fireside radio chats and ringing phrases ('the only thing we have to fear is fear itself'), he has generally been glimpsed only fleetingly on the big screen. The one exception was Ralph Bellamy's remarkable portrayal in *Sunrise At Campobello* which related in detail Roosevelt's inspiring fight against the disease which struck him down in 1921.

Captain Jack Young	*Yankee Doodle Dandy* (Curtiz) USA, 42
Captain Jack Young	*This Is The Army* (Curtiz) USA, 43
Godfrey Tearle	*The Beginning Or The End* (Taurog) USA, 46
Nikolai Cherkasov	*The First Front* (Petrov) USSR, 49
Ralph Bellamy	*Sunrise At Campobello* (Donehue) USA, 60
Richard Nelson	*The Pigeon That Took Rome* (Shavelson) USA, 62
Stephen Roberts	*First To Fight* (Nyby) USA, 67
Stanislav Yaskevich	*The Great Battle* (Ozerov) USSR/Pol/Yug/E.Ger/It, 69
Dan O'Herlihy	*MacArthur* (Sargent) USA, 77
Howard Da Silva	*The Private Files Of J. Edgar Hoover* (Cohen) USA, 78
Edward Herrmann	*Annie* (Huston) USA, 82

Note: Roosevelt has received far more detailed treatment on American TV. Edward Herrmann starred in two major TV films of the mid-70s – *Eleanor And Franklin* (76) which dealt with Roosevelt's early youth to his death in 1945 and *Eleanor And Franklin: The White House Years* (77) – and in 1980 Jason Robards featured as the president in *F.D.R.: The Last Year* (80). Stephen Roberts in *Ring of Passion* (77) and *Enola Gay* (80), Ralph Bellamy in *The Winds Of War* (83), and David Ogden Stiers in *J. Edgar Hoover* (87) are among the performers who have also played Roosevelt on TV.

Roosevelt, Theodore [R]

(1858–1919) Extrovert American President whose exploits as a Roughrider in the Spanish-American war e.g. in the famous charge up San Juan Hill in Cuba, earned him as much fame as his subsequent years as President when his motto was 'speak softly and carry a big stick'. Character actor Sidney Blackmer appeared several times as Roosevelt in minor roles; John Alexander pretended he was the president in *Arsenic And Old Lace;* and Brian Keith developed his bullish personality at length in John Milius' *The Wind And The Lion,* based on a true incident in which Roosevelt sent the marines to Morocco to rescue an American widow and her children, kidnapped by a desert chieftain.

Actor	Film	Country, Year
Sidney Blackmer	*This Is My Affair* (Seiter)	USA, 37
Wallis Clark	*Yankee Doodle Dandy* (Curtiz)	USA, 42
Wallis Clark	*Jack London* (Santell)	USA, 43
Sidney Blackmer	*In Old Oklahoma* (Rogell)	USA, 43
Sidney Blackmer	*Buffalo Bill* (Wellman)	USA, 44
John Alexander	*Arsenic And Old Lace* (Capra)	USA, 44
John Merton	*I Wonder Who's Kissing Her Now* (Bacon)	USA, 47
Sidney Blackmer	*My Girl Tisa* (Nugent)	USA, 48
John Alexander	*Fancy Pants* (Marshall)	USA, 50
Edward Cassidy	*The First Travelling Saleslady* (Lubin)	USA, 56
Karl Swenson	*Brighty Of The Grand Canyon* (Foster)	USA, 66
Brian Keith	*The Wind And The Lion* (Milius)	USA, 75
Robert Boyd	*Ragtime* (Forman)	USA, 81

Note: W. E. Whittle in *General Pershing* (19), Jack Ridgeway in *The Copperhead* (19), E. J. Radcliffe in *Sundown* (24), Buck Black in *Lights Of Old Broadway* (25) and Frank Hopper in *The Rough Riders* (27) all featured as Roosevelt on the American silent screen. On TV William Phipps in *Eleanor And Franklin* (76) and David Healy in *Eleanor And Franklin: The White House Years* (77) both featured as the president. The 1978 TV film *Bully* (78), directed by Peter H. Hunt, was a recording of James Whitmore's two hour stage performance as Roosevelt.

Rose, Billy [R]

(1899–1966) Brash American showman and night-club owner, who began his Broadway career producing revues then graduated to long-running hit musicals, e.g. 'Jumbo' (1935) and 'Carmen Jones' (1943). James Caan's screen performance in *Funny Lady* revolved around Rose's marriage to comedienne Fanny Brice.

Actor	Film	Country, Year
James Caan	*Funny Lady* (Ross)	USA, 75

Rose-Marie

Melodious belle of a Canadian trading post, loved by both a mountie and a French trapper in the Rudolf Friml/Herbert Stothart stage musical of 1924. The first version of the story was silent; the subsequent versions included substantial story changes and allowed 'Indian Love Call', 'Only A Kiss' and 'The Door Of Her Dreams'.

Actor	Film	Country, Year
Jeanette MacDonald	*Rose-Marie* (Van Dyke)	USA, 36
Ann Blyth	*Rose-Marie* (LeRoy)	USA, 54

Note: Joan Crawford was the silent Rose-Marie, appearing in Lucien Hubbard's 1928 film for MGM.

Rosenberg, Julius and Ethel

The only American civilians to be put to death for espionage in peace time, a 35-year-old New York engineer and his wife who were accused of passing atomic secrets to the Russians and, after a much publicized trial conducted in McCarthy-type hysteria, executed in January 1953. Sidney Lumet's film *Daniel* (based on the novel 'The Book Of Daniel' by E. L. Doctorow), renamed the Rosenbergs Paul and Rochelle Isaacson and looked at their lives in flashback as their two adult children try to come

Arguably the most effective portrayal of President Teddy Roosevelt yet put on the screen—Brian Keith as the adventurous president who sends troops to Morocco when a Berber chieftain kidnaps an American widow and her son, holds them hostage and sparks off an international incident. Sean Connery played the Arab chief, Candice Bergen his victim. The film: John Milius' *The Wind And The Lion*

to terms with the knowledge that their parents were convicted spies.

Mandy Patinkin (Paul) and Lindsay Crouse (Rochelle)	*Daniel* (Lumet)	USA, 83

Note: The two children, Daniel and Susan, were played by Timothy Hutton and Amanda Plummer respectively; the character of David Greenglass whose evidence helped convict the Rosenbergs and who was secretly a courier for the British physicist/spy Klaus Fuchs, was renamed Selig Mindish. He was played in Lumet's film by Joseph Leon.

Roth, Lillian R

(1910–80) A former child star who joined Paramount in the 20s and featured in several early musicals (*The Love Parade, The Vagabond King*) before losing her battle with alcoholism. Her harrowing experiences and courageous fight back were revealed in a frank autobiography 'I'll Cry Tomorrow', later made into a realistic film by Daniel Mann.

Susan Hayward	*I'll Cry Tomorrow* (Mann)	USA, 55

Note: Susan Hayward sang all her own songs in the film.

Rousseau, Jean Jacques 

(1712–78) French novelist and political theorist who rebelled against the social orders of his time and profoundly influenced the course of the revolution which occurred just a decade after his death. Claude Goretta's 200-minute film covered his last years when he was forced to leave France and live abroad in poverty and near solitude.

André Laurent	*Champs-Elysées* (Guitry)	Fra, 39
François Simon	*Roads Of Exile* (Goretta)	Fra, 78

Ruggles Of Red Gap 

An English gentleman's gentleman, won as a prize in a poker game in Europe and transported by his 'nouveau riche' American master to a new life (and independence) in the Old West. Created in the 1915 play by Harry Leon Wilson; memorably portrayed by Charles Laughton in McCarey's film of 1935.

Charles Laughton	*Ruggles Of Red Gap* (McCarey)	USA, 35
Bob Hope	*Fancy Pants* (Marshall)	USA, 50

Note: Taylor Holmes featured in the 1918 Essanay production and Edward Everett Horton in Paramount's 1923 film. The 1950 Bob Hope movie was a loose remake with Ruggles renamed Humphrey.

Rupert Of Hentzau 

A conspirator for the throne of Ruritania in Anthony Hope's 'The Prisoner Of Zenda' and one of the most engaging villains in the swashbuckling genre. Played with charm by Douglas Fairbanks Jr and suave menace by James Mason, he engages in a climactic duel with hero Rudolf Rassendyll and is always allowed (quite rightly) to escape with his life. Hope must have tired of him, however. In his sequel, 'Rupert Of Hentzau' (1898), filmed only in the silent days, the dashing Rupert at last meets his demise – at the hands of Rassendyll!

Douglas Fairbanks Jr	*The Prisoner Of Zenda* (Cromwell)	USA, 37
James Mason	*The Prisoner Of Zenda* (Thorpe)	USA, 52
Stuart Wilson	*The Prisoner Of Zenda* (Quine)	USA, 79

Note: Alan Hale (USA, 13), Gerald Ames (GB, 15) and Ramon Novarro (USA, 22) played Rupert in silent versions of *The Prisoner Of Zenda;* Gerald Ames (GB, 15) and Lew Cody (USA, 23) in *Rupert Of Hentzau.*

Russell, Lillian 

(1868–1922) Colourful musical star of the Gay Nineties, renowned for her hour-glass figure, feathered hats and legendary exploits off stage, which included the taking and discarding of four husbands. The Fox studio filmed her story in 1940 with Alice Faye as 'Luscious Lillian'. Among her songs: 'Come Down, Ma Evenin' Star', 'After The Ball' and 'Rosie, You Are My Posie'.

Ruth Gillette	*The Great Ziegfeld* (Leonard)	USA, 36
Ruth Gillette	*The Gentleman From Louisiana* (Pichel)	USA, 36
Alice Faye	*Lillian Russell* (Cummings)	USA, 40

Louise Allbritton	*Bowery To Broadway*	(Lamont) USA, 44
Andrea King	*My Wild Irish Rose*	(Butler) USA, 47

Ruth, Babe

R

(1895–1948) Baseball's most famous player and the greatest hitter of home runs in the history of the game. Just about the perfect athlete – he could run, field, throw and bat – he hit 714 home runs during his spectacular career. Appeared in several silent baseball comedies and light dramas, *Headin' Home* (20), *Babe Comes Home* (26), etc. and as himself in Harold Lloyd's *Speedy* (27) and *Pride Of The Yankees* (42).

William Bendix	*The Babe Ruth Story*	(Del Ruth) USA, 48

Sacco And Vanzetti [R]

Italian immigrants to America, well-known for their anarchist activities, who were convicted of the murder of a cashier and guard during a payroll robbery in Massachusetts in April, 1920. Both men vainly protested their innocence but, after seven years of appeals, were executed in the electric chair. Doubts about their guilt remained and, in 1977, both had their names cleared in a special proclamation signed by the Governor of Massachusetts. The 1971 film of Giuliano Montaldo retold their story.

Riccardo Cucciolla (Nicola Sacco)	*Sacco And Vanzetti* (Montaldo) It, 71
Gian Maria Volonte (Bartolomeo Vanzetti)	

Sade, Marquis de [R]

(1740–1814) Infamous French writer whose cruelty and sexual perversions brought the word sadism into the English language. Spent 30 years of his life in prison, had a quarter of his literary output burned by the police, and died insane. Keir Dullea was the actor chosen to interpret De Sade's mental torment in the Richard Matheson-scripted biography of 1969; tinted orgies in slow motion represented the sexual decadence.

Patrick Magee	*The Persecution And Assassination Of Jean-Paul Marat, as performed by the inmates of the Asylum Of Charenton under the direction of the Marquis De Sade* (Brook) GB, 67
Klaus Kinski	*Marquis De Sade: Justine* (Franco) W.Ger/It, 68
Michel Piccoli	*The Milky Way* (Bunuel) Fra/It, 69
Keir Dullea	*De Sade* (Endfield) USA/W.Ger, 69

Note: Conrad Veidt appeared as De Sade in Abel Gance's silent masterpiece *Napoleon* (Fra, 27).

Saint, The [F]

Amateur detective (real name Simon Templar), more famous on TV – through the likeable personality of Roger Moore – than in the movies. A debonair Englishman, he is half-crook, half-detective, and spends most of his time on the Continent and in America, constantly involving himself with villains, police and beautiful women. His nickname is derived from his calling card which shows a stick figure with a halo. First appeared in print in Leslie Charteris' 'Meet The Tiger' in 1929, but did not attract the attention of film-makers until almost a decade later.

Louis Hayward	*The Saint In New York* (Holmes) USA, 38
George Sanders	*The Saint Strikes Back* (Farrow) USA, 39
George Sanders	*The Saint In London* (Carstairs) GB, 39
George Sanders	*The Saint's Double Trouble* (Hively) USA, 40
George Sanders	*The Saint Takes Over* (Hively) USA, 40
George Sanders	*The Saint In Palm Springs* (Hively) USA, 41
Hugh Sinclair	*The Saint's Vacation* (Fenton) GB, 41
Hugh Sinclair	*The Saint Meets The Tiger* (Stein) GB, 41
Louis Hayward	*The Saint's Girl Friday* (Friedman) GB, 53
Felix Marten	*Le Saint mene la Danse* (Nahum) Fra, 59

Salome [R]

The seductive daughter of Herodias who slipped off seven veils whilst dancing for her stepfather, Herod Antipas, and gained the head of John the Baptist as a prize. A minor figure in biblical epics (she was barely glimpsed in *The Greatest Story Ever Told*), but featuring in several film biographies of both the silent and sound cinema.

Rita Hayworth	*Salome* (Dieterle) USA, 53
Brigid Bazlen	*King Of Kings* (Ray) USA, 61
Paola Tedesco	*The Gospel According to St. Matthew* (Pasolini) It/Fra, 64
Donyale Luna	*Salome* (Bene) It, 72
Jo Champa	*Salome* (d'Anna) Fra/It, 86
Imogen Millais-Scott	*Salome's Last Dance* (Russell) GB, 88

Note: Theda Bara (18), Nazimova (22) and Diana Allen (23) all starred in American silent productions of *Salome*.

Sand, George R

(1804–76) French writer, as famous for her scandalous love affairs as for her literary accomplishments. Her romance with Polish composer Frederic Chopin has been the subject of several films, notably *A Song To Remember*, a high camp movie with dialogue that only Hollywood at its most flamboyant would have the audacity to deliver, e.g. Sand to Chopin: 'You could make miracles of music in Majorca'.

Sybille Schmitz	*Abschiedswalzer* (Bolvary)	Ger, 34
Merle Oberon	*A Song To Remember* (Charles Vidor)	USA, 45
Patricia Morison	*Song Without End* (Charles Vidor)	USA, 60
Lucia Bose	*Jutrzenka: A Winter In Majorca* (Camino)	Spa, 71
Anne Wiazemsky	*Georges Qui?* (Rosier)	Fra, 73
Imogen Claire	*Lisztomania* (Russell)	GB, 75

Note: Dagny Servaes in *Die Lachende Grille* (Ger, 26) and Germaine Laugier in *La Valse de L'Adieu* (Fra, 27) both featured as Sand in European silent productions.

Sansom, Odette

(1912–) Undercover agent and radio operator for Peter Churchill in occupied France during World War II. Eventually captured and handed over to the Gestapo, she was tortured but kept alive by the Nazis who believed her to be a relation of Winston Churchill. Awarded a George Cross for bravery after the war, she was the subject of perhaps Anna Neagle's most convincing screen performance.

Anna Neagle	*Odette* (Wilcox)	GB, 50

Savage, Doc

Pulp fiction superman of the 30s who appeared in 181 stories (début 1933) but failed to find favour with film-makers until some 40 years later when George Pal produced a tongue-in-cheek account of his adventures. The 'strongest and most intelligent man in the world', he works in conjunction with a personal brains trust called, 'The Amazing Five', aims to conquer crime the world over and keeps himself solvent by borrowing from a vast store of gold in a secret valley in South America. Lester Dent wrote the majority of the stories under the pseudonym of Kenneth Robeson. Savage later enjoyed continuing popularity in the pages of 'Marvel Comics' and was played on screen by TV's Tarzan, Ron Ely.

Ron Ely	*Doc Savage – Man Of Bronze* (Anderson)	USA, 75

Sawyer, Tom

Mark Twain's Missouri schoolboy whose adventurous instincts invariably get the better of him and lead him into all kinds of exploits with his pipe-smoking friend Huckleberry Finn. The pair's visit to a graveyard at midnight, their escape to a tiny island by raft and Tom's encounter with Injun Joe in an underground cavern belong with the immortal moments in American literature. Some decidedly shaky adaptations of Twain's novel have been redeemed by Selznick's classic of 1938 and the sprightly musical of 1973.

Jackie Coogan	*Tom Sawyer* (Cromwell)	USA, 30
Jackie Coogan	*Huckleberry Finn* (Taurog)	USA, 31
Kostya Koltchitsky	*Tom Soyer* (Frenkel)	USSR, 36
Billy Cook	*Tom Sawyer, Detective* (Louis King)	USA, 38
Tommy Kelly	*The Adventures Of Tom Sawyer* (Taurog)	USA, 38
Roland Demongeot	*Tom Sawyer* (Iacob)	Fra/Rum, 69
Johnny Whitaker	*Tom Sawyer* (Taylor)	USA, 73

Note: Jack Pickford featured as Tom in the silents *Tom Sawyer* (17) and *Huck And Tom* (18) and Gordon Griffith in *Huckleberry Finn* (20). Recent TV portrayals have been by Josh Albee in *Tom Sawyer* (73), Donny Most in *Huckleberry Finn* (75), Dan Monahan in *The Adventures Of Huckleberry Finn* (81) and Eugene Oakes in Peter Hunt's 1986 TV Movie *The Adventures Of Huckleberry Finn*.

The murderous half breed Injun Joe has been portrayed by Charles Stevens (30), Victor Jory (38), Kunu Hank (73) and, on TV, by Vic Morrow (73).

Scaramouche [F]

Swashbuckling hero of Rafael Sabatini during the days of the French Revolution. A romantic swordsman, he seeks revenge on the man responsible for the death of his revolutionary friend only to discover that his mortal enemy is his own half-brother. In the now much acclaimed 1952 version, Stewart Granger participates in the longest duel in screen history – six and a half minutes – as he fights with Mel Ferrer around the interiors of a lavish French theatre.

Stewart Granger	*Scaramouche* (Sidney) USA, 52
Gerard Barray	*The Adventures Of Scaramouche* (Isásmendi) Fra/It/Spa, 63
Michael Sarrazin	*The Loves And Times Of Scaramouche* (Castellari) It/Yug, 76

Note: Ramon Novarro played Scaramouche in a lavish silent production by Rex Ingram.

Scarlet Pimpernel, The [R]

English dandy who leads a double life during the days of the French Revolution, masquerading as the foppish Sir Percy Blakeney in English high society and, on the other side of the channel, rescuing aristocrats from the terrors of the guillotine. A dashing hero of Baroness Orczy's 1905 novel and several films since the silent days. Definitive screen portrait: Leslie Howard in Alexander Korda'a 1934 production. The most recent: that of Anthony Andrews in the 1983 TV version of Clive Donner.

Leslie Howard	*The Scarlet Pimpernel* (Young) GB, 34
Barry K. Barnes	*The Return Of The Scarlet Pimpernel* (Schwartz) GB, 38
David Niven	*The Elusive Pimpernel* (Powell/Pressburger) GB, 50
Anthony Andrews	*The Scarlet Pimpernel* (Donner) TVM/USA, 83

Note: Dustin Farnum starred in a 1917 version of *The Scarlet Pimpernel;* Cecil Humphrey in *The Elusive Pimpernel* (GB, 19), Holmes Herbert in *I Will Repay* (GB, 23) and Matheson Lang in *The Triumph Of The Scarlet Pimpernel* (GB, 28) were others who featured in the role.

Citizen Chauvelin, the arch enemy of Blakeney and modelled after several real-life revolutionary leaders, has been played by Norman Page (19), Raymond Massey (34), Francis Lister (38), Cyril Cusack (50) and Ian McKellen (TV, 83).

Schultz, Dutch [R]

New York gangster, in charge of bootlegging in the Bronx and Manhattan in the 20s and 30s, who was also responsible for the murder of Legs Diamond. Met his own death shortly afterwards (1935) when he was shot down 'Godfather style', i.e. over dinner in a New Jersey restaurant, by Alberto Anastasia's executioners from Murder, Inc. Vic Morrow played Schultz in a full-length biography, *Portrait Of A Mobster,* in 1961.

Vic Morrow	*Portrait Of A Mobster* (Pevney) USA, 61
Vincent Gardenia	*Mad Dog Coll* (Balaban) USA, 61
John Durren	*Lepke* (Golan) USA, 75
James Remar	*The Cotton Club* (Coppola) USA, 84

Schumann, Robert [R]

(1810–56) German symphonic composer whose original ambition to become the 'Paganini of the piano' was thwarted when he became paralyzed in his right hand. The composer of four symphonies and a piano concerto, he later fell victim to mental illness and died at the early age of 46. His career and affair with (and later marriage to) the 16-year-old Clara Wieck were recreated in the 1947 Hollywood film *Song Of Love* and the more recent West German production *Spring Symphony*.

Paul Henreid	*Song Of Love* (Brown) USA, 47
Herbert Gronemeyer	*Spring Symphony* (Schamoni) W.Ger, 83

Note: Clara Wieck, a brilliant pianist who outlived Schumann by some 40 years and who interpreted his works in the concert hall, was played by Katharine Hepburn in 1947 and Nastassia Kinski in 1983.

Schweitzer, Dr Albert [R]

(1875–1965) French medical missionary, theologian and musician who, in 1913, set up a riverside hospital in the heart of French Equatorial Africa and devoted his life to treating leprosy and being of service to the Africans. Described as the noblest figure of the twentieth century, he has been portrayed just once on celluloid – by Pierre Fresnay in a French biography of the early 50s.

Pierre Fresnay	*The Story Of Albert Schweitzer* (Haguet)	Fra, 52

Note: The leprosy doctor played by Niall MacGinnis in *The Nun's Story* (59) had vague connections with Schweitzer.

Scott, Robert Falcon [R]

(1868–1912) British Antarctic explorer who reached the South Pole on 18 January, 1912, just a few weeks after the Norwegian Roald Amundsen. Died with his party when trapped by fierce blizzards on the return journey. Charles Frend's Ealing film chronicled the expedition in detail.

John Mills	*Scott Of The Antarctic* (Frend)	GB, 48

Note: The other members of Scott's ill-fated party were played by Harold Warrender (Dr Wilson), James Robertson Justice (Taff Evans), Reginald Beckwith (Lt Bowers) and Derek Bond (Captain Oates).

Scrooge, Ebenezer [F]

Charles Dickens' grasping old skinflint, visited one memorable Christmas Eve by three spirits who show him the error of his ways and change his future life. Along with Fagin the most coveted of all Dickens roles although, ironically, it was as an animated character in Richard Williams' 1972 cartoon that he was most realistically portrayed. Alastair Sim, who had played the role 20 years earlier, voiced the character in Williams' film. 'A Christmas Carol' was published in 1843; the first known film version released in 1901.

Seymour Hicks	*Scrooge* (Edwards)	GB, 35
Reginald Owen	*A Christmas Carol* (Marin)	USA, 38
Alastair Sim	*Scrooge* (Desmond Hurst)	GB, 50
Albert Finney	*Scrooge* (Neame)	GB, 70
Alastair Sim (voice only)	*A Christmas Carol* (Williams)	GB, 72
George C. Scott	*A Christmas Carol* (Donner)	GB, 84

Note: Seymour Hicks also played Scrooge in a British silent production of 1913. Charles Rock (GB, 14) and Rupert Julian in an American adaptation, *The Right To Be Happy* (16) both featured in the role.

Alan Young voiced Scrooge McDuck in Walt Disney's animated featurette *Mickey's Christmas Carol* in 1983; in 1988 Bill Murray appeared as a modern day miser – an 80s business executive – in an updated version of Dickens' tale *Scrooge*.

Scrooge's luckless clerk Bob Cratchit, his former partner Jacob Marley, and the three spirits have been played by the following:

Bob Cratchit

Donald Calthrop	*Scrooge* (Edwards)	GB, 35
Gene Lockhart	*A Christmas Carol* (Marin)	USA, 38
Mervyn Johns	*Scrooge* (Desmond Hurst)	GB, 50
David Collings	*Scrooge* (Neame)	GB, 70
Melvyn Hayes (voice only)	*A Christmas Carol* (Williams)	GB, 72
David Warner	*A Christmas Carol* (Donner)	GB, 84

Silent: George Bellamy (GB, 14) and John Cook in *The Right To Be Happy* (USA, 16).

Jacob Marley

Leo G. Carroll	*A Christmas Carol* (Marin)	USA, 38
Michael Hordern	*Scrooge* (Desmond Hurst)	GB, 50
Alec Guinness	*Scrooge* (Neame)	GB, 70
Michael Hordern (voice only)	*A Christmas Carol* (Williams)	GB, 72
Frank Finlay	*A Christmas Carol* (Donner)	GB, 84

(Not featured in the 1935 version)
Silent: Edward O'Neill (GB, 14) and Harry Carter in *The Right To Be Happy* (USA, 16).

The Spirit Of Christmas Present

Oscar Asche	*Scrooge* (Edwards)	GB, 35
Lionel Braham	*A Christmas Carol* (Marin)	USA, 38
Francis DeWolff	*Scrooge* (Desmond Hurst)	GB, 50
Kenneth More	*Scrooge* (Neame)	GB, 70
Edward Woodward	*A Christmas Carol* (Donner)	GB, 84

(Above) The only actor to portray both the young and old Scrooge on screen – Albert Finney in Ronald Neame's 1970 film musical *Scrooge;* (right) an animated skinflint, voiced by Alastair Sim, in Richard Williams' 25 minute featurette, *A Christmas Carol*

(Not voiced in Richard Williams' cartoon)
Silent: Windham Guise (GB, 14).

The Spirit Of Christmas Past

Marie Ney	*Scrooge* (Edwards)	GB, 35
Ann Rutherford	*A Christmas Carol* (Marin)	USA, 38
Michael Dolan	*Scrooge* (Desmond Hurst)	GB, 50
Edith Evans	*Scrooge* (Neame)	GB, 70
Angela Pleasence	*A Christmas Carol* (Donner)	GB, 84

(Not voiced in Richard Williams' cartoon)
Silent: Arthur Cullin (GB, 14).

The Spirit Of Christmas Yet To Come

C. V. France	*Scrooge* (Edwards)	GB, 35
D'Arcy Corrigan	*A Christmas Carol* (Marin)	USA, 38
C. Konarski	*Scrooge* (Desmond Hurst)	GB, 50
Paddy Stone	*Scrooge* (Neame)	GB, 70
Michael Carter	*A Christmas Carol* (Donner)	GB, 84

(Not voiced in Richard Williams' cartoon)
Silent:Assheton Tonge (GB, 14).

Al Pacino as Frank Serpico, the undercover cop who exposed corruption in the New York police force and was later isolated by his colleagues

Serpico, Frank [R]

Honest rookie cop who encountered corruption among his New York colleagues and was then isolated when he refused to 'go on the take' and accept bribes to keep his mouth shut. His true story and how he eventually testified before a Special Commission after being left to die by his colleagues during a narcotics raid, was told in Sidney Lumet's hard-hitting 1973 film. Al Pacino earned an Oscar nomination for his portrayal of the unconventional cop; three years later David Birney repeated the role for TV in the remake *Serpico: The Deadly Game*. The TV film led to a thirteen-part TV series also starring Birney.

Al Pacino	*Serpico* (Lumet)	USA, 73
David Birney	*Serpico: The Deadly Game* (Collins)	TVM/USA, 76

Note: Serpico gave his testimony in 1970 and then resigned from the force for self-imposed exile in Switzerland. Peter Maas' best-selling novel based on his career was published in 1973.

Shaft, John [F]

Black New York private-eye who proved in the 70s that investigating the activities of racketeers wasn't strictly the prerogative of the white man. A slick, glossy character who lives high, fights hard and has no illusions about his limitations: 'I'm not James Bond, just Sam Spade!'

Richard Roundtree	*Shaft* (Parks)	USA, 71
Richard Roundtree	*Shaft's Big Score* (Parks)	USA, 72
Richard Roundtree	*Shaft In Africa* (Guillermin)	USA, 73

Shane [F]

Jack Schaefer's legendary gunfighter who rides into a Wyoming valley, helps a group of homesteaders in their fight against cattlemen, then rides out again as mysteriously as he came. As personified by Alan Ladd, the most attractive and satisfying hero ever to appear in a Western and one of the few unrepeatable roles in all cinema. Schaefer's novel first appeared in print in 1949.

Alan Ladd	*Shane* (Stevens)	USA, 53

Note: David Carradine featured as Shane in a short-lived TV series of 1966; in the 1985 western *Pale Rider,* Clint Eastwood's 'Preacher', a stranger who rides into a mining community and helps the miners in their battle with the mine-owners, had strong affinities with Schaefer's Shane character.

Sharp, Becky 

Thackeray's famed golddigger from 'Vanity Fair' (1848); an unprincipled schemer whose sole ambition is to rise as high as she can in the world, no matter what the cost. Several silent portrayals, but nothing since 1935 when Miriam Hopkins indulged not only in Becky's ruthless traits, but also became the first major actress to appear in three-colour Technicolor!

Myrna Loy	*Vanity Fair* (Franklin)	USA, 32
Miriam Hopkins	*Becky Sharp* (Mamoulian)	USA, 35

Note: Helen Gardner (USA, 11), Minnie Madden Fiske (USA, 15) and Mabel Ballin (USA, 23) featured as Becky in silent productions.

She 

2000-year-old ruler of the mountain city of Kuma, an African sorceress of ethereal mystery and beauty who enjoys the luxury of life everlasting by walking into the flame of eternal youth. Known also as Ayesha, she was created by Rider Haggard in his 1887 novel 'She, A History Of Adventure'. Helen Gahagan's 1935 performance remains the most convincing interpretation, Ursula Andress' the most beautiful to look at.

Helen Gahagan	*She* (Pichel/Holden)	USA, 35
Ursula Andress	*She* (Day)	GB, 65
Olinka Berova	*The Vengeance Of She* (Owen)	GB, 68
Sandahl Bergman	*She* (Nesher)	It, 85

Note: There were at least five silent versions of *She,* among them a 1908 Edison adaptation in seven scenes. Marguerite Snow (11) and Valeska Suratt (17) featured as Ayesha in subsequent American adaptations, Alice Delysia (16) and Betty Blythe (25) in British versions.

In the 1968 sequel *The Vengeance Of She,* Olinka Berova features as the reincarnation of the ageless queen.

Shelley, Mary Wollstonecraft 

(1797–1851) The creator of 'Frankenstein' and a lady who shocked the literary world of the early nineteenth century with her depiction of what science might accomplish in the years that lay ahead. Portrayed briefly (in a prologue) by Elsa Lanchester in Whale's *The Bride Of Frankenstein* and more recently in a trio of films that centred on the haunted summer of 1816 when she stayed with her husband and Lord Byron at a villa on the shores of Lake Geneva and first conceived the idea for *Frankenstein.* Ken Russell's *Gothic* turned the famous occasion into a wild house party, the essential ingredients of which were drugs, nightmares and sexual orgies!

Elsa Lanchester	*The Bride Of Frankenstein* (Whale)	USA, 35
Natasha Richardson	*Gothic* (Russell)	GB, 86
Alice Krige	*The Haunted Summer* (Passer)	??? 88
Lizzy McInnerny	*Rowing With The Wind* (Suarez)	Spa, 88

Note: Elsa Lanchester doubled as the 'she monster' in *The Bride Of Frankenstein;* the poet Shelley has been played by Douglas Walton (35), Julian Sands in *Gothic,* Philip Anglim in *The Haunted Summer* and V. Pelka in *Rowing With The Wind.*

Sheppard, Jack 

(1702–24) The most celebrated thief and escape artist of eighteenth century London, five times caught and four times escaped. Number five proved to be one too many, however, and although a crowd of 200,000 turned up at Tyburn to witness another possible escape, they were disappointed and Sheppard finished up dangling at the end of a rope, aged 22. Not so in the movie, *Where's Jack?;* Tommy Steele escaped with all the panache of a Tom Jones!

Tommy Steele	*Where's Jack?* (Clavell)	GB, 69

Note: Jonathan Wild, notorious receiver of stolen goods and informer, was played in *Where's Jack?* by Stanley Baker. Wild, too, met his death by hanging, just a year after Sheppard.

Sheriff Of Nottingham, The R

Robin Hood's chief adversary, a hireling of the scheming Prince John and the most frequent 'loser' of the swashbuckling screen. Peter Finch allowed him a touch of engaging black villainy in Disney's 1952 Film; a tired Robert Shaw battled to the death with an ageing Sean Connery in Richard Lester's *Robin And Marian*.

Melville Cooper	*The Adventures Of Robin Hood* (Curtiz/Keighley) USA, 38
Lloyd Corrigan	*The Bandit Of Sherwood Forest* (Sherman/Levin) USA, 46
Tiny Stowe	*Tales Of Robin Hood* (Tinling) USA, 51
Peter Finch	*The Story Of Robin Hood And His Merrie Men* (Annakin) GB, 52
Peter Cushing	*Sword Of Sherwood Forest* (Fisher) GB, 60
John Arnatt	*A Challenge For Robin Hood* (Pennington Richards) GB, 67
Robert Shaw	*Robin And Marian* (Lester) USA, 76
Neil Hallett	*The Zany Adventures Of Robin Hood* (Austin) TVM/USA, 84

Note: Pat Buttram voiced the character in Disney's 1973 cartoon *Robin Hood;* Victor Buono featured as the modern equivalent in the gangster version, *Robin And The Seven Hoods* in 1964.

Alec B. Francis in *Robin Hood* (USA, 12), John Dillon in *Robin Hood And Maid Marian* (USA, 14) and William Lowrey in Allan Dwan's lavish *Robin Hood* of 1922, were among the actors to play the role on the silent screen.

Shomron, General Dan R

Commando head of the Israeli Rescue Operation at Entebbe Airport in June, 1976, when Arab guerillas hijacked a plane and held to ransom 250 prisoners. Portrayed on screen three times within 18 months of the actual event!

Harris Yulin	*Victory At Entebbe* (Chomsky) USA, 76
Charles Bronson	*Raid On Entebbe* (Kershner) USA, 76
Arik Lavi	*Entebbe: Operation Thunderbolt* (Golan) Isr, 77

Note: 'Yonni' Netanyahu, the young colonel who led the assault (and the only soldier killed in the action) was played by Richard Dreyfuss in Marvin Chomsky's film, Stephen Macht in that of Irvin Kershner, and Yehoram Gaon in the 1977 picture.

Shostakovitch, Dimitri R

(1906–75) One of the twentieth century's finest symphonists, a Russian composer who lived through the turbulent Stalin years and whose works were often criticized in his home country for their 'western decadence'. Official Soviet approval was restored with the performance of his famous Symphony No 5. His Seventh Symphony depicting the German siege of Leningrad was performed frequently by the Allies during World War II. Tony Palmer's two and a half hour TV film *Testimony* featured Ben Kingsley as Shostakovitch and drew both a compelling portrait of the composer and also of his uneasy relationship with Stalin.

Ben Kingsley	*Testimony* (Palmer) TVM/GB, 87

Shylock 

One of Shakespeare's most controversial characters, an avaricious Jewish moneylender who demands his famous 'pound of flesh' when a rival merchant in Venice, Antonio, fails to repay his debt. On screen, portrayed just once, in robust style by Michael Simon in a French/Italian co-production of 1952. Shakespeare's play 'The Merchant of Venice' was first performed in 1595.

Michael Simon	*The Merchant Of Venice* (Billon) Fra/It, 52

Note: William V. Ranous (USA, 08), Ermete Novelli (It, 10), William J. Bowman (USA, 12), Harry Baur (Fra, 13), Phillips Smalley (USA, 14), Matheson Lang (GB, 16) and Werner Krauss (Ger, 22) all played Shylock on the silent screen; in 1980 Warren Mitchell appeared as the moneylender in a BBC/-Time Life TV production of *The Merchant Of Venice.*

Silkwood, Karen 

(1946–74) For some the first nuclear martyr; a young laboratory technician who worked in a nuclear processing plant in Oklahoma where she became politically active after discovering the dangers and lack of safety precautions at the plant. She eventu-

Meryl Streep as Karen Silkwood, a worker in a plutonium plant in Oklahoma in the early '70s and who met a mysterious death in a 'one-car accident' after discovering X-rays that revealed flaws in fuel rods manufactured for nuclear reactors

ally became seriously contaminated with plutonium and met a mysterious death in a car accident while driving to provide inside information to a New York Times reporter. Her personal and professional struggles were filmed by Mike Nichols in the 1983 film *Silkwood* (once a Jane Fonda project) with Meryl Streep in the leading role.

Meryl Streep — *Silkwood* (Nichols) — USA, 83

Silver, Long John [F]

A pair of crutches, one leg and a parrot screaming 'pieces of eight' brought this roguish pirate to life in Robert Louis Stevenson's classic pirate novel 'Treasure Island' (1883). On screen, just a leer and a roll of Robert Newton's eyes were enough to create the same character in a more benevolent but no less effective vein. Wallace Beery, in Victor Fleming's 1934 film, was probably closer to Stevenson's original conception but, in truth, there have been two Long John Silvers, one belonging to Stevenson, one to Newton.

Wallace Beery — *Treasure Island* (Fleming) — USA, 34

Osip Abdulov — *Treasure Island* (Vaynstok) — USSR, 37

Robert Newton — *Treasure Island* (Haskin) — GB, 50

Robert Newton — *Long John Silver* (Haskin) — USA, 54

Boris Andreyev — *Treasure Island* (Bazylev) — USSR, 71

Orson Welles — *Treasure Island* (Hough) — GB/Fra/W.Ger/Spa, 72

Note: Addison Rothermel (12) and Charles Ogle (20) both portrayed Silver on the silent screen; on TV Brian Blessed played the pirate in the sequel *Return To Treasure Island* (86) and Anthony Quinn featured as the Silver character in *Space Island* (It, 87) a sci-fi reworking of Stevenson's tale, set in the year 2300 and with the island being replaced by a planet.

The other major characters in Stevenson's pirate adventure include the boy Jim Hawkins who discovers the treasure map and through whose eyes the story is told, his companions Dr Livesey and Squire Trelawney, the castaway Ben Gunn and the pirates Billy Bones, Israel Hands and Blind Pew. They have appeared in most film versions of the story and have been played as follows:

Jim Hawkins

Jackie Cooper	*Treasure Island* (Fleming)	USA, 34
Bobby Driscoll	*Treasure Island* (Haskin)	GB, 50
Kit Taylor	*Long John Silver* (Haskin)	USA, 54
Aare Laanemets	*Treasure Island* (Bazylev)	USSR, 71
Kim Burfield	*Treasure Island* (Hough)	GB/Fra/W.Ger/Spa, 72

Silent: Shirley Mason (20)

Dr Livesey

Otto Kruger	*Treasure Island* (Fleming)	USA, 34
Denis O'Dea	*Treasure Island* (Haskin)	GB, 50
L. Norika	*Treasure Island* (Bazylev)	USSR, 71
Angel Del Pozo	*Treasure Island* (Hough)	GB/Fra/W.Ger/Spa, 72

Silent: Charles Hill Mailes (20)

Squire Trelawney

Nigel Bruce	*Treasure Island* (Fleming)	USA, 34
Walter Fitzgerald	*Treasure Island* (Haskin)	GB, 50
A. Massulis	*Treasure Island* (Bazylev)	USSR, 71
Walter Slezak	*Treasure Island* (Hough)	GB/Fra/W.Ger/Spa, 72

Silent: Sydney Dean (20)

Ben Gunn

Lewis Stone	*Treasure Island* (Fleming)	USA, 34
Geoffrey Wilkinson	*Treasure Island* (Haskin)	GB, 50
Jean Lefebvre	*Treasure Island* (Hough)	GB/Fra/W.Ger/Spa, 72

Billy Bones

Lionel Barrymore	*Treasure Island* (Fleming)	USA, 34
Finlay Currie	*Treasure Island* (Haskin)	GB, 50
Lionel Stander	*Treasure Island* (Hough)	GB/Fra/W.Ger/Spa, 72

Silent: Al Filson (20)

Israel Hands

Douglass Dumbrille	*Treasure Island* (Fleming)	USA, 34
Geoffrey Keen	*Treasure Island* (Haskin)	GB, 50
Rodney Taylor	*Long John Silver* (Haskin)	USA, 54
A. Pikialis	*Treasure Island* (Bazylev)	USSR, 71
Aldo Sambrell	*Treasure Island* (Hough)	GB/Fra/W.Ger/Spa, 72

Silent: Joseph Singleton (20)

Blind Pew

William V. Mong	*Treasure Island* (Fleming)	USA, 34
John Laurie	*Treasure Island* (Haskin)	GB, 50
Paul Muller	*Treasure Island* (Hough)	GB/Fra/W.Ger/Spa, 72

Silent: Lon Chaney (20)

Sinbad F

Arabian Nights adventurer, a favourite tongue-in-cheek swashbuckler of the 40s and 50s but somewhat overshadowed in more recent years by the terrifying Ray Harryhausen monsters he meets on his travels. Six-armed statues that come to life, sword-fighting skeletons and one-eyed Centaurs tend to remain in the memory longer than Messrs John Phillip Law and Patrick Wayne.

Shemp Howard	*Arabian Nights* (Rawlins)	USA, 42
Douglas Fairbanks, Jr	*Sinbad The Sailor* (Wallace)	USA, 47

Sebastian Cabot	*Babes In Bagdad* (Ulmer) USA, 52
Lon Chaney, Jr	*The Thief Of Damascus* (Jason) USA, 52
Dale Robertson	*Son Of Sinbad* (Tetzlaff) USA, 55
Gene Kelly	*The Magic Lamp* (Kelly) GB, 56
Kerwin Mathews	*The Seventh Voyage Of Sinbad* (Juran) USA, 58
Edward Stolar	*The Magic Voyage Of Sinbad* (Posco) USSR, 62
Guy Williams	*Captain Sinbad* (Haskin) USA, 63
Toshiro Mifune	*The Lost World Of Sinbad* (Taniguchi) Jap, 63
John Phillip Law	*The Golden Voyage Of Sinbad* (Hessler) GB, 74
Patrick Wayne	*Sinbad And The Eye Of The Tiger* (Wanamaker) GB, 77

Note: Gene Kelly appeared in the animated Sinbad The Sailor sequence from *The Magic Lamp*. He danced to the music of Rimsky Korsakov.

Sitting Bull [R]

(*c.* 1835–90) Chief of the Sioux Indians and the man who planned the destruction of Custer and his command at the Little Big Horn in 1876. Did not, as is sometimes believed, take part in the Custer massacre (the attack was led by Crazy Horse and Gaul) but did finish up a decade later as a celebrity of a different kind – as an attraction in Buffalo Bill's Wild West Show. Played twice on screen by J. Carrol Naish.

Chief Thunder Bird	*Annie Oakley* (Stevens) USA, 35
J. Carrol Naish	*Annie Get Your Gun* (Sidney) USA, 50
Michael Granger	*Fort Vengeance* (Selander) USA, 53
J. Carrol Naish	*Sitting Bull* (Salkow) USA, 54
John War Eagle	*Tonka* (Foster) USA, 58
Michael Pate	*The Great Sioux Massacre* (Salkow) USA, 65
Frank Kaquitts	*Buffalo Bill And The Indians, or Sitting Bull's History Lesson* (Altman) USA, 76

Note: Howling Wolf played the Indian chief in the 1936 serial *Custer's Last Stand;* on the silent screen Noble Johnson appeared as Sitting Bull in *The Flaming Frontier* (USA, 26).

Smiley, George [F]

The supreme spymaster of modern times; the central figure in many of John Le Carré's novels and a man who has frequently to grapple with the all-important question: how is it possible to defend a western society supposedly based on human values with inhuman methods? Alec Guinness, blinking and owl-like behind horn-rimmed spectacles has made the figure world-famous through his portrayals on TV; Rupert Davies, seen but briefly in the film *The Spy Who Came In From The Cold* and James Mason (renamed Charles Dobbs) in *The Deadly Affair,* had earlier played Smiley on the big screen.

Rupert Davies	*The Spy Who Came In From The Cold* (Ritt) GB, 65
James Mason	*The Deadly Affair* (Lumet) GB, 66

Note: Guinness appeared as Smiley in the two lengthy BBC serializations of *Tinker, Tailor, Soldier, Spy* (79) and *Smiley's People* (82) in which he first uncovers a mole betraying the British spy circus to the Russians and then ultimately tracks down his Russian counterpart Karla. Smiley is said to be based on Le Carre's old history tutor at Oxford, Vivian Green.

Smith, Cora 

The blonde femme fatale of James M. Cain's 1934 novel 'The Postman Always Rings Twice'; a sultry platinum schemer who seduces a wandering hobo and then talks him into murdering her husband, the middle-aged Greek owner of a roadside restaurant. A deadly lady of the Depression, she has been played four times on screen, most memorably by a smouldering Lana Turner in 1946, most realistically by Jessica Lange in Bob Rafelson's 1981 remake.

Corinne Luchaire	*Le Dernier Tournant* (Chenal) Fra, 39
Clara Calamai	*Ossessione* (Visconti) It, 42
Lana Turner	*The Postman Always Rings Twice* (Garnett) USA, 46
Jessica Lange	*The Postman Always Rings Twice* (Rafelson) USA, 81

Jessica Lange as Cora Smith and Jack Nicholson as the Depression drifter she seduces into murdering her elderly Greek husband. A scene from the 1981 version of James M. Cain's seamy novel, *The Postman Always Knocks Twice,* directed by Bob Rafelson and scripted by David Mamet

Smith, Madeleine

R

(1836–1928) Wealthy Scottish girl, the daughter of a prosperous member of the Scottish gentry, who was tried for the murder of her low-bred suitor in Glasgow during the 1850s. She was acquitted, but doubts about her guilt remained for the rest of her life. David Lean's stylish study of her ill-fated romance and trial remains one of his most serious and underrated films.

Ann Todd	*Madeleine* (Lean)	GB, 50

Smith, Nevada

F

One of Harold Robbins' more enduring creations; a former outlaw turned movie star who acts as mentor and confidante to the Howard Hughes styled studio head and plane manufacturer in 'The Carpetbaggers'. Alan Ladd, in his last film role, played Smith in his Hollywood days in the 1964 version of Robbins' novel, Steve McQueen essayed his earlier adventures in the Old West where he hunts down and executes the three killers who have murdered his parents.

Alan Ladd	*The Carpetbaggers* (Dmytryk)	USA, 64
Steve McQueen	*Nevada Smith* (Hathaway)	USA, 66

Note: The character of Nevada Smith was said to be an amalgam of the B movie cowboy heroes Tom Mix and Ken Maynard; in 1975 Cliff Potts starred as the outlaw in the routine TV movie, *Nevada Smith,* directed by Gordon Douglas.

Smith, Winston F

The courageous hero of George Orwell's horrific satire *1984;* a 'history reviser' who rebels against life in a futuristic totalitarian society in which 'Big Brother' is constantly on watch and truth has been replaced by propaganda. Played twice on the big screen – in 1955 by American Edmond O'Brien and more recently by John Hurt in Michael Radford's bleak adaptation, shot in London's East End and decaying docklands in the exact weeks of the year imagined in the novel.

Edmond O'Brien	*1984*	(Anderson)	GB, 55
John Hurt	*1984*	(Radford)	GB, 84

Note: O'Brien, the interrogator who tortures Smith into submission and admitting that 'two and two make five' has been played by Michael Redgrave (55) and, in his last film role, Richard Burton (84). Burton was signed just two weeks before he was due on set, Sean Connery, Rod Steiger, Paul Scofield and Jason Robards all having refused the role because of previous commitments. In the famous BBC TV version of December, 1954 Peter Cushing played Smith and André Morrell featured as O'Brien.

Smith, Perry and Hickock, Dick R

Two young ex-cons who, for no apparent reason, shot a Kansas farmer and his family in November, 1959, and later became the central subjects of Truman Capote's book 'In Cold Blood', which probed into the reasons behind the mystifying slaughter. Richard Brooks' semi-documentary film followed the lives of the two men from the time of the killing to their arrest, appeals and execution in April, 1965.

Robert Blake (Perry Smith) — *In Cold Blood*
Scott Wilson (Dick Hickock) — (Brooks) USA, 67

Smith, Stevie R

(1902–71) Depressive British poet and author whose uneventful suburban life and devotion to her maiden aunt were examined in a straight film adaptation of Hugh Whitemore's popular stage play. The film, set almost exclusively in a suburban living room, contains excerpts from Smith's poetic works.

Glenda Jackson	*Stevie*	(Enders)	GB, 78

Solo, Napoleon F

Smooth-talking American agent for the international organization UNCLE (United Network Command For Law and Enforcement) in its never-ending battle against terrorism and subversion. Accompanied in all his adventures by his Russian sidekick Illya Kuryakin (David McCallum) and permanently under the supervision of benign chief, Mr Waverly (Leo G. Carroll). All eight film releases were spinoffs from material used in MGM's four-year TV series.

Robert Vaughn	*To Trap A Spy*	(Medford)	USA, 65
Robert Vaughn	*The Spy With My Face*	(Newland)	USA, 66
Robert Vaughn	*One Of Our Spies Is Missing*	(Hallenbeck)	USA, 66
Robert Vaughn	*One Spy Too Many*	(Sargent)	USA, 66
Robert Vaughn	*The Spy In The Green Hat*	(Sargent)	USA, 67
Robert Vaughn	*The Karate Killers*	(Shear)	USA, 67
Robert Vaughn	*The Helicopter Spies*	(Sagal)	USA, 68
Robert Vaughn	*How To Steal The World*	(Roley)	USA, 68

Note: Robert Vaughn and David McCallum reprised their roles in Ray Austin's TV film, *The Return Of The Man From Uncle* (83).

Sousa, John Philip R

(1854–1932) American composer and military bandmaster. Known as The March King, he composed over 100 popular marches including 'Semper Fidelis', 'The Washington Post' and 'Stars And Stripes Forever', all of which were included in Fox's 1952 biography with Clifton Webb.

Clifton Webb	*Stars And Stripes Forever*	(Koster)	USA, 52

Spade, Sam F

Tough private-eye, as ruthless with females ('When you're slapped you'll take it and like it') as with the

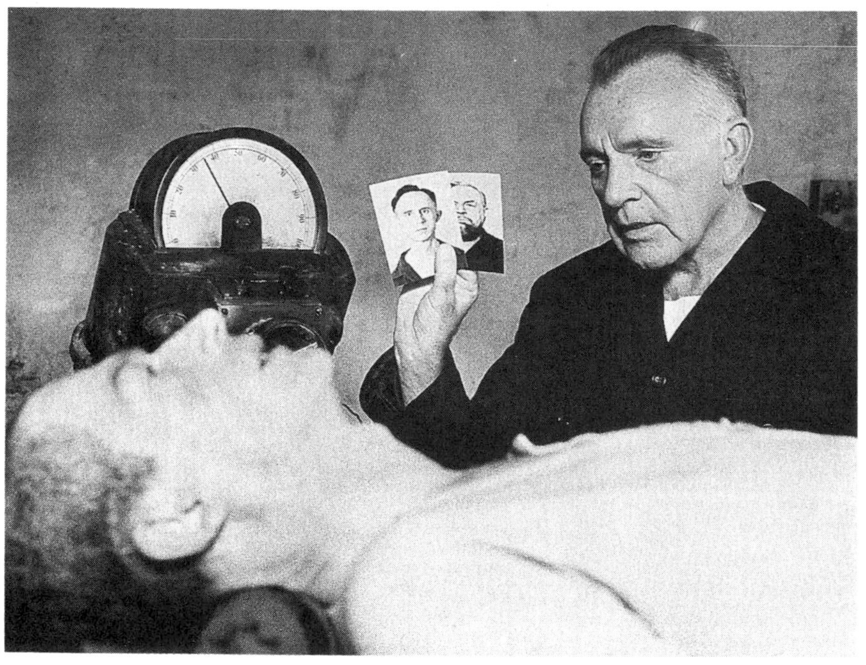

Winston Smith, the history revisor in George Orwell's prophetic novel of life in a totalitarian state, as portrayed by Edmond O'Brien (above) and John Hurt (left) in the two film versions made fom the novel *1984*. Enjoying their moments of triumph—Michael Redgrave and Richard Burton

hoods who get in his way. The central figure in Dashiell Hammett's 1930 novel 'The Maltese Falcon', he is cynical, mercenary and very different, despite some views to the contrary, to Chandler's subsequent Philip Marlowe. Forever associated with Humphrey Bogart even though Bogie was not the first choice for the role, George Raft having turned the part down in 1941. George Segal played Sam Spade Jr in the spoof sequel *The Black Bird* in 1975.

Ricardo Cortez	*The Maltese Falcon* (Del Ruth)	USA, 31
Warren William	*Satan Met A Lady* (Dieterle)	USA, 36
Humphrey Bogart	*The Maltese Falcon* (Huston)	USA, 41

Note: In William Dieterle's 1936 version the character was renamed Ted Shayne.

Sparrow, Simon

F

The hero of Richard Gordon's popular series of comedy 'Doctor' books. Began his screen career in 1954 as a student at St Swithin's Hospital then continued as a fully-fledged doctor in three subsequent movies. Romantic and anatomical misadventures in all four!

Dirk Bogarde	*Doctor In The House* (Thomas)	GB, 54
Dirk Bogarde	*Doctor At Sea* (Thomas)	GB, 55
Dirk Bogarde	*Doctor At Large* (Thomas)	GB, 57
Dirk Bogarde	*Doctor In Distress* (Thomas)	GB, 63

Note: Sparrow featured in only four of the 'Doctor' movies. Michael Craig starred as Dr Richard Hare in *Doctor In Love* (60), Leslie Phillips as Gaston Grimsdyke and Simon Burke in the last two in the series *Doctor In Clover* (65) and *Doctor In Trouble* (70).

Spartacus

R

(*d.* 71 BC) Thracian slave and gladiator who led a rebellion of slaves during the last decades of the tyrannical Roman republic. Finally defeated and killed by Crassus, he was the central figure in Howard Fast's historical novel of 1951, turned into a memorable epic a decade later by Stanley Kubrick.

Massimo Girotti	*Spartacus, The Gladiator* (Freda)	It, 53
Kirk Douglas	*Spartacus* (Kubrick)	USA, 60

Note: Steve Reeves featured as the *Son Of Spartacus,* an Italian film directed in 1962 by Sergio Corbucci.

Spock, Mr

F

Part human/part Vulcan crew member of the spaceship *U.S.S. Enterprise,* noted for his vast scientific knowledge, lack of humour and sharp pointed ears. A small screen hero of the late 60s when he was played by Leonard Nimoy, he was later resurrected, along with the rest of the crew, when the cinema turned its attention to the *Star Trek* characters in 1979. To-date he has helped Kirk and company combat a lethal force field headed towards the Earth, battle with the 'Space Seed' villain Khan, and save the Earth from the future with the help of humpbacked whales! Along the way he has also been rescued in the nick of time from the disintegrating planet Genesis.

Leonard Nimoy	*Star Trek – The Motion Picture* (Wise)	USA, 79
Leonard Nimoy	*Star Trek II: The Wrath Of Khan* (Meyer)	USA, 82
Leonard Nimoy	*Star Trek III: The Search For Spock* (Nimoy)	USA, 84
Leonard Nimoy	*Star Trek IV: The Voyage Home* (Nimoy)	USA, 86

Note: The other key members of the spacecrew – Captain, subsequently Admiral Kirk and Dr 'Bones' McCoy – have been played in all four movies by their TV originators, William Shatner and DeForrest Kelley. The TV series ran for 78 episodes from 1966 to 1969. In 1987 a new TV series with a crew minus Spock, Kirk and the others was launched by executive producer Gene Rodenberry. In command in the new series: the bald-headed Patrick Stewart as Captain Jean-Luc Picard and first officer William Riker (Jonathan Frakes).

Spratt, Sir Lancelot

F

Bombastic head surgeon of Richard Gordon's 'Doctor' books, played to the hilt by James Robertson Justice in the popular film series of the 50s and 60s. A man whose bark is often worse than his bite, although the bark is frequently worth listening to: 'Hang on to your swabs gentlemen. You can cut the patient's throat while he is under an anaesthetic and nobody will mind. But if you leave anything inside you will be in the Sunday papers in no time!'

James Robertson Justice	*Doctor In The House* (Thomas) GB, 54
James Robertson Justice	*Doctor At Sea* (Thomas) GB, 55
James Robertson Justice	*Doctor At Large* (Thomas) GB, 57
James Robertson Justice	*Doctor In Love* (Thomas) GB, 60
James Robertson Justice	*Doctor In Distress* (Thomas) GB, 63
James Robertson Justice	*Doctor In Clover* (Thomas) GB, 65
James Robertson Justice	*Doctor In Trouble* (Thomas) GB, 70

Note: In *Doctor At Sea* Justice featured not as Sir Lancelot but as his naval equivalent, the blustering Captain Hogg.

Stalin, Josef

R

(1879–1953) Soviet dictator who took over supreme power after the death of Lenin in 1924 and ruled Russia for the next 30 years. Portrayed on screen most often by M. Gelovani, a Russian actor-director who between 1937 and 1953 made a successful career out of playing this one role.

I. Golshtab	*Lenin In October* (Romm) USSR, 37
M. Gelovani	*The Man With A Gun* (Yutkevich) USSR, 38
M. Gelovani	*Great Dawn* (Chiaureli) USSR, 38
M. Gelovani	*Lenin in 1918* (Romm) USSR, 39
M. Gelovani	*The Vyborg Side* (Kozintsev/Trauberg) USSR, 39
M. Gelovani	*Manhood* (Kalatozov) USSR, 39
M. Gelovani	*Fortress On The Volga* (Ginsburg) USSR, 42
M. Gelovani	*Defence Of Tsaritsin* (Vasiliev) USSR, 42
Manart Kippen	*Mission To Moscow* (Curtiz) USA, 43
M. Gelovani	*The Vow* (Chiaureli) USSR, 46
M. Gelovani	*Light Over Russia* (Yutkevich) USSR, 47
M. Gelovani	*The Fall Of Berlin* (Chiaureli) USSR, 49
A. Dieky	*The Battle Of Stalingrad* (Petrov) USSR, 50
M. Gelovani	*The Unforgettable Year, 1919* (Chiaureli) USSR, 52
Maurice Manson	*The Girl In The Kremlin* (Birdwell) USA, 57
A. Kobaladze	*In The October Days* (Vasiliev) USSR, 58
Buhuti Zakariadze	*The Great Battle* (Ozerov) USSR/Pol/Yug/E.Ger/It, 69
Saul Katz	*Why Russians Are Revolting* (Sullivan) USA, 70
James Hazeldine	*Nicholas And Alexandra* (Schaffner) USA, 71

Note: Nehemiah Persoff in *F.D.R.–The Last Year* (80) and Anatoly Shaginyan in *The Winds Of War* (83) have both played Stalin on the TV screen.

Stanley, Sir Henry Morton

R

(1841-1904) British explorer and journalist who was commissioned by his newspaper, The New York Herald, to make a hazardous expedition into Central Africa to find David Livingstone. In 1871 he did just that and supposedly uttered the immortal words, 'Dr Livingstone, I presume'. A suitably determined Spencer Tracy spoke them on screen in Henry King's full scale adventure movie, *Stanley And Livingstone*.

Hugh McDermott	*David Livingstone* (Fitzpatrick) GB, 36
Spencer Tracy	*Stanley And Livingstone* (Henry King) USA, 39

Note: Henry Walton featured in the role in M. A. Wetherell's silent film *Livingstone* (GB, 25).

Starr, Belle

R

(1848–89) Another of the Wild West's so-called glamorous heroines, in reality no more than a hard-bitten horse stealer from Missouri, but in Hollywood's never-never land, a beauty, first in the shape of Gene Tierney and then in the even more impressive physique of Jane Russell. Belle (real name Myra Belle Shirley) met her death at the hands of a bushwhacker after enjoying violent careers with Cole Younger in Texas and her own rustling gang in Oklahoma. Like Buffalo Bill, she was given legendary acclaim through the newspaper accounts of her exploits.

Gene Tierney	*Belle Starr* (Cummings) USA, 41

Isabel Jewell	*Badman's Territory* (Whelan)	USA, 46
Isabel Jewell	*Belle Starr's Daughter* (Selander)	USA, 48
Jane Russell	*Montana Belle* (Dwan)	USA, 52
Merry Anders	*Young Jesse James* (Claxton)	USA, 60
Sally Starr	*The Outlaws Is Coming* (Maurer)	USA, 65
Pat Quinn	*Zachariah* (Englund)	USA, 71
Pamela Reed	*The Long Riders* (Hill)	USA, 80

Note: Betty Compson featured as Belle Starr in the 1929 silent *Court Martial;* Elizabeth Montgomery appeared as the outlaw in John Alonzo's 1980 TV Movie *Belle Starr* (scripted by James Lee Barrett) which dealt with the final days in the life of the bandit queen.

Stauffenberg, Colonel Claus von [R]

(1907–44) Not a name that immediately springs to mind, but a key member of the July plot of 1944 when some German officers attempted to assassinate Hitler and bring to an end World War II. Von Stauffenberg was the man selected to plant the bomb (in a suitcase) next to the Führer during a conference. The bomb exploded but succeeded only in injuring Hitler. The officers in the plot were summarily executed, including von Stauffenberg who was shot in a courtyard. The two German films of 1955 concentrated on the assassination attempt in detail.

Eduard Franz	*The Desert Fox* (Hathaway)	USA, 51
Bernhard Wicki	*Es Geschah Am 20. Juli* (Pabst)	Ger, 55
Wolfgang Preiss	*Der 20 Juli* (Harnack)	Ger, 55
William Sargent	*Hitler* (Heisler)	USA, 62
Gerard Buhr	*The Night Of The Generals* (Litvak)	Fra/GB, 66

Stavisky, Serge Alexandre [R]

(*c.* 1886–1934) French swindler whose huge bond frauds in Paris in the 30s made sensational headlines and resulted in the exposure of widespread corruption in French government circles. Stavisky's life, motives and suicide were the subject of a 1974 film by Alain Resnais.

Jean-Paul Belmondo	*Stavisky* (Resnais)	Fra/It, 74

Strangelove, Dr [F]

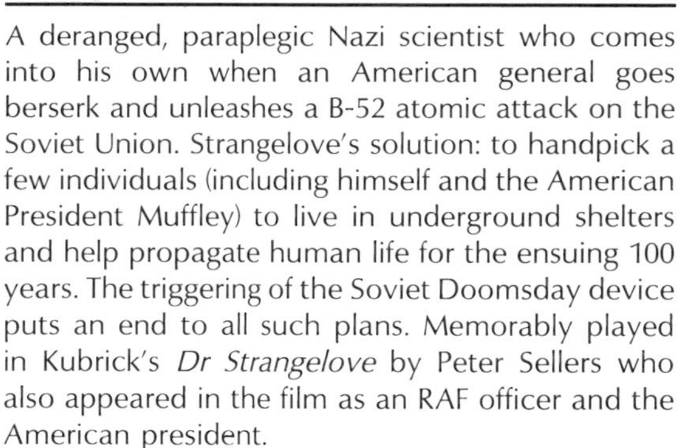
A deranged, paraplegic Nazi scientist who comes into his own when an American general goes berserk and unleashes a B-52 atomic attack on the Soviet Union. Strangelove's solution: to handpick a few individuals (including himself and the American President Muffley) to live in underground shelters and help propagate human life for the ensuing 100 years. The triggering of the Soviet Doomsday device puts an end to all such plans. Memorably played in Kubrick's *Dr Strangelove* by Peter Sellers who also appeared in the film as an RAF officer and the American president.

Peter Sellers	*Dr Strangelove: Or How I Learned To Stop Worrying And Love The Bomb* (Kubrick)	GB, 64

Note: Sellers was also to have played a fourth role, that of the Texas pilot who releases the Bomb, but a cracked ankle prevented him from making it a quartet of performances. Kubrick's film derived from the dramatic novel 'Two Hours To Doom' (58) – known as 'Red Alert' in the United States – by former air force officer Peter George. George also wrote 'Commander I' (65) which followed the desperate struggles of a group of people left alive after a nuclear war. He committed suicide in 1966.

Stratten, Dorothy [R]

A Canadian 'Playboy Centrefold' who looked all set for the big time after appearing in her one starring role in *They All Laughed* but was then murdered by her estranged husband Paul Snider who had used her as his meal ticket to get to Hollywood. Director Bob Fosse turned her tragic tale into a modern day horror story about exploitation, basing his film on Teresa Carpenter's Pulitzer Prize winning article in 'The Village Voice'. Mariel Hemingway featured as the ill-fated Stratten just two years after Jamie Lee Curtis had played her in the TV movie *Death Of A Centrefold.*

Jamie Lee Curtis	*Death Of A Centrefold: The Dorothy Stratten Story* (Beaumont)	TVM/USA, 81
Mariel Hemingway	*Star 80* (Fosse)	USA, 83

Note: Paul Snider, Stratten's sleazy hustler husband, was played by Eric Roberts in Fosse's film and Bruce Weitz in the TV Movie; Mitchell Ryan (81) and Cliff Robertson (83) featured as playboy boss Hugh Heffner.

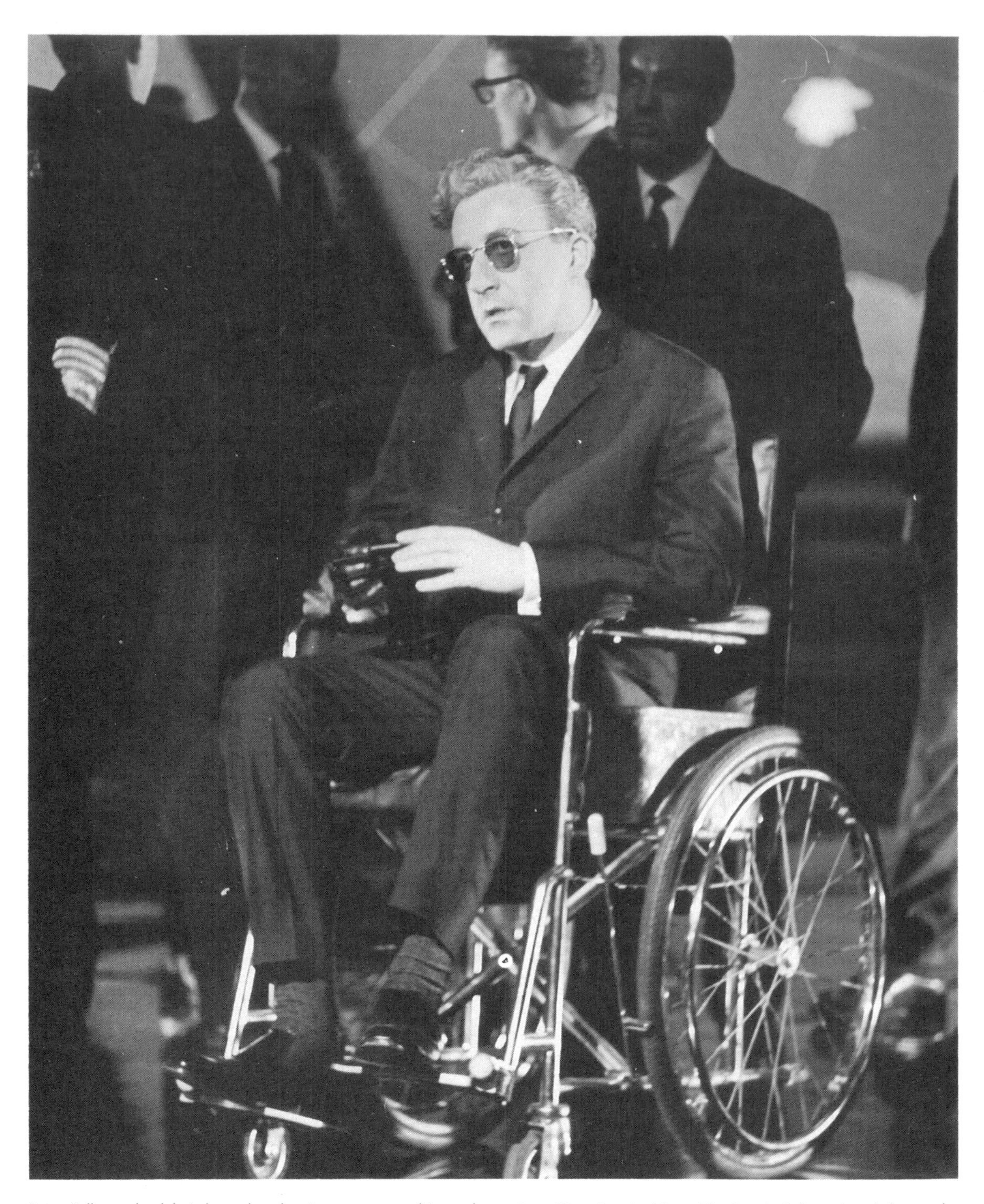

Peter Sellers, wheelchair bound and trying to prevent his steel hand from rising to give a Hitler salute, in Stanley Kubrick's brilliant black comedy *Dr Strangelove: Or How I Learned To Stop Worrying And Love The Bomb*. Sellers played three roles in the film—the deranged German scientist of the title, the American president and an RAF officer

Strauss, Johann, Jr R

(1825–99) Austrian composer-conductor whose beautiful waltzes reflected the romance and gaiety of nineteenth century Vienna. Fernand Gravet starred in the most lavish account of his life, Horst Buchholz in the most vulgar and Oliver Tobias in the most recent. In all film biographies, the music has won hands down!

Gustav Fröhlich	*So lang noch ein Walzer von Strauss erklingt* (Conrad Wiene) Ger, 31
Esmond Knight	*Waltzes From Vienna* (Hitchcock) GB, 34
Anton Walbrook	*Waltztime In Vienna* (Berger) Ger, 34
Fernand Gravet	*The Great Waltz* (Duvivier) USA, 38
Fred Liewehr	*Unsterbliche Walzer* (Emo) Ger, 39
Kerwin Mathews	*The Waltz King* (Previn) USA, 63
Horst Buchholz	*The Great Waltz* (Stone) USA, 72
Oliver Tobias	*Johann Strauss, The King Without A Crown* (Antel) Aust/Hung, 88

Note: Johann Strauss Sr has been played by Hans Junkermann in Conrad Wiene's 1931 film, Edmund Gwenn in *Waltzes From Vienna* (34), Paul Horbiger in *Unsterbliche Walzer* (39), Anton Walbrook in *Vienna Waltzes* (Austria, 51), Brian Aherne in *The Waltz King* (63) and Nigel Patrick in *The Great Waltz* (72).

Stroud, Robert 

The famous 'Birdman Of Alcatraz' who spent most of his adult life in American prisons, using his long solitary confinement to become a renowned world authority on bird-life. One of the most complex of American criminals, he was originally convicted of manslaughter when he killed a man in a fight over a dance-hall girl and was later responsible for killing a prison guard. He died in prison in 1963, aged 76. Burt Lancaster, in a restrained, moving performance, played him on film.

Burt Lancaster	*Birdman Of Alcatraz* (Frankenheimer) USA, 62

Note: Art Carney featured as Stroud in Paul Krasny's 1980 TV film, *Alcatraz: The Whole Shocking Story.*

Burt Lancaster as Robert Stroud, the famous 'Birdman of Alcatraz' who, during his long years in prison became a world-renowned authority on bird life

Student Prince, The 

Royal hero of the 1924 operetta by Sigmund Romberg, a young German prince who enjoys a fleeting romance with a tavern waitress whilst finishing his education at Heidelberg University. Strictly a hero of his time, but retaining a certain amount of schmaltzy glamour through the Romberg melodies, 'Deep In My Heart', 'Serenade' and 'The Drinking Song'. Edmund Purdom replaced an overweight Mario Lanza in the 1954 version, although Lanza recorded the songs.

Edmund Purdom	*The Student Prince* (Thorpe) USA, 54
Christian Wolff	*Alt-Heidelberg* (Marischka) Ger, 59

Note: The three silent versions of the story were derived from the non-musical play 'Old Heidelberg' (1902) by Rudolf Bleichman, the source of the Romberg operetta. Wallace Reid in *Old Heidelberg* (USA, 15), Paul Hartmann in *The Student Prince* (Ger, 23) and Ramon Novarro in *The Student Prince In Old Heidelberg* (USA, 27) all featured as Prince Karl Heinrich.

Sullivan, John L. [R]

(1858–1918) One of the great heavyweight champions in American boxing history, a man who weighed in at 200 lbs and began his career when bare knuckle fighting was still the name of the game. His massive contest with Jim Corbett was the highlight of Raoul Walsh's *Gentleman Jim;* his rise to the top and subsequent fall from grace the subject of a not ineffective biography, *The Great John L.*

George Walsh	*The Bowery* (Walsh)	USA, 34
Bill Hoolahahn	*Diamond Jim* (Sutherland)	USA, 35
John Kelly	*My Gal Sal* (Cummings)	USA, 42
Ward Bond	*Gentleman Jim* (Walsh)	USA, 42
Greg McClure	*The Great John L.* (Tuttle)	USA, 45

Sundance Kid, The [R]

Fast-shooting member of Butch Cassidy's outlaw gang, 'The Wild Bunch'. Figured in several routine westerns of the 40s and 50s before reaching heroic stature in the now classic *Butch Cassidy and The Sundance Kid.* Historical photographs reveal Sundance to be far removed from the golden-haired Robert Redford, but his relationship with the non-violent Butch and schoolteacher Etta Place is an intriguing one and was retold with great historical accuracy by George Roy Hill. Sundance, who supposedly died in Bolivia in 1908, was christened Harry Longbaugh.

Arthur Kennedy	*Cheyenne* (Walsh)	USA, 47
Robert Ryan	*Return Of The Badmen* (Enright)	USA, 48

Robert Redford in action as 'Sundance', the role that made him a superstar in George Roy Hill's *Butch Cassidy And The Sundance Kid.* The film traced the last months of the two outlaws who robbed banks in the turn-of-the-century West and finished their career violently in the jungles of Bolivia!

Ian MacDonald	*The Texas Rangers*	(Karlson)	USA, 51
William Bishop	*Wyoming Renegades*	(Sears)	USA, 55
Scott Brady	*The Maverick Queen*	(Kane)	USA, 56
Alan Hale, Jr.	*The Three Outlaws*	(Newfield)	USA, 56
Russell Johnson	*Badman's Country*	(Sears)	USA, 58
Robert Redford	*Butch Cassidy And The Sundance Kid*	(Hill)	USA, 69
William Katt	*Butch And Sundance – The Early Days*	(Lester)	USA, 79

Note: John Davis Chandler appeared as The Sundance Kid in *Return Of The Gunfighter*, a TV movie made by James Neilson in 1967; Etta Place, the wife of Sundance, played by Katharine Ross in George Roy Hill's 1969 film, has been portrayed by Elizabeth Montgomery in *Mrs Sundance* (Chomsky, 73) and again by Ross in *Wanted, The Sundance Woman* (Philips, 76).

Superman

F

The flying strongman from the planet Krypton – an ineffectual newspaper reporter (Clark Kent) by day, a red-caped heroic man of steel by night. The subject of several early film cartoons, two serials, a 50s movie and a TV series, before reaching big budget super-status in Richard Donner's 1978 film. First appeared in print in a comic strip in 'Action Comics' in 1938.

Kirk Alyn	*Superman*	(Bennet/Carr)	USA, 48
Kirk Alyn	*Atom Man vs Superman*	(Bennet)	USA, 50
George Reeves	*Superman And the Mole Men*	(Sholem)	USA, 51
Christopher Reeve	*Superman*	(Donner)	GB, 78
Christopher Reeve	*Superman II*	(Donner)	GB, 80
Christopher Reeve	*Superman III*	(Lester)	GB, 83
Christopher Reeve	*Superman IV: The Quest For Peace*	(Furie)	USA, 87

Note: Both films starring Kirk Alyn were 15-episode Columbia serials; George Reeves later went on to play Superman in a long-running TV series (53–57).

Lois Lane, girl friend of Clark Kent on The Daily Planet, was played by Noel Neill in the two serials, Phyllis Coates in *Superman And The Mole Men*, and Margot Kidder in the recent spectaculars starring Christopher Reeve. In 1984 Helen Slater featured as Superman's cousin Kara/Linda Lee in Jeannot Szwarc's *Supergirl* (GB).

Svengali

Sinister Hungarian musician who uses his strange hypnotic powers to transform a beautiful young artist's model into a great singing star. Created by George du Maurier in his 1894 novel 'Trilby' and the central figure in no fewer than seven screen adaptations of the story. Donald Wolfit replaced Robert Newton in the most recent version when the latter walked out halfway through production.

John Barrymore	*Svengali*	(Mayo)	USA, 31
Donald Wolfit	*Svengali*	(Langley)	GB, 54

Note: Viggo Larsen was the first silent screen Svengali in the Danish film of 1908. Sir Herbert Beerbohm Tree (GB, 14), Wilton Lackaye (USA, 15), Arthur Edmund Carew (USA, 23) and Paul Wegener (Ger, 27) all played the role on the silent screen. The story was reworked and updated for TV in 1983 (director: Anthony Harvey) when Peter O'Toole appeared as a faded musical performer who takes a young rock singer (Jodie Foster) and turns her into a star.

Syn, Dr

Eighteenth century vicar, leader of smuggling activities in the small English coastal village of Dymchurch. A creation of novelists Russell Thorndike and William Buchanan ('Christopher Syn'), he has been portrayed three times on screen, Peter Cushing's performance differing from the others in that the character was renamed Dr Blyss, a cover name for the notorious pirate Captain Clegg.

George Arliss	*Dr Syn*	(Neill)	GB, 38
Peter Cushing	*Captain Clegg*	(Scott)	GB, 62
Patrick McGoohan	*Dr Syn–Alias The Scarecrow*	(Neilson)	GB, 63

The rebirth of Superman! Christopher Reeve as the flying strongman from the planet Krypton, first created in the comic strip in 'Action Comics' in 1938 and given contemporary life by Reeve in four large-scale movies of the last decade. Sharing things with him—Margot Kidder (above right)

Szabo Violette [R]

(1918–45) Half-English, half-French widow who in 1942 became a Secret Service Agent for the Allies and was parachuted into France. Following several successful missions she was captured by the Gestapo and finally executed in January, 1945, after failing to reveal the identity of her contacts. A courageous heroine whose story is told in R. J. Minney's book 'Carve Her Name With Pride'.

Virginia McKenna *Carve Her Name With Pride* (Gilbert) GB, 58

T

Taras Bulba

F

Heroic figure of the 1835 novel by Nikolai Gogol; a famed, sword-swinging adventurer who joins the Cossacks in their campaign against the Poles in seventeenth century Ukraine. Mostly portrayed in European and Asian films, Yul Brynner's performance in the 1962 spectacular of J. Lee Thompson being the one exception.

Harry Baur	*Taras Bulba*	(Granovski) Fra, 36
Vladimir Medar	*Taras Bulba*	(Zaphiratos/Baldi) Fra/It, 61
Yul Brynner	*Taras Bulba*	(Lee Thompson) USA, 62

Note: Taras Bulba was played on the silent screen by N. Vassiliev in a Russian version of 1910 and Duvan Torzov in Vladimir Strizhevski's German adaptation of 1923.

Tarzan

Possibly the world's best-known fictional hero, the son of an English nobleman who is abandoned in Africa and raised by apes who teach him their language. Hence the famous jungle call, 'aaah-eee-aaah!' The first screen Tarzan, Elmo Lincoln, appeared just four years after the publication of Edgar Rice Burroughs' 'Tarzan Of The Apes' in 1914; Johnny Weismuller, who worked his way through a dozen loincloths, played Tarzan more times than any other actor.

Lex Barker, the successor to Johnny Weismuller as the screen's Tarzan and who played the 'Ape Man' on five occasions in the early 50s

Johnny Weismuller	*Tarzan The Ape Man*	(Van Dyke) USA, 32
Buster Crabbe	*Tarzan The Fearless*	(Hill) USA, 33
Johnny Weismuller	*Tarzan And His Mate*	(Gibbons) USA, 34
Herman Brix	*The New Adventures Of Tarzan*	(Kull) USA, 35
Johnny Weismuller	*Tarzan Escapes*	(Thorpe) USA, 36
Herman Brix	*Tarzan And The Green Goddess*	(Kull) USA, 38
Glenn Morris	*Tarzan's Revenge*	(Lederman) USA, 38
Johnny Weismuller	*Tarzan Finds A Son*	(Thorpe) USA, 39
Johnny Weismuller	*Tarzan's Secret Treasure*	(Thorpe) USA, 41
Johnny Weismuller	*Tarzan's New York Adventure*	(Thorpe) USA, 42
Johnny Weismuller	*Tarzan Triumphs*	(Thiele) USA, 43
Johnny Weismuller	*Tarzan's Desert Mystery*	(Thiele) USA, 43
Johnny Weismuller	*Tarzan And The Amazons*	(Neumann) USA, 45
Johnny Weismuller	*Tarzan And The Leopard Woman*	(Neumann) USA, 46
Johnny Weismuller	*Tarzan And The Huntress*	(Neumann) USA, 47
Johnny Weismuller	*Tarzan And The Mermaids*	(Florey) USA, 48
Lex Barker	*Tarzan's Magic Fountain*	(Sholem) USA, 49

Christopher Lambert, a somewhat more realistic Tarzan, in Hugh Hudson's 1984 version of Edgar Burrough's tale 'Greystoke'. *The Legend of Tarzan, Lord of the Apes*

Lex Barker	*Tarzan And The Slave Girl* (Sholem) USA, 50
Lex Barker	*Tarzan's Peril* (Haskin) USA, 51
Lex Barker	*Tarzan's Savage Fury* (Endfield) USA, 52
Lex Barker	*Tarzan And The She-Devil* (Schuster) USA, 53
Gordon Scott	*Tarzan's Hidden Jungle* (Schuster) USA, 55
Gordon Scott	*Tarzan And The Lost Safari* (Humberstone) USA, 58
Gordon Scott	*Tarzan's Fight For Life* (Humberstone) GB, 59
Gordon Scott	*Tarzan And The Trappers* (Humberstone) USA, 58
Gordon Scott	*Tarzan's Greatest Adventure* (Guillermin) GB, 59
Denny Miller	*Tarzan The Ape Man* (Newman) USA, 59
Gordon Scott	*Tarzan The Magnificent* (Day) GB, 60
Jock Mahoney	*Tarzan Goes To India* (Guillermin) GB, 62
Jock Mahoney	*Tarzan's Three Challenges* (Day) USA 63
Mike Henry	*Tarzan And The Valley Of Gold* (Day) USA/Swi, 66
Mike Henry	*Tarzan And The Great River* (Day) USA, 67
Mike Henry	*Tarzan And The Jungle Boy* (Day) USA/Swi, 68
Ron Ely	*Tarzan's Jungle Rebellion* (Witney) USA, 70
Ron Ely	*Tarzan's Deadly Silence* (Friend/Dobkin) USA, 70
Miles O'Keefe	*Tarzan, The Ape Man* (Derek) USA, 81
Christopher Lambert	*Greystoke: The Legend Of Tarzan, Lord Of The Apes* (Hudson) GB/USA, 84

Note: The Indian actor Azad appeared in eleven Tarzan adventures (none of them released in Britain or the USA) during the 60s and 70s, among them *Toofani Tarzan* (62), *Tarzan And Captain Kishore* (64), *Tarzan And Delilah* (64) and *Tarzan And The Circus* (64); Herman Brix, who played Tarzan twice in the 30s, subsequently changed his name to Bruce Bennett.

Elmo Lincoln played The Ape Man three times on the silent screen—in *Tarzan Of The Apes* (USA, 18), *The Romance Of Tarzan* (USA, 18) and the 15-episode serial *The Adventures Of Tarzan* (USA, 21). Gene Pollar (20), P. Dempsey Tabler (20), James Pierce (27) and Frank Merrill (28) were other silent Tarzans.

Prior to appearing as a screen Tarzan in 1970 Ron Ely featured in nearly 60 TV adventures in a popular Tarzan series of 1966–7.

Tauber, Richard

(1892–1948) Austrian-born opera singer who established himself as one of the leading tenors of the pre-war period, first in Mozart opera and then in light opera by Lehar. Appeared in several British musicals of the 30s, e.g. *Blossom Time, Hearts Desire, Land Without Music.*

Rudolf Schock	*The Richard Tauber Story* (Morischka) Aus, 53

Tchaikovsky, Peter Ilyich

(1840–93) Russian composer of many of the world's most melodic symphonies and ballets. His homosexual problems, coupled with the demands of his nymphomaniac wife, led, not surprisingly, to a life full of torment and anguish. They also helped create 'Romeo And Juliet', 'Swan Lake' 'The Sleeping Beauty' and 'The Nutcracker Suite'. Talankin's overblown 191-minute Russian film treated the composer with due reverence; Ken Russell's vivid *The Music Lovers* cast aside the solemnity and opted for the torment!

Hans Stuwe	*Es War Eine Rauschende Ballnacht* (Froelich) Ger, 39
Frank Sundstrom	*Song Of My Heart* (Glazer) USA, 48
Innokenti Smoktunovsky	*Tchaikovsky* (Talankin) USSR/USA, 70
Richard Chamberlain	*The Music Lovers* (Russell) GB, 71

Tess Of the D'Urbervilles F

One of Thomas Hardy's most tragic (and typical) victims; a Dorset peasant girl whose seduction by the aristocratic D'Urberville leads to the birth of a dead child, a disastrous marriage to an unforgiving clergyman's son and ultimately to the crime of murder and death on the gallows. Nastassia Kinski starred in the only sound version of Hardy's powerful tale, shot by Roman Polanski in the farms and villages of Normandy and Brittany which substituted for the author's beloved Wessex.

Nastassia Kinski	*Tess* (Polanski)	Fra/GB, 79

Note: A 1924 MGM film starred Blanche Sweet as Tess; in 1913 an American film with Minnie Maddern Fiske, based on the stage version of the novel, was released by Famous Players. Both films carried the title of the original novel which was published in 1891.

Thalberg, Irving G. R

(1899–1936) American film producer, long known as the boy wonder, who graduated to legendary

Forbidden fruit! Thomas Hardy's beautiful 16-year-old Tess of the D'Urbervilles about to embark on her tragic young life, one that leads to seduction, despair, a loveless marriage and finally murder. Natassia Kinski played Tess in Roman Polanski's 1979 film

status at MGM after an apprenticeship at Universal. Robert Evans' minor portrait in *Man Of A Thousand Faces* showed Thalberg during his years at Universal with Lon Chaney; Robert De Niro's performance as Monroe Stahr (a prototype for Thalberg) in *The Last Tycoon* revealed him in full command of a major studio. An arrogant, ruthless yet brilliant man, Thalberg encouraged MGM to pursue a literary trend in their movies of the 30s.

Robert Evans — *Man Of A Thousand Faces* (Pevney) USA, 57
Robert De Niro — *The Last Tycoon* (Kazan) USA, 76

Note: Louis B. Mayer, boss of MGM during Thalberg's period as production head, has been played on screen by Jack Kruschen in Alex Segal's *Harlow* (65), Martin Balsam (as Everett Redman) in Gordon Douglas' *Harlow* (65) and Allen Garfield in *Gable And Lombard* (76).

Thaw, Harry K. R

A man who earned himself a place in the annals of American crime when he walked into the Madison Square Garden dining theatre on a June night in 1906 and, in full view of everybody, put three bullets through the head of architect Stanford White. The events leading up to the murder i.e. White's supposed liaison with Thaw's wife, Evelyn Nesbitt, and the subsequent trial, were reconstructed in Richard Fleischer's *The Girl In The Red Velvet Swing* and, more briefly, in Milos Forman's *Ragtime.* Thaw, a millionaire, was found to be insane but was eventually released from prison and lived for another 25 years. He died, aged 76, in February 1947.

Farley Granger — *The Girl In The Red Velvet Swing* (Fleischer) USA, 55
Robert Joy — *Ragtime* (Forman) USA, 81

Note: Stanford White was played by Ray Milland in Fleischer's 1955 film and Norman Mailer in *Ragtime;* Evelyn Nesbitt by Joan Collins (55) and Elizabeth McGovern (81).

Thief of Bagdad, The 

Magical Arabian Nights figure of adventure and romance who has enjoyed encounters with Oriental villains, giants, dragons, winged horses, etc., ever since Douglas Fairbanks turned him into one of the most famous heroes of the silent screen.

Sabu — *The Thief Of Bagdad* (Powell/Berger/Whelan) GB, 40
Steve Reeves — *The Thief Of Bagdad* (Lubin) Fra/It, 61
Kabir Bedi — *The Thief Of Bagdad* (Donner) GB, 79

Note: Fairbanks' silent version, directed by Raoul Walsh, was released by United Artists in 1924.

Thompson, Sadie 

South Seas island prostitute, converted to religion by a repressed missionary, who quickly resorts to her former way of life when the missionary himself seduces her. First created by Somerset Maugham in the 1921 short story 'Rain'; updated into a song-and-dance trollop in the 1953 film of Curtis Bernhardt.

Joan Crawford — *Rain* (Milestone) USA, 32
Rita Hayworth — *Miss Sadie Thompson* (Bernhardt) USA, 53

Note: Gloria Swanson played Sadie in the 1928 film of Raoul Walsh; the Rev. Alfred Davidson, the fire and brimstone preacher who succumbs to the pleasures of the flesh has been played by Lionel Barrymore (28), Walter Huston (32) and Jose Ferrer (53).

Thorpe, Jim 

(1886–1953) One of America's greatest athletes, an Oklahoma Indian who won pentathlon and decathlon gold medals at the 1912 Olympics in Stockholm but was later relieved of his medals because he had taken part in some professional baseball matches and was deduced not to be an amateur. Michael Curtiz's 1951 film followed his initial triumphs and also his alcoholic decline after the death of his son but did not cover his subsequent arrival in Hollywood where he was reduced to working as an extra in bit parts.

Burt Lancaster — *Jim Thorpe – All American* Curtiz) USA, 51

Note: Thorpe acted as technical adviser on the Curtiz film. Among the movies in which he appeared were *Road To Utopia* (45), Cagney's *White Heat* (49)

Assassination in Madison Square Garden! (left) Farley Granger (as Harry K. Thaw) guns down architect/socialite Stanford White (Ray Milland) in Richard Fleischer's *The Girl In The Red Velvet Swing.* (Above) Robert Joy carries out the same crime in the 1981 production *Ragtime*

and John Ford's *Wagonmaster* (50) in which he played a Navajo Indian. In 1982 Thorpe's gold medals were restored posthumously by the International Olympic Committee. His grandson Bill Thorpe was a torch carrier for the 1984 Olympics in Los Angeles.

Three Men In A Boat F

Or, in other words, Harris, George and J., Jerome K. Jerome's trio of British incompetents who attempt a peaceful boating holiday on the Thames only to find themselves involved in a series of unmitigated disasters with tents, rain, girls and the Hampton Court Maze. Jerome's special brand of literary humour has yet to be satisfactorily transferred to the screen despite three attempts by British film-makers.

Harris

William Austin	*Three Men In A Boat* (Cutts)	GB, 33
Jimmy Edwards	*Three Men In A Boat* (Annakin)	GB, 56

George

Edmond Breon	*Three Men In A Boat* (Cutts)	GB, 33
Laurence Harvey	*Three Men In A Boat* (Annakin)	GB, 56

J

Billy Milton	*Three Men In A Boat* (Cutts)	GB, 33
David Tomlinson	*Three Men In A Boat* (Annakin)	GB, 56

Note: Manning Haynes (Harris), Johnny Butt (George) and Lionelle Howard (J) featured in Challis Sanderson's 1920 British silent version.

Thumb, Tom F

Five-inch hero of an old sixteenth century nursery tale, turned into a woodland musical figure in the 1958 fantasy of George Pal, who combined ingenious puppet and animation techniques with the film's live-action sequences. The film marked one of the last appearances of the acrobatic Russ Tamblyn in an MGM musical role.

Russ Tamblyn	*Tom Thumb* (Pal)	GB, 58
Titoyo	*Tom Thumb* (Boisrond)	Fra, 72

Tibbetts, Colonel Paul R

(1915–) The man who trained and commanded the specialist crew who dropped the atomic bombs on Hiroshima and Nagasaki in August, 1945. His own plane dropped the bomb 'Little Boy' on Hiroshima. The full story of the training of the crew and the mission itself is recounted in the Norman Panama/Melvin Frank production *Above And Beyond*.

Barry Nelson	*The Beginning Or The End?* (Taurog)	USA, 47
Robert Taylor	*Above And Beyond* (Panama/Frank)	USA, 53

Note: Patrick Duffy featured as Tibbetts in *Engola Gay,* a 1980 TV movie directed by David Lowell Rich, which looked at the same story some 35 years after the event. The TV film was scripted by two noted screenwriters, James Poe and Millard Kaufman. It was dedicated to Poe who died before its completion.

Tibbs, Virgil F

The best-known black cop in films, first brought to life on screen in the Oscar-winning *In The Heat Of The Night,* a tale of two detectives, one white, one black, reluctantly working in harness to solve a murder in the Deep South. Other film cases, involving prostitution and drug-running, set in San Francisco. A creation of novelist John Ball.

Sidney Poitier	*In The Heat Of The Night* (Jewison)	USA, 67
Sidney Poitier	*They Call Me MISTER Tibbs* (Douglas)	USA, 70
Sidney Poitier	*The Organization* (Medford)	USA, 71

Tolstoy, Count Leo R

(1828–1910) One of the great figures of world literature (*War And Peace, Resurrection*) who, together with Dostoievsky, helped raise the Russian realistic novel to the level of Greek tragedy. A philosopher and champion of non-violent protest, he was an influential factor in the social restlessness that swept Russia before the 1917 revolution. Sergei Gerasimov directed and starred in the three hour film biography which recreated the last days of Tolstoy's life when his thoughts were wrapped in peasant mysticism. The film concentrated on his emotional conflicts with his wife, his long-standing relationship with his doctor-friend and his final flight (at the age of 82) to the railway station at Astapovo where he died at the stationmaster's house.

Sergei Gerasimov	*Leo Tolstoy* (Gerasimov)	USSR, 84

Topaze [F]

Mild mannered, scrupulously honest French provincial schoolteacher who is used as a front by a corrupt city official, suddenly sees the error of his ways and rises to undreamed heights as the biggest swindler of them all! The central character in Marcel Pagnol's satirical stage play of 1928; portrayed on six occasions on screen, each time memorably.

Louis Jouvet	*Topaze* (Gasnier)	Fra, 33
John Barrymore	*Topaze* (d'Arrast)	USA, 33
Nagib El-Rihani	*Yacout Effendi* (El-Rihani)	Egypt, 33
Arnaudy	*Topaze* (Pagnol)	Fra, 36
Fernandel	*Topaze* (Pagnol)	Fra, 50
Peter Sellers	*Mr Topaze* (Sellers)	GB, 60

Topper, Cosmo [F]

Unassuming hero of Thorne Smith's novels, a timid, henpecked little banker who suddenly finds himself plagued by a couple of ghosts determined to liberate him from his nagging wife and humdrum career. During the three films made about the character the ghosts changed frequently, but Roland Young was always the long-suffering Topper.

Roland Young	*Topper* (McLeod)	USA, 37
Roland Young	*Topper Takes A Trip* (McLeod)	USA, 39
Roland Young	*Topper Returns* (Del Ruth)	USA, 41

Note: Leo G. Carroll took over the role of Topper in a 1953/54 TV series; Jack Warden appeared as the character (changed to a lawyer) in a 1979 update directed by Charles Dubin.

Toulouse-Lautrec, Henri [R]

(1864–1901) Parisian artist and lithographer whose stunted growth caused him to be a figure of ridicule for most of his adult life and who found solace only amongst the whores and dancers of Montmartre. His lonely, alcoholic life and brilliant skill as a painter were recreated with affection by John Huston in the biography *Moulin Rouge*.

Jose Ferrer	*Moulin Rouge* (Huston)	GB, 52
Jerry Bergen	*Lust For Life* (Minnelli)	USA, 56

Tracy, Dick [F]

The first comic strip detective hero, conceived by Chester Gould in 1931 and brought to the screen in 1937 in the Republic serial *Dick Tracy*. Tough and square-jawed, he is remembered for two key phrases: 'Little crimes lead to big crimes' and 'Crime does not pay'.

Ralph Byrd	*Dick Tracy* (Taylor/James)	USA, 37
Ralph Byrd	*Dick Tracy Returns* (Witney/English)	USA, 38
Ralph Byrd	*Dick Tracy's G-Men* (Witney/English)	USA, 39
Ralph Byrd	*Dick Tracy vs Crime, Inc.* (Witney/English)	USA, 41
Morgan Conway	*Dick Tracy* (Berke)	USA, 45
Morgan Conway	*Dick Tracy vs Cueball* (Douglas)	USA, 46
Ralph Byrd	*Dick Tracy's Dilemma* (Rawlins)	USA, 47
Ralph Byrd	*Dick Tracy Meets Gruesome* (Rawlins)	USA, 47

Note: the first four Ralph Byrd films on the above list are all serials, the remaining four all features.

Trapp, Maria von 

The world-famous children's governess who taught her charges to sing, wed their stern father Captain von Trapp and finally escaped with them from a Nazi-dominated Austria to America. Portrayed on screen in two German films long before Julie Andrews set the hills alive with 'The Sound Of Music' in 1965. She died in 1987, aged 82.

Ruth Leuwerik	*The Trapp Family* (Liebeneiner)	Ger, 56
Ruth Leuwerik	*The Trapp Family In America* (Liebeneiner)	Ger, 58
Julie Andrews	*The Sound Of Music* (Wise)	USA, 65

Note: Hans Holt played Captain von Trapp in the two German pictures, Christopher Plummer in the 1965 musical.

'The hills are alive with the sound of music'; Julie Andrews as the musical Maria von Trapp in Fox's record-breaking film of 1965

Trilby

R

George du Maurier's tragic heroine of his novel 'Trilby', an artist's model and *habituée* of the Latin Quarter in Paris who falls under the influence of the musician Svengali and is hypnotized into becoming a great singer. When her mentor dies suddenly of a heart attack her voice dies also. A romantic, helpless character (full name Trilby O'Ferral), she has attracted actresses from Germany, Denmark, Britain and America.

Marian Marsh	*Svengali*	(Mayo)	USA, 31
Hildegarde Neff	*Svengali*	(Langley)	GB, 54

Note: Oda Alstrup (Den, 08), Viva Birkett (GB, 14), Clara Kimball Young (USA, 15), Andrée Lafayette (USA, 23) and Anita Dorris (Ger, 27) all played the role on the silent screen.

Trotsky, Leon

R

(1877–1940) Influential communist leader and a top member of Lenin's Bolshevik government; expelled after Lenin's death because of idealogical differences with Stalin. Screen portraits have been surprisingly few although his final weeks in exile in Mexico, where he was assassinated in 1940, were examined in some detail in Joseph Losey's film of 1972.

D. F. Barry	*Why Russians Are Revolting*	(Sullivan)	USA, 70
Brian Cox	*Nicholas And Alexandra*	(Schaffner)	USA, 71
Richard Burton	*The Assassination Of Trotsky*	(Losey)	Fra/It/GB, 72
Yves Peneau	*Stavisky*	(Resnais)	Fra/It, 74
Stuart Richman	*Reds*	(Beatty)	USA, 81

Note: Ken McMullen's 1985 British film *Zina* probed into the unhappy life of the daughter of Trotsky, believed to have committed suicide in Berlin in 1931, shortly before the advent of National socialism. Domiziana Giordano featured in the title role.

Truman, Harry S.

(1884–1972) American President who proved to be a much tougher cookie than most people bargained for when he succeeded to the Presidency on the death of Franklin Roosevelt in April, 1945. Famous for his 'The buck stops here' remark, he was honoured with a one man performance by James Whitmore in the 1975 film, *Give 'Em Hell, Harry!* Truman made the decision to use the atomic bomb to end the war against Japan, an event depicted in *The Beginning Or The End?*

Art Baker	*The Beginning Or The End?*	(Taurog)	USA, 46
James Whitmore	*Give 'Em Hell, Harry!*	(Binder)	USA, 75
Ed Flanders	*MacArthur*	(Sargent)	USA, 77

Note: In *Alias Jesse James,* a small boy is shown playing 'The Missouri Waltz' on the James family's piano. When Bob Hope asks the youngster his name, he replies, 'Harry Truman, sir'.

On TV Truman has been played by E. G. Marshall in *Collision Course* (76), a film which dealt with the President's clash with General MacArthur, Robert Symonds in *Tail Gunner Joe* (77) and Richard McKenzie in *Eleanor, First Lady Of The World* (82).

Turpin, Dick

R

(1706–39) Famed highwayman of eighteenth century England. In real life, no more than a common horse thief and housebreaker who was hanged for murder on the gallows at York; in legend, the man who rode his gallant steed Black Bess from London to York in a single night. A hero figure in all the several movies made about his adventures.

Victor McLaglen — *Dick Turpin* (Stafford/Hanbury) GB, 33
Louis Hayward — *Dick Turpin's Ride* (Murphy) USA, 51
Philip Friend — *Dick Turpin – The Highwayman* (Paltenghi) GB, 56
David Weston — *The Legend Of Young Dick Turpin* (Neilson) GB, 65

Note: Turpin was also a popular screen figure in the silent days. Among the actors who played him were Percy Moran in four British films of 1912; Matheson Lang in the 1922 British production, *Dick Turpin's Ride To York;* and Tom Mix in John Blystone's *Dick Turpin* (USA, 25).

Tutankhamen

(*c.* 1371–52 BC) Egyptian Pharaoh, aged just nineteen years when he died, whose magnificent tomb was discovered at Thebes by Lord Carnarvon and Howard Carter in November, 1922. The discovery gave rise to the famous horror tale, *The Mummy,* first filmed with Boris Karloff, in 1932. It was also the background to a British film about a Pharaoh's curse and a young girl who sees visions of the boy during her tour of the Tutankhamen exhibition in London.

Seif El Din — *A Story Of Tutankhamen* (Scott) GB, 73

Twain, Mark

(1835–1910) American novelist and humorist (real name, Samuel Clemens) who earned worldwide fame for creating 'Tom Sawyer' and 'Huckleberry Finn' and satirizing established institutions and traditions. A former Mississippi riverboat pilot, he adapted his pen name from a well-known river call ('mark twain' meaning 'by the mark of two fathoms'). He drew on his boyhood experiences along the Mississippi for many of his literary characters and was afforded a respectful 130-minute Warner Bros tribute in 1944.

Fredric March — *The Adventures Of Mark Twain* (Rapper) USA, 44

Note: Ronald Adam appeared as Samuel Clemens in the 1954 version of Twain's story, *The Million Pound Note;* Karl Formes in *A Connecticut Yankee In King Arthur's Court* (21), Leslie King in *Broadway Broke* (23) and Charles Gerson in *The Pony Express* (25) all featured briefly as the author on the silent screen.

In Will Vinton's 1986 claymation feature *The Adventures Of Mark Twain* Clemens was voiced by James Whitmore.

Twelve Angry Men

Twelve of the most famous characters in American cinema, a group of assorted jurors who spend most of Sidney Lumet's 1957 film sweltering in a New York jury room trying to decide whether a black teenager is guilty of murdering his father. During 95 highly charged minutes their hatreds and prejudices are drawn to the surface as they are forced by Henry Fonda to rethink what had appeared to be an open and shut case. Apart from Fonda, the best known actors in the film were Lee J. Cobb (as the bullying owner of a messenger service), Martin Balsam (as the jury foreman), E. G. Marshall (as a calculating businessman), Ed Begley (as an aged bigot) and Jack Warden as a man who wants the case wrapped quickly so that he can catch a ball game!

For the record, the full twelve, never referred to by name, were as follows:

Martin Balsam (*Juror 1*); John Fiedler (*Juror 2*); Lee J. Cobb (*Juror 3*); E. G. Marshall (*Juror 4*); Jack Klugman (*Juror 5*); Edward Binns (*Juror 6*); Jack Warden (*Juror 7*); Henry Fonda (*Juror 8*); Joseph Sweeney (*Juror 9*); Ed Begley (*Juror 10*); George Voskovec (*Juror 11*); Robert Webber (*Juror 12*).

Twelve Angry Men (Lumet) USA, 57

Uncle Remus

F

Whimsical black storyteller (created by Joel Chandler Harris), noted for his tales of the adventures of Brer Rabbit. Just one screen interpretation – by James Baskett in Disney's *Song Of The South*, a live-action/animated production featuring three cartoon Brer Rabbit stories – 'The Tar Baby', 'The Briar Patch' and 'The Laughing Place'. Harris' tales of the Deep South were first collected together in 1880 in the book 'Uncle Remus, His Songs And Sayings'.

James Baskett	*Song Of The South* (Foster)	USA, 46

Usher, Roderick

Edgar Allan Poe's decaying nobleman who determines that the madness that has plagued his family for generations shall at last come to an end with the deaths of his sister and himself in their crumbling mansion. A role hammed to perfection by Vincent Price in Roger Corman's 1960 film, *The House Of Usher.*

Kay Tendeter	*The Fall Of The House Of Usher* (Barnett)	GB, 50
Vincent Price	*The House Of Usher* (Corman)	USA, 60
Howard Vernon	*The Fall Of The House Of Usher* (Franco)	Spa, 83

Note: Melville Webber and Jean Debucourt (in a French film by Jean Epstein) both featured as Usher in silent films released in 1928; on TV Martin Landau appeared in the role in a 1982 Classics Illustrated adaptation, directed by James L. Conway.

Valachi, Joseph [R]

Not the most important member of the Cosa Nostra, but one of the few Mafia members to break the organization's code of silence. An enforcer, numbers runner and narcotics peddler for the Luciano 'Family', he turned informer in 1959 when sentenced to 15 years in Atlanta for violation of narcotics laws. He died of a heart attack in 1971 in a Texas prison. His life was portrayed by Charles Bronson in Terence Young's film *The Valachi Papers* (also known as *Cosa Nostra*).

Charles Bronson	*The Valachi Papers* (Young)	Fra/It, 72

Valens, Ritchie 

(1942–59) Fifties rock star who died in the same plane crash as Buddy Holly and J.P. ('Big Bopper') Richardson and whose brief life – he was just 17 when he died – was afforded the familiar rags to riches treatment by Luis Valdez in 1987. Lou Diamond Phillips starred as the Mexican teenage idol (real name: Richard Valenzuela) who shone briefly in the charts in 1958; Los Lobos recreated the sounds of late 50s rock including Valens' three chart-toppers 'Come On Let's Go', 'Donna' and 'La Bamba'.

Lou Diamond Phillips	*La Bamba* (Valdez)	USA, 87

Note: Howard Huntsberry as Jackie Wilson, Brian Setzer as Eddie Cochran and Marshall Crenshaw as Buddy Holly performed both the music and appeared in cameo roles as their musical mentors.

Lou Diamond Phillips in *La Bamba*, the story of Ritchie Valens who became a rock 'n' roll sensation at the age of 17

Valentino, Rudolph 

(1895–1926) *The* romantic movie star of the early 20s, a 'Sheik of the Silver Screen' who caused female fainting fits and male boredom with his amorous escapades in a series of famous silent films: *The Four Horsemen Of The Apocalypse* (21), *The Sheik* (21), *Blood And Sand* (22), etc. His life on and off the screen has been the subject of two film biographies, the first starring look-alike Anthony Dexter, the second featuring Rudolf Nureyev and directed in flamboyant style by Ken Russell.

Anthony Dexter	*Valentino* (Allen)	USA, 51
Rudolf Nureyev	*Valentino* (Russell)	GB, 77
Matt Collins	*The World's Greatest Lover* (Gene Wilder)	USA, 77

Note: Franco Nero starred as the silent screen idol in Mel Shavelson's TV movie *The Legend Of Valentino* (75); in the Gene Wilder spoof Matt Collins played a neurotic baker from Milwaukee who changes his name to Valentino and auditions for 'The World's Greatest Lover'. A proposed 50s biography to star Tyrone Power never materialized.

Valjean, Jean 

One of literature's most pitiable victims, a French peasant who escapes from a living hell (over 20 years imprisonment for stealing a loaf of bread) to spend the rest of his life eluding his fanatical pursuer

Valentino look alike Anthony Dexter in Columbia's 1951 life story of the silent screen's greatest lover

Inspector Javert. The leading figure in Victor Hugo's scathing indictment of injustice in nineteenth century France, 'Les Miserables' (1862).

Harry Baur	*Les Misérables* (Bernard)	Fra, 34
Fredric March	*Les Misérables* (Boleslawski)	USA, 35
Domingo Soler	*Les Misérables* (Rivero)	Mex, 44
Gino Cervi	*Les Misérables* (Freda)	It, 46
T. S. Baliah	*Ezhai Padum Padu* (Ramanath)	Ind, 50
Sessue Hayakawa	*Les Misérables* (Dasuke/Masahiro)	Jap, 50
Michael Rennie	*Les Misérables* (Milestone)	USA, 52
Sohrab Modi	*Kundan* (Modi)	Ind, 55
Jean Gabin	*Les Misérables* (Le Chanois)	Fra/It, 58
Richard Jordan	*Les Misérables* (Glenn Jordan)	GB, 79
Lino Ventura	*Les Misérables* (Hossein)	Fra, 82

Note: Robert Hossein's 1982 film was a ten million dollar cinema/TV production running for three hours in cinemas and for six 50 minute episodes on TV; on the silent screen Henry Krauss featured as Valjean in Albert Capellani's 1913 French version; William Farnum in Frank Lloyd's 1917 adaptation and Gabriel Gabrio in Henry Fescourt's film of 1925. Earlier versions of the story were released in France in 1909 and America in 1910.

Vance, Philo [F]

Debonair private detective of S. S. Van Dine, first introduced to the reading public in 1926 ('The Benson Murder Case') and to the screen three years later. The epitome of the elegant dilettante-sleuth, he was best represented on film by the polished characterizations of William Powell who played him on four occasions. During Powell's heyday he featured in at least one classic crime film, Michael Curtiz's *The Kennel Murder Case* (33).

William Powell	*The Canary Murder Case* (St Clair)	USA, 29
William Powell	*The Greene Murder Case* (Tuttle)	USA, 29
Basil Rathbone	*The Bishop Murder Case* (Grinde/Burton)	USA, 30
William Powell	*The Benson Murder Case* (Tuttle)	USA, 30
William Powell	*The Kennel Murder Case* (Curtiz)	USA, 33
Warren William	*The Dragon Murder Case* (Humberstone)	USA, 34
Paul Lukas	*The Casino Murder Case* (Marin)	USA, 35
Edmund Lowe	*The Garden Murder Case* (Marin)	USA, 36
Wilfrid Hyde White	*The Scarab Murder Case* (Hankinson)	GB, 36
Grant Richards	*Night Of Mystery* (Dupont)	USA, 37
Warren William	*The Gracie Allen Murder Case* (Green)	USA, 39
James Stephenson	*Calling Philo Vance* (Clemens)	USA, 40
William Wright	*Philo Vance Returns* (Beaudine)	USA, 47
Alan Curtis	*Philo Vance's Gamble* (Wrangell)	USA, 47
Alan Curtis	*Philo Vance's Secret Mission* (LeBorg)	USA, 47

Van Gogh, Vincent 

(1853–90) Tormented Dutch artist, a pioneer of Expressionism, whose tortured, depressed life, first as a Methodist preacher and finally as a painter among the Provençal landscapes at Arles, was faithfully recreated by Vincente Minnelli in *Lust For Life.* Much of the film was shot in the actual places where Van Gogh lived and worked.

Kirk Douglas	*Lust For Life* (Minnelli)	USA, 56
John Hurt (voice only)	*Vincent – The Life And Death Of Vincent Van Gogh* (Cox)	Austral/Holl, 87

Note: In the 1987 film *Vincent,* Van Gogh was heard but not seen, John Hurt reading letters written by Van Gogh to his brother during the last ten years of his life when he produced some 1800 works but at the time of his death had sold only one and was unknown and impoverished. Barrie Houghton featured as the artist in Fielder Cook's 1980 TV film, *Gauguin The Savage.*

Van Helsing, Professor 

Count Dracula's deadliest foe, a vampire hunter with all the necessary tricks of the trade needed to rid the world of the bloodsucking tyrant of Transylvania. The two actors most associated with holding a trembling crucifix in front of bared fangs and driving a stake through Dracula's heart, are Edward Van Sloan and Peter Cushing. But despite their determination and noble intentions the count has steadfastly refused to die.

Edward Van Sloan	*Dracula* (Browning)	USA, 31
Edward Van Sloan	*Dracula's Daughter* (Hillyard)	USA, 36
Peter Cushing	*Dracula* (Fisher)	GB, 58
Peter Cushing	*Brides Of Dracula* (Fisher)	GB, 60
Herbert Lom	*El Conde Dracula* (Franco)	Spa, 70
Peter Cushing	*Dracula AD 1972* (Gibson)	GB, 72
Peter Cushing	*The Satanic Rites Of Dracula* (Gibson)	GB, 73
Nigel Davenport	*Dracula* (Cohen)	USA, 73
Peter Cushing	*The Legend Of The Seven Golden Vampires* (Baker)	GB/Hong Kong, 74
Walter Ladengast	*Nosferatu – The Vampyre* (Herzog)	W.Ger, 79
Laurence Olivier	*Dracula* (Badham)	USA, 79

Verloc 

Anarchist villain of Joseph Conrad's 1907 novel 'The Secret Agent'. He operates with his fellow conspirators in the back streets of London where he plans to overthrow the forces of law and order and is eventually murdered by his wife. In Hitchcock's 1936 adaptation *Sabotage,* the character was brought up to date and turned into the manager of a small cinema. The net result was the same however, a knife in the back from Sylvia Sidney!

Oscar Homolka	*Sabotage* (Hitchcock)	GB, 36

Vicious, Sid

The lead singer of the notorious punk group The Sex Pistols, a controversial performer who earned something of a reputation in the late 70s with his provocative, anarchistic songs and stage exhibitionism. Alex Cox's 1986 film looked at his affair with his drug-addicted girl-friend Nancy Spungen (who was subsequently found stabbed to death in their New York hotel room) and also concentrated in flashback on The Sex Pistols' rise to fame.

Gary Oldman	*Sid And Nancy* (Cox)	GB, 86

Note: Julian Temple's documentary parody *The Great Rock And Roll Swindle* (80) charted the rise and fall of the group, utilizing original cinema-verité footage of The Sex Pistols at different stages of their brief one and a half year career – early concerts, interviews, TV appearances, etc. Vicious died of a heroin overdose in February 1979.

Victoria, Queen 

(1819–1901) British monarch and Empress of India who reigned for most of the nineteenth century and whose life inspired two Anna Neagle film biographies of the late 30s. Only an occasional, minor character on the modern screen, but portrayed in some depth in the post-war period – by Romy Schneider in *The Young Victoria* and Irene Dunne in *The Mudlark* – a unique movie about a London orphan who smuggles himself into Windsor Castle and persuades the ageing queen to emerge from her lengthy seclusion after the death of her husband, Prince Albert.

Margaret Mann	*Disraeli* (Green)	USA, 29

Madeleine Ozeray	*La Guerre Des Valses* (Berger) Ger/Fra, 33
Hanna Waag	*Waltz: Time In Vienna* (Berger) Ger, 34
Pamela Stanley	*David Livingstone (Fitzpatrick) GB, 36*
Anna Neagle	*Victoria The Great* (Wilcox) GB, 37
Anna Neagle	Sixty Glorious Years (Wilcox) GB, 38
Pamela Stanley	*Marigold* (Bentley) GB, 38
Gaby Morlay	*Entente Cordiale* (L'Herbier) Fra, 38
Beryl Mercer	*Alexander Graham Bell* (Cummings) USA, 39
Beryl Mercer	*The Little Princess* (Lang) USA, 39
Hedwig Wangel	*Ohm Krüger* (Steinhoff) Ger, 41
Fay Compton	*The Prime Minister* (Dickinson) GB, 41
Evelyn Beresford	*Annie Get Your Gun* (Sidney) USA, 50
Irene Dunne	*The Mudlark* (Negulesco) GB, 50
Helena Pickard	*The Lady With The Lamp* (Wilcox) GB, 51
Muriel Aked	*The Story Of Gilbert And Sullivan* (Gilliat) GB, 53
Sybil Thorndike	*Melba* (Milestone)
Anna Neagle	*Lilacs In The Spring* (Wilcox) GB, 54
Romy Schneider	*The Young Victoria* (Marischka) Ger, 55
Mollie Maureen	*The Private Live Of Sherlock Holmes* (Billy Wilder) GB, 70
Susan Field	*The Adventures Of Sherlock Holmes' Smarter Brother* (Gene Wilder) USA, 75

Villa, Pancho

R

(1877–1923) Mexican revolutionary leader, for some a ruthless bandit, for others a noble champion of the people. Unlike Zapata, who was also active in the 1910 revolution, he survived the conflict only to be brought down by an assassin's bullet in 1923. Recent portrayals have been of heroic stature, i.e. Yul Brynner in *Villa Rides!* and Telly Savalas in *Pancho Villa*; Wallace Beery's more fiery portrait in the pre-war *Viva Villa!* allowed Villa a higher degree of sadism and cruelty.

Wallace Beery	*Viva Villa!* (Conway) USA, 34
Domingo Soler	*Let's Go With Pancho Villa* (de Fuentes) Mex, 36
Leo Carrillo	*Pancho Villa Returns* (Contreras) Mex, 50
Alan Reed	*Viva Zapata!* (Kazan) USA, 52
Rodolfo Hoyos	*Villa!* (Clark) USA, 58
Pedro Armendariz	*This Was Pancho Villa* (Rodrigues) Mex, 59
Pedro Armendariz	*Pancho Villa and Valentina* (Rodrigues) Mex, 60
Yul Brynner	*Villa Rides!* (Kulik) USA, 68
Eraclio Zepeda	*Reed: Insurgent Mexico* (Leduc) Mex, 71
Telly Savalas	*Pancho Villa* (Martin) Spa, 72

Virginian, The

F

Archetypal western hero; a stoic Virginian cowboy whose battles with rustling bad guy Trampas occupied film-makers for several decades during the hey-day of the western. Dustin Farnum was the first Virginian in DeMille's 1914 silent but Gary Cooper remains the best known mainly for his uttering of one of the most famous lines in movies, spoken to Trampas with quiet threat: 'If you want to call me that, smile!'

Dustin Farnum	*The Virginian* (DeMille) USA, 14
Kenneth Harlan	*The Virginian* (Forman) USA, 23
Gary Cooper	*The Virginian* (Fleming) USA, 29
Joel McCrea	*The Virginian* (Gilmore) USA, 46

Note: The cowboy hero was first created by Owen Wister in 'The Virginian: A Horseman Of The Plains' (1902); Trampas has been played by Billy Elmer (14), Russell Simpson (23), Walter Huston (29) and Brian Donlevy (46). The TV series starring James Drury as The Virginian ran for seven seasons from 1962 to 1969. Doug McClure played a now friendly Trampas and the episodes bore no relation to Wister's original novel.

Voltaire [R]

(1694–1778) French satirist and novelist whose literary works and crusading ideas helped foster the French Revolution of 1789. A constant source of irritation to the political and religious establishment figures of his time, he was the 'embodiment of eighteenth century enlightenment'. Just one screen biography to date and a half-hearted one at that, John Adolfi's 1933 film with George Arliss.

Karl Meinhardt	*Trenck* (Paul and Neubach)	Ger, 32
George Arliss	*Voltaire* (Adolfi)	USA, 33
Fernand Bercher	*Adrienne Lecouvreur* (L'Herbier)	Fra, 38
Maurice Schutz	*Le Diable Boiteux* (Guitry)	Fra, 48
Jacques de Feraudy	*Versailles* (Guitry)	Fra, 54

Von Werra, Franz [R]

A German pilot who earned a minor place in the history of World War II when he became the only German prisoner of war in Britain to escape from captivity and make it back to Germany. He broke free at his third attempt, jumping from a train after being sent with other POWs to Canada and then fleeing across the snow and ice to the then neutral USA. All the effort didn't do him much good however for when he finally arrived back in Germany via Mexico, Peru and Spain he was eventually killed in action on the Russian front. Hardy Kruger played Von Werra in an intriguing 1957 film directed by Roy Baker.

Hardy Kruger	*The One That Got Away* (Baker)	GB, 57

Wagner, Richard [R]

(1813–83) Fiercely nationalistic German composer whose sweeping dramatic works – 'Tannhäuser', 'Tristan und Isolde', 'Nibelungen' – revolutionized the world of opera and whose egotism and emotional instability earned him a notoriety that went side by side with his fame as a musician. The subject of a low budget biography by William Dieterle, he has also been featured prominently in films about his patron, Ludwig II of Bavaria. In 1983 he was afforded a spectacular five hour treatment (nine hours for the TV version) by director Tony Palmer.

Robert Pizani	*Champs-Elysées* (Guitry)	Fra, 39
Paul Bildt	*Ludwig II* (Kautner)	Ger, 55
Alan Badel	*Magic Fire* (Dieterle)	USA, 56
Lyndon Brook	*Song Without End* (Charles Vidor)	USA, 60
Gerhard Marz	*Ludwig – Requiem For A Virgin King* (Syberberg)	W.Ger, 72
Trevor Howard	*Ludwig* (Visconti)	It/Fra/W.Ger, 73
Paul Nicholas	*Lisztomania* (Russell)	GB, 75
Richard Burton	*Wagner* (Palmer)	GB/Hung/Austria,83

Note: Giuseppe Becce featured as the composer in the 1913 German silent, *Richard Wagner*.

Walker, Jimmy [R]

(1881–1946) One of New York's most celebrated mayors (and also the hundredth), a jaunty, colourful character who reigned over the city during the dizzy days and nights of the 20s and made the headlines by frequently mixing with top Broadway and entertainment personalities of the time. Also in his favour was his sponsorship of a bill that legalized prizefighting in New York. The 1957 Paramount movie was more an affectionate valentine to Walker than a probing examination of his eventual fall because of corruption but it did allow Bob Hope to indulge in one of his few straight roles.

Bob Hope	*Beau James* (Shavelson)	USA, 57

Wallis, Sir Barnes Nevill 

(1887–1979). The most famous of the World War II boffins, an English aircraft designer whose invention of a revolutionary bouncing bomb enabled the RAF to destroy the vital Möhne and Eder dams in Germany in 1943. Portrayed in some depth and with considerable skill by Michael Redgrave in the 1955 film *The Dam Busters*.

Michael Redgrave	*The Dam Busters* (Anderson)	GB, 55

Note: Guy Gibson, the British Wing Commander who led the low flying bomber raid and was awarded the Victoria Cross for bravery, was played by Richard Todd.

Watson, Dr 

Famed chronicler of the adventures of Sherlock Holmes and, unquestionably, one of the most difficult characters to play convincingly on screen. Generally emerges as a bluff, likeable buffoon (e.g. Nigel Bruce) if only to accentuate the brilliance of his famous partner. Colin Blakely's younger Watson in *The Private Life Of Sherlock Holmes* and James Mason's more mature doctor in the recent *Murder By Decree* stand perhaps as the most believable interpretations.

H. Reeves Smith	*The Return Of Sherlock Holmes* (Dean/Brook)	USA, 29
Ian Fleming	*The Sleeping Cardinal* (Hiscott)	GB, 31
Athole Stewart	*The Speckled Band* (Raymond)	GB, 31
Fred Lloyd	*The Hound Of The Baskervilles* (Gundrey)	GB, 32
Ian Fleming	*The Missing Rembrandt* (Hiscott)	GB, 32
Ian Hunter	*The Sign Of Four* (Cutts)	GB, 32
Reginald Owen	*Sherlock Holmes* (Howard)	USA, 32
Warburton Gamble	*A Study In Scarlet* (Marin)	USA, 33

Michael Redgrave (second from the left) in one of his most notable film roles as Dr Barnes Wallis, a World War II scientist whose experimental bouncing bomb was dropped by low flying RAF aircraft and helped destroy the Mohne and Eder dams in Germany. A scene from the 1955 British hit, *The Dam Busters*

Ian Fleming	*The Triumph Of Sherlock Holmes* (Hiscott) GB, 35
Fritz Odemar	*Der Hund Von Baskerville* (Lamac) Ger, 37
Ian Fleming	*Silver Blaze* (Bentley) GB, 37
Heinz Ruhmann	*The Man Who Was Sherlock Holmes* (Hartl) Ger, 37
Nigel Bruce	*The Hound Of The Baskervilles* (Lanfield) USA, 39
Nigel Bruce	*The Adventures Of Sherlock Holmes* (Werker) USA, 39
Nigel Bruce	*Sherlock Holmes And The Voice Of Terror* (Rawlins) USA, 42
Nigel Bruce	*Sherlock Holmes And The Secret Weapon* (Neill) USA, 42
Nigel Bruce	*Sherlock Holmes In Washington* (Neill) USA, 43
Nigel Bruce	*Sherlock Holmes Faces Death* (Neill) USA, 44
Nigel Bruce	*Spider Woman* (Neill) USA, 44
Nigel Bruce	*The Scarlet Claw* (Neill) USA, 44
Nigel Bruce	*The Pearl Of Death* (Neill) USA, 44
Nigel Bruce	*The House Of Fear* (Neill) USA, 45
Nigel Bruce	*The Woman In Green* (Neill) USA, 45
Nigel Bruce	*Pursuit To Algiers* (Neill) USA, 45
Nigel Bruce	*Terror By Night* (Neill) USA, 46

Nigel Bruce	*Dressed To Kill* (Neill) USA, 46
Campbell Singer	*The Man with The Twisted Lip* (Grey) GB, 51
André Morell	*The Hound Of The Baskervilles* (Fisher) GB, 59
Thorley Walters	*Sherlock Holmes And The Deadly Necklace* (Fisher) W.Ger, 62
Donald Houston	*A Study In Terror* (Hill) GB, 65
Colin Blakely	*The Private Life Of Sherlock Holmes* (Billy Wilder) GB, 70
Vaclav Voska	*Sherlock Holmes' Desire* (Skalsky) Czech, 71
Thorley Walters	*The Adventures Of Sherlock Holmes' Smarter Brother* (Gene Wilder) USA, 75
Robert Duvall	*The Seven-Per-Cent Solution* (Ross) USA, 76
Dudley Moore	*The Hound Of The Baskervilles* (Morissey) GB, 78
James Mason	*Murder By Decree* (Clark) GB, 79
David Healy	*The Sign Of Four* (Davis) GB, 83
Donald Churchill	*The Hound Of The Baskervilles* (Hickox) GB, 83
Alan Cox	*Young Sherlock Holmes* (Levinson) USA, 85

Note: Val Bettin voiced the mouse Dr David Q. Dawson in Disney's animated feature *The Great Mouse Detective* (USA, 86), a film loosely derived from the Sherlock Holmes adventures.

Bernard Fox in *The Hound Of The Baskervilles* (72), Patrick MacNee in *Sherlock Holmes In New York* (77), Richard Woods in *Sherlock Holmes* (81) and John Mills in *The Mask Of Death* (84) have all starred as the doctor in TV movies. In television series adapted from the Doyle short stories Raymond Francis (51), Nigel Stock (65 and 68), David Burke (84–85) and Edward Hardwicke (86–88) have all featured as Watson.

Chief among the silent screen Watsons were those of Arthur M. Cullin in *The Valley Of Fear* (GB, 16), Hubert Willis in the Stoll series of the 20s, Roland Young in *Sherlock Holmes* (USA, 22) and George Seroff in *Der Hund Von Baskerville* (Ger, 29).

Reginald Owen remains the only actor to play both Holmes and Watson on screen.

Wellington, Duke Of [R]

(1769–1852) English general and statesman, victor over Napoleon at Waterloo and Prime Minister from 1828–30. For film-makers, a less appealing figure than Bonaparte and warranting only one full-length biography by Victor Saville in 1935. Christopher Plummer's suave, witty Wellington in Bondarchuk's *Waterloo* went some way to redressing the balance in 1970.

Humberstone Wright	*Congress Dances* (Charell) Ger, 31
C. Aubrey Smith	*The House Of Rothschild* (Werker) USA, 34
William Faversham	*Becky Sharp* (Mamoulian) USA, 35
George Arliss	*The Iron Duke* (Saville) GB, 35
Matthew Boulton	*The Firefly* (Leonard) USA, 37
James Dale	*Victoria The Great* (Wilcox) GB, 37
C. Aubrey Smith	*Sixty Glorious Years* (Wilcox) GB, 38
Torin Thatcher	*The Miracle* (Rapper) USA, 59
Christopher Plummer	*Waterloo* (Bondarchuk) It/USSR, 70
John Neville	*The Adventures Of Gerard* (Skolimowski) GB/It/Swi, 70
Laurence Olivier	*Lady Caroline Lamb* (Bolt) GB/It, 72

Wells, H.G. [R]

(1866–1946) Brilliant British novelist and scientific prophet who, like Jules Verne, predicted many things that came to pass in the twentieth century including World War II (although his version lasted for 30 years) and a trip to the moon. His personal life and romantic encounters (with Rebecca West and others) would alone make for an intriguing screen biography but to date Wells has been featured in only two films: *The Time Machine* in which Rod Taylor (under the name of George) travelled into the future, and *Time After Time*, a

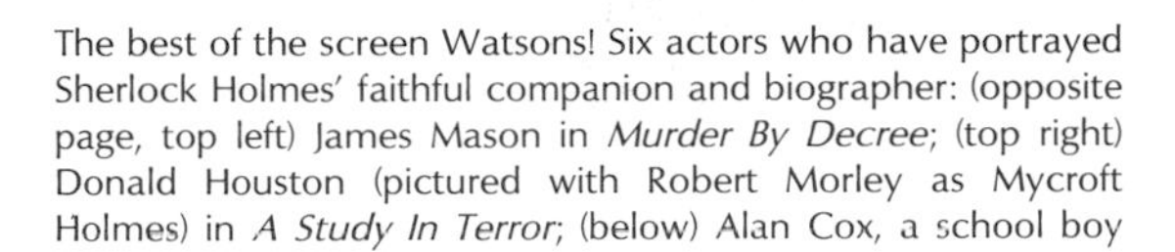

The best of the screen Watsons! Six actors who have portrayed Sherlock Holmes' faithful companion and biographer: (opposite page, top left) James Mason in *Murder By Decree*; (top right) Donald Houston (pictured with Robert Morley as Mycroft Holmes) in *A Study In Terror*; (below) Alan Cox, a school boy Watson in *Young Sherlock Holmes*; (this page, top left) Robert Duvall in *The Seven-Per-Cent Solution;* (top right) Colin Blakely in Billy Wilder's *The Private Life of Sherlock Holmes*; (bottom left) John Mills in *The Mask Of Death* and (bottom right) David Healy in *The Sign Of Four*

fantasy in which Malcolm McDowell took advantage of the same vehicle to pursue Jack The Ripper from the murky streets of Victorian London to modern day San Francisco.

Rod Taylor — *The Time Machine* (Pal) USA, 60

Malcolm McDowell — *Time After Time* (Meyer) USA, 79

Note: John Beck (as Neil Perry) starred in an updated TV version of *The Time Machine* in 1978.

Author H.G. Wells (Malcolm McDowell) haunted by the spectre of Jack The Ripper in the ingenious 1979 fantasy-thriller *Time After Time*

Werewolf, The

F

A reluctant member of the horror scene, just any old John Doe during the daylight hours, but a hairy-faced long toothed killer when the moon is full. Supposedly derived from Greek superstition, he made his first sound screen appearance in 1935 when botanist Henry Hull was bitten by a werewolf while searching for a mysterious flower in Tibet. Since then, college boys, young girls, even politicians (*The Werewolf Of Washington*) have had the bite put on them, been changed into werewolves and despatched by the traditional silver bullet. Lon Chaney gave the definitive portrayal in the 1941 production *The Wolf Man.* He subsequently played the role on another five occasions. In 1981 David Naughton, hidden behind Rick Baker's Oscar-winning make-up, was perhaps the most fearsome of all the wolf men in John Landis' *An American Werewolf In London.*

Henry Hull — *The Werewolf Of London* (Walker) USA, 35

Lon Chaney, Jr — *The Wolf Man* (Waggner) USA, 41

Lon Chaney, Jr — *Frankenstein Meets The Wolf Man* (Neill) USA, 43

Matt Willis — *The Return Of The Vampire* (Landers) USA, 43

Nina Foch — *Cry Of The Werewolf* (Levin) USA, 44

Lon Chaney, Jr — *House Of Frankenstein* (Kenton) USA, 44

Lon Chaney, Jr — *House Of Dracula* (Kenton) USA, 45

June Lockhart — *She-Wolf Of London* (Yarbrough) USA, 46

Lon Chaney, Jr — *Abbott And Costello Meet Frankenstein* (Barton) USA, 48

Inventor Rod Taylor venturing into an unknown future in George Pal's 1960 screen version of Wells' *The Time Machine*

Steven Ritch	*The Werewolf* (Sears) USA, 56
Michael Landon	*I Was A Teenage Werewolf* (Fowler, Jr) USA, 57
Lon Chaney, Jr	*Face Of The Screaming Werewolf* (Warren) Mex, 60
Oliver Reed	*Curse Of The Werewolf* (Fisher) GB, 61
Curt Lowens	*Werewolf In A Girl's Dormitory* (Benson) It, 62
Ursula Howells	*Dr Terror's House Of Horrors* (Francis) GB, 64
Paul Naschy	*Frankenstein's Bloody Terror* (Equiluz) Spa, 68
Paul Naschy	*Las Noches Del Hombre* (Gover) Spa, 68
Paul Naschy	*Shadow Of The Werewolf* (Klimovsky) Spa/W.Ger, 70
Paul Naschy	*The Fury Of The Wolf Man* (Zabalazar) Spa, 70
Paul Naschy	*Doctor Jekyll And The Werewolf* (Klimovsky) Spa, 71
Paul Naschy	*Curse Of The Dead* (Alonzo) Spa/Mex, 73
Dean Stockwell	*The Werewolf Of Washington* (Ginsberg) USA, 73
Kerwin Mathews	*The Boy Who Cried Werewolf* (Juran) USA, 73
David Rintoul	*Legend Of The Werewolf* (Francis) GB, 74
Michael Gambon	*The Beast Must Die* (Annett) GB, 74
Earl Owensby	*Wolfman* (Keeler) USA, 79
Roger Sloman	*The Monster Club* (Baker) GB, 80
Robert Picardo and Christopher Stone	*The Howling* (Dante) USA, 81

David Rintoul lurching his way through the sewers in the Tyburn horror film *Legend of the Werewolf,* and following in the footsteps of such earlier werewolves as Lon Chaney Jnr, Paul Naschy and Henry Hull who back in 1935 was the first screen actor to be bitten when the moon was full

David Naughton — *An American Werewolf In London* (Landis) GB, 81
Adam Arkin — *Full Moon High* (Cohen) USA, 82

Note: Two variations of the werewolf theme were released in the 1980s; *Wolfen* (81) the story of a series of murders committed by marauding wolves in New York's South Bronx, and Neil Jordan's fantasy *The Company Of Wolves* (84), a version of Perrault's 'Little Red Riding Hood'. Micha Bergese featured in the latter film as a huntsman who undergoes the transformation of man into wolf.

White, Pearl [R]

(1889–1938) Silent movie queen who was tied screaming to railway tracks, flung from cliff tops and generally manhandled in several silent serials during the ten-year period, 1914–23: *The Exploits Of Elaine* (14), *The Perils Of Pauline* (14), *The Fatal Ring* (17), etc. A former stunt girl, she was played on screen in a loose, much fictionalized biography, by Betty Hutton.

Betty Hutton — *The Perils Of Pauline* (Marshall) USA, 47

Wicked Lady, The 

As corny a *femme fatale* (real name Barbara Skelton) as has ever vamped her way across the cinema screen; a seventeenth century seductress who marries for luxury but turns to highway robbery once things get a bit on the dull side and finds love and night-time adventure with a fellow king of the road. A ludicrous role but one that both Margaret Lockwood and Faye Dunaway have revelled in and that still offers plenty of cleavage, female sadism and over the top hysterics. James Mason in 1945 and Alan Bates in 1983 have been those privileged to play the highwayman who satisfies Lady Barbara's sexual appetites.

Margaret Lockwood — *The Wicked Lady* (Arliss) GB, 45
Faye Dunaway — *The Wicked Lady* (Winner) GB, 83

Wilde, Oscar 

(1854–1900) The wittiest author of his generation, noted for his brilliant epigrams and sophisticated writings ('The Importance Of Being Earnest', 'The Picture Of Dorian Gray'), and notorious for his homosexual association with Lord Alfred Douglas. The affair caused headlines in the 1890s when Douglas' father, The Marquis of Queensbury, accused Wilde of sodomy and perversion and was the focal point of both 1960 screen biographies. Ken Hughes' version emerged as the most successful of the two, not least for the performance of Peter Finch who movingly brought out both the wit and moral decay of the writer. Wilde died in exile in Paris in 1900.

Faye Dunaway—masked and unmasked—but either way very much *The Wicked Lady* in Michael Winner's camp remake of the 1945 historical romance starring Margaret Lockwood

Robert Morley — *Oscar Wilde* (Ratoff) GB, 60
Peter Finch — *The Trials Of Oscar Wilde* (Hughes) GB, 60
John De Marco — *The Best House In London* (Saville) GB, 69

Wilson, Thomas Woodrow 

(1856–1924) A former schoolmaster who brought dignity, courage and quiet honesty to his eight-year term as the twenty-eighth President of the United States. Zanuck's 154-minute tribute, with

Alexander Knox playing the President, covered Wilson's entire political life, from his years at Princeton University to when he took America into World War I and helped found the League Of Nations. Despite its unimaginative approach, the film remains the most detailed chronicle of a Presidential career ever put on celluloid.

Actor	Film	Country, year
Alexander Knox	*Wilson* (Henry King)	USA, 44
Earl Lee	*The Story Of Will Rogers* (Curtiz)	USA, 52
L. Korsakov	*The Unforgettable Year – 1919*	USSR, 52
Frank Forsyth	*Oh! What A Lovely War* (Attenborough)	GB, 69
Jerzy Kaliszewski	*Polonia Restituta* (Poreba)	Pol/USSR/Hung/Cz/GDR, 81

Note: Wilson appeared as himself in the silent films *The Battle Cry Of Peace* (USA, 15), *Womanhood, The Glory Of A Nation* (USA, 17) and *The Great Victory* (USA, 18); R. A. Faulkner played the President in the 1919 American production *General Pershing.* On TV Robert Webber featured as Wilson in the 1983 movie *Shooting Star.*

Wizard Of Oz, The

F

Or, in other words, a phoney, a sham wizard to whom Dorothy, along with the Scarecrow, the Tin Woodman and the Cowardly Lion, travels for help after a cyclone has transported her from Kansas to the magical land of Oz. Frank Morgan portrayed him in the Judy Garland classic, Graham Matters in the Australian updated rock film, and Richard Pryor (as a failed politician) in the all-black musical *The Wiz.* The Wizard did not feature in the 1985 *Return To Oz* which derived from three subsequent Baum books – 'The Land Of Oz', 'Ozma Of Oz' and 'Tik-Tok Of Oz'.

Actor	Film	Country, year
Frank Morgan	*The Wizard Of Oz* (Fleming)	USA, 39
Graham Matters	*Oz* (Lofven)	Austral, 76
Richard Pryor	*The Wiz* (Lumet)	USA, 78

Note: Todd Wright appeared as the Wizard in the 1914 silent production *The Patchwork Girl Of Oz* (USA) and Charles Murray in Larry Semon's 1925 film.

The other major characters in Frank Baum's famous story, first published in 1900, have been played as follows:

Dorothy

Actor	Film	Country, year
Bebe Daniels	*The Wizard Of Oz* (Turner)	USA, 10
Violet MacMillan	*His Majesty, The Scarecrow Of Oz* (Baum)	USA, 14
Dorothy Dwan	*The Wizard Of Oz* (Semon)	USA, 25
Judy Garland	*The Wizard Of Oz* (Fleming)	USA, 39
Joy Dunstan	*Oz* (Lofven)	Austral, 76
Diana Ross	*The Wiz* (Lumet)	USA, 78
Fairuza Balk	*Return To Oz* (Murch)	USA, 85

Note: Liza Minnelli voiced the character of Dorothy in Hal Sutherland's full-length animated feature, *Journey Back To Oz* in 1972.

The Scarecrow

Actor	Film	Country, year
Herbert Glennon	*The Patchwork Girl Of Oz* (MacDonald)	USA, 14
Frank Moore	*His Majesty, The Scarecrow Of Oz* (Baum)	USA, 14
Larry Semon	*The Wizard Of Oz* (Semon)	USA, 25
Ray Bolger	*The Wizard Of Oz* (Fleming)	USA, 39
Bruce Spence	*Oz* (Lofven)	Austral, 76
Michael Jackson	*The Wiz* (Lumet)	USA, 78
Justin Case	*Return To Oz* (Murch)	USA, 85

Note: Mickey Rooney voiced The Scarecrow in the cartoon, *Journey Back To Oz* (72); in the Australian rock movie the character was renamed Surfie.

The Tin Woodman

Actor	Film	Country, year
Lon Musgrave	*The Patchwork Girl Of Oz* (MacDonald)	USA, 14
Pierre Couderc	*His Majesty, The Scarecrow Of Oz* (Baum)	USA, 14
Oliver Hardy	*The Wizard Of Oz* (Semon)	USA, 25
Jack Haley	*The Wizard Of Oz* (Fleming)	USA, 39
Michael Carmen	*Oz* (Lofven)	Austral, 76
Nipsey Russell	*The Wiz* (Lumet)	USA, 78
Deep Roy	*Return To Oz* (Murch)	USA, 85

Note: Danny Thomas voiced The Tin Woodman in *Journey Back To Oz;* in the Australian movie the character was renamed Mechanic.

(Opposite page, above) Judy Garland's Dorothy meets Scarecrow Ray Bolger on the road to the Emerald City. A scene from the 1939 version of Frank Baum's *The Wizard Of Oz;* (this page, above) Diana Ross as Dorothy in the all-black musical *The Wiz,* directed by Sidney Lumet and based on the Broadway show by William F. Brown and Charlie Smalls. Her co-stars: Michael Jackson as the Scarecrow (opposite page, bottom left) Ted Ross as the Cowardly Lion (opposite bottom right) and Nipsey Russell as the Tin Man (left)

The Cowardly Lion

Al Roach	*The Patchwork Girl Of Oz* (MacDonald)	USA, 14
Fred Woodward	*His Majesty, The Scarecrow Of Oz* (Baum)	USA, 14
Bert Lahr	*The Wizard Of Oz* (Fleming)	USA, 39
Gary Waddell	*Oz* (Lofven)	Austral, 76
Ted Ross	*The Wiz* (Lumet)	USA, 78
John Alexander	*Return To Oz* (Murch)	USA, 85

Note: Milton Berle voiced the character in *Journey Back To Oz.* Larry Semon and Oliver Hardy played farmhands who masquerade as a scarecrow and tin woodman in the 1925 silent version of the story which did not include the Cowardly Lion. Frank Baum authored 14 Oz books between 1900 and 1920.

Wolsey, Cardinal Thomas [R]

(1471–1530) Sixteenth-century English cardinal and Lord Chancellor, for a period all powerful, but finally a humiliated figure when he failed to secure the Pope's agreement to Henry VIII's divorce from Catherine Of Aragon. Orson Welles made him a figure of decay and frustrated ambition in *A Man For All Seasons;* Anthony Quayle a pathetic and ineffectual character in *Anne Of The Thousand Days.*

Percy Marmont	*The Pearls Of The Crown* (Guitry-Jaque)	Fra, 37
D. A. Clarke-Smith	*The Sword And The Rose* (Annakin)	GB, 53
Orson Welles	*A Man For All Seasons* (Zinnemann)	GB, 66
Anthony Quayle	*Anne Of The Thousand Days* (Jarrott)	GB, 69
Terry Scott	*Carry On Henry* (Thomas)	GB, 71
John Bryans	*Henry VIII And His Six Wives* (Hussein)	GB, 72

Note: Herbert Tree in *Henry VIII* (GB, 11), Hal Reid in *Cardinal Wolsey* (USA, 12) and Arthur Forrest in *When Knighthood Was In Flower* (USA, 22) were among the actors who played Wolsey in the silent era.

Women, The [F]

A bitchy group of 'ladies' who gather to snipe and crow when the marriage of one of their best friends is nearly destroyed when the woman's husband has an affair with an opportunistic salesgirl. First created (by Clare Booth Luce) for the stage in 1936 they were brought to the screen three years later in a film that boasted an all-female cast. No man was seen from beginning to end. A unique set of credit titles portrayed the ladies as animals prior to the film's first sequence. Norma Shearer played the luckless victim, Joan Crawford the predatory vamp and Rosalind Russell the chief tormentor. The full cast list, plus animal parallels, was as follows:

Norma Shearer	Mary Haines (fawn)
Joan Crawford	Crystel Allen (leopard)
Rosalind Russell	Sylvia Fowler (panther)
Mary Boland	Countess DeLage (chimp)
Paulette Goddard	Miriam Aarons (fox)
Joan Fontaine	Peggy Day (lamb)
Lucile Watson	Mrs. Morehead (owl)
Phyllis Povah	Edith Potter (cow)
Virginia Weidler	Little Mary (doe)
Marjorie Main	Lucy (donkey)

The Women (Cukor) USA, 39

Note: In 1956 MGM refilmed the story as *The Opposite Sex* with music and men. The equivalent roles were played by the following (original stars in parenthesis): June Allyson (the Norma Shearer role), Joan Collins (Crawford), Dolores Gray (Russell), Ann Sheridan (Fontaine), Ann Miller (Goddard), Joan Blondell (Povah), Charlotte Greenwood (Main) and Agnes Moorehead (Boland).

Yamamoto, Admiral Isoroku

R

(1884–1943) Japanese naval strategist and commander who planned the attack on Pearl Harbour in December, 1941, and then quickly suffered reversals at the hands of the Americans in the Pacific, i.e. at the Battle of Midway. Eventually killed when shot down by American aircraft in 1943; played many times on screen by Japanee actor Toshiro Mifune.

James T. Goto	*The Gallant Hours* (Montgomery)	USA, 60
Toshiro Mifune	*I Bombed Pearl Harbour* (Matsubayashi)	Jap, 60
Toshiro Mifune	*Admiral Yamamoto* (Maruyama)	Jap, 68
Shogo Shimada	*Gateway To Glory* (Murayama)	Jap 69
Toshiro Mifune	*The Militarists* (Horikawa)	Jap, 70
Soh Yamamura	*Tora! Tora! Tora!* (Fleischer)	USA/Jap, 70
Toshiro Mifune	*Midway* (Smight)	USA, 76

Yeager, Chuck

R

World War II fighter pilot who, on 14 October, 1947, became the fastest man alive when he crashed the sound barrier in the rocket-boosted X-I after several of his colleagues had died in previous attempts. Sam Shepard portrayed Yeager in Philip Kaufman's version of Tom Wolfe's bestseller *The Right Stuff* which revealed how the pilot was passed over for the Mercury astronaut programme because he lacked a college degree and then went on to pay elegaic homage to the 'Magnificent Seven' who made the ultimate journey into space.

Sam Shepard	*The Right Stuff* O (Kaufman)	USA, 83

Note: Yeager served as technical advisor on *The Right Stuff* and also played a small role as the barman in Pancho Barnes' ramshackle saloon on the Airforce base in California's Mohave Desert. The seven Mercury astronauts were played by Ed Harris (John Glenn), Lance Henriksen (Schirra), Dennis Quaid (Cooper), Charles Frank (Carpenter), Scott Glenn (Shepard), Scott Paulin (Slayton) and Fred Ward (Grissom).

York, Alvin C.

R

Deeply religious and pacifist Tennessee farmer who was obliged to go against his beliefs in World War I and finished up being acclaimed 'the greatest civilian soldier of the war'. His heroic exploits reached almost unbelievable proportions when he killed 25 of the enemy and captured 132 prisoners single-handed. Howard Hawks' film, which won Gary Cooper an Oscar, was an adaptation of York's diaries.

Gary Cooper	*Sergeant York* (Hawks)	USA, 41

Younger, Cole

R

(1844–1916) The most notorious of the three Younger brothers. A rider with Quantrill in the American Civil War and later with the Jesse James gang, he was a casualty of the ill-fated raid on the bank of Northfield (1876) and spent his next 25 years in jail, reputedly with 17 bullets still resting harmlessly in his body. Generally a second string western character but examined at length in Philip Kaufman's *The Great Northfield Minnesota Raid*.

Glenn Strange	*Days Of Jesse James* (Kane)	USA, 39
Dennis Morgan	*Bad Men Of Missouri* (Enright)	USA, 41
Steve Brodie	*Return Of The Badmen* (Enright)	USA, 48
Wayne Morris	*The Younger Brothers* (Marin)	USA, 49
James Best	*Kansas Raiders* (Enright)	USA, 50
Bruce Bennett	*The Great Missouri Raid* (Douglas)	USA, 51
Bruce Cabot	*Best Of The Badmen* (Russell)	USA, 51
Jim Davis	*Woman They Almost Lynched* (Dawn)	USA, 53
Sam Keller	*Jesse James' Women* (Barry)	USA, 54
Alan Hale Jr.	*The True Story Of Jesse James* (Ray)	USA, 56

(Opposite page, below) Sam Shepard as Chuck Yeager, the first man to break the sound barrier on 14 October, 1947, pictured in Philip Kaufman's *The Right Stuff*; (opposite page, above) General Chuck Yeager (right) with Sam Shepard; (this page, above) the Seven Mercury astronauts in *The Right Stuff*; Scott Glenn (Alan Shepard), Ed Harris (John Glenn), Dennis Quaid (Gordon Gordo' Cooper), Fred Ward (Gus Grissom), Scott Paulin (Deke Slayton), Lance Henriksen (Wally Schirra) and Charles Frank (Scott Carpenter)

GLENNIS

AD INEXPLORATA

(Left to right) Robert, David and Keith Carradine as the gunfighting Younger brothers, Bob, Cole and Jim in Walter Hill's *The Long Riders,* a realistic account of the outlaw activities of the James and Youngers in post Civil War Missouri

Myron Healy	*Hell's Crossroads* (Andreon)	USA, 57
Frank Lovejoy	*Cole Younger, Gunfighter* (Springsteen)	USA, 58
Willard Parker	*Young Jesse James* (Claxton)	USA, 60
Bruce Sedley	*The Outlaws Is Coming* (Maurer)	USA, 65
Cliff Robertson	*The Great Northfield Minnesota Raid* (Kaufman)	USA, 72
David Carradine	*The Long Riders* (Hill)	USA, 80

Zapata, Emiliano [R]

(*c.* 1879–1919) Mexican revolutionary who joined with Pancho Villa to overthrow the Diaz regime in 1911. An idealized but excitingly cinematic biography by Elia Kazan (script by John Steinbeck) followed Zapata from his years as a bandit outlaw and general, to his short term as President and subsequent assassination by the military. Brando's Zapata stands high amongst his finest work.

Marlon Brando	*Viva Zapata!* (Kazan) USA, 52
Tony Davis	*Guns Of The Magnificent Seven* (Wendkos) USA, 69

Note: The Tony Davis performance was of Zapata as a child.

Zaroff, Count 

Richard Connell's bizarre sadist, a fanatical big game hunter who becomes bored with killing animals and turns to hunting humans instead. Operates from his own private island and chooses his victims from those shipwrecked on the rocky coasts. There have been many variations of the role down the years – with several changes of name – but Leslie Banks' original performance remains the authoritative portrayal.

Leslie Banks	*The Most Dangerous Game* (Schoedsack/Pichel) USA, 32
Edgar Barrier	*A Game Of Death* (Wise) USA, 46
Trevor Howard	*Run For The Sun* (Roy Boulting) USA, 56

Note: Both *Johnny Allegro* (49) and *Kill Or Be Killed* (50) were loose adaptations of the Zaroff story; *To Kill A Clown* (72), based on a novel by Algis Budrys, featured Alan Alda as a crippled Vietnam veteran who hunts down a young couple on an island off the New England coast.

Ziegfeld, Florenz [R]

(1869–1932) The most celebrated of all American showmen impresarios, producer of such Broadway shows as 'Sally', 'Rio Rita' and 'Show Boat', but best-known for his lavish series of Follies 'glorifying the American girl'. Appropriately enough, the subject of the first three hour Hollywood musical biography, the Oscar-winning *The Great Ziegfeld,* produced by MGM in 1936.

William Powell	*The Great Ziegfeld* (Leonard) USA, 36
William Powell	*Ziegfeld Follies* (Minnelli) USA, 45
Eddie Kane	*The Jolson Story* (Green) USA, 46
William Forrest	*I'll See You In My Dreams* (Curtiz) USA, 52
William Forrest	*The Eddie Cantor Story* (Green) USA, 53
Wilton Graff	*The I Don't Care Girl* (Bacon) USA, 53
Paul Henreid	*Deep In My Heart* (Donen) USA, 54
Walter Woolf King	*The Helen Morgan Story* (Curtiz) USA, 57
Walter Pidgeon	*Funny Girl* (Wyler) USA, 68
Paul Stewart	*W. C. Fields And Me* (Hiller) USA, 76

Note: Bernard Randall in *Polly Of The Follies* (22) and Bertram Marburgh (as Lew Kline) in *An Affair Of The Follies* (27) both featured as Ziegfeld on the silent screen. Paul Shenar played the showman in Buzz Kulik's 1978 TV biography, *Ziegfeld: The Man And His Women.*

Zola, Emile 

(1840–1902) Nineteenth century novelist, regarded by many as the French Charles Dickens in his never-ending quest for social reform and for his compassionate portraits of the lower classes. 'L'Assommoir', 'Nana' and 'Therese Raquin' are among those of his novels filmed; the Oscar-winning *The Life Of Emile Zola* retold his life, Hollywood style, in 1937. Zola figures prominently in the films made about the famous Dreyfus case.

Heinrich George	*The Dreyfus Case* (Oswald) Ger, 30
George Merritt	*Dreyfus* (Kraemer/Rosmer) GB, 31

Paul Muni	*The Life Of Emile Zola* (Dieterle)	USA, 37
Emlyn Williams	*I Accuse!* (Jose Ferrer)	GB, 58

Zorro

F

The masked avenger (real name: Don Diego de la Vega) of Johnston McCulley's serial *The Curse Of Capistrano,* a champion of the oppressed who operates in nineteenth century California posing as a fop by day but donning a mask and cape when dealing with despots and all those involved in corrupt rule. Trademark: Carving with his rapier the letter Z on walls and the foreheads of his luckless opponents. The athletic frames of Douglas Fairbanks, Tyrone Power and Frank Langella have filled the role over the years; in recent times George Hamilton has spoofed the part, playing the foppish son of the legendary Zorro and also his look-alike gay brother Bunny Wigglesworth. Johnston McCulley's serial, fashioned after *The Scarlet Pimpernel,* was first published in 'All-Story' magazine in 1919.

Tyrone Power	*The Mark Of Zorro* (Mamoulian)	USA, 40
Pedro Armendariz	*El Zorro de Jalisco* (Benavides, Jr)	Mex, 40
Guy Williams	*Sign Of Zorro* (Lewis R & Norman Foster)	USA, 60
Guy Williams	*Zorro The Avenger* (Barton)	USA, 60
Frank Latimore	*Zorro* (Marchient)	Spa, 62
Giorgio Ardisson	*Zorro The Intrepid* (Capueno)	It, 62

Villain Basil Rathbone looks to have the upperhand in this scene from Rouben Mamoulian's 1940 swashbuckler *The Mark of Zorro,* but as usual, poor Basil lost out in the end and finished up being pierced through the heart by the rapier of Tyrone Power!

Sean Flynn	*The Mark of Zorro* (aka *Duel At The Rio Grande)* (Caiano)	Spa/It/Fra, 62
Pierre Brice	*The Invincible Masked Rider* (Lenzi)	It, 63
Gordon Scott	*Zorro And The Three Musketeers* (Capuano)	It, 63
Douglas Frey	*The Erotic Adventures Of Zorro* (Freeman)	W.Ger/Fra, 72
Frank Langella	*The Mark Of Zorro* (McDougall)	TVM/USA, 74
Alain Delon	*Zorro* (Tessari)	Fra/It, 75
George Hamilton	*Zorro, The Gay Blade* (Medak)	USA, 81

Note: On the silent screen Douglas Fairbanks featured as the black clad avenger in Fred Niblo's *The Mark Of Zorro* (20) and Donald Crisp's *Don Q. Zon Of Zorro* (25); in the 30s and 40s numerous serials were based on Zorro's adventures i.e. *Zorro Rides Again* (37) with John Carroll, *Zorro's Fighting Legion* (39) with Reed Hadley, *Zorro's Black Whip* (44) with George J. Lewis, *Son Of Zorro* (47) with George Turner and *Ghost Of Zorro* (49) with Clayton Moore.

The two Guy Williams performances as Zorro derived from episodes originally shown in the Walt Disney TV series of 1958. The TV comedy *Zorro And Son* (83) featured Henry Darrow as an ageing Don Diego and Paul Regina as his son Zorro, jr.